FROM THE LIBRARY OF

POST-COMMUNIST STUDIES AND POLITICAL SCIENCE

POST-COMMUNIST STUDIES AND POLITICAL SCIENCE

Methodology and Empirical Theory in Sovietology

EDITED BY

Frederic J. Fleron, Jr.
AND
Erik P. Hoffmann

Foreword by
Robert C. Tucker

Westview Press
BOULDER • SAN FRANCISCO • OXFORD

Published in 1993 in the United States of America by Westview Press, Inc., 5500 Central Avenue, Boulder, Colorado 80301-2877, and in the United Kingdom by Westview Press, 36 Lonsdale Road, Summertown, Oxford OX2 7EW

Library of Congress Cataloging-in-Publication Data
Post-Communist studies and political science : methodology and
empirical theory in Sovietology / edited by Frederic J. Fleron, Jr.,
Erik P. Hoffmann ; foreword by Robert C. Tucker.
    p. cm.
  Includes bibliographical references.
  ISBN 0-8133-1685-5.—ISBN 0-8133-1686-3 (pbk.)
  1. Soviet Union—Study and teaching (Higher) 2 Political
science. I. Fleron, Frederic J., 1937– . II. Hoffmann, Erik P.,
1939– .
DK38.8.P64 1993
947´.001—dc20   92-38893
                                                                                    CIP

Printed and bound in the United States of America

  The paper used in this publication meets the requirements of the American National Standard for Permanence of Paper for Printed Library Materials Z39.48-1984.

10 9 8 7 6 5 4 3 2 1

To
Julian and Ingeri
and in loving memory of
Anders

CONTENTS

FOREWORD

Serious stock-taking is in progress now among practitioners of what has been called Sovietology, meaning studies of the Union of Soviet Socialist Republics. The reason is that the field for the most part had not been expecting what happened in 1991: The USSR collapsed and went out of existence as a unified state system governing a sixth of the world's territory, having allowed its East European empire to free itself from Soviet dominance somewhat earlier.

It might be said in defense of Sovietology that, by the beginning of the 1980s, it understood that economic and political crises were brewing in the Soviet Union and its outer empire. But the field as a whole failed to grasp the full depth of the systemic crisis in Soviet Russia and the destructive or self-destructive potentialities inherent in it. As the editors of this valuable volume write in the Introduction: "Sovietology was not prepared for perestroika and postcommunism."

Perestroika is the name that was given to the reform course adopted by Mikhail S. Gorbachev soon after he came to power in 1985 as general secretary of the Soviet Communist Party. He envisaged a radical reformation of the deeply ailing Soviet order, an effort to cure it of its ills through some measure of liberalizing change. Instead of curing the system, however, *perestroika* unleashed centrifugal and other forces that in the seventh year of Gorbachev's reign brought the Soviet state formation down to destruction. Now, in late 1992, the ex-USSR consists of the Russian Federation (still a huge country unto itself) and fourteen other Soviet successor states, and communism no longer exists as the official ideology of any of them (although, naturally, no few individuals remain loyal to it).

To say that Sovietology was unprepared for what happened in and to the Soviet Union after 1985 is true if we have in mind the field of Soviet studies as a whole, or the great majority of its members. But fields as a whole are normally characterized by diversity of thinking. Some scholars are likely to arrive at views that differ from widely accepted ones, and in some cases these diverging minds turn out later to have been right. In this instance too, there were a few who, around 1980 or earlier, grasped that the Soviet

Union was in a stagnant internal condition with mounting serious problems; that reform was urgently needed; and that radical reform, if instituted, could endanger the system or even lead to its downfall. For such a downfall had happened before in Russian history after a new young tsar, Alexander II, came to the throne in 1855 and instituted some far-reaching reforms, beginning with the abolition of serfdom in 1861. These reforms led to the rise of an antistate revolutionary movement, which in 1917, under wartime conditions, managed to seize power in a coup some months after the tsarist regime had collapsed upon the abdication of Tsar Nicholas II.

One exceptional mind was that of a Soviet dissident named Andrei Amalrik, who decided to become a Sovietologist by analyzing the condition of his own country's established order. In 1969 he wrote a short treatise called *Will the Soviet Union Survive Until 1984?* Since such a writing could not be published, due to strict censorship, Amalrik put some copies into hand-to-hand circulation (this practice was called *samizdat* and had a tradition in tsarist Russia too). For this he was later forced by the authorities into exile abroad. A copy of his essay found its way abroad, however, where it was published and widely read.

Amalrik grasped that the Soviet system was in deep internal crisis and hence in need of radical reform. But he also saw that the systemic crisis had an explosive potential in the event that the country, under conservative rule such as Leonid Brezhnev then offered, should blunder into a foreign war (as it later did in Afghanistan). He imagined that the foreign war would be with China and pictured the USSR self-destructing under its pressure. No war with China came about, of course, yet many events, the Afghan war among them, brought new leadership under Gorbachev, the beginnings of radical reform, and systemic collapse in 1991.

What explains Amalrik's capacity to foresee what Soviet Russia's future might contain? A part of the answer lies in his professional specialization as a historian of tsarist Russia along with his understanding of the fact that, in some fundamental ways, the Soviet Union after 1917 had retraced the path taken by that earlier Russia of the tsars. What Amalrik saw and intuitively grasped was the potential in twentieth-century Soviet Russia for a repetition of the sequence of events, beginning with Alexander II's *perestroika* and ending during World War I, that had brought about the collapse of tsarism.

But all this is just history, the reader may be saying to himself or herself by now. What does it have to do with the subjects of this book—post-Communist studies and political science, methodology and empirical theory in Sovietology? To this question there is a threefold answer. First, the relation of Soviet Russia to earlier Russian history is the subject of two essays in this volume and hence is properly a topic in which the editors invite the student to take an interest.

Second, one recognized field of political science is called "comparative politics." It involves the analytic comparison of different political systems or different kinds of political systems, normally in two different countries. But there can be a comparative politics across time as well as a comparative politics across space. In the former, the scholar is comparing the political systems and the development of the political systems of two "countries," as it were, that inhabit the same geopolitical space: the two systems that existed before and after a far-reaching event such as the Russian Revolution of 1917–1920. To compare Soviet Russia with tsarist Russia, as Amalrik was implicitly doing, is to engage in a study of comparative Russian politics across time.

Third, a generally accepted form of analysis in contemporary political science, as more than one essay in this volume can testify, is the study of what goes by the name of "political culture," and political-culture study is closely related to historical thinking. A political culture is a society's complex of real and ideal culture patterns, the former comprising the accepted ways of political acting (such as voting in competitive elections in a democracy) and the latter comprising the accepted ways of political belief, i.e., the norms or values (such as the belief that citizens *should* vote in elections even though few, in this or that society, may do so). It can happen that certain patterns of political culture persist or revive after a revolutionary transition to another sociopolitical system. Revolutionary leaders can try to resist such a revival, as Lenin did when, in the early 1920s, he declared war on "bureaucratism," a familiar old Russian pattern (or cluster of patterns) of political culture that was making a comeback in Soviet Russia. One cause of his failure was that some other prominent Bolshevik leaders, among them Stalin, found it in their self-interest to support and promote the bureaucratic tendencies that he sought to combat. Later on, by means of what is known as the Great Terror of 1934–1939, Stalin revived some other patterns of tsarist political culture, most notably absolute autocracy with himself in the role of a new tsar-autocrat (although not officially called that).

And now political-culture analysis can be useful to the student of post-Communist or post-Soviet political life in the successor states of the USSR. For although communism as a belief system, meaning a set of ideal culture patterns, norms, ideals, or values, is dying out there, very many of the real culture patterns of the Soviet period, including that very "bureaucratism" that made a comeback after the revolutionary break in 1917, are still tenaciously holding on. Now it becomes possible for the student of post-Communist politics to go at the study of it with an awareness that the historical background of the present period is of great importance and continuing relevance. Indeed, the study of post-Communist politics is a most exciting field of inquiry for the serious younger social scientist or historian, and this ably chosen and edited set of essays is an excellent guide to the subject.

Robert C. Tucker

CONTRIBUTORS

Gabriel A. Almond	Stanford University
John A. Armstrong	University of Wisconsin
Mark R. Beissinger	University of Wisconsin
Joseph R. Berliner	Brandeis University
Russell Bova	Dickinson College
Susan Bronson	Social Science Research Council
Alexander Dallin	Stanford University
Daniel Deudney	University of Pennsylvania
Frederic J. Fleron, Jr.	State University of New York at Buffalo
Jeffrey W. Hahn	Villanova University
Laura Roselle Helvey	Stanford University
Erik P. Hoffmann	State University of New York at Albany
Jerry F. Hough	Duke University
Robert T. Huber	Social Science Research Council
G. John Ikenberry	Princeton University
Alfred G. Meyer	University of Michigan
James R. Millar	George Washington University
Alexander J. Motyl	Columbia University
Thomas F. Remington	Emory University
J. Thomas Sanders	United States Naval Academy
Jack Snyder	Columbia University
Robert C. Tucker	Princeton University

CREDITS

The editors wish to thank Addie Napolitano of the State University of New York at Albany for her superb job of word processing the entire manuscript.

The chapters in this book are reprinted from the following sources. Permission from the authors and publishers to reprint is gratefully acknowledged.

Chapter 2: Gabriel A. Almond and Laura Roselle, "Model Fitting in Communism Studies," in Thomas F. Remington, ed., *Politics and the Soviet System* (London: Macmillan, 1989), pp. 170–224. Copyright © 1989 by Thomas F. Remington.

Chapter 3: Alexander J. Motyl, "The Dilemmas of Sovietology" and "The Labyrinth of Theory," in Alexander J. Motyl, *Sovietology, Rationality, Nationality: Coming to Grips with Nationalism in the USSR* (New York: Columbia University Press, 1990), pp. 1–29, 197–202. Copyright © 1990 by Columbia University Press, New York. Reprinted by permission of the publisher and the author.

Chapter 4: Jack Snyder, "Science and Sovietology: Bridging the Methods Gap in Soviet Foreign Policy Studies," *World Politics,* 40, 2 (1988), pp. 169–193.

Chapter 5: Alexander Dallin, "The Uses and Abuses of Russian History," in Terry L. Thompson and Richard Sheldon, eds., *Soviet Society and Culture: Essays in Honor of Vera S. Dunham* (Boulder: Westview, 1988), pp. 181–194.

Chapter 6: J. Thomas Sanders, "Historical Consciousness and the Incorporation of the Soviet Past," *Problems of Communism,* 40, 6 (November-December 1991), pp. 115–123.

Chapter 7: Alfred G. Meyer, "Politics and Methodology in Soviet Studies." This article was first published in *Studies in Comparative Communism,* 24, 2, June 1991, pp. 127–136, and is reproduced here with the permission of Butterworth-Heinemann, Oxford, UK.

Chapter 8: Joseph R. Berliner, "Foreword," in James R. Millar, ed., *Politics, Work, and Daily Life in the USSR: A Survey of Former Soviet Citizens* (Cambridge, England, and New York: Cambridge University Press, 1987), pp. vii–xii. Copyright © Cambridge University Press 1987. Reprinted with the permission of Cambridge University Press.

Part One

INTRODUCTION

FREDERIC J. FLERON, JR.
ERIK P. HOFFMANN

1

COMMUNIST STUDIES AND POLITICAL SCIENCE:

Cold War and Peaceful Coexistence

In 1969 the Institute of the World Economy and International Relations (IMEMO) in Moscow convened a roundtable conference to discuss general methodological issues and the relevance of Western social science approaches such as game theory for the Soviet study of international relations.[1] Ironically, the first collection of essays explaining, advocating, and demonstrating the application of Western social science concepts, theory, and methodology to Soviet politics and international behavior appeared in the West the same year. The title of that book was *Communist Studies and the Social Sciences: Essays on Methodology and Empirical Theory,* and it even included a chapter on game theory.

In his introduction to that book, Frederic J. Fleron, Jr. argued that the study of the Soviet political system (indeed, all Communist systems) had proceeded in isolation from developments in social science concepts, theory, and methodology and that this had occurred in large part because Sovietologists tended to view the object of their affection, disaffection, or defection as sui generis—a unique phenomenon in the history of humankind and, therefore, irrelevant to the methodology and empirical theory of the social sciences. In the late 1960s, the editors of this book felt that Communist studies *and* the social sciences could benefit from concerted and systematic efforts to link the two.

Parts of this chapter have been adapted from Frederic J. Fleron, Jr., and Erik P. Hoffmann, "Sovietology and Perestroika: Methodology and Lessons from the Past," *Harriman Institute Forum,* 5, 1 (September 1991), pp. 1–12. The authors wish to thank Guoli Liu, Allen Lynch, Alexander Motyl, and Robert Sharlet for their thoughtful comments on drafts of that article.

Imagine our surprise when, some twenty years later, we read the following passage in *Daedalus,* the prestigious quarterly journal of the American Academy of Arts and Sciences:

> It is precisely because during the past twenty-odd years mainline Western Sovietology has concentrated on the sources of Soviet "stability" as a "mature industrial society" with a potential for "pluralist development" that it has prepared us so poorly for the present crisis, not only in the Soviet Union but in communist systems everywhere. Instead of taking the Soviet leadership at its ideological word—that their task was to *"build socialism"—Western Sovietology—has by and large foisted on Soviet reality social science categories derived from Western realities,* with the result that the extraordinary, indeed surreal, Soviet experience has been rendered banal to the point of triviality.[2]

Martin Malia, the author of the article, cited four books as the main culprits responsible for leading Soviet studies astray during the past two decades. The editors of this volume edited and/or contributed to two of those books.[3]

On one hand, we could be flattered that the power to initiate such a dramatic shift in Sovietology has been attributed to us. On the other hand, we might then have to share the blame for having poorly prepared the academic and policy communities for Gorbachev's domestic and international innovations, for the dramatic transformation of Eastern Europe in 1989, and for the disintegration of the Soviet Union in 1991. However, we do not believe that any one group of scholars was responsible for the direction of Sovietology. Whether Sovietology would have been better prepared for perestroika and postcommunism had our colleagues heeded the call some twenty years ago to join forces with the social sciences is a moot point. But we do know that Sovietology was not prepared for perestroika and postcommunism. Instead, multidisciplinary area studies and policy-oriented research dominated Sovietology in the 1970s and 1980s. Many specialists on Soviet politics learned more about Soviet economics or East-West military competition. Some produced comparative research on different stages of Soviet and Russian history or creative contextual analyses at the interstices of various disciplines. Others parlayed their geographical area expertise into political influence and pecuniary reward through government and business consulting. A few senior academic specialists eagerly pursued temporary government assignments and business opportunities, and many junior specialists involuntarily abandoned academic careers because of the vagaries of the job market. Fewer and fewer Sovietologists sought to "construct" social science theory (macro-, middle-, or microlevel), and their professional ties to core disciplines diminished.

It is high time to reassess the traditional methodologies of Sovietology because the nature of the subject matter and the available

It is high time to reassess the traditional methodologies of Sovietology because the nature of the subject matter and the available data are dramatically changing. It is also time to move toward the integration of Sovietology and the social sciences by striving to produce more theoretically oriented and empirically grounded studies. Rivalry has stunted Sovietology and the social sciences; partnership can strengthen them both. Multiple-sum thinking should replace zero-sum thinking in scholarship as well as in politics.

This volume examines new theoretical approaches and research methodologies that may further our understanding of perestroika and postcommunism, and it aims to stimulate thoroughgoing and judicious reevaluation of previous and current approaches and techniques. We focus on the Soviet Union and its successor states, but much of our analysis applies to other Communist and post-Communist systems, especially in east-central Europe.

POST–WORLD WAR II SOVIETOLOGY

Since the late 1940s and 1950s, scholars have attempted to use Western social science approaches to elucidate Soviet realities. Some of these efforts, perhaps especially in the late 1960s and early 1970s, imposed questionable Western approaches on recalcitrant Soviet realities, as Jerry F. Hough pointed out a decade and a half ago in his too-little-read book, *The Soviet Union and Social Science Theory*.[4] In Hough's view and in ours, the comparative politics generalists were much worse offenders than the Soviet area specialists. Many of the theoretically grounded as well as atheoretical works by Sovietologists have enhanced our knowledge of the polity, economy, and society of the former Soviet Union and have withstood the test of time. Less successful attempts at theoretical and conceptual innovation were of an admittedly experimental nature and, despite their meager fruits or outright failure, were probably worth the effort. Because Sovietologists have frequently ignored and sometimes discarded irrelevant theoretical approaches and conceptual frameworks—their own and others'—it is hard to sustain Malia's argument that social science theories and methodologies have harmed Soviet studies, a few self-inflicted wounds notwithstanding.

It is worth recalling that two of the earliest post–World War II studies of the Soviet Union stressed the evolving interrelationships between the Soviet political system and its socioeconomic environment—namely, Barrington Moore, Jr.'s *Soviet Politics—The Dilemma of Power* and Merle Fainsod's *How Russia Is Ruled*.[5]

Moore's work had a significant central theme—the impact of ideas on social change and vice versa. Implicit was the approach of a social scientist who viewed both sets of factors as independent variables. Moore's study was particularly forceful because he carefully analyzed the reciprocal influences of the ideas and actions of Soviet leaders in different contexts. He also judiciously emphasized the situational constraints on Soviet policymakers, their adaptability and responsiveness to rapidly changing events and conditions, and the changing functions performed by the values and beliefs of important Communist Party figures. For example, Moore affirmed that the Bolshevik "ideology of means," exemplified in the words and actions of Lenin and in the Russian revolutionary tradition, exerted a tremendous influence on the evolution of the Soviet political system. This instrumental ideology, according to Moore, had a vastly greater impact on the behavior of Party officials than did the much less authoritarian and less clearly thought-out goals and ideals of classical Marxism and Russian Marxism.

Fainsod, too, presented a distinctive and prodigiously documented theoretical analysis and interpretation of the Soviet system. His emphasis on the concept of "totalitarianism" helped to produce an even more macrotheoretical study than Moore's—perhaps more macrotheoretical than Fainsod himself intended—and one that profoundly influenced the questions posed by a generation of Western scholars. Rereading Fainsod, one is likely to evaluate even more highly than before his abilities as a social scientist and a "middle-range" social theorist, especially in the spheres of mobilization, conflict, and communication theories. Fainsod is not usually thought of as a conflict theorist because of his stress on the dictatorial nature of Soviet policymaking. But he was acutely aware of the importance of inter- and intraorganizational conflict in the implementation of national policies and of the top leaders' continuous efforts to prevent "the pluralization of authority." Also, Fainsod fully understood that Stalin relied heavily on terror to spur socioeconomic and political transformation and that Stalin adroitly altered career incentives and the legal system to stabilize and institutionalize many new socioeconomic and political relationships.

Moore's book devoted insufficient attention to Stalinist coercion, which he subsequently analyzed in *Terror and Progress—USSR*.[6] Fainsod deemphasized organizational input into the policymaking process, and he tended (in the 1963 edition) to overstress the similarities between the purposes and powers of Stalin and Khrushchev. Nonetheless, the sophistication and scholarship of these two early broad-gauged studies are of a very high order indeed.

Of the "second-generation" postwar studies of the Soviet system (it is difficult, because of multiple editions, to provide precise dates), the works of John N. Hazard, Zbigniew Brzezinski, and Alfred G. Meyer deserve special mention. All offer fresh approaches to their subject and some new answers to both new and old questions.

Hazard, in *The Soviet System of Government*,[7] stressed the explanatory, comparative, and normative advantages of viewing the

Soviet polity as one in which "democratic forms" are subject to "counterweights" at key "peril points." Developing the theory of totalitarianism, Hazard identified the crucial characteristics of the Soviet system that inhibit "the democratic functioning of democratic forms" (e.g., the nomenklatura and election systems, a judiciary that was subject to Communist Party domination in political cases, and other controls that prevented the emergence of potentially independent institutional and associational pressure groups). Hazard's study was informed by his deep knowledge of legal sources and of the practical problems involved in translating general Party policies into specific legislation. Hazard was keenly aware of political changes after Stalin—for example, increasing recruitment of technical specialists into the Party and broader elite participation in policy formulation through the standing committees of the USSR Supreme Soviet. But he insisted that if there were to be substantial change in the polity as a whole, it must come in a few vital areas (i.e., at specific "peril-points"). Significantly, Hazard did not consider "an expansion of the circle of the ruling elite" to be one of these areas, and he did not foresee changes in the "essentials" of the political order.

Brzezinski and Samuel P. Huntington's study, *Political Power: USA/USSR,*[8] is well known for its systematic comparisons of the Soviet and U.S. polities and for its rejection of "convergence" theories. Brzezinski and Huntington offered a comparative analysis of the political consequences of modernization, particularly industrialization and urbanization. Stressing that "a multiplicity of expertises . . . is not the same thing as socio-political pluralism based on group autonomy," the authors forcefully argued that economic and political relationships depended heavily on specific characteristics of the existing political system. In the Soviet case, the political vision and skills of professional Party officials and their capacity "to combine economic rationalization . . . with ideological revitalization" were thought to be key variables (p. 424).

With over a quarter century's hindsight, one is inclined to conclude that an even more significant contribution of the Brzezinski-Huntington study was its theoretical focus on the policymaking process. Of particular importance were its emphases on policy initiation, consensus-building, and decisionmaking in different issue areas as well as on the vital role of Soviet leaders' goals, beliefs, perceptions, calculations, career experience, and formal and informal relations with one another. Fainsod had relatively little to say about the interrelationships of power, ideology, and issues as input into policymaking in different periods of Soviet history. In contrast, Brzezinski viewed Soviet politics as a "bargaining" process, and he analyzed the nature, stakes, and outcomes of this process in light of the "political resources" available to various participants and would-be participants (groups and individuals) at different stages in the formulation, execution, and reformulation of public policies in the post-Stalin era.

Meyer's *The Soviet Political System*[9] is best known for viewing the USSR as "bureaucracy writ large" and for its striking comparison of the Soviet Union to a modern Western business corporation dominating a "company town." Meyer considered the Communist Party of the Soviet Union (CPSU) to be the directing nucleus ("The Board of Directors" and "stockholders") of a giant, highly complex, and differentiated bureaucracy. By conceptualizing the Soviet system as a single huge unit, Meyer focused attention on what he considered to be the essentially *intra*organizational, rather than *inter*organizational, nature of Soviet politics. In particular, he stressed that CPSU leaders could frequently change the structure and personnel of all the major bureaucracies and could adjust quickly to new domestic and foreign opportunities, problems, and power relationships. What distinguished Meyer's approach from the "totalitarian model" were his emphases on the contradictory, unclear, and unattainable characteristics of the Soviet polity's central commands as well as on the formidable bureaucratic obstacles to transforming national Party goals into workable policies and laws that lower-level officials could and would carry out. Industrialization and urbanization made these factors even more important, he believed, and placed qualitatively new demands on the policymaking process. In short, Meyer was keenly sensitive to the importance of policymaking and administrative procedures and to the reciprocal influences of decisionmaking practices and substantive decisions. He contended, for example, that "open debate has begun in the USSR on many issues of public policy . . . covering matters of vital importance" and that "ever more frequent and open disputes are taking place among the various elites" and institutional "interest groups" (pp. 188, 231, 470).

Elsewhere, Meyer deliberately jostled our thinking by suggesting that "there is no such thing as The Soviet Political System," only "a succession of systems sharply differing from each other in purpose, structure, and functioning."[10] Meyer's emphasis on the Soviet polity's capacity and propensity for change is strikingly different from Hazard's emphasis on the durability and resilience of the polity's core elements.

Such theories about change and continuity were central features of Sovietology in the Khrushchev and early Brezhnev years. The reformability of Stalinist policymaking practices and domestic and international policies was an issue of immense intellectual and practical significance.

The decade of the 1960s began and ended with apocalyptic dichotomy. Writing in 1960 about the post-Stalin reforms, Robert C. Tucker stated:

> But it is doubtful that a policy of reform operating within these narrow limits (e.g., reorganizational schemes, the decentralization of the bureaucracy, the restoration of Party rule, the relaxation of police terror) can

repair the rupture between the state and society that is reflected in the revival of the image of a dual Russia. A moral renovation of the national life, a fundamental reordering of relations, a process of genuine "unbinding," or, in other words, *an alteration in the nature of the system,* would be needed.[11]

Much later in the decade, Zbigniew Brzezinski formulated the now classic version of the apocalypse: transformation or degeneration? Answering his own question, Brzezinski concluded that "it is the absence of basic institutional development in the Soviet political system that has posed the danger of the system's degeneration."[12] Tucker and Brzezinski have not often agreed in their analyses of Soviet politics and foreign policy, but during the 1960s they agreed on at least the following key point: The most pressing problems of the Soviet polity could not be solved without fundamental transformation of the nature of the polity itself.

Hoping to shed light on these central issues and armed with some innovative approaches and techniques from the behavioral sciences, a new generation of Sovietologists entered academe and government service in the late 1960s. But these scholars never really produced a "behavioral revolution in communist studies."[13] Even those who tried to spark such a revolution respected the high quality of the best Sovietological research of the 1950s and early 1960s.[14] Some of the young generation of Sovietologists saw three basic issues emerging: (1) the potential of Western social science theories to add to our understanding of Soviet society and the need for Soviet data to help verify, reject, or refine these mostly middle-range theories; (2) the promise of philosophies of social science, especially logical positivism, to help Sovietologists explain rather than merely describe events and trends as well as to develop new patterns of explanation and methods of concept formation; and (3) the decreasing value of "totalitarian models" in describing and explaining the Khrushchev and Brezhnev periods.

Young Sovietologists were much more convinced than their elders of the increasing liabilities of totalitarian approaches. But junior scholars did not agree among themselves about the Soviet Union's destination, path, or pace as it moved away from totalitarianism. They did not agree about whether essential features of the Soviet political system were changing or merely adapting to new domestic and international conditions. They did not agree on criteria and standards to resolve these disputes. And they did not espouse a uniform new paradigm, ideal type, model, or conceptual orientation to identify and study key questions.

These "young Turks" of the 1960s called for theoretical and methodological experimentation, with emphasis on theories about bureaucracies, interest groups, modernization, communication, and political culture. They also advocated *qualitative* content analysis of all of the above subjects and favored *quantitative* techniques for only a few specialized topics such as elite recruitment patterns, demographic trends, and economic growth and productivity rates. Furthermore, virtually all young analysts agreed on the need for greater clarity and consistency in forming and applying (not necessarily "operationalizing") concepts such as "role," "culture," "elite," "participation," and "influence."

With the benefit of hindsight, the chief impact of the "behavioral revolution" in Sovietology probably lay in increased conceptual lucidity and interdisciplinary communication, not in creative macro- and middle-range theorizing or in rigorous application of new research methodologies and data-gathering techniques. Greater care in the formation and use of old and new concepts was surely worthwhile because it made it much easier to understand and evaluate propositions and arguments employing these concepts. Novel theories and methods were often much less useful.

For example, Erik P. Hoffmann's criticism of the conceptual ambiguities in Hough's *The Soviet Prefects* seems well founded.[15] More problematical was Hoffmann's overly general appeal for the construction of conceptual frameworks *prior* to data collection. This research strategy is most useful in relatively well-defined and data-rich fields, where incremental change is probable and puzzle solving has been largely completed. But such a strategy can be burdened by positivist and conservative assumptions. It is generally inappropriate for an analyst new to a rapidly changing subject. And it is counterproductive if it distorts political actors' perceptions of their aims and environment or homogenizes the political behavior of groups and individuals, thereby minimizing or disregarding contexts such as particular geographical and issue areas or time periods.[16]

Many of us writing over a quarter century ago were trying to grapple with an evident contradiction: The post-Stalinist society had become increasingly differentiated as the result of industrialization and urbanization, and the political system purported to be monolithic but in some important ways was not. One group of scholars continued to deal with this problem within the conceptual confines of the totalitarianism-pluralism dichotomy. Others rejected this dichotomy implicitly or explicitly and ventured in different directions conceptually, theoretically, and empirically.[17] Everything considered, there was little silliness in the aims and output of the fledgling Sovietologists of the late 1960s. Most had historically grounded and multidisciplinary interests as well as methodological and epistemological concerns. Occasionally their exhortations were shrill, and their confidence in particular approaches and techniques was excessive. But they committed themselves to "methodological pluralism"—that is, they scrutinized alternative concepts, theories, and techniques and tried to tailor them to appropriate topics. Not surprisingly, certain innovations succeeded (fully or partially) and others failed (miserably or barely) to enhance our understanding of basic and secondary characteristics of Soviet society. Many senior scholars encouraged this experimentation and participated in it. Some, however, were rankled by the newcomers' calls to explicate widely used but generally unexamined methodological assumptions and to refine or reject them in response to changing circumstances. Others were concerned that a preoccupation with political science might diminish one's feel for politics and one's ability to communicate persuasively with policymakers.

Today, the former young Turks of the 1960s bring to their analysis of perestroika and postcommunism most of the strengths and weaknesses of other Western analysts. Our interdisciplinary skills are surely beneficial. But our focus on elites and bureaucracies has ill-prepared us for comprehending powerful social forces and popular movements, and our perspective "from the top" rather than "from the bottom" has been of little help in explaining, let alone predicting, the demise of the Soviet bloc and of the Soviet political system. Our incremental and bargaining approaches may be of decreasing relevance in understanding the conflicts among and within the new polities of the former USSR. Such approaches will probably be of greater value when and if the new countries and new institutions more fully understand the many benefits of voluntary cooperation as well as the high costs of complete independence. There are a lot of hidden assumptions underlying Western research on the Soviet Union and Russia. Are we sufficiently aware of them? A sage once said that Sovietologists give very little thought to methodology; they just use it. But what is the "it" they use? Surely we should reflect more on this question, because even some of our most illustrious predecessors insufficiently adapted their research methodologies and theories to new circumstances. For example, E. H. Carr's textual analysis of Soviet documents was much more fruitful in interpreting the Lenin era than the Stalin era, and Fainsod's totalitarian model was much more useful in comprehending Stalinism than Khrushchevism.

Sovietologists are now consciously and subconsciously applying the methodologies and theories of the past to the dynamically changing conditions of the present. Surely these methodologies and theories should undergo their own kinds of reform or revolution. That would seem to be part of a quite natural and welcome process in the advancement of knowledge, no less desirable in the social sciences than in the physical sciences. Since virtually no one predicted the disintegration of the USSR and the Soviet bloc, the least we can do is to use all the techniques and models at our disposal to try to develop a "big bang" theory that explains the causes and consequences of one of the most remarkable political implosions in world history.

ABOUT THE BOOK

The essays in Part Two of this volume address a variety of methodological issues in Sovietology, and they enable us to draw some lessons from the past that can increase our understanding of the present and the future. We have juxtaposed competing viewpoints, and readers are sure to draw diverse lessons.

The lengthy review essay by Gabriel A. Almond and Laura Roselle (Chapter 2) is a comprehensive analysis applauding the use of social science theory in Soviet studies. The authors provide us with an overview of various models, theories, and conceptual frameworks that have been employed to comprehend Communist systems, including the totalitarian model, structural functionalism and decision theories, political culture, the developmental model, pluralist models, the interest group model, corporatism, issue networks and policy communities, bureaucratic politics, patron-client relations, and communications theory. In their view, this literature "describes a rich and complex interaction between communism studies and empirical political theory." Almond and Roselle praise Sovietology for its methodological and theoretical sophistication, and in turn they earn Alfred G. Meyer's praise for their "endorsement of methodological eclecticism."[18]

Almond and Roselle fail to point out that much of what they term "model fitting" has operated in what philosophers of science term the "realm of discovery," not in the "realm of verification."[19] It is quite true that many of the models, theories, and approaches they describe have enabled Sovietologists to look at their subject in a new way, but they have expended very little effort in the systematic testing of propositions from these theories. Part of the problem has been undue emphasis on novelty in the reward structure for academics—a point well taken by Alexander J. Motyl (Chapter 3) and Meyer (Chapter 7). The emphasis on novelty has led to the ever-increasing proliferation of new concepts, theories, and approaches rather than to the testing and retesting of existing theories. As Almond and Roselle affirm, "This may very well be due to the scarcity of data about communist societies, and the effort to enhance insight through experimenting with different perspectives." By the early 1990s, however, that argument no longer holds. Post-Communist studies must take advantage of the new accessibility of previously closed systems. The closest Almond and Roselle come to pointing in the direction of the realm of verification is at the end of their chapter, when they observe that "perhaps a more systematic use of case studies is to be recommended, a more deliberate effort to sample communist politics-cum-policy reality."

In our view, post-Communist studies should spend more time in the realm of verification and less time in the realm of discovery. We are awash in models and conceptual frameworks. What we need is abundant empirical research on post-Communist polities, economies, and societies. This research should be guided by the models and conceptual frameworks previously employed in Soviet studies and by the rich and not-so-rich theories of social science literature in general. Some will prove quite useful in strengthening explanations and furthering understanding; others less so, or not at all. But their utility can be determined only by testing with empirical data, not by armchair speculation or by a priori acceptance or rejection.

Alexander J. Motyl (Chapter 3) applauds the efforts of some Sovietologists in the 1950s and 1960s "not merely to collect data but to generate theory." "In contrast," he argues, "the ossified behavioralism that has come to replace the original behavioralist vision has halted Sovietology's admirable effort to keep pace with theory; by largely abandoning the quest for theory, it has also deprived its practitioners of the capacity to explain what they purport to describe. At its worst, this deification of data, or what I call routine behavioralism, has reduced much of Sovietology to a form of political journalism." Motyl's essay identifies central methodological issues in Soviet studies and their relation to contemporary philosophy of science, and his analysis elevates discussion of methodological problems in Sovietology to a higher level of sophistication—a direction that we heartily endorse.

In juxtaposing the Almond-Roselle and Motyl essays, we take note of the curious fact that the former praises Sovietology for its emphasis on model fitting while the latter criticizes Sovietology for its "current obsession with facts." Are they referring to the same general field of study? Or are there big differences among the disciplines that make up Sovietology?

Jack Snyder (Chapter 4) examines the strengths and weaknesses of holistic and positivist approaches to the study of Soviet foreign policy. Stressing the tension between these two approaches, he notes that "a scholar's regionalist culture pulls him toward holism, while his disciplinary culture of political science pulls him toward positivism." After analyzing examples of each approach, Snyder concludes that "both positivism and holism can make valuable contributions to the study of Soviet foreign policy." In his view, they are not incompatible and can work synergistically, despite the fact that "some irreducible disagreements between the practitioners of holist and positivistic methods are likely to persist." Because "the positivist side of Soviet foreign policy studies has remained underdeveloped," Snyder asserts that "the most pressing task is to use the opportunity presented by recent developments in international relations theory to correct that weakness."[20]

Alexander Dallin (Chapter 5) and J. Thomas Sanders (Chapter 6) examine the nature and consequences of recent efforts to utilize the Russian past to explain the Soviet and post-Soviet present. Dallin draws on David Hackett Fischer's "fallacy of presumptive causality," Herbert Butterfield's caution "against reading the present back into the past by discovering 'false continuity,'" and Gordon Craig's warning not "to confuse chance likeness and similarities of formulation with identity in essence." Dallin urges that we "opt first of all for parsimony in causality, rather than for more devious, remote, complex, or overdetermined alternatives." He reminds us that "this seems to be done without dispute" in the study of other societies. But some Sovietologists adopt a hard-line syndrome of historical determinism that for Dallin has no more validity than economic or technological determinism.

At the same time, Dallin is quite aware that there are important continuities in Russian history.

1. The readiness to accept authority
2. The axiomatic acceptance of a powerful centralized state
3. The role of the state as the principal source and instrument of change as well as its paternalistic function as dispenser of welfare
4. The paucity of voluntary associations mediating between state and individual
5. The weakness of individualism
6. The frailty of representative institutions at the national level
7. The absence of values and forms of a *Rechtsstaat,* or society based on the rule of law
8. Other persistent prejudices, stereotypes, and customs

J. Thomas Sanders (Chapter 6) examines the question of historical continuity between tsarist and Soviet Russia from an altogether different angle by focusing on "a pattern of historical rejectionism specific to the Russian past." This pattern finds contemporary expression in what Sanders terms the current fad of "anti-Sovietism," which "draws sustenance from a wildly radical and poorly considered rejection of the totality of the Soviet experiment on the part of observers within the Soviet Union." He calls on Western observers, and Sovietologists in particular, not to participate in this "practice of denying a significant component" of Russian national life experience. Rather than participating in that denial and thereby losing "equilibrium in the quest for contemporaneity," Sanders challenges Western Sovietologists to facilitate what he terms an "incipient development with incalculable significance for Soviet studies—the emergence of *Soviet* Soviet studies as a legitimate, respectable enterprise." He suggests that systems theory may help Russian and Western analysts ascertain the links between tsarist and Soviet Russia, especially elements of political culture—a topic addressed by both Dallin (Chapter 5) and Russell Bova (Chapter 12). Indeed, systems theory may help to reconceptualize paths to modernity, one of the eight promising areas of study discussed by Robert T. Huber and Susan Bronson (Chapter 10).

According to Alfred G. Meyer (Chapter 7), "there is not all that much that Soviet studies can learn from our colleagues in the discipline" of political science. He sees commitments to quantification and overarching models as serious drawbacks. The emphasis on quantification means "that important information either is lost to our view or is distorted to fit into quantitative moulds." Overarching models have little utility for students of the USSR and the former USSR because they are "mostly abstractions—and idealized ones at that—from Western history and institutions." Meyer thinks these models are more useful to ideologists than to serious scholars, because they perpetuate ideological and cultural biases in our research. Instead, he calls for "an approach that combines institutional or behavioral analysis with cultural empathy."

As if to contradict his own conclusion, Meyer reminds us of the important ways in which the findings of the Harvard Refugee Interview Project (HIP) of the late Stalin years were "in conflict with the images conveyed by the totalitarian model." HIP documented much "informal behavior and informal organizations underneath the totalitarian facade, a second economy, beginnings of a civil society, social stratification, including the persistence of pre-revolutionary status advantages, role conflicts, and ethical notions opposed to Party doctrine." These were vitally important findings that greatly advanced our knowledge of the USSR, and they were findings produced by social scientists employing the concepts, theories, and methodologies of their respective social science disciplines. They were not the findings of professional Sovietologists employing arcane methods to study a "unique" system.

As Meyer points out, "The relationship between Soviet studies and the several social science disciplines has been uneasy and troubled." Foremost among these difficulties is the compulsion of many disciplines to set "certain standards of performance by which works and their creators are judged"—a point explored also by Motyl (Chapter 3). While both area studies and the social sciences (especially political science) must share blame for this pattern of isolation, it is now time to reassess what each can do for the other.

Today Sovietologists are overwhelmed by an abundance of information, unprecedented access to political officials, and the opportunity to conduct survey research in the USSR and its successor states. Joseph R. Berliner (Chapter 8) reminds us of earlier times when this was not the case and, therefore, we had to rely heavily on interview data from Soviet refugees. The two major and systematic efforts in that genre were the Harvard Refugee Interview Project of the late 1940s and the Soviet Interview Project (SIP) of the early 1980s. Berliner and James R. Millar (Chapter 9) compare the results of these two projects. HIP found that social class was the most important factor in explaining response differences. SIP, on the other hand, found that generational differences were the most important explanatory variables, although educational attainment, material incentives, and political conformity were also important. SIP provided insights into Soviet society at a microlevel not available from HIP.

The findings of these two projects have substantive and methodological significance. According to Millar, the most significant and surprising substantive finding of SIP was "a transformation in the structure of support for the Soviet regime" since HIP. Although the earlier project had found that support for the regime came from those who were younger and well educated, the SIP found that regime support came from those who were older and less well-educated. As Berliner and Millar suggest, these findings had major ramifications for our understanding of change and continuity in the Soviet polity.

SIP, in Millar's view, had important methodological implications as well. Not only did the findings tend to confirm "hypotheses put forward by other methods and using other sources," but they demonstrated "that the Soviet social system *is* amenable to analysis with standard Western disciplinary tools." Millar noted that "Soviet society differs in quite specific ways from other societies," but those "differences are in degree rather than in kind." These are significant and comforting thoughts as we enter a period of abundant data and look to the social sciences for assistance in analyzing these data.

Meyer holds that "the study of society and politics is not a science in the strict sense of the word but it is at least to some degree an art." Others will disagree and insist that conceptual clarity, theory testing, and rigorous methodology are essential to advance our knowledge of the USSR and its successor states. The argument over scientific method among social scientists is not unique to Soviet area studies and is not likely to be resolved in the foreseeable future. Nor is it necessary to resolve this question in order to get on with fruitful academic or policy-oriented research. After all, the proof is in the pudding; a priori agreement on methodology is both impossible and undesirable. Different orientations will produce both useful and not-so-useful results.

We need not agree on methodology to realize that Sovietology is in need of its own restructuring and revitalization, as a number of scholars have argued in recent years. Both the social sciences and post-Communist studies can benefit from increased interaction that transcends the barriers and prejudices of the past. Huber and Bronson (Chapter 10) suggest that "dramatically enhanced access to data has facilitated and given life to the concept of the Soviet Union as a vast new laboratory for social science research. To use the assets of the laboratory requires training in the tools of science and a stress on replicability, intersubjective verifiability, and a comparative focus for interpreting results." In their view, these techniques enable "scholars to use the Soviet experience as a means for illuminating and contributing to our understanding of core issues in the social sciences and humanities. In turn, more scholars in the field have begun to put their work in a comparative context, much like research communities that study other complex regions of the world." All of these observations and prescriptions take on even greater force now that the former Soviet Union has spawned many different kinds of successor countries.

The essays in Part Three of this book are efforts to use social science concepts and theory to further our understanding of the Soviet past and the post-Soviet present.

Reminiscent of Daniel Bell's famous 1958 article, "Ten Theories in Search of Reality," the contribution by Daniel Deudney and G. John Ikenberry (Chapter 11) examines ten theories that attempt to explain recent events in the USSR in light of general patterns not unique to that country:

- Three variants of realism (hard realism, soft realism, and statism) that "share assumptions about the primacy of the state, power, and conflict in world politics"
- Three variants of globalism (nuclear one-worldism, international institutionalism, and ecological environmentalism) that "share the view that the state-centric world order has been rendered less viable by powerful and broad underlying trends and forces operating on a global scale"
- Four socioeconomic theories (democratic liberalism, capitalism, neo-Marxism, and industrial modernism) that "have in common the idea that the spread of originally Western political and economic institutions is propelled by deep historical forces"

Some colleagues may view these theories as examples of what Meyer debunked as overarching models, which have little utility because they constitute idealized abstractions from Western theory and institutions. For Deudney and Ikenberry, however, such macrohistorical theorizing is necessary to make sense out of the major events now unfolding in the successor states to the USSR. Their important conclusion is that "no one theory can explain the causes and consequences of these contemporary events" because of "the irreducibly plural nature of the historical phenomena." They also conclude that "the shortfall of the theories reveals a theoretical insight, namely that these events are *conjunctural:* the outcome of multiple, distinctive processes" occurring simultaneously.

Russell Bova (Chapter 12) and Thomas F. Remington (Chapter 13) analyze the post-Communist transition in the former USSR through the lenses of political development and modernization literature in comparative politics and comparisons to transitions to democracy in other authoritarian regimes (the Iberian and Latin American experiences in particular). Both authors recognize that the transition from communism may be unique. At the same time, Bova affirms that the transition may "be usefully viewed as a sub-category of a more generic phenomenon of transition from authoritarian rule."

Remington draws our attention to the pitfalls of attempting to "'normalize' the study of politics in communist systems by adapting concepts borrowed from the noncommunist world"—a theme also discussed by Meyer (Chapter 7) and John A. Armstrong (Chapter 15). The result of such adaptations was a tendency to focus on the statics and structures rather than on the dynamics and functions of such systems. This problem has been underscored by Richard Pipes, Martin Malia, and other critics of efforts to apply social science theory and methodology to Communist regimes. In seeking to overcome this problem, Bova and Remington address issues of context and process. They argue that the direction and speed of systemic transition can be understood only through the interaction of context and process factors. Bova's context variables are the level of economic development, the character of the national political culture, the degree of national integration, and the nature of the country's class structure. Remington focuses on such contextual factors as urbanization, educational achievements, occupational structure, and communications. Bova's process variables focus on the choices and strategies adopted by key actors in the democratic transition; Remington's process variables focus on the concentration of grievances and the construction of political parties (both of which can be subsumed by Bova's more general category of democratization).

The Bova and Remington essays are initial efforts to integrate Sovietology and post-Communist studies with the field of comparative politics. As Bova aptly puts it, "The best way to make the case for the utility of comparison is to produce at least a sample of what a comparative analysis can provide." Comparison, he stresses, illuminates both differences and similarities.

Jeffrey W. Hahn (Chapter 14) presents the results of the first major attempt to test propositions from the Sovietological literature about the impact of the Russian past (especially Russian political culture) on the post-Soviet present in Russia. Through detailed empirical research on contemporary political culture in Yaroslavl, he addresses some of the methodological and substantive questions raised by Dallin (Chapter 5), Sanders (Chapter 6), and Meyer (Chapter 7). Hahn's findings directly challenge the received wisdom in much of Sovietology—namely, that traditional Russian cultural patterns persist in such a form and to such a degree as to frustrate rather than facilitate the transition to democracy. Hahn's findings "provide little support for the argument that continuity rather than change is the chief characteristic of Russian political culture." On the contrary, "the evidence suggests that Russians come closer to what we find in Western industrial democracies than to what we would expect to find if the traditional cultural patterns ascribed to the period of Russian autocracy had persisted." Although Hahn is quick to point out that the conclusions from his Yaroslavl study cannot be generalized to all of Russia, they are important and provocative and merit further exploration.

John A. Armstrong's critique (Chapter 15) of his own 1968 article, "The Ethnic Scene in the Soviet Union," illustrates the benefits of periodic reassessments of our conceptual frameworks, typologies, and theories. Working from the framework of structural functionalism and the single rational actor model, Armstrong had developed a functional typology of ethnic groups in the USSR based on three quantitative indicators: (1) "the extent of social mobilization (change from traditional to modernized ways of life)"; (2) "the specific objectives and tactics of Soviet policy"; and (3) "the degree of Russification achieved."[21] Five distinct types were identified based on these indicators: the internal proletariat, mobilized diasporas, younger brothers, state nations, and colonials. Each of the various ethnic groups of the USSR was then located in one of these categories and the common traits analyzed. A quarter century later, Armstrong concludes that "the typology presented in 'The Ethnic Scene' and many of its practical implications have held up, whereas the broader theoretical underpinnings had to be discarded." Such paradoxes, Armstrong argued, "are not uncommon in the social sciences, where mistaken efforts to produce elegant systematic frameworks are often remedied by pragmatic diagnoses based on intimate knowledge of specific situations." For Armstrong, the lesson to be learned relates directly to major themes in this book: "Exercise caution about applying general theories to contemporary situations, while continuing the search for conceptual schemes which can be tested against the greater range of historical evidence."

Mark R. Beissinger (Chapter 16) thinks that "Armstrong's classification has held up surprisingly well against the events of the *glasnost*' period." The success of this "predictive model of political attitudes and behavior," he argues, can be attributed to three factors in Armstrong's approach: (1) "Armstrong was sensitive to the enormous variety and complexity of the Soviet ethnic scene" and to the need for a multiplicity of analogies "that would fit the variety of Soviet circumstances" (a theme developed by Deudney and Ikenberry in Chapter 11); (2) Armstrong "consistently followed a holistic approach" (an approach explored by Snyder in Chapter 4); and (3) Armstrong utilized a "rigorous comparative focus beyond Soviet borders" (Deudney and Ikenberry, Chapter 11; Bova, Chapter 12; Remington, Chapter 13).

Jerry F. Hough (Chapter 17) explores the utility of Mancur Olson's "logic of collective action" for an understanding of patterns of revolutionary behavior in the USSR. While critics argue that social science approaches have produced no new insights about Soviet politics, Hough demonstrates that Olson's theory helps us to arrive at nonintuitive explanations of concrete events by drawing attention to both nonrational factors and the causes of "irrational" action, neither of which are altogether obvious by other means. For Hough, these nonrational factors include (1) the effort of every society to inculcate into its citizens "values such as collective responsibility, professionalism, and honesty that transcend individual rationality (narrowly defined)"; (2) irrationality itself ("People are not simply rational beings"); and (3) personal enjoyment. "These are all the kind of nonrational factors that should be expected to overcome the logic of collective action on a short-term basis. Action, especially collective action, could easily release psychological tension and not be 'irrational' from an individual's point of view even if it is 'non-rational.'"

PAST AND PRESENT

The subtitle of this chapter—"Cold War and Peaceful Coexistence"—refers to periods of Soviet history and to relations between social science theory and Sovietology. Roughly speaking, the worst of the actual Cold War coincided with the greatest isolation of Sovietology from the social sciences in the final peacetime years of Stalin's rule (1945–1953). But it is worth recalling that Russian and Soviet studies during and prior to World War II were almost entirely atheoretical. Also, the postwar theories of totalitarianism, which were grounded on the presumed similarities between Stalinist Russia and Nazi Germany, were nonetheless theories. Furthermore, the Harvard Project included a number of fine social scientists, some of whom soon left the field of Sovietology to pursue their broader theoretical interests (e.g., Barrington Moore, Jr., and Alex Inkeles).

The Khrushchev and Brezhnev years of peaceful coexistence and detente generally parallel the uneasy coexistence between social science and Soviet area studies. Western analysts made periodic efforts to reduce the conflicts, distrust, and misunderstandings among the two competing intellectual orientations and to expand the spheres of cooperation, reconciliation, and reconstruction. To be sure, there were no academic U-2 incidents or Cuban missile crises, a few minor flareups notwithstanding. But the USSR began a two-decade military buildup in the mid-1960s, used force to establish several new third-world client states in the 1970s, and persistently rejected peaceful coexistence in the "ideological" sphere. Analogously, some deep-rooted suspicions derailed detente between Western social science and Sovietology throughout the Khrushchev and Brezhnev periods. Like the top Soviet and U.S. leaders, Western social scientists and Sovietologists could never agree on the type or degree of relaxation of tensions, to say nothing of the mutual benefits of sustained collaboration.

Fortunately, some Sovietologists and social scientists tried to communicate, compromise, and create, and a few Sovietologists became "social science literate." The net result was new insights, information, and techniques that added to our understanding of Soviet politics and, to a much lesser extent, incorporated data from Soviet experience into middle-range social science theories. These accomplishments, together with considerable inertia, occasional failures and foolishness, and persistent barriers between Sovietology and social science, deserve to be scrutinized for both academic and pragmatic reasons.

We believe that political scientists, area specialists, and policy advisors can profit from reading the following thoughtful essays. The authors' differing assumptions, approaches, and conclusions attest to the diversity of opinions and skills of Sovietologists. It is to be hoped that theoretical and methodological pluralism can continue to advance our understanding of the Communist past, the transitional present, and the post-Communist future.

NOTES

1. Allen Lynch, *The Soviet Study of International Relations* (Cambridge, England: Cambridge University Press, 1987), p. 43.

2. Z [Martin Malia], "To the Stalin Mausoleum," *Daedalus,* 119, 1 (Winter 1990), pp. 295–344 (italics added). See also Malia's "From Under the Rubble, What?" *Problems of Communism,* XLI, 1 (January-April 1992), pp. 89–106, and the commentaries that follow, pp. 106–120.

3. The four books cited are: Frederic J. Fleron, Jr. (ed.), *Communist Studies and the Social Sciences: Essays on Methodology and Empirical Theory* (Chicago: Rand McNally, 1969); Susan Gross Solomon (ed.), *Pluralism in the Soviet Union* (London and New York: The Macmillan Press Ltd., 1983); Erik P. Hoffmann and Robbin F. Laird (eds.), *The Soviet Polity in the Modern Era* (New York: Aldine de Gruyter, 1984); and Samuel P. Huntington, *Political Order in Changing Societies* (New Haven: Yale University Press, 1968).

4. Jerry F. Hough, *The Soviet Union and Social Science Theory* (Cambridge, MA: Harvard University Press, 1977).

5. Barrington Moore, Jr., *Soviet Politics—The Dilemma of Power* (Cambridge, MA: Harvard University Press, 1951); Merle Fainsod, *How Russia Is Ruled,* 2d ed. (Cambridge, MA: Harvard University Press, 1965). See also Julian Towster, *Political Power in the USSR, 1917–1947* (New York: Oxford University Press, 1948).

6. Barrington Moore, Jr., *Terror and Progress—USSR (Cambridge, MA: Harvard University Press, 1954).*

7. John N. Hazard, *The Soviet System of Government*, 5th ed. (Chicago: University of Chicago Press, 1980).

8. Zbigniew Brzezinski and Samuel P. Huntington, *Political Power: USA/USSR* (New York: Viking Press, 1964). See also Zbigniew Brzezinski, *Ideology and Power in Soviet Politics*, 2d ed. (New York: Praeger, 1967) and *Between Two Ages: America's Role in the Technotronic Era* (New York: Viking Press, 1970), especially Part III, "Communism: The Problem of Relevance."

9. Alfred G. Meyer, *The Soviet Political System* (New York: Random House, 1965).

10. Alfred G. Meyer, "The Soviet Political System," in Samuel Hendel and Randolph Braham (eds.), *The USSR After 50 Years* (New York: Knopf, 1967), pp. 39–60.

11. Robert C. Tucker, "The Image of Dual Russia," in Robert C. Tucker (ed.), *The Soviet Political Mind: Studies in Stalinism and Post-Stalin Change* (New York: Praeger, 1963), p. 89 (italics added). An earlier version of this essay appeared in Cyril E. Black (ed.), *The Transformation of Russian Society: Aspects of Social Change Since 1861* (Cambridge, MA: Harvard University Press, 1960).

12. Zbigniew Brzezinski, "The Soviet Political System: Transformation or Degeneration?" in Zbigniew Brzezinski (ed.), *Dilemmas of Change in Soviet Politics* (New York: Columbia University Press, 1969), p. 33.

13. For early attempts to stimulate such a revolution, see the essays printed and reprinted in Fleron (ed.), *Communist Studies and the Social Sciences*, and Roger E. Kanet (ed.), *The Behavioral Revolution and Communist Studies: Applications of Behaviorally Oriented Political Research on the Soviet Union and Eastern Europe* (New York: The Free Press, 1971).

14. Works by George Kennan, Merle Fainsod, Barrington Moore, Jr., E. H. Carr, Robert Conquest, Leonard Schapiro, Alex Inkeles, John N. Hazard, Robert C. Tucker, Alfred G. Meyer, John A. Armstrong, Adam Ulam, Zbigniew Brzezinski, and many other political analysts were perceived to have made lasting contributions to our understanding of Soviet domestic politics and foreign policy. For succinct summaries and assessments of many seminal books, see Byron Dexter (ed.), *The Foreign Affairs 50-Year Bibliography: New Evaluations of Significant Books on International Relations, 1920–1970* (New York: R. R. Bowker Co., 1972), pp. 633–686. For a brief comparative analysis of some of these works, including major textbooks, see Erik P. Hoffmann, "The Soviet Union: Consensus or Debate?" *Studies in Comparative Communism*, VIII, 3 (Autumn 1975), pp. 230–244, and Alexander Dallin's rejoinder, pp. 245–247.

15. Erik P. Hoffmann, "Social Science and Soviet Administrative Behavior," *World Politics*, XXIV, 3 (April 1972), pp. 444–471.

16. As Hough suggested in his comment on Hoffmann's critique. See Hough, *The Soviet Union and Social Science Theory*, pp. 228–230.

17. In addition to the work of George Fischer and Michael P. Gehlen, Fleron's work on cooptation falls into this category. See George Fischer, *The Soviet System and Modern Society* (New York: Atherton Press, 1968); and Michael P. Gehlen, *The Communist Party of the Soviet Union: A Functional Analysis* (Bloomington and London: Indiana University Press, 1969). Fleron's work on cooptation appeared as follows: "Toward a Reconceptualization of Political Change in the Soviet Union: The Political Lead-

ership System," *Comparative Politics,* I, 2 (1969), pp. 228–244; "Cooptation as a Mechanism of Adaptation to Change: The Soviet Political Leadership System," *Polity,* II, 2 (1969), pp. 176–201; "Representation of Career Types in the Soviet Political Leadership," in R. Barry Farrell (ed.), *Political Leadership in Eastern Europe and the Soviet Union* (Chicago: Aldine Publishing Company, 1970), pp. 108–139; and "System Attributes and Career Attributes: The Soviet Leadership System, 1952–1965," in Carl Beck et al., *Comparative Communist Political Leadership* (New York: David McKay Co., 1973), pp. 43–85.

18. Alfred G. Meyer, book review, *Soviet Studies,* 42, 3 (July 1990), p. 603.

19. For an earlier discussion of these two realms in Soviet studies, see Fleron (ed.), *Communist Studies and the Social Sciences,* pp. 8–9.

20. For a discussion of multiple advocacy in foreign policy decisions, see Condoleezza Rice, "Is Gorbachev Changing the Rules of Defense Decision-Making?" in Frederic J. Fleron, Jr., Erik P. Hoffmann, and Robbin F. Laird (eds.), *Soviet Foreign Policy: Classic and Contemporary Issues* (New York: Aldine de Gruyter, 1991), pp. 488–508.

21. John A. Armstrong, "The Ethnic Scene in the Soviet Union: The View of the Dictatorship," *Journal of Soviet Nationalities,* I, 1 (Spring 1990), pp. 17–18. Reprinted from Erich Goldhagen (ed.), *Ethnic Minorities in the Soviet Union* (New York: Praeger, 1968).

Part Two

METHODOLOGY AND LESSONS FROM THE PAST

GABRIEL A. ALMOND
LAURA ROSELLE

2

MODEL FITTING
IN COMMUNISM STUDIES

The interaction between political theory and area studies in the last
several decades has taken the form of model fitting—crude, clumsy,
and, sometimes sanguine at the outset, increasingly deft and experimental as time went on and experience accumulated. Soviet, East
European (and now Chinese) political studies, of all area studies,
have been more open to this model-fitting process. This may very
well be due to the scarcity of data about communist societies, and
the effort to enhance insight through experimenting with different
theoretical perspectives.

The argument that we make in this paper is that this model-fitting experience is not to be set aside as ethnocentrism and cultural
imperialism on the one hand, or methodologically gauche "conceptual traveling . . . conceptual misformation . . . conceptual stretching
. . . or conceptual straining" on the other.[1] Both Binder and Sartori
miss the point. Binder surely does not accurately describe the works
of his colleagues when he speaks of "Modernization theory . . ." as
. . . "an academic, and pseudo-scientific transfer of the dominant,
and ideologically significant, paradigm employed in research on the
American political systems" to foreign and particularly non-Western
areas.[2] And Giovanni Sartori in his praiseworthy pursuit of careful,
precise, logically arranged conceptualization, suppresses the messy,
everyday interaction between theory and data which lies at the
heart of creative scholarship.[3]

An early example of self-conscious model fitting in political science was Karl Deutsch's *Nerves of Government* which employed
the analogy of a cybernetic system as a way of illuminating political
processes and concepts.[4] The analogy of communications flows, feedback loops and "steering" produced suggestive insights and hypotheses. Deutsch reviews the experiences with modelling in the
history of political theory citing the model of mechanism—of balance, tension, and equilibrium—in the theories of Machiavelli,

27

Hobbes, Locke, Montesquieu, and the Founding Fathers; the model of organism in classical and Catholic political theory, in Rousseau, and Burke; the grand philosophy of history models—the cyclical model of growth and decay of Plato and Aristotle, of Spengler and Toynbee; and the enlightenment model of progress. He also briefly reviews contemporary social science modelling—formal mathematical systems of equations, game theory, Weberian ideal-typical analysis, and the like.

Deutsch deals primarily with large scale "macro-models" of total societies, political systems, economies, the shape of history, though it is quite clear that he has in mind the experimental model-fitting process that we shall be describing. Models, he points out, have to be tested for relevance; they must be matched against reality. The "model-matching" process is the way to get at the shape of reality. Surely the history of science demonstrates the value of this trial and error, back and forth process, between physical and conceptual imagination, drawing analogies from one subject-matter to another, and experimental tests of these physical, or conceptual models against reality. The development of high energy physics, modern cosmology, and molecular biology with their "charm theories," their "string," "black hole," "meat ball," and "sponge" theories, their "double helix" theories, are illustrative.

The history of communism studies, more than any other of the area studies (except American studies, which are area studies too), reflects the growth of this methodological sophistication. The history of communism studies may be written in terms of these experiments with macro-modelling efforts to capture the whole phenomenon so to speak, and with micro-modelling of aspects of communist politics. The notion of modelling has more than one meaning. In quantitative studies the term "model" is reserved for relations that are expressible in mathematical equations. But the term is also used generically to refer to explanatory mental constructs. The mind has no choice in relating to, adapting to, or attempting to master reality, but to select, summarize, and compare the unfamiliar with the familiar. In what follows we discuss totalitarianism, developmental theories of communist systems, the various treatments of communist politics in terms of pluralism, interest group theory, bureaucratic politics, and patron-client relations, as applications of explanatory models coming from other parts of the political science discipline, as efforts to explain the puzzling, the unfamiliar, by the known, by the familiar. This use of the model concept is relatively clear-cut. An interest group explanation of Soviet or Chinese politics seeks to explain the political process and its outputs by the action and interaction of groups defined in some way. Do actions of groups and coalitions of groups add up to a particular decision process and policy outcome? Group process concepts have been used with some effect in studies of American and European politics. Do they explain political processes and policy decisions in communist systems?

But the interaction of communism studies with other parts of the political and social science disciplines is not simply via explanatory models. Communism studies have also been influenced by theoretical frameworks drawn from sociological, anthropological, and political theories such as structural-functionalism, decision process theory, modernization theory. We discuss these imports into communism studies as heuristic theories, as conceptual frameworks of variables which enable us to formulate questions and hypotheses. Thus structural-functionalism and decision process frameworks, by requiring communism specialists to assume the existence of political processes, led to the experimentation with specific schemes such as bureaucratic politics, interest group, and patron-client theory.

THE TOTALITARIAN MODEL

The first model used in the study of communism was "dictatorship." Indeed the Soviet regime referred to itself as a "dictatorship of the proletariat" (or of its "vanguard," the Communist Party), a stage in the development of communism, before the state gave way to simple administration in the post-class struggle phase, first of socialism, and then of communism. For political scientists in the 1920s and 1930s it was classed with Italian Fascism and National Socialism. The comparative government of the interwar period had two classes of political systems—democracies and dictatorships. Dictatorship was defined in essentially negative terms; it eliminated effective popular participation and representation, the rule of law, division and separation of powers.

The first inkling that something new was afoot was in some speeches of Mussolini in the mid-1920s when he referred to Fascist Italy as *uno stato totalitario,* meaning by that, national unity, the elimination of opposition, and the end of special interest domination. As Fascist power became more penetrative and Nazi Germany came on the scene, the term became generic, at first including only Germany and Italy. In the later 1930s "there was at least some disposition . . ." to include the Soviet Union, ". . . a disposition which was muffled during the war period, but which revived with the onset of the cold war."[5] In the mood of World War II Japanese military authoritarianism was assimilated to the model.

Perhaps the first self-conscious recognition that totalitarianism was a new form of government was a lecture by the historian Carlton J.H. Hayes entitled "The Novelty of Totalitarianism in the History of Western Civilization" delivered at a meeting of the American Philosophical Society in November 1939.[6] Hayes lists four novel characteristics of this governmental system: (1) its monopoly of all powers within society; (2) its mobilization of popular support; (3) its effective use of techniques of education and propaganda; and (4) its emphasis on national power and the use of force.

The two works, however, which established totalitarianism as a unique type of political system appeared in the aftermath of the Second World War, Hannah Arendt's *Origins of Totalitarianism,* and Friedrich's and Brzezinski's *Totalitarian Dictatorship and Autocracy.*[7] Both studies described totalitarianism as a uniquely twentieth-century occurrence and both singled out the combination of terror, coercion, propaganda, and manipulation as the distinctive instruments of totalitarian rule. Arendt sought the origins of the system in anti-semitism, nationalism and imperialism, while Friedrich and Brzezinski focused on the distinctive institutions and practices of totalitarian rule. Perhaps Arendt's most important insight into the politics of totalitarianism was her thesis that rather than being a stable monocratic distribution of power, it was inherently arbitrary in the interest of maximizing power at the center. Generalizing from the Hitler and Stalin cases, she pointed out that the extraordinary concentration of power in their hands was associated with maintenance of several competing organizations—a mass party, a secret police, and military services—and the refusal to make stable delegations of power and function to any one of them.[8] Friedrich and Brzezinski presented a general model of totalitarian dictatorship based on six criteria: (1) an official, monopolistic ideology; (2) a single mass party; (3) terroristic police control; (4) a monopoly of the communication of ideas; (5) a monopoly of weapons; (6) a centrally directed economy. These six characteristics formed the "syndrome" of the pattern of interrelated traits common to totalitarian dictatorships.

During the decade of the 1950s the totalitarian model dominated Soviet studies. The leading texts tended to interpret Soviet institutions and political processes primarily, if not solely, in terms of this extreme concentration of power.[9] The focus was on the central role of the Communist party, the personal role of Stalin, and the reliance on political terror.

The totalitarian model ran into rough water in the 1960s. The changes in the Soviet Union that followed the death of Stalin, and the emergence and development of other communist systems raised questions as to the model's applicability, first to the Soviet Union and second, to other communist systems. The lessening of the use of terror under Khrushchev called into question, for example, the totalitarian model's emphasis on terror. The Sino-Soviet split, which came into the open during the early 1960s, led some scholars to doubt the applicability of the totalitarian model in the study of communist China. The disorders in Eastern Europe in the 1950s created a similar problem.

There were noteworthy efforts during the 1960s to modify and amend the model. An early example is an article by Allen Kassof entitled "The Administered Society: Totalitarianism Without Terror," written in 1964. Kassof observed that the "administered society is thus a variant of modern totalitarianism, with the important difference that it operates by and large without resort to those elements of gross irrationality . . . that we have come to associate with totalitarian systems in recent decades."[10] Carl Friedrich, in his revised edition of *Totalitarian Dictatorship*, de-emphasized terror as well. Similarly Arendt in a later edition of her book downplays terror as a necessary and permanent feature of this kind of regime.[11] These efforts at repair retained most of the early features of the model, but treated the terroristic and mobilizational aspects as modifiable in degree.

But the scholarly community was not ready to accept the concept with those minor repairs. There were too many problems with it, too many definitions; too much cold war coloration; failure to explain change over time; and failure to distinguish totalitarianism from other types of autocracy.[12] Linz tried to remedy this situation by distinguishing totalitarian regimes which he confined to Hitler's Germany and Stalin's Russia, from "pre-mobilizational" totalitarian regimes, and "post-totalitarian" regimes under which category he would include the contemporary Soviet Union.

Studies of communism in Eastern Europe and communist China generally eschewed the use of the term "totalitarianism." It is striking that Brzezinski simply does not use the term in his *The Soviet Bloc*;[13] and Townsend in the leading text on Communist China points out that the six criteria of Friedrich and Brzezinski did not fit well.[14] Control rested less on political terror than it did on persuasion and organization.

This intellectual history of communism studies reflects the earlier more naïve use of models; first, the effort to capture the essence of political reality in a simple model (and not in the self-conscious, Weberian "ideal type" sense), and then the disillusionment at the failure of the model accompanied by the rejection of all modelling in favor of the "barefooted empiricism" of area studies. Some of the papers in the Lucian Pye volume, *Political Science and Area Studies*, reflect this disappointment and disillusionment with theory.[15] But this disillusionment with theorizing was rejected, for example, by George Breslauer, who asserts the need for modelling even after the failure of the totalitarian model.[16] "Western frustration with the shortcomings of the totalitarian model has led to a backlash against the use of labels per se, but this is a shortsighted response. Labels can be useful, and one measure of their utility is the dimensions of the system to which they draw attention."[17] The importance of theory in the learning process is also stressed by Abbott Gleason, who pointed out,

It is one thing to criticize the totalitarian model. It would be quite another if the rejectors had not already thoroughly absorbed its insights. . . . The insights of one generation, especially the crucial ones that define its vision of the world, are often sitting ducks for those who speak for the next generation. From a scholarly point of view, the rejection of the idea of totalitarianism may be crucial to whatever the successor generation of scholars achieves in the way of understanding the Soviet Union and other Communist states.[18]

There had, however, been a more conceptually imaginative multi-model minor trend in Soviet studies beginning in the 1950s. Barrington Moore in his perceptive study, *Terror and Progress—USSR,* employed three models in combination as a way of explaining and forecasting Soviet development.[19] Many aspects of Soviet political and economic life lent themselves to a patron-client, traditionalistic interpretation—factionalism, "cliquism," "familistic" behavior and the like. Other aspects lent themselves to an industrializing rational-technical pattern of explanation. And finally, there were aspects which lent themselves to an ideological, totalitarian model of explanation. Moore argued that all three dynamisms were present in Soviet politics; their relative dominance varied by issue and sphere, and over time in response to external and internal pressures.

Daniel Bell published an article enumerating some ten different approaches to the study of Soviet politics including social culture and personality theories, Marxist and non-Marxist industrialization theories, totalitarianism, geopolitical approaches, and the like.[20] He explores the ways these various approaches illuminate different aspects of Soviet politics, and advocates an eclectic approach in Soviet studies.

Alex Inkeles, more parsimoniously, suggests three models rather similar to those of Barrington Moore: (1) totalitarianism; (2) industrialization; and (3) developmental.[21] He points out that some aspects of Soviet development can be explained by the totalitarian model, some by the generic industrialization model, and some by the requirements of an effective national administrative structure and economic growth. He observed that other models, such as the national characterological, also had useful insights to offer.

But the move into experimental model fitting in communism studies actually began in the discontent in the sub-discipline as it moved into the post-Stalin era when much of what was happening in the politics of communist countries could not be explained by the totalitarian model, when decentralizing, legalistic, and pluralist bargaining features began to manifest themselves. Abbott Gleason, for example, claims that "with passage of time the Soviet Union seems more and more understandable in terms of rather traditional categories."[22] Hence, it is not accidental that the first major alternative model to be tried out was that of pluralism or "interest group" theory. Similarly it is not surprising that experimentation began with case studies of policy processes in efforts to test various models for fit. But before concluding the discussion of totalitarianism it should be noted that after having been set aside for some two decades, there has been a small step back toward acknowledgment of the usefulness of the totalitarian model. It is still widely viewed as quite appropriate in analyzing the historic Stalinist and Nazi systems, and as a tendency in contemporary communist countries.[23] The limited utility that the totalitarianism concept still retains is reflected in discussions in Frederic Fleron's *Communist Studies and the Social Sciences,* as well as in such leading texts as Barghoorn on Soviet politics, Jerry Hough and Merle Fainsod on Soviet politics, and James Townsend on Chinese politics.[24] Leonard Schapiro offers a history of the use of the totalitarian concept and makes an important argument in favor of its continued limited utility.[25] Joseph LaPalombara offers a trenchant review of this polemic and points out that the pluralist writers qualify their revisionism by acknowledgment of the unitary and coercive features of these regimes. He takes a skeptical view of pluralist reinterpretations, and adopts the modified view of totalitarianism of Juan Linz.[26]

HEURISTIC THEORY AND FRAMEWORKS

What follows in this chapter is a brief account of the interplay of political theory and communism studies since the 1960s. Not all of it can be strictly accommodated under the modelling metaphor. There have been conceptual imports into communism studies which are "mapping" or heuristic devices facilitating description and comparison, and thus ultimately contributing to explanation, but not in themselves explanatory competitors. System theory, structural functionalism, decision theory, and political culture theory are examples of these heuristic imports from political, sociological, psychological, and anthropological theory. They are conceptual frameworks suitable for the description and comparison of any political system, or explanatory variables as in the case of the political culture concept. Such frameworks and concepts enable us to do the job of explanation of politics and policy systematically and rigorously. They are of a different order from the patron-client model, interest group model, the bureaucratic politics model, and the like, which have been put forward as tentative explanations of communist political processes. Thus a patron-client factional model of communist politics would explain it in terms of the rivalry and competition of patron-client factions concerned with power and patronage, with policy a secondary concern. An interest group model would seek to explain communist politics in terms of group conflict and bargaining over power and policy. A bureaucratic politics model of communism would explain power and policy in terms of propensities and standard operating procedures of bureaucratic organizations. A rational choice, game theoretic model would seek to explain communist politics in terms of competing actors with different resources calculating short-term material interests and pursuing strategies and forming coalitions on the basis of those interests. Another heuristic export from social science theory has been political culture theory which stresses the importance of subjective or psychological variables in the explanation of politics. Political culture theory has had an unusually successful "run" in communism studies, helping to explain the survival, even the vitality, of pre-communist and non-communist attitudes and values, despite powerful efforts to eliminate them.

STRUCTURAL FUNCTIONALISM AND DECISION THEORIES

The first major postwar text on Soviet politics, Fainsod's *How Russia Is Ruled,* dominated the field for more than a decade.[27] It was an authoritative, essentially historical-institutional-descriptive study oriented around the totalitarian model, though not minimizing important lines of cleavage and dissent. Barrington Moore's early study of *Soviet Politics* is an impressive account of the interplay of ideology and historical circumstance in the shaping of the Soviet economic, social, and political system.[28] His *Terror and Progress* to which we have already referred is a logical extension of his argument in this earlier work that historical reality—internal and external—has produced a social system differing in fundamental ways from what was predicted in Soviet ideology. However, the categories he employs in this earlier work are essentially historical and institutional.

Three other texts that first appeared in the 1950s and early 1960s—those of Adam Ulam, John Hazard, and John Armstrong—also were essentially historical institutional studies.[29] While sociological and anthropological theory had some impact on the work of Barrington Moore in the 1950s it was not until the appearance of David Easton's *The Political System,* and Lasswell's *Decision Process,* and Almond's "Comparative Political Systems," that system and functional concepts began to penetrate comparative politics and studies of communist systems.[30] Frederick Barghoorn's *Politics in the USSR* was the first major experiment in the application of functional categories in the analysis of Soviet politics, and James Townsend's *Politics in China* applies a similar functional scheme to Communist China's politics.[31]

Other text treatments of Soviet and Chinese politics have adapted in varying degrees to system-functional and decision-process analysis. Thus Jerry Hough's adaptation of the Fainsod text involves employing a policy-process perspective in the second half of the book, dealing with such themes as citizen participation and political inputs, agenda setting and support building, factional conflict and pluralist tendencies, policy initiation, policy debates, and the like. Hough justifies this shift in the volume's emphasis by arguing that "research and writing about Western governments has centered on the policy-process and the factors associated with responsiveness in political systems, and meaningful comparative political science requires that a conscious attempt be made to ask the same questions about the Soviet Union."[32] Mary McAuley's Penguin book, *Politics and the Soviet Union*, deals with the contemporary Soviet political system in terms of the new policy-process approach, using a policy case study technique.[33] The influence of Dahl, Allison, Skilling, Almond, and Powell is evident in her work. The current edition of David Lane's *Politics and Society in the USSR* has two substantial chapters (7 and 8) presenting a system-functional approach to Soviet politics and the group basis of Soviet politics. In his preface he describes his approach in the following terms: "I have sought to bring together the fruits of research, conducted both in the West and in the USSR, to give a synoptic view of Soviet society studied from the viewpoint of the social sciences. While the political process is examined as a political 'system,' other more traditional ways of study, such as the description of political 'institutions' have not been excluded . . ."[34] In his more recent textbook focused more particularly on politics, the approach used in analyzing the political process is also in part a system-functional one.[35] A more recent text on communist systems by Stephen White and others follows a system-structural, policy-process format, and deals at length with the significance of political cultural factors in explaining differences in political patterns.[36] White and his colleagues suggest a trial and error model-fitting approach similar to the one developed in this chapter, but they deal only briefly with the totalitarian, modernization, and bureaucratic models.

The diffusion of system-functional concepts into continental European Soviet studies is reflected in the work of Georg Brunner who relies heavily on the American literature for his concepts and categories. After reviewing other functional categorizations he presents a three-fold functional scheme: (1) basic decision; (2) implementation; and (3) control. On the structural side the party dominates the decision and control functions, while the state and social organizations perform the implementation function. A later chapter on interest groups does not quite fit into this scheme.[37]

Two important conceptual steps have been taken in these structural-functional and decision-process studies. The first is the separation of the policy-process from structure and institutions. To understand a single country's political process, to say nothing of comparing it with others, requires asking functional or process questions. How is policy made and implemented? What institutions and agencies are involved in what ways in the articulation, communication, and aggregation of demands, and the making and implementation of decisions? A purely historical, structural approach tends to impute particular functions to particular structures, whereas in actual fact the typical pattern is one of multifunctionality of structure. A structural approach to communist systems would leave us with the dilemma of how to characterize the significant changes in communist political processes which have occurred while institutions have substantially remained the same. The second conceptual step is to require students of communist systems to assume a political and policy process. Daniel Tarschys has shown how the adoption of systemic and functional notions in the 1960s directed the attention of communist scholarship to the input side of the political process, rendering the older model of a purely administered "output" society obsolete.[38] T. H. Rigby, in a study of the changing composition of party leadership and membership in the Soviet Union in the half century from 1917 to 1967, shows how these changes were related to policy initiation, aggregation, communication, socialization, and recruitment.[39]

The conceptual models which have been employed by students of communist politics have come from the Almond-Powell threefold scheme of system, process, and policy functions, or from administrative decision theory which breaks the policy process down into phases which typically include agenda setting, issue analysis, decision-taking, implementation, evaluation, and termination.[40] Decision theoretic approaches may be normative or prescriptive, that is, they may examine a decision process from the point of view of its rationality, the extent to which ends are clearly formulated, and means chosen to attain those ends; or explanatory, that is, the extent to which the decision process is rigorously described, and its phases explained and related to outcomes. Case studies of Soviet foreign policy-making may exemplify the prescriptive approach to foreign policy decision-making. Examples of this approach would be the various studies of the Berlin crises of the 1948–1962 period, the Middle East crises of the 1950s and 1960s, the Cuban Missile crisis, the Czech crisis and others. This work and the larger decision theoretic literature is reviewed in Horelick et al.[41] The explanatory decision theoretic approach is exemplifed by William Potter who breaks the decision process down into five phases: (1) initiation; (2) controversy; (3) formal decision; (4) implementation; and (5) termination.[42] Potter then evaluates the literature on Soviet foreign policy-making from the point of view of its effective coverage of these five phases. Aspaturian in a recent analysis of Soviet foreign policy decision-making uses a similar scheme, but does not include termination.[43]

POLITICAL CULTURE

While interest in attitudes and values as an explanation for political behavior is an ancient theme in political theory, in recent decades research and theoretical speculation about political culture has been associated with four historical puzzles. The first of these was the fall of the Weimar Republic and the rise of National Socialism in Germany; the second, the decline of civic culture in Britain and the United States, and the rise of consensual democratic political culture in Germany in the 1960s and 1970s; the third development was the frustration of efforts to export democratic attitudes and practices to third world countries. The fourth puzzle was the remarkable persistence in communist countries of ethno-linguistic-national particularisms, religious commitments, and political opposition and dissent, despite the enormous effort mounted in these countries to eliminate these propensities and replace them with a new Marxist-Leninist political culture.

The collapse of democracy in Germany in the 1930s shook confidence in the relationship between industrialization, education, and democratization. What could explain this brutalization of politics and opinion in a country which had excelled in its trained and talented labor force, in scientific discovery, technological invention, and in artistic creativity? The decline of consensual politics in Britain and the United States during the 1960s and the 1970s and its rise in Germany during the same decades raised questions about the stability and persistence of political attitudes, given sharp fluctuations in governmental effectiveness and performance. The rapid collapse of democratic institutions in third world countries demonstrated the "stickiness" of traditional attitudes and values. Finally, the intermittent popping up of dissenting nationalistic, religious, ethno-linguistic, and political movements in communist countries despite the sustained, massive, and penetrative efforts on the part of the communist elites to develop a homogeneous "communist man" political culture, stimulated political culture research and speculation among scholars specializing in these areas.

In fact the political culture bibliography in the last decade has more entries from communism studies than from other areas. The first full length treatment of communist political culture, sub-culture, and political socialization was in Barghoorn's study of Soviet politics. Within a few years Richard Fagen published a study of the effort of the communist movement to create a new "Cuban man," urging that the concept of political culture be broadened to include behavior as well as attitudes.[44] This polemic over the definition of the political culture concept has been continued by Robert C. Tucker, Stephen White, and others.[45] In a thoughtful analysis of this issue, Archie Brown, drawing on anthropological debates about the definition of culture, shows that the more inclusive "kitchen sink" definition of culture has been increasingly set aside by anthropologists in recent decades in favor of a subjective definition (one limited to cognitive, affective, and evaluative factors) rather than including behavior and even artifacts. This shift among anthropologists "represents a recognition that making an analytical distinction between the cognitive world of the actors and the realm of events and transactions in which they engage points up the problematic nature of the relationship between the subjective and cognitive realm, on the one hand, and the behavior on the other, in a way conducive to reflection and research on the nature of the interactions."[46]

The bibliography dealing with communism and political culture theory in general terms includes Fagen, Tucker, Brown, Jack Gray, McAuley, Stephen White, and Almond, among others.[47] The main theoretical issues have to do with definition and methodology. What should be included under the political culture rubric; and, given the difficulties of access for the collection of data, how is it possible to determine the extent of persistence of pre-communist, or the creation of non-communist propensities? Stephen White suggests an ingenious method of determining the significance of historical-cultural factors in the political life of communist countries.[48] He draws on John Stuart Mill's approach to comparative analysis, combining the methods of agreement and difference in contrasting the historical and contemporary experience of communist countries.

Barghoorn is the acknowledged pioneer in the treatment of political culture in the Soviet Union. All three editions of his *Politics in the USSR* deal with historical patterns, subcultural tendencies, elite political culture, and socialization and communication processes.[49] A book-length treatment of Soviet political culture by Stephen White emphasizes mass political culture, presenting substantial empirical data produced by Soviet social scientists on popular attitudes and beliefs.[50] He makes the argument that the acceptance of absolutism on the part of the Soviet masses is largely explained by Russia's historical pattern of absolutism. This point is disputed by Barghoorn who insists that the extreme coercion and terror of the Stalin years as well as the monopoly of communication and organization are important contributing factors.

Another polemic in the Soviet political culture field deals with the nature of popular participation in Soviet politics. Barghoorn and Friedgut emphasize the mobilized and subject-participatory character of mass participation.[51] Di Franceisco and Gitelman, on the basis of a substantial number of interviews with Soviet emigres, assert that mass participation, while focused on the implementation side of the policy process, includes both a ritual conformity component and a quantitatively significant component of "particularized contacting" *à la* Verba and Nie.[52] In other words, there is greater activism in Soviet politics than is suggested in the notion of subject participation, but it takes the form of approaching party and governmental authorities on private and personal needs.

The political cultures of the Eastern European countries demonstrate the extraordinary staying power of nationalist and liberal tendencies, and traditional ethnic and religious propensities in the face of the most penetrative efforts to eliminate them or assimilate them into the communist system. Czechoslovakia, Poland, Hungary, and Romania each in their own way have managed to force a compromise on the Soviet-backed communist efforts to create homogeneous "socialist" cultures.[53] The Yugoslavian experience suggests how these socio-political systems might modify themselves if Soviet pressure were withdrawn.[54]

In this connection it is of interest that the concept of political culture has been widely adopted in the Soviet Union itself and with a definition not too far removed from that used in the West. While Soviet scholars assume that socialist political culture is the normative version of political culture toward which human history tends, they acknowledge the persistence of older historical tendencies, and the socialization processes which preserve them, in the Soviet Union, in the Eastern European countries, in the Third World and the West. Soviet scholars have used survey research particularly in the study of the political culture of youth in Russia.[55] Empirical studies of attitudes and opinion on political, ideological, and social issues have been carried out in a number of Eastern European countries as well.

THE DEVELOPMENTAL MODEL

Quite early in communism studies different versions of modernization and development theory were applied in efforts to explain and predict the course of political change. Thus the industrial development model was one of the three models used by Barrington Moore and Alex Inkeles in speculating about the dynamics of Soviet politics.[56] Huntington and Brzezinski in their comparative study of the US and USSR explained converging political tendencies in terms of the common impact of industrialization and modernization, while at the same time arguing that differing historical and ideological patterns would prevent a complete convergence.[57]

Social mobilization theory in its earlier version predicted that political mobilization would follow upon social mobilization (industrialization, urbanization, education, mass communication). Karl Deutsch, S.M. Lipset, James Coleman, Inkeles and Smith, and many others contributed to a literature which anticipated tendencies toward democratization in communist countries as they succeeded in industrializing.[58] The conceptual apparatus of modernization theory was applied to Eastern European communist countries by Jan Triska and his associates.[59] Paul Johnson, in particular, presented a set of hypotheses about the relationships among economic, social, and political modernization variables in Eastern European countries, and suggested a research design which might be used to test the validity of these hypotheses.[60]

Huntington explained the development of the "Leninist party" in terms of the political-economic dynamics of modernization. The Leninist party provided an organizational framework capable of containing a society mobilized by industrialization, urbanization, spreading literacy, and the mass media.[61] Richard Lowenthal argued more than fifteen years ago that we ought to expect a profound alteration in the functions and operations of the CPSU as it shifted from its earlier penetrative, mobilizing, and transformative role, to that of reacting and interacting with a basically transformed socio-economic base. "Yet though the totalitarian institutional framework has been preserved, the basic relation between the political system and the development of society has been reversed. Formerly the political system was in command, subjecting an underdeveloped society to forced development and to a series of revolutions from above. Now the political system has to respond to the pressures generated by an increasingly advanced society."[62] Lowenthal anticipated a political transformation which would include the legitimation of policy conflict within a framework of bureaucratic rationality, but which would be marked by tension between pluralist impulses and efforts to contain them and avoid instability and the threat of systemic change. Kenneth Jowitt advanced the theory that there were only two routes to the modern world—the liberal route, historically unique and no longer available, and the Marxist-Leninist route of forced modernization. He saw no future for reformist incrementalism.[63] But in later writing as he reflected on the experience of such communist countries as Yugoslavia, Poland, and Romania, he introduces the category of neo-traditionalism to explain the stagnation and corruption of communist regimes.[64]

Broadly speaking, the development model, the historical persistence-cultural model, and the ideological model have been the principal competitors in efforts to explain future political change in communist societies. The development model predicts that given industrial-technical development, historical-cultural differences and ideological differences would gradually lose their explanatory power to the point of insignificance. The historical-cultural persistence model argues that no matter how powerful and homogeneous these technocratic-industrial developments are, historical-cultural propensities would produce significant differences in development patterns. An ideological model argues that political ideological goals could both significantly modify historic-cultural propensities, and contain the unintended consequences of technical-industrial change. It is a tribute to the originality of Barrington Moore's original formulation that this threefold approach still survives as the most inclusive explanation of the dynamics of communist systems and change.

Andrew Janos in his recent *Politics and Paradigms* goes beyond Barrington Moore, arguing that he and, indeed, the entire classical Marxian-Weberian-Parsonian modernization tradition can no longer explain developmental processes in the modern world, that a global division of labor and system of communications has been reached in which international political-economic forces have important explanatory power. Janos foresees a new paradigm which will recognize the looseness of the relationship between internal mobilization variables and cultural-political change.[65] Innovations and ideas

> float freely from society to society and from continent to continent . . . and as ideas move from core to periphery, they will encounter different configurations of interest, giving rise to different institutional responses and patterns of behavior. The ideas of modern secularism and popular sovereignty are cases in point. Whereas in the West they gave rise to parliamentary democracy, elsewhere the corresponding institutional expression is most frequently bureaucratic authoritarianism.[66]

Janos overlooks the fact that the international environment was of enormous importance in the shaping of the European states and their institutions, and that this has been recognized and elaborated in the work of Hintze, Tilly, and many others.[67] Similarly the importance of international demonstration effect and of diffusion in western development has been elaborated in Heclo and debated in Flora and Heidenheimer and others.[68] It is not clear how Janos' new paradigm differs from the positions taken by other development theorists, in particular those listed in his table who postulate different development outcomes attributable to differences in internal characteristics, historical timing, and international context.[69]

In an earlier, more focused treatment of the prospects for Soviet development, George Breslauer lists some five "images" of the Soviet future to be found in the literature of Soviet dissent, and Western Soviet scholarship.[70] These are, working from left to right, socialist democracy, elitist liberalism, welfare state authoritarianism, Russite fundamentalism, and various forms of instability and fragmentation. On Dahl's polyarchy scale, socialist democracy would involve transformation in the direction of both participation and contestation; while elitist liberalism would represent movement in the direction of pluralism limited primarily to technocrats and intellectuals.[71] On the right, Russite fundamentalism would represent the coming to dominance of chauvinistic, anti-semitic, anti-intellectual propensities present among some sections of the military, the police and even in some sections of the party. Breslauer finds a number of different varieties of instability predicted in the literature. These include ethnic fragmentation occurring in a context of economic stagnation, military conflict, and Russite favoritism; and recurrent political crises resulting from economic and political immobilism. Breslauer's left and center alternatives are similar to the predictions of the development school which anticipated political mobilization and pluralist tendencies resulting from modernization; while Russite fundamentalism is one version of the traditionalist or neo-traditionalist alternative described in Moore, Jowitt and others.

In the center of Breslauer's continuum is "welfare state authoritarianism" which approximates contemporary Soviet reality. Breslauer describes a "leftist" and "rightist" version of welfare state authoritarianism. The leftist version would involve a budgetary shift toward a consumer economy, expanded opportunity for ethnic minorities, opening up of the political process to some participation and a narrower definition of political deviance; this moderate leftward movement would be associated with detente and increased foreign trade and cultural exchange. The rightist version would involve moves in contrary directions on all these dimensions. Breslauer expects the foreseeable future to oscillate between these two welfare authoritarian tendencies.

PLURALIST MODELS

Discontent with the totalitarian model as a description of the communist political process led to a willingness to experiment with a family of pluralist models—interest group theory, corporatism, and issue network and policy community theories.

The concept of pluralism entered political science as an attack on the theory of sovereignty. The theory of sovereignty in turn emerged in the state-building processes of the fifteenth to nineteenth centuries, affirming and justifying the central state authority of the absolutist regimes. In its extreme form, as in Hobbes, the sovereign was viewed as the fashioner of law and as unlimited by any other source of law, human or divine. And in the middle and late nineteenth century in connection with the late development of the nation-state in Germany and Italy, and the general rise of trade unions, democratic, and socialist parties, a theoretical polemic developed affirming the ultimate sovereignty of the central state on the one hand, and the autonomy and legitimacy of such other institutions as churches, communities, regions, professions, the family on the other. Otto Gierke, John Figgis, Leon Duguit, Harold Laski, Ernest Barker and others argued that rather than viewing society as an association of individuals dominated by the central state, it ought to be viewed as an organization of co-equal and cooperating groups—churches, professional associations, trade unions, local communities as well as the state.[72] These constituent groups had their own legitimacy which ought not to be set aside by the central state. Such theorists as Bentley and Mary Parker Follett went even further, reducing government and the state to interest group phenomena, and viewing public policy as the product of the free play of group pressures.[73]

The relationship between this "pluralism" of political theory, and the pluralist models that were employed in, and rose out of, the empirical interest group research of the decades since the First World War, is more complex than is suggested in the work of Berger, Manley, and Krasner.[74] These empirical interest group approaches, as in Merriam and Schattschneider, did not attribute equality to the various interests, nor did they decry the "autonomy" of the state.[75] Samuel Huntington describes the history of American political science in terms of the succession of three paradigms—the progressive, the pluralist-conflictual, and the pluralist-consensual.[76] The progressive historians such as Beard, Parrington, and Turner, interpreted American politics as a conflict between a narrow economic elite, and a populist mass.[77] The early empirical pluralist tradition represented in the works of such political scientists as Merriam and Schattschneider took a critical view of the group interest basis of American politics, arguing that while groups influenced the government, business interests were far more powerfully organized and effective than other groups.

The pluralist-consensual model was developed in the work of Herring, Truman, and others in the New Deal and post–Second World War period.[78] Here the pluralist model took into account the rise of organized labor and the development of the welfare state. Pluralism was viewed as a relatively open system in which workers as well as farmers and businessmen, blacks as well as whites, had access to the political process.

What the Herrings and Trumans did was to modify the earlier conflictual pressure group model of Merriam and Schattschneider. They saw interest groups as functional to democracy. In the contemporary debate about pluralism in American democracy, the earlier muckraking model has been forgotten. Thus we would have to correct John Manley's Pluralism I and II.[79] He really is contrasting Pluralism II with Pluralism III; and Pluralism II has much in common with Pluralism I. The Pluralism I of Merriam and Schattschneider is by no means the equilibrium, balanced model of Bentley and Latham. It is a model in which democracy is biased by a concentration of political resources in the business class; quite similar to the picture drawn in Lindblom's *Politics and Markets,* and Dahl's *Dilemmas of Democratic Pluralism.*[80]

The empirical models of pluralism in American political studies have been caricatured in still another respect. The political scientists of the decades of the 1930s to the 1960s produced a very large literature on the Congress, the Presidency, and public administration. Thus, the same writers associated with the pluralist position have also produced studies illustrative of the autonomy and importance of governmental institutions. Thus Pendleton Herring wrote *Presidential Leadership* and *Public Administration and the Public Interest.*[81] V.O. Key, Jr. wrote *The Administration of Federal Grants in Aid to the States,* and David Truman wrote *Administrative Decentralization.*[82] We may argue that prior to going abroad, interest group models were the focus of the principal polemic in American political studies.

In its voyages abroad, *pace* Sartori, interest group theory had a similarly constructive polemical and theoretical effect. In the 1950s and the 1960s interest group studies moved to the European and then to the Latin American areas. Henry Ehrmann and Almond chronicle the European trip, and Stepan and Schmitter the Latin American.[83] These last two voyages produced the corporatist models which we discuss below.

THE INTEREST GROUP MODEL
IN COMMUNIST STUDIES

But interest group theory had one of its most interesting stopovers in communism studies. H. Gordon Skilling was one of the first students of communist countries to suggest that interest groups also function there as well.[84] In a later symposium a number of Soviet specialists applied interest group theory to various aspects of Soviet politics.[85] Some argued that not only do groups exist in communist systems, but that they initiate policy ideas in competition with other groups, and that Soviet leaders take the demands of groups into account in making policy. This was a sharp break from the totalitarian model, and its significance was emphasized in a new version of Fainsod's early book by Jerry Hough who argued that "The basic insights of the interest group and factional conflict approaches about the presence of conflict in the Soviet policy process should be seen as a valuable supplement to other models and should not be considered controversial."[86] A flurry of attacks on Skilling's work and on Hough's more extreme version of the interest group approach to communism studies followed, suggesting that the approach was indeed controversial. Thus William Odom wrote "A Dissenting View," Andrew Janos took a "Second Look," and David Powell had problems "In Pursuit of Interest Groups in the Soviet Union."[87] LaPalombara in his "Monoliths or Plural Systems: Through Conceptual Lenses Darkly" implied that communism specialists were suffering from blurred vision.[88]

Some of these critics were assuming that Skilling had advanced the interest group approach as *the* explanatory model of Soviet politics. But as Skilling explains in his most recent discussion of the issue "interest groups were not asserted to be the most significant feature of the Soviet polity, still less was policy considered an automatic product of group pressures."[89] Using the interest group model illuminated important aspects of Soviet politics. Skilling also argued that interest groups are compatible with an authoritarian system, although they are subject to restrictions imposed by the state. Some scholars doubted the appropriateness of the group concept in treating communist political phenomena. Griffiths, for example, spoke of "tendencies" rather than groups.[90]

One of the most constructive developments coming out of this polemic regarding the "totalism-pluralism" of communist systems was the resort to policy case studies as a way of testing the validity of the interest group approach. Thus Joel Schwartz and William Keech examined group influences in the educational policy processes in the Soviet Union; Philip Stewart has investigated the politics of industrial education; Peter Solomon has written about the politics of Soviet criminal policy, and Thane Gustafson has examined Soviet land and water policy.[91]

The interest group approach has also entered into the China field. Early examples would be the work of Oksenberg, Liu and Esmein on the Cultural Revolution.[92] Goldman and Pye have also used group theory implicitly in their work on Chinese political processes.[93] Most group studies, however, were limited to the analysis of the Chinese political elite. David Goodman sought to remedy this situation in an edited symposium on groups and politics in the PRC.[94] Goodman notes the reliance in China studies on the use of the totalitarian model, although the term itself was rarely employed. He argues that experimentation with a group perspective may be "a necessary stage of development because it is thought probable that it will provide some obvious (and sharp) contrasts with the dominant totalitarian model(s)."[95] By initially focusing on elite behavior and not testing alternative pluralist models, China studies failed to generate the kinds of empirical data that had enriched Soviet and communism studies. The death of Mao and the example of Soviet studies set the stage for the incorporation and testing of interest group models in China studies. By focusing on groups one is able to focus on political process and the relationship between political and social systems. Contributors to this Goodman symposium presented case studies on the military, economists, teachers, peasants, workers, intellectuals and the political elites.

An important contribution to the interest group literature, treating the various communist countries of Eastern Europe, is the study of the "blue collar" workers edited by Jan Triska and Charles Gati.[96] The workers had previously been neglected in the literature. The book focuses on working class attitudes and political behavior. There are a number of case studies of specific problems in East European countries. One theme is that in the absence of working class organizations articulating their interests, informal and anomic activities predominate. Alex Pravda's contribution to the volume reports on labor disorders and strikes, through which workers attempt to articulate their interests.

Another group-focused contribution to the study of Eastern Europe is the symposium edited by Zvi Gitelman and Walter Connor which examines public opinion and interest groups in the USSR,

Poland, Czechoslovakia and Hungary.[97] Gitelman argues that the "modernization of East European society has resulted in the partial emergence of publics—collectivities that confront issues, discuss them, and divide over them."[98] Knowledge of these groups, their attitudes and propensities is essential to the understanding of the political processes of these countries.

In a lucid and comprehensive review of the debate about pluralism as it relates to Soviet studies, Archie Brown concludes that the work on interest group theory has greatly expanded our knowledge of the politics of communist countries. But the picture does not justify calling it pluralism. The groups are not open or autonomous.

Archie Brown acknowledges that Czechoslovakia in 1968, and Poland in 1980–1981, were de facto pluralist-socialist states in the sense in which Dahl defines pluralism.[99] On the other hand efforts to rescue pluralism by qualifying it as "institutional-pluralism" or "bureaucratic-pluralism," fail to distinguish communist patterns from non-communist ones. Departmental particularism, and bureaucratic crypto-politics are well-nigh universal phenomena.

CORPORATISM

One offshoot of the totalitarian-pluralist polemic was a search for a model which would combine features of both, and would take into account the empirical complexity of communist regimes. "Corporatism," a theme out of Latin American and European studies, has appeared promising to some students of communist countries. Corporatism, as a political theory, emerged in the nineteenth and early twentieth centuries in two versions; a "guild socialist" kind of corporatism elaborated in the work of the British political theorist, G.D.H. Cole and a corporatist version developed in Catholic political theory.[100] The pluralist version of corporatism led to various proposals for functional representation such as adding a special legislative chamber to represent economic and professional "interests" to existing parliamentary chambers, or formally introducing interest representation into existing legislative chambers. There have been some experiments with functional representation in one or two European countries. The Catholic version, expressed first in the Papal Encyclical, *Rerum Novarum* issued in 1892, was the Church's answer to Marxist class struggle doctrine on the one hand, and liberal capitalist individualism on the other. The social reality of mankind could not be expressed simply in class terms, nor in isolated individual terms, but rather in the complex of groupings in which men and women are associated—families, communities, regions, professions and occupations, and the like. The state must accommodate the legitimacy and autonomy of these groupings, and they must have a share in public decision-making. The appropriation of corporatist ideas and institutional arrangements by Fascist Italy, Nazi Germany, as well as authoritarian Austria, Spain and Portugal, discredited corporatism in the first postwar decades.

Contemporary corporatist theory rests on the discovery that in many European countries and in Latin America, interest group activity differs from the open, relatively unregulated competition familiar in American politics. Stein Rokkan and Robert Kvavik had made this point earlier with regard to the Scandinavian countries.[101] In these countries, in the Low Countries, in Austria, to a lesser extent in Germany, the interest group–government bargaining process is a more orderly, more regulated matter. It typically involves a limited number of economic-occupational organizations "recognized by the state" and "enjoying a representation monopoly within their respective categories."[102] It involves regularized bargaining over wage, price, and investment policy between these interest groups and relevant parts of the government bureaucracy. Cameron has demonstrated that this pattern of industrial and economic policy-making is associated with greater stability, slow but continuous economic growth, less inflation, and more substantial welfare benefits, than is the case with the more competitive interest group countries such as the United States.[103] Katzenstein attributes this pattern of interest group relations to the vulnerability of small nations to international political, military, and economic threat and pressure, primarily since the great depression of the 1930s.[104] Schmitter distinguishes between societal and state corporatism, and it is the statist version of corporatism that has had some appeal to communism specialists.

Bunce and Echols viewed state corporatism rather than pluralism as a more apt description of the Soviet system under Brezhnev.[105] The evidence that they adduced is largely based on Brezhnev's efforts to balance and accommodate the interests of the party professionals, the industrial managers, the government bureaucracy, the scientists, and the agricultural sector, in the aftermath of the Khrushchev era. In a later discussion Valerie Bunce argues that corporatism in the Soviet political process fluctuates in relation to pressure on the Soviet economy. Thus in the early Brezhnev era there "was a mode of interest intermediation that sought to minimize conflict and maximize productivity by incorporating dominant economic and political interests directly into the policy process, while cultivating the support of the mass public through an expanding welfare state."[106] In the latter years of the Brezhnev regime pressure on Soviet resources from Eastern Europe, from increasing involvement in costly foreign ventures, and the accelerating arms race, skewed the political process towards the military and heavy industry, foreclosing the bargaining power of light industries and labor. Bunce concludes that "corporatism does not live easily with large international commitments, both because of their costs and because of the contradictions in domestic class alliances that such commitments generate."[107] She disagrees with Archie Brown's argument that in the Soviet system these "interests" lack the legitimacy and autonomy that a corporatist regime would require—even in its statist version. According to Bunce periods of international relaxation and lowered military costs may move the Soviet polity in a corporatist direction with relatively open bargaining processes.

Hough objects to the application of the corporatist model to the Soviet case on the grounds that it ignores the fact that the state itself is segmented, and "that this segmentation has to be understood in terms of different societal interests."[108] Skilling complains that too little research has been done in terms of corporatism to test its utility.[109]

Archie Brown, along with Schmitter, Linz, and Stepan, has argued that the corporatist model may be applicable to Yugoslavia and perhaps other Eastern European communist countries.[110] With regard to the broad applicability of corporatism to the analysis of communist politics, Brown concludes tentatively that, "A transition from a Communist Party state, organized to maintain the party's control within and vis-a-vis every other organization, to a corporatist one is not, in principle, impossible, and one could argue that in Yugoslavia, and perhaps in Hungary, we have begun to see a new type of corporatism emerging."[111]

ISSUE NETWORKS AND POLICY COMMUNITIES

Another model coming from American studies is "issue network" or "policy community" theory. This approach has its origins in the recognition that political processes vary according to issue or policy areas. The concept was first seriously advanced in Dahl's *Who Governs* in which he demonstrated that the structure of political power in New Haven varied according to the substance of the issues in conflict.[112] Theodore Lowi argued more explicitly that there were four relatively distinctive political process patterns according to whether the issues were extractive, regulative, distributive, or redistributive.[113] Freeman and others advanced the argument that there were many sub-governments or "iron triangles"—persistent relationships between administrative bureaus, congressional committees and their staffs, and interest group officials and technicians—that controlled access to the political process as it affected tax policy, welfare policy, health, transportation, conservation, and defense and other spheres of public policy.[114] Heclo viewed the "iron triangle" phenomenon as an unusual rather than a typical phenomenon, and preferred the looser formulation "issue networks" as more descriptive of the tripartite interaction among legislative, administrative, and interest group personnel.[115] His point was that the movement of policy specialists into and out of issue areas was too fluid to be captured by the "iron triangle" metaphor.[116] John Kingdon uses the term "policy community" to describe this loosely "corporatist" phenomenon; but it is not clear that this term differs very substantially in meaning from the issue network concept.[117]

An early application of issue network theory to Soviet studies was Zimmerman's "Issue Area and Foreign Policy Process."[118] Perhaps the most extensive application of the issue network model is to be found in Nina Halpern's study of the role of economists in the making of Chinese economic policy.[119] She also provides an excellent review of the literature dealing with interest group, bureaucratic, and patron-client models. John Lewis makes an interesting connection between issue network and clientelist theory which we discuss below.[120]

Students of Soviet politics employ related concepts. Thus John Lowenhardt writes about "policy coalitions" in his study of Soviet decision-making.[121] Hough associates his notion of institutional pluralism with issue "whirlpools" and complexes.[122] Political conflicts "tend to be compartmentalized with the debate in each policy area or whirlpool being largely limited to those whose careers are related to the issue, and others who have developed a special interest in it."[123] Skilling, on the other hand, views network theory as a variation on the interest group theme. It may, however, turn out to be a more appropriate model for communism studies since it does not carry the connotation of formal organization and autonomy.

BUREAUCRATIC POLITICS

In the questioning about the "fit" of the totalitarian model in the 1960s another option that received attention was that of bureaucratic politics. Bureaucracy has been a central theme in the history of Marxism-Leninism. In Marx the state and bureaucracy were associated with class domination. Eliminate class, eliminate the state and bureaucracy. This was the Leninist utopia as well. Once class exploitation was eliminated any washerwoman would be able to carry out the simple administrative tasks required in the communist society. In the early years of the Soviet Union Lenin, and Trotsky in particular, viewed the emergence of Soviet bureaucracy as a threat to, or actual betrayal of the revolution.

Early scholarship on Soviet politics also developed the bureaucratic theme. Barrington Moore's threefold scheme of tendencies in Soviet politics included bureaucratic politics as one of the three. This was the rational-technocratic impulse, the instrumental rationality of Max Weber, that Moore imputed to the emerging bureaucracy in the Soviet industrializing process. In the post-Stalin era, when some of the features of totalitarianism had subsided, the view was expressed that the technocratic bureaucracy now dominated the whole of Soviet society. Thus Alfred Meyer described the whole of the USSR as "a large bureaucracy comparable in its structure and functioning to giant corporations, armies, government agencies, and similar institutions."[124] The whole system, he claims, is a vast bureaucracy united by common goals which the central hierarchy guides and controls. Meyer's view of the role of bureaucracy in Soviet politics is similar in many ways to the view presented by those who describe the Soviet Union as an "administered" society, or as an "organized" or "command" society. Kassof sees, for example, one powerful ruling group as having a monopoly of the knowledge necessary to plan and coordinate the system. In Rigby's command society there is one group (the party and its leader) which has control, while the rest of the system is obedient and fulfills the ruling group's plans.[125] Armstrong also depicted hierarchical administration as being characteristic of the bureaucracy, but he insisted that the structure was not rigid and uniform.[126] In his comparison of bureaucracy in the Soviet Union and Western Europe he takes into account informal and personal relationships and utilitarian motivations common to both, as well as significant differences such as the relative lack of efficient communication in Soviet bureaucracy.

In his book, *The Soviet Union and Social Science Theory,* Jerry Hough offers a critical review of the literature on bureaucratic politics.[127] He asks how bureaucrats and bureaucracy are to be defined as applying to the Soviet Union. Does the definition include the whole managerial stratum—political, governmental, military, industrial, scientific? The career patterns of all these managerial groups are similar, and Hough concludes that they are all parts of a bureaucracy. He then asks whether a bureaucratic model which stresses hierarchy and uniformity really captures the essence of the Soviet policy-making process. His conclusion is in agreement with Barghoorn's formulation that "We should not make the mistake of assuming that uniform socialization, centralized recruiting of executives, and the hierarchical structure of the political bureaucracy ensure unity of perspective or purpose among Soviet decision-makers. On the contrary, much evidence indicates that discord, conflict, and political infighting may play a larger, though concealed, role in one-party systems, than in democracies."[128]

Hough concludes that only case studies of Soviet institutions, and public policy areas, can begin to reveal the complexity of the Soviet decision-making process. He cites studies of industrial management by Granick, Berliner, and Azrael as examples of the kind of research likely to bring our understanding of Soviet politics to a higher level of resolution.[129]

The bureaucratic model has been frequently used in studies of Soviet foreign policy. Horelick, Johnson, and Steinbruner discuss the applicability of the bureaucratic politics model to Soviet decision-making in their Rand study.[130] William Potter demonstrates the value of using an organizational decision-making approach in the study of Soviet foreign policy-making.[131] Distinguishing between the initiating, deliberating, legitimating, implementing, and terminating phases of foreign policy decision-making enables one to locate the political actors in the relevant organizations, and spell out their roles in the decision process.[132] Jiri Valenta experimented with the bureaucratic politics paradigm in a case study of Soviet decision-making in the Czech crisis of 1968.[133] Gail Lapidus recommends the use of a bureaucratic pluralist model in the analysis of Soviet policy toward China.[134]

The bureaucratic politics model has had an interesting encounter in Chinese political studies. Thus Lucian Pye points out that because of Chinese political cultural and structural factors, the bureaucratic politics model does not work well.

> Instead of having bureaucratic politics that involve the clashes of functionally specific interests, the Chinese political system remains a "bureaucratic polity," that is, a small hierarchically organized elite of officials whose attitudes, values, and personal relationships shape all decisions. In a bureaucratic polity, the decisionmakers do not have to respond to pressures from the society at large, and no interests outside of the state (or single party) hierarchy are allowed.[135]

There is an emphasis on personal relationships. Oksenberg and Lieberthal have both examined linkages in Chinese politics.[136] Oksenberg examined the communications process in particular, finding horizontal communications he did not expect to find which suggested the importance of informal, lateral interaction in Chinese politics. These questions among China specialists as to the aptness of the bureaucratic politics model lead to the "patron-client" model to which we now turn.

PATRON-CLIENT RELATIONS

Each of these models in its exclusive form claims to be able to explain the output of political processes. A totalitarian model explains outputs as initiated by the central leader, and as implemented through the political process without significant modification. A pluralist model explains outputs as related to the strength of competing groups and their coalitions, and their access to the political process. A bureaucratic politics model explains outputs in terms of the standard operating procedures and policy propensities of bureaucratic agencies. It is the rare exception these days that any one of these models is advanced in exclusive terms.

The patron-client model came into prominence in the 1970s. What led to the experimentation with clientelism in communism studies was the evident importance of factionalism, power struggles, patronage, and corruption in these countries, and the failure of the totalitarian or pluralist models to account for these phenomena. Studies of this kind had emerged in the Soviet field independently of theory, as exemplified in the "kremlinology" studies. The most elegant example of this tradition was Robert Conquest's extraordinary analysis of "Soviet dynasties."[137] By the 1970s patron-clientelism as an analytical model had emerged all across the area disciplines, and there was a theoretical literature as well.

The patron-client model had its origin in anthropological and sociological theory, and it has been described and analyzed in a substantial ethnographic and historical literature covering the first, second, and third worlds, the present, the recent, and more remote pasts. James Scott's masterful bibliographical essay on clientelism includes more than a thousand items.[138] The principal theoretical analyses of political clientelism are to be found in the writings of Carl Lande, and in his work reprinted in Schmidt *et al.,* and in those of James C. Scott, Rene Lemarchand and Keith Legg, Eisenstadt and Lemarchand, and others.[139] The general theoretical point made in these writings is that the ultimate unit of political interaction in all societies is the *dyad,* the interaction of two persons, normally a dominance dependence, or patron-client relationship. Factions are made up of constellations of dyads with differing structures and different relationships, operating within such formal organizations as parties, interest groups, parliaments, and bureaucracies. Power and patronage are the currency of clientelist systems; policy is a secondary matter.

While factional power groups and cliques have been well known in Soviet studies since early on, it was not until the publication of a paper by Andrew Nathan, presenting a factional model for Chinese politics, that the explicit link-up with patron-client theory was made.[140] Two of the seminal influences on Nathan's work were Lande's study of clientelism in the Philippines and James Scott's paper on patron-client politics in South-east Asia.[141] Nathan's analysis of politics in China was also substantially influenced by Nathan Leites' "operational code" analysis of factional politics in Fourth Republic France.[142] Nathan presents an operational code of Chinese factionalism which includes some fifteen propositions. These stress the essentially defensive and limited nature of factional struggle, the consensual basis of decision-making, and the secondary nature of policy and ideology. While he found that analyzing the Cultural Revolution in these terms was illuminating, it was essential to recognize that

> factional struggle occurs within the context of a broad consensus on goals and methods. It would therefore be a mistake to identify the factionalism model with a crude power struggle theory, if the latter assumes that leaders are cynical in their ideological statements. But it

would be equally foolish to believe that in China alone men's perspectives on ideological and policy issues are not influenced by their individual political vantage points. The occasional impression that this is so may be the result of our knowing so much more about the issues than about the vantage points.[143]

In a thoughtful and theoretically informed monograph on clientelism in Chinese policy-making, John Lewis argues that "informal networks are pervasive in the Chinese policy process."[144] Citing the literature of anthropological network theory which posits networks as universal units of social structure, Lewis first makes the point that "networks underlie all strategies for coalition building in political as well as other social situations."[145] He then distinguishes between dense and loose networks.

In a relatively closed or 'dense' network, the component members interact frequently, and network 'gatekeepers' tightly control information from and to individuals outside the network including officials. Although dense networks may blunt or distort any leadership's implementation and monitoring of policies, the more extreme (or successful) forms of loose networks can also deflect centralized policy control since they can become alternative leadership systems of vast scope and influence. Dense networks of small scope can act as impenetrable fortresses, or to change the metaphor, as rival tribes, whereas large, loose networks can function as actual governing regimes. Both types of network coexist in China.[146]

There is substantial evidence that there are dense networks in China of the kind described by Lewis, and that they are viewed by the Deng regime as subversive of reformist and developmental plans. Locally based networks are able to establish "regional economic blockades." Privilege-seeking clientelism is pervasive throughout China, extending into the higher reaches of authority, and it frequently goes beyond privilege seeking and influence peddling into criminal behavior. Lewis hints at the importance of regime-supportive clientelism—using influence networks to enhance productivity and otherwise implement regime goals. Thus the struggle in Chinese communist politics would seem to be between power and privilege-oriented clientelism, and issue network clientelism, between power and privilege on the one hand, and policy orientation on the other. Lewis argues,

The task for Chinese studies beyond generating important questions, can start only with the aberrant behavior of networks. Eventually, however, we must deal directly with the roles that social networks play throughout the policy process. Often troublesome and destructive to policy implementation in the past, these networks may be the key to policy innovation and problem solving in the future. To make this possible, China's national leaders have made the transformation of political networks a priority task.[147]

Lucian Pye in his recent *Asian Power and Politics* describes the varieties of patron-clientelism to be found in the politics of Asian countries, their dependence on different political cultures, and their consequences for power and politics in East, South-east, and South Asia. He points out,

> In the East Asian societies which were once infused with Confucian values, political associations are themselves seen as being properly modelled after the family and the clan, and hence participants are expected to act as though they were banded together in a blood relationship. . . . The patterns in South and Southeast Asia, while not so explicitly modelled on the family, are also strongly group-oriented, but according more to the ties of patron-client relationships. In South Asia, and especially in India, this has meant that the politics of patronage generally prevails over the politics of policy implementation. In Southeast Asia the politics of entourages and cliques, of personal networks, and associations, are critical for the building of coherent national power structures. Thus, even such hierarchical institutions as national bureaucracies and military establishments tend to be facades for pyramids of informal, but enduring, patron-client groupings.[148]

The importance of patron-client relations for Indian politics is suggested by Pye as explaining the absence of demoralization when grandiose plans go awry. "In this society of nurturing superiors and their dependent inferiors it is possible for people to find satisfying rewards in spite of failed grand designs."[149] The uniquely accommodative mode of adaptation to change which characterized Japanese historical development is explained by Lucian Pye as attributable to a propensity to build power "upward from the motivations of subordinate and local networks of relationships. . . . The same patterns of mutual dependency between superiors and subordinates were at work when the Japanese made their distinctive adaptations of Confucianism, and finally of American democracy. With each adaptation leaders and followers have deferred collectively to what they have taken to be a better, larger system, even while preserving the essence of their basic approach to power."[150]

A symposium published in *Studies in Comparative Communism* presents a patron-client analysis of Soviet politics by John Willerton with comments on Eastern Europe by Zygmunt Bauman, on China by John Burns, on Japan by Nobutake Ike, on advanced industrial societies by Keith Legg, and general comments by T.H. Rigby.[151] As evidence of the importance of patron-client networks in the Soviet Union, Willerton examines the clustering of members of the Central Committee around members of the Politburo.[152] Evidence of clustering into clientelistic networks is inferred from associated upward and downward shifts of Central Committee members as their patrons in the Politburo rise and fall.

Bauman confirms the importance of these lateral patronage linkages in Eastern European politics, but he is less confident of Willerton's measuring of these linkages simply by coinciding regional origins, and related upward and downward movements of upper and lower party figures.[153] John Burns reports the polemic in Chinese political studies which followed on Andrew Nathan's clientelistic interpretation of the Cultural Revolution. He argues that any clientelistic approach has to be reconciled with organizational, cultural, and ideological factors in explaining political behavior and public policy.[154] Nobutake Ike in his discussion of clientelism in Japan makes the general point that no political system can function without an element of trust, friendship and personal loyalty, and that whenever and wherever there is distrust and insecurity, protective relationships form.[155] From this point of view the universality of clientelism may be safely assumed. The interesting question is how it combines with other criteria such as ideology and formal organization in the making of public policy. Finally Rigby draws this useful symposium to a conclusion by pointing out that, "Patronage is a widespread, perhaps almost universal dimension of social systems, although it is perhaps only in feudal and quasi-feudal societies that it assumes a central organizing importance."[156] At the same time he points out that

> it would be foolish to assume that the causes and character of clientelism in western industrial bureaucracies and bureaucracies of Soviet type systems are identical. The point rather is that the systematic comparison may help elucidate just how far and in what respect the latter are *sui generis*. Further, to the extent that common features are established, the Western industrial bureaucracy literature may throw some light on the Soviet case, which is not open to direct field study.[157]

A symposium edited by Rigby and Harasymiw on leadership recruitment and clientelism in the Soviet Union and Yugoslavia brings together a great deal of information on the communist *nomenklatura* system of controlling and regulating staffing and promotion at the upper levels of the communist employment hierarchy.[158] It also deals with the ways in which clientelism works within this framework. Gyula Josza imaginatively likens patron-clientelism in the USSR to a *Seilschaft,* a roped party of mountain climbers. He points out that in the Soviet Union and other communist countries patron-client studies have largely been confined to the upper levels of the hierarchy. The farther down one goes the more inadequate biographical details become. He summarizes the data yielded in various studies of various central and local networks, and concludes that these networks are tolerated by top leaders since they may "contribute substantially to the functional capacity of the system in so far as they loosen the rigidity of rules and thereby ease the mutual blocking of each other's efforts by the different bureaucracies . . . and finally, they are able to patch up conflicts between local and central interests."[159]

This last collection of papers dealing primarily with the Soviet Union, John Lewis's treatment of this theme in the context of China studies, and Lucian Pye's concern with the ways in which differences in culture affect patterns of clientelism, reflect the growing sophistication of communism studies.[160] Students of these phenomena now systematically place them in the context of theories of political recruitment and policy-making.

OTHER MODELS

There are, of course, other models which have been generated in the social sciences, and which have only been tested in limited ways in communism studies. Thus, communications theory in at least two senses has been applied in Soviet and communism studies. In the first sense there is an overlap with bureaucratic or organization theory. Oksenberg and others (see above) have been concerned with the nature of information flows in the Chinese bureaucracy. The predominance of informal communication suggested to Oksenberg that factional and patron-client interactions might be dominating issue-oriented policy-making and implementation. Erik Hoffmann suggests that a combination of communications theory, organization theory, and role theory applied in communism studies would be productive of insights into the effectiveness of the Soviet polity and economy.[161] Thus the responsiveness and effectiveness of Soviet decision-making would be dependent on flows of information from and to the international and domestic environments. The cybernetic model would lead one to observe the "feedback" and "steering" mechanisms of Soviet institutions. A predominance of vertical communication and restrictions on lateral communication in economic decisions might seriously affect efficiency and productivity by limiting feedback. A communications model would lead one to look for blocks and biases in Soviet information and communications processes, and ask questions as to the effect of such blocks and biases on industrial policy, security policy, and the like.

Ellen Mickiewicz, viewing Soviet communications patterns developmentally, concludes that the older "two-step flow" theory which was adapted to Soviet politics by Alex Inkeles, is no longer applicable to Soviet communication, just as it is no longer accorded validity in American studies.[162] A combination of mass education and the spread of electronic media, particularly television, has reduced the importance of opinion leaders and agitators. Hence the image of the

Soviet polity as thoroughly penetrated and manipulated by the oral agitation of party local and cell leaders may no longer be applicable. The party cannot so thoroughly pre-empt the air waves; and the information transmitted by these means cannot be carefully interpreted by party members as was previously the case. Lacking the organizational means of directly penetrating policy processes, the Soviet mass public surely is not as important as in Western democracies; nevertheless there may be significant changes in Soviet policy processes attributable to the media revolution.

Very little use has been made of the public choice or rational choice model of political analysis in communism studies. This approach to political research, which applies models taken from economic theory to electoral, political, and legislative processes, and which has had substantial success in generating hypotheses about American political processes and institutions, has not as yet been given much of a test in foreign contexts. Economists specializing in the Soviet and other communist economies, have done a certain amount of modelling of economic decisions in centrally managed economies. But a real test of this approach in illuminating communist political processes is still to be made. From this point of view William Welsh's game theoretic analysis of the Hungarian Revolt of 1956 was an isolated research initiative, and his recommendations as to how the formal theory of games would have to be adapted to be useful in empirical research seem to have fallen on deaf ears.[163]

CONCLUSIONS

The literature which we have reviewed describes a rich and complex interaction between communism studies and empirical political theory. Figure [2].1 suggests the sources and directions of this process of diffusion. From the social science disciplines—political science, sociology, social psychology, and anthropology—came the developmental and modernization models, structural-functionalism, and political culture. From American and European political studies came the pluralist family of models—interest group theory, issue network and policy community theory—and the bureaucratic politics model. We might with equal justice attribute the bureaucratic model to Weberian sociological and political theory, but it came to communism studies via American models of organizational process and decision-making. From European and Latin American studies came the neocorporatist model; and from South-east Asian studies came the patron-client model. The only internally generated model in communism studies was the totalitarian one; and as our discussion suggests it still retains a limited utility.

How other area studies rank in openness to theoretical experimentation is a matter of separate and careful inquiry. A preliminary

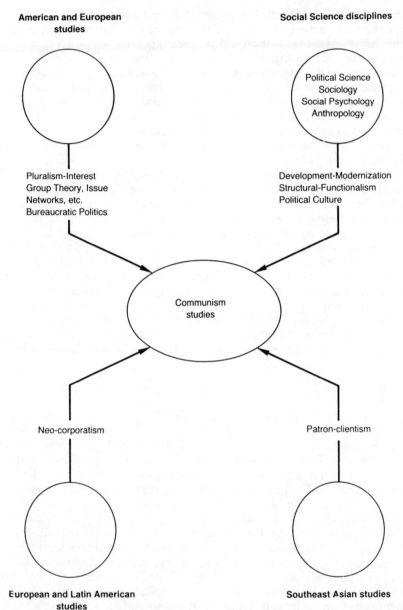

FIGURE [2].1 Diagramming interaction among communism studies, the social science disciplines and other area studies

impression suggests that communism studies ranks highest in this theoretical ecumenism, while Latin American studies would rank at the low end of the scale, though recent surveys suggest that this isolation may be abating.[164]

This conceptual experimentation in western studies of communist systems has stirred up some curiosity among Soviet and Eastern European scholars. There is a kind of dialogue going on between western scholarship and its communist counterparts. There have been more than echoes among Soviet political theorists of the concept of political culture. Political culture research has been defined by leading Soviet political scientists as one of the major subfields of political science, and a number of books have been published dealing with theoretical and empirical aspects of this theme.[165] Soviet political theorists are currently facing the problem of defining the state and the political system, and locating the state within the larger political system. They are seeking to escape from class reductionism, by attributing autonomy to the state, the capitalist state as well as the Soviet state. There is a partly covert, but occasionally overt polemic around the issue of monism-pluralism. In a review of the writings of Soviet theorists on the state and the political system, Archie Brown argues that

> What makes the work of these writers both significant and controversial in the Soviet context is their attempt . . . to put on the scholarly agenda the real political process and real political relations within the Soviet Union and elsewhere, and to break away from the legalistic approach which has been far more dominant in Soviet writing on the state and on political institutions than the so-called legal-institutional approach ever was in Western political science prior to the 'behavioral revolution'.[166]

Soviet theorists have added their voices to the pluralistic polemic, in Rousseauan and populist terms. Thus, Archie Brown quotes Shakhnazarov, on the concept of pluralism,

> In recent times one has met with the assertion that socialist democracy is also pluralist in nature. It seems hardly necessary to use an alien concept to characterize the features of the political system of socialism which for a long time have been quite adequately defined in Marxist-Leninist scholarship by such concepts as the needs and interests of classes and social groups, the unity and diversity of these interests, the coincidence or contradiction between them, their defense and expression, coordination, etc. So far as a general definition is concerned, to that vague and ambiguous term, "pluralism," which may be interpreted in all sorts of ways, one ought to prefer the clear concept, "sovereignty of the people," (narodovlastie).[167]

On the broader issue of the creative impact on communism studies of this almost three-decade-long model-fitting experience, we are led to ask what alternative theories and methods might have been employed in efforts to explain communist political reality? There were, of course, the classic methodological antinomies, the nomothetic and the idiographic approaches to explanation—the search, on the one hand, for lawful regularities among variables, for necessary and sufficient causation; and on the other, there is the deep, Geertzian, "thickly descriptive," clinical search for the inward reality of individual cases.[168] Przeworski and Teune in their treatise on the comparative method go furthest in recommending the assimilation of area studies into general theory. In their own language "the role of comparative research in the process of theory building and theory testing consists of replacing proper names of social systems (in this instance, countries) by the relevant variables."[169] From this point of view the Soviet Union, China, Poland, Czechoslovakia, etc. are of interest to us simply insofar as they can serve as experimental "trials" of the relationships among variables, on the one hand, or insofar as they can be explained by laws derived from comparative research, on the other.

If we suppose that a Przeworskian strategy had been adopted, the area study approach would have had to make do with that diminishing part of a nation's behavior not yet explained by general laws. Studies of communist countries would be reducible to events explainable and predictable by these generalizations. Aberrant events might lead to modifications in these generalizations, or to the addition of corollary theories. Albert Hirschman excoriates this extreme behavioral determinism in his "Search for Paradigms as a Hindrance to Understanding."[170] In this paper Hirschman compares two then recently published books—John Womack's *Zapata and the Mexican Revolution,* and James Payne's *Patterns of Conflict in Colombia.*[171] The Payne study, based on interviews and questionnaires, forecasts with great certainty a depressing and conflictual future for Colombian politics and economics attributable to the venality and lack of program orientation of its politicians. Hirschman is critical of the extreme behavioral determinism of the Payne interpretation, and its failure to recognize the "open-endedness" of history. He does not reject the usefulness of "models, paradigms, and ideal types." Without such abstractions, he acknowledges, "we cannot even start to think."[172] It is the exaggerated belief in the complete explanatory and predictive power of these models that Hirschman is inveighing against.

Hirschman contrasts Womack's biography of Zapata with the approach in the Payne study. He says, "what is remarkable about the book is the continuity of the narrative and the almost complete, one might say Flaubertian, absence from its pages of the author who could have explained, commented, moralized, or drawn conclusions.

Yet whoever reads through the book will have gained immeasurably in his understanding not only of the Mexican Revolution, but of peasant revolutions everywhere, and Womack's very reticence and self-effacement stimulate the reader's curiosity and imagination."[173] Hirschman's celebration of the Womack book, of course, makes the very best case for the clinical, in depth, empathic approach to political studies. But in his zeal to give a well-earned spanking to Payne, Hirschman leaves not unmentioned but somewhat unelaborated the role played by models and theories in the growth of social knowledge. Womack may not have made his models explicit, but surely a Harvard PhD in history in the 1960s could not have escaped some exposure to sociological and anthropological theory. As Hirschman pointed out there is much theory implicit in it. And everyone seeking to exploit research such as that of Womack's would have had to explicate appropriate generalizations from his study, and compare and combine them with insights acquired from other studies. Had the Womack idiographic strategy been the only strategy pursued in communism studies we would have ended up with a great many in-depth, clinical studies, not adding up to conclusions—it would be neither a cumulative, nor progressive, strategy.

Eckstein explores the methodological ground, left as *terra incognita* by Hirschman, between the idiographic and nomothetic extremes.[174] In an elegant essay on case studies Eckstein describes five points on this continuum, or five types of case studies. The first—the idiographic-configurative has already been exemplified in the Womack study; there are biographies of communist leaders, as well as historical studies which would also exemplify this genre. The intellectual history of communism studies which we have been recounting exemplifies three of Eckstein's types of case studies: the "disciplined configurative," the "heuristic," and the "plausibility probe." Disciplined configurative studies are the least ambitious of these theory-oriented types of case studies. They apply theories to individual cases. Thus "frustration-aggression" theory may be applied to the frequency of disorder in a particular country, and may illuminate events in that country, and may even lead to questioning the theory if the expected interaction does not occur. If this type of case study theory is employed to illuminate the case, the feedback to the validation of the theory itself is fortuitous. Eckstein cites the application of structural-functionalism and political culture theory to individual country studies as examples of the disciplined configurative variety of case study. "Heuristic" case studies, on the other hand, are deliberate theory-testing undertakings. They may, and often do, involve a multiple case-study strategy. The experience in communism studies with the family of pluralist theories exemplifies this type of case study strategy. Thus interest "group" theory has been rejected by some scholars, and "issue network" or political tendency theory proposed instead, on the basis of policy case studies. Valerie Bunce's testing of the corporatist model in the early and late Brezhnev era, is another example of this strategy.

Eckstein's fourth type of case study—"the plausibility probe" is related to the third type, and may actually be a preliminary step intended to estimate the promise of a theory before a substantial investment is made. The "crucial case study" is the most theoretically ambitious type of case study, involving the selection of a case least likely to support the theory. Roberto Michels' "Iron Law of Oligarchy" exemplifies this strategy.[175] If the tendency toward oligarchic domination in all organizations is a "scientific law," then it ought to hold even in situations where deliberate efforts are made to democratize political control. His study of the German Social Democratic Party in the late nineteenth century—where ideology and institutional structure were supportive of democratic process—he viewed as a "crucial" test of the hypothesis. There do not seem to be any examples of crucial case studies in the communist field.

There have also been other substantive strategies pursued in communism studies. These would include the variety of monistic theories—those stemming from Marxism, or from Marxism-Leninism and propounded by communist political theorists; the culture-personality interpretations which were popular in the late 1940s and 1950s; the totalitarian model whose history we have reviewed above; and the modernization-convergence theories which held sway in the Khrushchev era. Our review of the literature makes it clear that all these theories fall substantially short of accounting for Soviet politics and political trends, and that the multi-model theoretical approach and the systematic theory-informed case study approach gives us a more secure understanding of political patterns and potentialities.

But, if we are left with the eclectic, model-fitting approach as the preferred one, we still have to deal with the question of whether these various models fit together in a logic of explanation, and if so, what is the larger logic in which they fit. Ronald Amann in a recent article suggests such a multi-model logical concept of Soviet politics. He divides these interpretations of Soviet politics into Group A and Group B theories: "Group A theories place a heavy stress on the maximization of the power and privilege of the elite and of the nation over which they preside."[176] The variants of the Group A theories include: (1) totalitarianism (a Messianic all-dominant elite); (2) state capitalism (an acquisitive elite exploiting public assets); and (3) neo-traditionalism (systematic venal abuse of office). The variants of the Group B theories include: (1) developmentalism, or institutional change impelled by technological imperatives and leading to democratization; (2) economic decentralization, in which a differentiated economy and society lead to bargaining propensities; and (3) state corporatism in which major social groups are incorporated into a planned framework of bargaining and decision-making. Broadly speaking, the Group A models present a pessimistic view of Soviet potentialities; they add up to the "evil empire" model of Ronald Reagan. There is little prospect for improvement in the climate of international politics. Group B theories, on the other hand, present the Soviet Union as moving to a more open and responsive system, and amenable to negotiation and compromise. Amann comes to the conclusion that none of the variants of the A or the B version of Soviet politics captures its essential characteristics. In their place Amann offers the notion of "hesitant modernizers" as describing the Soviet elite caught between system maintenance and reform. The modernization to which Amann refers includes movement away from extreme central planning in the direction of market incentives, enterprise autonomy, the encouragement of creativity and novelty, and in the political sphere a movement away "from traditional stress on discipline and obedience to greater reliance on material incentives and 'output participation'."[177]

What Amann's analysis misses is the point that while neither conservative Group A theories, nor liberal Group B theories fully capture the dynamics of Soviet politics, a strategy which employs them all in a battery, so to speak, can bring us closer to an understanding of how the system works, and how it might respond to different kinds of environmental changes. Both Group A theories and Group B theories, as well as some which Amann has overlooked, make some contribution to the illumination of communist politics. As we have seen in our brief intellectual history of communism studies, no one of the models could capture the whole of the political reality; but each one generated different questions about it, and brought into relief different aspects of Soviet politics.

Thus the family of pluralist models in their interest group, issue network, policy community, corporatist, and political tendency versions, came to grips with the shortfall in the totalitarian conception. It enabled scholars to deal in a relatively orderly way with conflict and process in the making of Soviet policy. If political conflict Soviet style could not be accommodated to the interest group model, was the "issue network" concept, the policy community model, the "tendency" notion a better match? Functional and decision-theoretic concepts drew attention to the phasing of communist policy-making, the importance of initiation, the structure of policy-making and implementation, and the importance of termination.

The bureaucratic politics model drew attention to the enormous importance of formal organization in the politics of communist countries, but by itself it exaggerated the orderliness and hierarchy of these systems. Here the pluralist family of models and the patron-client model provided the needed correctives, drawing attention to the multiplicity of informal relationships—partly of a task-oriented variety, partly of a self-interested variety—which made it possible for these vast systems of interrelated formal organizations to function in response to leadership goals, on the one hand, or subverted them to personal demands for safety or advantage, on the other. Working with this battery of models, students of communist politics are in a position to observe how changes in the domestic and international environments of communist political systems are connected with changes in their political processes. They may bring out the point that under one set of environmental conditions pluralist or corporatist propensities may manifest themselves; while under another set, centralizing, bureaucratic tendencies may result; and under still a third set of conditions patron-client propensities may become dominant. This kind of model-fitting points the way to dynamic and developmental theories of communist politics.

We should not exaggerate the accomplishments in communism studies which have resulted from this conceptual experimentation. On the eve of these developments—in 1963—Zbigniew Brzezinski and Samuel Huntington published their book, *Political Power: USA/USSR*.[178] It is to the great credit of these then young scholars that practically the entire armamentarium of theoretical innovations described above were applied in this trail-breaking study. Thus, (1) they present a functional or process scheme; (2) in different language they deal with political cultural differences; (3) they employ an interest group model; (4) a bureaucratic politics model; and (5) a patron-client model. And they present five case studies of public policy as a way of discovering the similarities and differences in the policy-making processes of the United States and the Soviet Union. Yet if one compares their treatments of these themes with comparable treatments in more recent work, it is evident that we have reached a higher level of conceptual sophistication, and interpretive capacity. This is in no way to the discredit of these pioneers. Contemporary specialists on communist politics have available to them, in addition to these models and analytical schemes—what is at least as important—a rich collection of events and decisions of the later 1960s, 1970s, and 1980s on which to try them out.

Some of the best examples of contemporary state of the art analysis of Soviet and communist political processes are to be found in the recent writings of Alexander Dallin and Archie Brown, the first reviewing our knowledge of Soviet political processes as they affect foreign policy, the second more broadly generalizing about pluralist, corporatist, and bureaucratic politics interpretations of European communist countries in general. Dallin concludes that "while the handicaps have been immense, a review of the record shows a formidable accumulation of instances supporting and illustrating the hypothesis of Soviet political conflict and, in spite of a frequent sense of frustration (and a number of false starts) on the part of many observers, a remarkable increase over time in insight and sophistication in analysis and interpretation."[179] His chapter on domestic sources of Soviet foreign policy in the Seweryn Bialer volume is a subtle, and analytically sharp review and synthesis of the literature, reflecting the three-decade long experimentation with the bureaucratic, interest group, and issue network models.

Archie Brown's summary of the state of knowledge with respect to interest groups in the politics of communist countries tells the story without exaggerating its theoretical implications.

> If scholars are better aware than they used to be that within the Soviet Union institutional rivalries are tacitly accepted, that certain party and state institutions may have common interests which differ from those of other party and state institutions, that departmentalism and localism exist, that there is covert competition for political office on the basis of what the Czech reformists called "Cabinet politics," that federation provides an institutional base for a limited amount of ethnic diversity and promotion of "national interests" on the part of those ethnic groupings within the party, within the intelligentsia and within the wider society, then this body of work has been of value not only for its general corrective to the totalitarian interpretation, but for the concrete details of political life that it has adduced in areas that did not attract much attention from proponents of the view that the Soviet Union was totalitarian. Yet, for all that it does not constitute pluralism.[180]

But even if the case has not been made out for pluralism in the Soviet Union, students of communist politics, including Brown, view Yugoslavia and other Eastern European countries as having corporatist tendencies. Valerie Bunce argues a plausible case for corporatist phases in the Soviet developmental process, and Brown concedes that there may be such a potentiality. The pluralist polemic, and the polemics over the other models which we have discussed have enabled us to ask more and better questions about communist politics. Systematic knowledge grows through the accumulation of evidence, but the very definition of what is evidence, and the orderly accumulation of evidence, depends on the kinds of questions we ask and the way we go about seeking answers. And here we come to the nub of our argument, that new models generate new questions, and stir up new polemics. And these polemics and the empirical research they stimulate are the life blood of creative scholarship.

Our comments would be incomplete if we did not draw some inferences from this review of the literature that might bear on future studies of communist politics. The use of theoretically informed case studies is already well established in the field. Perhaps a more systematic use of case studies is to be recommended, a more deliberate effort to sample communist politics-cum-policy reality. The ultimate reality of any political system consists of a universe or a population of policy decisions and implementations. It is a "stratified" universe or population. We know that the principal cause of stratification in the policy universe is the substance of issues—"different issues, different politics" as Dahl and Lowi have taught us. The next steps in the development of rigor in communism studies will consist of more systematic research programs—multiple case study research designs intended to sample the variety of communist policy processes—foreign and security policy, fiscal and economic policy, education, health, family, and welfare policy.

NOTES

[This paper has been revised in the light of criticisms and suggestions by Alexander Dallin, Nina Halpern, Joseph LaPalombara, Gail Lapidus, Seymour Martin Lipset, and Thomas Remington.]

1. Giovanni Sartori, "Concept Misformation in Comparative Politics," *American Political Science Review* 64:3 (December 1970), p. 1034.
2. Leonard Binder, "The Natural History of Development Theory," *Comparative Studies in Society and History* 28:1 (January 1986), p. 3.
3. Giovanni Sartori (ed.) *Social Science Concepts: A Systematic Analysis* (Beverly Hills, CA: Sage, 1984).
4. Karl Deutsch, *The Nerves of Government* (New York: Free Press, 1966).
5. Robert Orr, "Reflections on Totalitarianism, Leading to Reflections on Two Ways of Theorizing," *Political Studies* 21:4 (December 1973), p. 481; also see Abbott Gleason, "Totalitarianism in 1984," *Russian Review* 43:2 (April 1984), pp. 145–60, for a review of the origins of the concept.
6. Carlton J.H. Hayes, "The Novelty of Totalitarianism in the History of Western Civilization," *Proceedings of the American Philosophical Society* (Philadelphia, PA, 1940).
7. Hannah Arendt, *The Origins of Totalitarianism* (New York: Harcourt, Brace, 1951, 1966) and Carl J. Friedrich and Zbigniew Brzezinski, *Totalitarian Dictatorship and Autocracy* (Cambridge, MA: Harvard University Press, 1956, 1965).
8. Arendt, pp. 393 ff.
9. Merle Fainsod, *How Russia Is Ruled* (Cambridge, MA: Harvard University Press, 1953); Leonard Schapiro, *The Communist Party of the Soviet Union* (New York: Vintage, 1960); J.L. Talmon, *Political Messianism: The Romantic Phase* (New York: Praeger, 1960); Bertram D. Wolfe, *Three Who Made a Revolution* (Boston, MA: Beacon Press, 1948); Zbigniew Brzezinski, *The Permanent Purge—Politics in Soviet Totalitarianism* (Cambridge, MA: Harvard University Press, 1956); John A. Armstrong, *Ideology, Politics and Government in the Soviet Union* (New York: Praeger, 1962).
10. Allen Kassof, "The Administered Society; Totalitarianism Without Terror," *World Politics* 16:4 (July 1964), p. 559.
11. Carl J. Friedrich and Zbigniew Brzezinski, *Totalitarian Dictatorship and Autocracy* (Cambridge, MA: Harvard University Press, 1956); Hannah Arendt, *The Origins of Totalitarianism* (New York: Harcourt, Brace, 1966).
12. Frederic J. Fleron, Jr., "Soviet Area Studies and the Social Sciences: Some Methodological Problems in Communist Studies," in Fleron, *Communist Studies and the Social Sciences: Essays in Methodology and Empirical Theory* (Chicago: Rand McNally, 1965); Benjamin Barber, "Conceptual Foundations of Totalitarianism," in C.J. Friedrich (ed.) *Totalitarianism in Perspective* (New York: Praeger, 1969); Jeremy Azrael, "Varieties of Destalinization," in Chalmers Johnson (ed.) *Change in Communist Systems* (Stanford, CA: Stanford

University Press, 1970); Juan J. Linz, "Totalitarian and Authoritarian Regimes" in Greenstein and Polsby (eds.) *Handbook of Political Science* (Reading, MA: Addison Wesley, 1975), vol. 3.

13. Zbigniew Brzezinski, *The Soviet Bloc: Unity and Conflict* (Cambridge, MA: Harvard University Press, 1960).

14. James R. Townsend, *Politics in China* (Boston, MA: Little, Brown, 1974).

15. Lucian Pye (ed.) *Political Science and Area Studies* (Bloomington, IN: Indiana University Press, 1975).

16. George Breslauer, *Five Images of the Soviet Future* (Berkeley, CA: Institute of International Studies, 1978).

17. Ibid., p. 6.

18. Abbott Gleason, "Totalitarianism in 1984," p. 158.

19. Barrington Moore, *Terror and Progress, USSR* (Cambridge, MA: Harvard University Press, 1954).

20. Daniel Bell, "Ten Theories in Search of Reality: The Prediction of Soviet Behavior in the Social Sciences," *World Politics* 10:3 (April 1958), pp. 327–65.

21. Alex Inkeles, "Models and Issues in the Analysis of Soviet Society," *Survey* 60 (July 1968), pp. 3–17.

22. Gleason, p. 154.

23. Ernest A. Menze (ed.) *Totalitarianism Reconsidered* (Port Washington, NY: Kennikat Press, 1981); and Stephen J. Whitefield, *Into the Dark: Hannah Arendt and Totalitarianism* (Philadelphia, PA: Temple University Press, 1980).

24. Frederick C. Barghoorn, *Politics in the USSR* (Boston, MA: Little, Brown, 1966, 1972); Frederick C. Barghoorn and Thomas F. Remington, *Politics in the USSR* (Boston, MA: Little, Brown, 1986), pp. 18–19; Jerry Hough and Merle Fainsod, *How the Soviet Union Is Governed* (Cambridge, MA: Harvard University Press, 1979), p. 518; and James R. Townsend, *Politics in China* (Boston, MA: Little, Brown, 1974, 1980, 1986), pp. 191–95.

25. Leonard Schapiro, *Totalitarianism* (New York: Praeger, 1972).

26. Juan J. Linz, "Totalitarian and Authoritarian Regimes," in Greenstein and Polsby (eds.) *Handbook of Political Science* (Reading, MA: Addison Wesley, 1975), vol. 3.

27. Fainsod, *How Russia Is Ruled*; Merle Fainsod, *How Russia Is Ruled*, rev. ed. (Cambridge, MA: Harvard University Press, 1963).

28. Barrington Moore, *Soviet Politics: The Dilemma of Power* (Cambridge, MA: Harvard University Press, 1950).

29. John Hazard, *The Soviet System of Government* (Chicago, IL: University of Chicago Press, 1957); John A. Armstrong, *Ideology, Politics and Government in the Soviet Union* (New York: Praeger, 1962); Adam Ulam, *The New Face of Soviet Totalitarianism* (Cambridge, MA: Harvard University Press, 1963).

30. David Easton, *The Political System* (Chicago, IL: University of Chicago Press, 1953); H.D. Lasswell, *The Decision Process* (Bureau of Governmental Research, University of Maryland, 1956); and Gabriel A. Almond, "Comparative Political Systems," *Journal of Politics* 18:3 (August 1956), pp. 391–409.

31. James R. Townsend, *Politics in China* (Boston, MA: Little, Brown, 1974, 1980, 1986).

32. Hough and Fainsod, *How the Soviet Union Is Governed*, p. vii.

33. Mary McAuley, *Politics and the Soviet Union* (New York: Penguin, 1977).

34. David Lane, *Politics and Society in the USSR* (New York: New York University Press, 1978), p. xiii.
35. David Lane, *State and Politics in the USSR* (New York: New York University Press, 1985).
36. Stephen White *et al., Communist Political Systems* (New York: St. Martin's Press, 1982).
37. Georg Brunner, *Politische Soziologie der USSR* (Wiesbaden, Akademische Gesellschaft, 1977).
38. Daniel Tarschys, *The Soviet Political Agenda: Problems and Priorities, 1950–1970* (White Plains, NY: M.E. Sharpe, 1979).
39. T.H. Rigby, *Communist Party Membership in the USSR, 1917–1967* (Princeton, NJ: Princeton University Press, 1968).
40. Gabriel A. Almond and G. Bingham Powell, Jr., *Comparative Politics: System, Process and Policy,* 2nd ed. (Boston, MA: Little, Brown, 1978); Judith May and Aaron Wildavsky, *The Policy Cycle* (Beverly Hills, CA: Sage, 1978).
41. Arnold Horelick, Ross A. Johnson and John D. Steinbruner, *The Study of Soviet Foreign Policy: Decision Theory Related Approaches* (Beverly Hills, CA: Sage Publications, 1975).
42. William Potter, "Sources of Foreign Policy Change: Insights from the Policy Sciences," *Conference on the Domestic Sources of Soviet Foreign Policy,* UCLA Project on Politics and War, October 11, 1985.
43. Vernon V. Aspaturian, "The Soviet Decision-makers: Where, How, and By Whom Decisions Are Made," UCLA Project on Politics and War, October 10–11, 1985.
44. Richard Fagen, *The Transformation of Political Culture in Cuba* (Stanford, CA: Stanford University Press, 1969).
45. Robert Tucker, "Culture, Political Culture, and Communist Society," *Political Science Quarterly* 88:2 (June 1973), pp. 173–90, and Stephen White, *Political Culture in Soviet Politics* (London: Macmillan, 1979).
46. Archie Brown, "Conclusions," in Archie Brown (ed.) *Political Culture and Communist Studies* (Armonk, NY: M.E. Sharpe, 1985), p. 154.
47. Richard Fagen, *The Transformation of Political Culture in Cuba* (Stanford, CA: Stanford University Press, 1969); Robert C. Tucker, "Culture, Political Culture, and Communist Society"; Archie Brown and Jack Gray, *Political Culture and Political Change in Communist States,* 2nd ed. (New York: Holmes and Meier, 1979); Archie Brown, *Political Culture and Communist Studies* (Armonk, NY: M.E. Sharpe, 1985); Jack Gray, "Conclusions," in Brown and Gray (eds.) *Political Culture and Political Change in Communist States;* Mary McAuley, "Political Culture and Communist Politics: One Step Forward, Two Steps Back," in Brown (ed.) *Political Culture and Communist Studies;* Stephen White, "Political Culture in Communist States: Some Problems of Theory and Method," *Comparative Politics* 16:3 (April 1984), pp. 351–65; and Gabriel A. Almond, "Communism and Political Culture Theory," *Comparative Politics* 15:2 (January 1983), pp. 127–38.
48. White, "Political Culture in Communist States."
49. Barghoorn, *Politics in the USSR.*
50. White, *Political Culture in Soviet Politics.*
51. Barghoorn and Remington, *Politics in the USSR* (1986) and Theodore Friedgut, *Political Participation in the USSR* (Princeton, NJ: Princeton University Press, 1979).

52. Wayne DiFranceisco and Zvi Gitelman, "Soviet Political Culture and 'Covert Participation' in Policy Implementation," *American Political Science Review* 78:3 (September 1984), pp. 603–21; and Sidney Verba and Norman Nie, *Participation in America* (New York: Harper and Row, 1972).

53. Brown and Gray, *Political Culture and Political Change in Communist States;* Brown (ed.) *Political Culture and Communist Studies.*

54. David A. Dyker, "Yugoslavia: Unity Out of Diversity?" in Brown and Gray (eds.) *Political Culture and Political Change in Communist States.*

55. Archie Brown, "Soviet Political Culture Through Soviet Eyes," in Brown (ed.) *Political Culture and Communist Studies*, pp. 100–14.

56. Moore, *Terror and Progress, USSR;* Inkeles, "Models and Issues in the Analysis of Soviet Society."

57. Zbigniew Brzezinski and Samuel P. Huntington, *Political Power, USA/USSR* (New York: Viking, 1965).

58. Karl Deutsch, "Social Mobilization and Political Development," *American Political Science Review* 55:3 (September 1961), pp. 493–514; Seymour Martin Lipset, "Some Social Requisites of Democracy: Economic Development and Political Legitimacy," *American Political Science Review* 53:1 (January 1959), pp. 69–105; James Coleman, "Conclusion: The Political Systems of the Developing Areas," in Gabriel A. Almond and James Coleman (eds.) *The Politics of the Developing Areas* (Princeton, NJ: Princeton University Press, 1960); and Alex Inkeles and David Smith, *Becoming Modern* (Cambridge, MA: Harvard University Press, 1974).

59. Jan F. Triska and Paul M. Cocks (eds.) *Political Development in Eastern Europe* (New York: Praeger, 1977).

60. Paul M. Johnson, "Modernization as an Explanation of Political Change in East European States," in Triska and Cocks (eds.) *Political Development in Eastern Europe.*

61. Samuel P. Huntington, "Social and Institutional Dynamics of One-Party Systems," in Samuel Huntington and Clement Moore, *Authoritarian Politics in Modern Society* (New York: Basic Books, 1970), pp. 3–47.

62. Richard Lowenthal, "Development vs. Utopia in Communist Policy," in Chalmers Johnson (ed.) *Change in Communist Systems* (Stanford, CA: Stanford University Press, 1970), p. 112.

63. Kenneth Jowitt, *The Leninist Response to National Dependency* (Berkeley, CA: Institute of International Studies, 1978).

64. Kenneth Jowitt, "Soviet Neotraditionalism," *Soviet Studies* 35:3 (July 1983), pp. 275–97.

65. Andrew Janos, *Politics and Paradigms* (Stanford, CA: Stanford University Press, 1986), p. 155.

66. Ibid., p. 155.

67. Otto Hintze, *Staat und Verfassung* (Gottingen, Vandenhoeck and Ruprecht, 1962) and Charles Tilly, *The Formation of National States in Western Europe* (Princeton, NJ: Princeton University Press, 1975).

68. Hugh Heclo, *Modern Social Politics in Britain and Sweden* (New Haven, CT: Yale University Press, 1974) and Peter Flora and Arnold Heidenheimer (eds.) *The Development of Welfare States in Europe and America* (New Brunswick, NJ: Transaction Books, 1981).

69. Janos, *Politics and Paradigms,* p. 60.

70. George Breslauer, *Five Images of the Soviet Future* (Berkeley, CA: Institute of International Studies, 1978).

71. Robert A. Dahl, *Polyarchy* (New Haven, CT: Yale University Press, 1970).

72. Otto Gierke, *Political Theories of the Middle Ages* (Cambridge, UK: University of Cambridge Press, 1900); John Neville Figgis, *The Churches in the Modern State* (London, 1913); Leon Duguit, *Traite de Droit Constitutionnel* (Paris: Boccard, 1925); Harold Laski, *Studies in the Problem of Sovereignty* (New Haven, CT: Yale University Press, 1917); Ernest Barker, *Political Thought in England from Herbert Spencer to the Present Day* (London: Williams and Norgate, 1915).

73. Arthur Bentley, *The Process of Government* (Chicago, IL: University of Chicago Press, 1908); and Mary Parker Follett, *The New State, Group Organization and the Solution of Popular Government* (New York: Longmans, Green, 1918).

74. Suzanne Berger (ed.) *Organizing Interests in Western Europe* (Cambridge, MA: Harvard University Press, 1957); John Manley, "Neo-Pluralism: A Class Analysis of Pluralism I and Pluralism II," *American Political Science Review* 77:2 (June 1983), pp. 368–83; and Stephen Krasner, "Approaches to the State: Alternative Conceptions and Historical Dynamics," *Comparative Politics* 16:2 (January 1984), pp. 223–46.

75. Charles E. Merriam and Harold F. Gosnell, *The American Party System* (New York: Macmillan, 1933); Elmer E. Schattschneider, *Party Government* (New York: Farrar and Rhinehart, 1942).

76. Samuel Huntington, *American Politics: The Promise of Disharmony* (Cambridge, MA: The Belknap Press of Harvard University Press, 1981).

77. Charles Beard, *The Economic Basis of Politics* (New York: Knopf, 1922); Vernon Parrington, *Main Currents in American Thought,* 3 vols. (New York: Harcourt, Brace, 1927–1930); and Frederick Jackson Turner, *The Frontier in American History* (New York: Henry Holt, 1920).

78. Pendleton Herring, *The Politics of Democracy* (New York: Norton, 1940); and David Truman, *The Governmental Process* (New York: Knopf, 1951).

79. Manley, "Neo-Pluralism: A Class Analysis of Pluralism I and Pluralism II."

80. Charles E. Lindblom, *Politics and Markets* (New York: Basic Books, 1977); and Robert A. Dahl, *Dilemmas of Democratic Pluralism* (New Haven, CT: Yale University Press, 1981).

81. Pendleton Herring, *Public Administration and the Public Interest* (New York: McGraw Hill, 1936); *Presidential Leadership: The Political Relations of Congress and the Chief Executive* (New York: Farrar and Rhinehart, 1940).

82. V.O. Key, *The Administration of Federal Grants in Aid to the States* (Chicago, IL: Public Administration Services, 1937); and David Truman, *Administrative Decentralization* (Chicago, IL: University of Chicago Press, 1941).

83. Henry Ehrmann, "Interest Groups," vol. XII, *International Encyclopedia of the Social Sciences* (New York: Macmillan, 1968), pp. 241 ff.; Gabriel A. Almond, "Corporatism, Pluralism, and Professional Memory," *World Politics* 35:2 (January 1983), pp. 245–60; Alfred Stepan, *The State and Society: Peru in Comparative Perspective* (Princeton, NJ: Princeton University Press, 1978); and Phillippe Schmitter, *Interest Conflict and Political Change in Brazil* (Stanford, CA: Stanford University Press, 1971).

84. H. Gordon Skilling, "Interest Groups and Communist Politics," *World Politics* 18:3 (April 1966), pp. 435–51.

85. H. Gordon Skilling and Franklyn Griffiths (eds.) *Interest Groups in Soviet Politics* (Princeton, NJ: Princeton University Press, 1971).

86. Hough and Fainsod, *How the Soviet Union Is Governed*, p. 528.

87. William Odom, "A Dissenting View on the Group Approach to Soviet Politics," *World Politics* 28:4 (July 1976), pp. 542–67; David Powell, "In Pursuit of Interest Groups in the USSR," *Soviet Union/Union Sovietique* 6 (Part 1, 1979), pp. 99–124; Andrew Janos, "Interest Groups and the Structure of Power: Critiques and Comparisons," *Studies in Comparative Communism* 12:1 (Spring 1979), pp. 6–20; and Andrew Janos, "Group Politics in Communist Society: A Second Look at the Pluralistic Model," in Huntington and Moore, *Authoritarian Politics in Modern Society*, pp. 437–50.

88. Joseph LaPalombara, "Monoliths or Plural Systems: Through Conceptual Lenses Darkly," *Studies in Comparative Communism* 8:3 (Autumn, 1975), pp. 305–32.

89. H. Gordon Skilling, "Interest Groups and Communist Politics Revisited," *World Politics* 36:1 (October 1983), p. 5.

90. Franklyn Griffiths, "A Tendency Analysis of Soviet Policy-Making," in Skilling and Griffiths (eds.) *Interest Groups in Soviet Politics.*

91. Joel Schwartz and William Keech, "Group Influence and the Policy Process in the Soviet Union," *American Political Science Review* 62:3 (September 1968), pp. 840–51; Philip D. Stewart, "Soviet Interest Groups and the Policy Process: The Repeal of Production Education," *World Politics* 22:1 (October 1969), pp. 29–51; Peter Solomon, *Soviet Criminologists and Criminal Policy: Specialists in Policy Making* (New York: Columbia University Press, 1978); Thane Gustafson, *Reform in Soviet Politics; Lessons of Recent Policies on Land and Water* (Cambridge, UK: Cambridge University Press, 1981).

92. Michel Oksenberg, "Occupational Groups in Chinese Society and the Cultural Revolution," *Chinese Studies* 2 (Ann Arbor, MI: University of Michigan, Center for Chinese Studies, 1968); Alan Liu, *Communication and National Integration in China* (Berkeley, CA: University of California Press, 1971); and J. Esmein, *The Chinese Cultural Revolution* (London: Deutsch, 1975).

93. Merle Goldman, *China's Intellectuals: Advise and Dissent* (Cambridge, MA: Harvard University Press, 1981); Lucian W. Pye, *Dynamics of Chinese Politics* (Cambridge, MA: Oelgeschlager, Gunn & Hain, 1981).

94. David S. Goodman (ed.) *Groups and Politics in the People's Republic of China* (Armonk, NY: M.E. Sharpe, 1984).

95. Ibid., p. 6.

96. Jan Triska and Charles Gati (eds.) *Blue Collar Workers in Eastern Europe* (London: Allen & Unwin, 1981).

97. Zvi Gitelman and Walter Connor (eds.) *Public Opinion in European Socialist Systems* (New York: Praeger, 1977).

98. Ibid., p. 5.

99. Archie Brown, "Pluralism, Power and the Soviet Political System: A Comparative Perspective," in Susan Gross Solomon (ed.) *Pluralism in the Soviet Union* (New York: St. Martin's Press, 1983), pp. 61–107.

100. G.D.H. Cole, *Guild Socialism* (London: Fabian Society, 1922).

101. Stein Rokkan, "Geography, Religion, and Social Class: Crosscutting Cleavages in Norwegian Politics," in Seymour Martin Lipset and Stein Rok-

kan, *Party Systems and Voter Alignments* (New York: Free Press, 1967); and Robert Kvavik, *Interest Groups in Norwegian Politics* (Oslo: Universitets Forlaget, 1976).

102. Phillippe Schmitter, "Still the Century of Corporatism," in Phillippe Schmitter and Gerhard Lehmbruch, *Trends Toward Corporatist Intermediation* (Beverly Hills, CA: Sage, 1974), p. 100.

103. David Cameron, "Social Democracy, Corporatism, Labor Quiescence, and the Representation of Economic Interests in Advanced Capitalist Societies," in David Goldthorpe (ed.) *Order and Conflict in Contemporary Capitalism* (Cambridge, UK: University of Cambridge Press, 1984).

104. Peter Katzenstein, *Small States in World Markets* (Ithaca, NY: Cornell University Press, 1985). See also Harold M. Wilensky, "Leftism, Catholicism, and Democratic Corporatism: The Role of Political Parties in Recent Welfare State Development," in Flora and Heidenheimer, *The Development of Welfare States in Europe and America;* and Phillippe Schmitter, "Interest Intermediation and Regime Governability in Contemporary Western Europe and North America," in Suzanne Berger (ed.) *Organizing Interests in Western Europe* (Cambridge, UK: Cambridge University Press, 1981).

105. Valerie Bunce and John M. Echols, "Soviet Politics in the Brezhnev Era: Pluralism or Corporatism," in Donald R. Kelley, *Soviet Politics in the Brezhnev Era* (New York: Viking, 1980).

106. Valerie Bunce, "The Political Economy of the Brezhnev Era," *British Journal of Political Science* 13:2 (April 1983), p. 131.

107. Ibid., p. 157.

108. Jerry F. Hough, "Pluralism, Corporatism and the Soviet Union," in Solomon (ed.) *Pluralism in the Soviet Union,* pp. 37–60.

109. H. Gordon Skilling, "Interest Groups and Communist Politics Revisited."

110. Archie Brown, "Political Power in the Soviet State," in Neil Harding (ed.) *The State in Society* (Albany, NY: State University of New York Press, 1984); Phillippe Schmitter, "Still the Century of Corporatism," in Schmitter and Lehmbruch, *Trends Toward Corporatist Intermediation,* pp. 90–100; Juan J. Linz, "Totalitarian and Authoritarian Regimes," in Greenstein and Polsby (eds.) *Handbook of Political Science,* vol. 3 (Reading, MA: Addison Wesley, 1975), p. 312; and Alfred Stepan, *The State and Society: Peru in Comparative Perspective* (Princeton, NJ: Princeton University Press, 1978), p. 15.

111. Brown, "Political Power in the Soviet State," p. 68.

112. Robert A. Dahl, *Who Governs* (New Haven, CT: Yale University Press, 1962).

113. Theodore Lowi, "American Business, Public Policy, Case Studies, and Political Theory," *World Politics* 16:4 (July 1964), pp. 677–715.

114. J. Leiper Freeman, *The Political Process* (New York: Random House, 1965).

115. Hugh Heclo, "Issue Networks and the Executive Establishment," in Anthony King (ed.) *The New American Political System* (Washington, DC: American Enterprise Institute, 1978), pp. 87–124.

116. Ibid., p. 88.

117. John W. Kingdon, *Agendas, Alternatives, and Public Policies* (Boston, MA: Little, Brown, 1984).

118. William Zimmerman, "Issue Area and Foreign-Policy Process: A Research Note in Search of a General Theory," *American Political Science Review* 67:4 (December 1973), pp. 1204–12.

119. Nina Halpern, "Economic Specialists and the Making of Chinese Economic Policy, 1955–1983," PhD dissertation, University of Michigan, 1985.

120. John W. Lewis, *Political Networks and the Chinese Policy Process* (Stanford, CA: Northeast Asia Forum on International Policy, 1986).

121. John Lowenhardt, *Decision Making in Soviet Politics* (New York: St. Martin's Press, 1981).

122. Hough and Fainsod, *How the Soviet Union Is Governed.*

123. Ibid., p. 525.

124. Alfred Meyer, *The Soviet Political System: An Interpretation* (New York: Random House, 1965), p. 468.

125. Allen Kassof, "The Administered Society: Totalitarianism Without Terror," *World Politics* 16:4 (July 1964), pp. 558–75; T.H. Rigby, "Traditional, Market, and Organization Societies," *World Politics* 16:4 (July 1964), pp. 539–57.

126. John A. Armstrong, "Sources of Administrative Behavior: Some Soviet and Western European Comparisons," *American Political Science Review* 59:3 (September 1965), pp. 643–55.

127. Jerry Hough, *The Soviet Union and Social Science Theory* (Cambridge, MA: Harvard University Press, 1977).

128. Barghoorn, *Politics in the USSR* (1972), p. 202; see also Barghoorn and Remington, *Politics in the USSR* (1986), pp. 403–4.

129. David Granick, *Management of the Industrial Firm in the USSR* (New York: Columbia University Press, 1954); Joseph Berliner, *Factory and Manager in the USSR* (Cambridge, MA: Harvard University Press, 1957); and Jeremy Azrael, *Managerial Power and Soviet Politics* (Cambridge, MA: Harvard University Press, 1966).

130. Arnold Horelick, A. Ross Johnson and John D. Steinbruner, *The Study of Soviet Foreign Policy: Decision Theory Related Approaches* (Beverly Hills, CA: Sage, 1975).

131. William Potter, "Sources of Foreign Policy Change: Insights from the Policy Sciences," *Conference on the Domestic Sources of Soviet Foreign Policy,* UCLA Project on Politics and War, October 11, 1985.

132. Ibid.

133. Jiri Valenta, "Soviet Decisionmaking and the Czechoslovak Crisis of 1968," *Studies in Comparative Communism* 8:1 and 2 (Spring-Summer 1975), pp. 147–73.

134. Gail Lapidus, "The Making of Russia's China Policy: Domestic/Foreign Policy Linkages in Sino-Soviet Relations," UCLA Project on Politics and War, 1985.

135. Pye, *Dynamics of Chinese Politics,* p. 86.

136. Michel Oksenberg, "Methods of Communication Within the Chinese Bureaucracy," *China Quarterly* 57 (January–March 1974), pp. 1–39; Michel Oksenberg, "Economic Policy Making in China: Summer 1981," *China Quarterly* 90 (September 1982), pp. 165–94; and Kenneth Lieberthal, *Central Documents and Politburo Politics in China* (Ann Arbor, MI: University of Michigan Chinese Studies, 1978).

137. Robert Conquest, *Power and Policy in the USSR* (London: Macmillan, 1961).

138. James C. Scott, "Political Clientelism: A Bibliographical Essay," in Steffen Schmidt, *et al., Friends, Followers, and Factions* (Berkeley, CA: University of California Press, 1977).

139. Carl Lande, *Leaders, Factions and Parties: The Structure of Phillippine Politics* 6 (New Haven, CT: Yale Southeast Asia Monograph Series, 1965); Schmidt, *et al., Friends, Followers, and Factions,* Introduction, pp. 75–100 and pp. 506–10; James C. Scott, "Corruption, Machine Politics, and Political Change," *American Political Science Review* 63:4 (December 1969), pp. 1142–58 and "Patron-Client Politics and Political Change in Southeast Asia," *American Political Science Review* 66:1 (March 1972), pp. 91–113; René Lemarchand and Keith Legg, "Political Clientelism and Development: A Preliminary Analysis," *Comparative Politics* 4:2 (January 1972), pp. 149–78; and S. Eisenstadt and René Lemarchand, *Political Clientelism, Patronage, and Development* (Beverly Hills, CA: Sage, 1981).

140. Andrew Nathan, "A Factionalism Model for CCP Politics," *China Quarterly* 53 (January–March 1973), pp. 34–66.

141. Lande, *Leaders, Factions and Parties;* and Scott, "Patron-Client Politics and Change in Southeast Asia."

142. Nathan Leites, *On the Game of Politics in France* (Stanford, CA: Stanford University Press, 1959).

143. Andrew Nathan, "A Factionalism Model for CCP Politics," p. 396.

144. John W. Lewis, *Political Networks and the Chinese Policy Process* (Stanford, CA: Northeast Asia Forum on International Policy, 1986), p. 5.

145. Ibid., p. 7.

146. Ibid.

147. Ibid., p. 25.

148. Lucian W. Pye, *Asian Power and Politics* (Cambridge, MA: The Belknap Press of the Harvard University Press, 1985), p. 27.

149. Ibid., p. 146.

150. Ibid., p. 177.

151. "Clientelism," Symposium in *Studies in Comparative Communism,* vol. XII, nos. 2 and 3 (Summer/Autumn 1979), pp. 159–211.

152. John Willerton, "Clientelism in the Soviet Union: An Initial Examination," *Studies in Comparative Communism* 12:1 and 2 (Summer–Autumn, 1979), pp. 159–83.

153. Zygmunt Bauman, "Comment on Eastern Europe," pp. 184–89.

154. John Burns, "Comment on China," pp. 190–94.

155. Nobutake Ike, "Comment on Japan," pp. 201–3.

156. T.H. Rigby, "The Need for Comparative Research," p. 207.

157. Ibid., p. 209.

158. T.H. Rigby and Bohdan Harasymiw, *Leadership Selection and Patron-Client Relations in the USSR and Yugoslavia* (London: Allen & Unwin, 1983).

159. Gyula Jozsa, "Political *Seilschaften* in the USSR," in Ibid., p. 169.

160. See n. 158, 144 and 148 above.

161. Erik P. Hoffmann, "Methodological Problems of Kremlinology," in Frederic J. Fleron, Jr. (ed.) *Communist Studies and the Social Sciences: Essays on Methodology and Empirical Theory* (Chicago, IL: Rand McNally, 1969).

162. Ellen Mickiewicz, "Managing Public Opinion and International News in the Soviet Union," in *Domestic Sources of Foreign and Defense Policy,*

UCLA Project on Politics and War, 1985. Cf. Alex Inkeles, *Public Opinion in Soviet Russia* (Cambridge, MA: Harvard University Press, 1950).

163. William A. Welsh, "A Game-Theoretic Conceptualization of the Hungarian Revolt: Toward an Inductive Theory of Games," in Fleron (ed.) *Communist Studies and the Social Sciences*.

164. Robert Packenham, "The Changing Political Discourse in Brazil," in Wayne Selcher (ed.) *Political Liberalization in Brazil* (Boulder, CO: Westview, 1986).

165. Brown, "Soviet Political Culture Through Soviet Eyes," in *Political Culture and Communist Studies,* pp. 106 ff.

166. Archie Brown, "Political Power in the Soviet State," in Neil Harding (ed.) *The State in Society,* p. 75.

167. Ibid., p. 74.

168. Clifford Geertz, *The Interpretation of Cultures: Selected Essays* (New York: Basic Books, 1973).

169. Adam Przeworski and Henry Teune, *The Logic of Comparative Social Inquiry* (New York: John Wiley, 1970), p. 30.

170. Albert Hirschman, "The Search for Paradigms as a Hindrance to Understanding," *World Politics* 22:3 (April 1970), pp. 329–43.

171. John Womack, *Zapata and the Mexican Revolution* (New York: Knopf, 1968); and James Payne, *Patterns of Conflict in Colombia* (New Haven, CT: Yale University Press, 1968).

172. Hirschman, p. 338.

173. Ibid., p. 331.

174. Harry Eckstein, "Case Study and Theory in Political Science," in Greenstein and Polsby, *Handbook of Political Science,* vol. 3 (Reading, MA: Addison Wesley, 1975).

175. Roberto Michels, *Political Parties: A Sociological Study of the Oligarchical Tendencies of Modern Democracy* (New York: Hearst International Library, 1915).

176. Ronald Amann, "Searching for an Appropriate Concept of Soviet Politics: The Politics of Hesitant Modernization?" *British Journal of Political Science* 16:4 (October 1986), pp. 475–94.

177. Ibid., p. 492.

178. Brzezinski and Huntington, *Political Power USA/USSR.*

179. Alexander Dallin, "The Domestic Sources of Soviet Foreign Policy," in Seweryn Bialer (ed.) *The Domestic Context of Soviet Foreign Policy* (Boulder, CO: Westview, 1981), p. 363.

180. Archie Brown, "Political Power in the Soviet State," in Harding (ed.) *The State in Society,* p. 179.

3

THE DILEMMAS OF SOVIETOLOGY AND THE LABYRINTH OF THEORY

Water, water everywhere, Nor any drop to drink.
—Samuel Taylor Coleridge

Difficilis facilis, iucundus, acerbus es idem
Nec tecum possum vivere, nec sine te.
—Catullus

Ironically, although most contemporary Sovietologists are political scientists, most of the Sovietology they practice is not contemporary political science.[1] Instead, contemporary Sovietology represents an awkward amalgam of data collection, policy analysis, and journalism that is as divorced from scholarship as sense impressions are from theory. The reasons for Sovietology's underdevelopment involve far more than some ingrained incapacity to a great leap forward to comparative communist studies or, even, to comparative politics.[2] Although the profession's proud refusal to acknowledge theory—and thereby to appreciate that its continued viability as a scholarly pursuit depends on its reintegration into political science—is a large part of the problem, no less important are the outside pressures that force Sovietology onto a Procrustean bed of their own making. As I shall argue, it is the influence of the university, the state, and the media that confronts Sovietology with dilemmas that it is, alas, unequipped to resolve in its own favor.

A brief excursion into the past reveals that things were not always this way. A theoretical gap between the study of the Soviet political system and political science emerged only in the aftermath of World War II. In the interwar years, the two fields occupied different conceptual worlds, rarely intersected, and were therefore incommensurable. While students of government were comparing legislatures, executives, judiciaries, and constitutions, most students of Russia remained devoted to their primary vocations—history, language, and literature. For a variety of reasons, many of which were associated with the postwar rise to superpower status of both the United States and the Soviet Union and the attendant need for policy-relevant information about various parts of the contested world, Sovietology and political science experienced both a takeoff and a rapprochement in the 1940s and 1950s. As soon as their trajectories approached each other, however, a theoretical time lag became evident. The first inclination of postwar Sovietology was to appropriate the formal-legal baggage of prewar political science and fill it with totalitarian content. Then, in the 1960s and 1970s, as totalitarianism went into eclipse, Sovietologists belatedly discovered the concepts that political scientists had utilized in the 1950s, among them systems, interest groups, modernization, and political culture.[3]

More recently, just as many of their colleagues in political science were choosing postbehavioral approaches, students of Soviet domestic politics have embraced behavioralism. At present, tragically, this process of playing catch-up has largely ceased. Joseph LaPalombara summed up the problem succinctly in 1975: "It is instructive, I believe, that so few of the textbooks on the Soviet Union or Eastern Europe are self-consciously theoretical or represent even modest efforts at theoretical innovation . . . Soviet and East European textbooks do not advance our theoretical understanding very far. Moreover, they are obviously time-lagged in the sense of not reflecting some of the methodologically and conceptually richer work on these political systems which has emerged in recent years."[4]

Not only, as Lawrence C. Mayer suggests, has behavioral and post-behavioral political science continued to develop conceptually and theoretically, while Sovietology has not, but also, with the notable exception of the best work of the best Sovietologists, the outstanding feature of the current "era of stagnation" is that Sovietology's version of behavioralism has become a routinized pursuit of numbers.[5] After all, when Roger E. Kanet defined behavioralism in 1971 as a "concentration on both the observable political action of individuals and groups and the psychological processes which influence these actions," with the expectation that the "result will be the identification of uniformities in political behavior that can be expressed in generalizations or theories with explanatory or predictive power," his goal was not merely to collect data but to generate theory.[6] In contrast, the ossified behavioralism that has come to replace the original behavioralist vision has halted Sovietology's admirable effort to keep pace with theory; by largely abandoning the quest for theory, it has also deprived its practitioners of the capacity to explain what they purport to describe. At its worst, this deification of data, or what I call routine behavioralism, has reduced much of Sovietology to a form of political journalism.

The essence of routine behavioralism is what Jacques Barzun perhaps too caustically refers to as "doing research"—the vigorous pursuit of data on the faulty rationale that, as only data can generate knowledge, more data must translate into more knowledge.[7] Doing research thus has the advantage of being its own justification: where there is a gap in the data—and there is always some gap waiting to be filled, say, the development of working-class protest songs in Orel in 1910—doing research is always ready to spring in. Clearly, an approach such as this is a boundless enterprise. Because the number of Soviet oblasts, raions, cities, towns, villages, status groups, nationalities, and classes runs into the thousands, and because each of these has a long and colorful history, the permutations and combinations for doing research verge on the infinite.

Unlike its routinization of behavioralism, which, as I argue below, is largely the result of factors external to it, Sovietology's halting theoretical development stems from its own professional and intellectual history. An important part of that history is pedagogical. Frederic J. Fleron, Jr. noted long ago that the vast majority of Sovietologists have never had—and, it seems, still lack—an adequate grounding in political science theories, concepts, and methods.[8] For the most part, Sovietologists are trained as area specialists with only minimal exposure to the larger intellectual universe they inhabit. Such pedagogical inclinations are understandable, both historically, in view of Sovietology's roots in Russian studies, and academically, in view of the peculiar intellectual challenges that the magnitude and complexity of the USSR represent. Given these limitations, it makes some practical sense for Sovietologists to eschew cosmic questions and focus their energies on the mystery that is wrapped in an enigma. To be sure, the mystery no longer appears so mysterious nor the enigma so enigmatic as Sovietologists once thought them to be; nonetheless, students of the Soviet Union continue to confront the kinds of empirical obstacles that have long since been surmounted in other fields.

The theoretical distance between Sovietology and political science is also a function of the dissimilar intellectual development of the two fields. Contemporary political science has its origins in the self-styled scientific study of more or less mundane American and West European political institutions and legal documents.[9] Sovietology, on the other hand, has traversed a politically divisive path beginning with the impassioned debates surrounding the establishment, consolidation, and growth of the USSR's brand of socialism in the 1920s and 1930s. The Russian Revolution and Stalinism opened vistas of liberation for some—especially the "political pilgrims" described by Paul Hollander[10]—and confirmed the worst fears of others. In so ideologically polarized an atmosphere, early students of the Soviet Union often were political activists, journalists, and exiles: people directly involved or concerned with Russia, such as Sidney and Beatrice Webb, Malcolm Muggeridge, W.H. Chamberlin, Louis

Fischer, Leon Trotsky, and Boris Nicolaevsky. Of course, the degree
to which nonscholars dominated the field in the interwar period was
also symptomatic of the adolescent state of Russian studies. Scholars,
journals, and research programs were few, to a large extent concentrated in Germany, while their understanding of the USSR was often
woefully inadequate. Walter Laqueur conveys nicely the then prevailing intellectual environment:

> The Russian experts, almost without exception, under-rated the impor-
> tance of the revolutionary movement. After the revolution their
> difficulties increased; they had now to deal with a country that in many
> essential respects had undergone radical change. Little had been known
> in the West about Russian socialism and communism; the comments on
> this subject published by German and British experts during the first
> world war must be read to be believed; one of them translated
> "Trudoviki" as "The Weary Ones" (this was not intended as a joke);
> another introduced Trotsky as a Ukrainian nationalist. In Germany,
> Staehlin, the leading historian of modern Russia, interpreted the
> Bolshevik revolution and subsequent events in terms of religious
> philosophy; Pares, after prolonged and bitter opposition to Lenin's Russia,
> came to display as much enthusiasm for Stalin's Russia as he had for
> Nikolai II's; in America Samuel Harper, the only American scholar to
> deal with contemporary Russian affairs, began by declaring the Sisson
> papers, that crudest of anti-Bolshevik forgeries, authentic, and twenty
> years later described the big purge as a necessary stage on Russia's road
> to constitutional government.[11]

We may smile at Laqueur's list of foibles, but we can also sym-
pathize with early scholars, who confronted the young Soviet state's
frightening newness and awesome impenetrability. Even the Stalinist
apologetics of the Webbs appear comprehensible, though no less
reprehensible,[12] in view of capitalism's seeming collapse, fascism's
seeming triumph, and the GPU's demonstrated ability to manipulate
even its sworn enemies.[13]

Pedagogical imperatives and historical origins may account for
Sovietology's perpetual lagging behind political science, but they do
little to explain its current obsession with facts. To be sure, the
radical rejection of totalitarianism as a conceptual mode pushed Sovietology away from theory; to a certain degree it may be argued that,
in ridding themselves of the bath water, Sovietologists also threw
out the baby. That is, in rejecting the so-called totalitarian model,
Sovietologists also rejected its healthy theoretical pretensions, indeed,
theory as a whole.[14] But this argument cannot make sense either of
the routinization of behavioralism or of its tenacity. Understanding
so intellectually counterproductive a turn in Sovietology's theoretical
development requires that we look outside of Sovietology at three
thoroughly familiar institutions, the university, the state, and the
media. As we shall see, changes within these institutions combined

with changes in Sovietology's theoretical inclinations to produce a confluence of powerful forces that encouraged the routinization by Sovietologists of behavioralism.

To its credit, the university's influence has been least pernicious. Nevertheless, although it aspires to promote genuine scholarship, the manner in which the university did so in the 1970s and 1980s became increasingly conducive to routine behavioralism. Unfortunately, market dynamics explain this trend best. With too many academics bidding for too few openings—the result of rapid educational expansion in the 1950s and 1960s and steady decline in the years thereafter—universities responded by raising the price of tenured slots. Simply put, the number of publications required for tenure rose dramatically.[15] Fearful that quantity might prove to be incompatible with quality, scholars resolved to overcome the pitfalls of the "publish or perish" syndrome by adopting the logic described below by David Ricci:

> Thus political scientists who aspire to advance professionally try to make scholarly contributions that can quickly earn them recognition. And within large organizations, one way of getting ahead is to invent something not yet being provided by any other member of the organization. It follows, in scholarly communities, that one tends to develop research projects which break ground that others have not tilled before, to stake out small areas of inquiry that other scholars have not yet invaded and conquered for their own. There is, therefore, a propensity constantly to refashion the scope of political science into smaller and smaller realms of expertise, so that some scholars can quickly stand forth as patently competent with regard to subjects that other scholars have somehow overlooked.[16]

Not only does a strategy such as this not sacrifice scholarly integrity to the pressures of the academic marketplace, but it is also interesting to the scholar engaged in unearthing past or present intrigues or collating statistics, very publishable, and—no small consideration—virtually above criticism. The structure of incentives is such that rational scholars are hardpressed not to subordinate their theoretical inclinations, if such there be, to the environmental constraints that encourage and reward routine behavioralism.

While the university's disequilibrated relationship with scholars is slated to improve in the 1990s, as the supply of academic positions more closely approaches the demand for them, no such favorable forecast can be made for the state's willful exploitation of Sovietology. Unfortunately, if unavoidably, all states have traditionally drawn on the advice, information, and expertise of patriotically inclined students of Russia who, for a variety of reasons, have been more than willing to provide it. Writes Laqueur of Sovietology's early years: "It is no exaggeration to say that all leading students of Russia at the time advised their governments in an official or unofficial capacity, though not all rose as high in rank as their erstwhile colleague Thomas Garrigue Masaryk."[17] After World War II, the relationship between Sovietologists and the state changed dramatically. The transformation of the United States and the Soviet Union into superpowers, together with Stalin's expansion into Eastern Europe, placed the USSR at the top of Western political agendas. Moreover, the growth of extensive intelligence apparatuses translated into a permanent demand for data on and analysis of the Soviet Union.[18] Understandably, the demand for Sovietologists grew apace, and vast sums of government money were poured into universities in the 1950s and 1960s. After slackening during the detente years, investments picked up in the 1980s, promising once again to convert Sovietology into a growth industry.[19]

The state's growing interest in Sovietology has encouraged routine behavioralism in two ways. First and most obviously, the state attempts to set Sovietology's research agenda. Thus, the bourgeoning need for policy-relevant data and the availability of funds for pursuing it have created strong incentives for Sovietologists to roll up their theoretical sleeves and just do research. More pernicious perhaps is the state's encouragement of policy analysis. Notwithstanding its importance for democratic government, policy analysis inclines Sovietologists to eschew the very stuff of theory—big questions with no simple answers. Stephen F. Cohen goes even further, arguing that "policy-oriented scholarship, which is designed for political consumption, can impose serious intellectual constraints. Complex political history must be rummaged for present-day relevance; 'lessons' and predictions become primary objectives. Such scholarship thus tends to grow narrow in focus and politically palatable in findings."[20] In a word, such scholarship is driven toward routine behavioralism.

The second way in which the state encourages routine behavioralism is far more subtle. The state confronts Sovietologists with a moral dilemma that is most easily resolved by flight into routine behavioralism. The state politicizes Sovietology, thus compelling it to consider what its attitude toward the Soviet Union should be: approbation or condemnation. A choice would have to be made in any circumstances, but state affiliation forces the issue. Although outward neutrality is generally the visage most scholars prefer to assume, it is unavailable to Sovietologists because of the nature of the beast they study. Naturally, one can love the peoples, languages, and cultures of the USSR, but it is difficult not to experience a sense of tragedy, if not shame or revulsion, with respect to the Soviet authorities.[21] Sovietologists cannot avoid confronting and living with the fact of the Soviet state's long-lasting involvement in terroristic practices and crimes against humanity. For most of their history, as even official Soviets increasingly admit, the "empire" was indeed "evil."[22] Tengiz Abuladze's film, *Repentance,* like the independent social organization *Memorial,* should persuade us that morality is an unavoidable question for everyone connected with the USSR.[23]

For all its excesses, the totalitarian "model" provided solid moral ground on which to stand: all totalitarian dictatorships were alike—be they Hitler's or Stalin's—and all deserved moral condemnation. The demise of totalitarianism left a moral vacuum at precisely the time that the state's interest in Sovietology assumed increasingly institutionalized forms. A moral response was imperative, yet exceedingly difficult, because behavioralism was premised on presumed scientific objectivity and *Wertfreiheit.* Not surprisingly, behaviorally inclined Sovietologists have sought refuge from this moral dilemma in routine behavioralism: when facts can speak for themselves, scholars are absolved from speaking out.

A less distressing Soviet system—a realistic possibility if *perestroika* proves successful—will help resolve part of the moral dilemma, but it will not dispel the state's interest in the Soviet Union and therefore in Sovietology. As long as the United States continues to share a world with a nuclear-armed Soviet Union, intelligence and policy analysis will be necessary, regardless of the condition of Soviet-American relations: indeed, the end of the Cold War may only increase the state's reliance on Sovietology for the data and policy advice it needs to steer in wholly uncharted waters. As the state's drafting of Sovietologists is unlikely to diminish anytime in the foreseeable future, the incentive to engage in routine behavioralism will remain strong.

The third source of Sovietology's infatuation with routine behavioralism is the media. The pervasiveness, influence, and prominence of the media—the result of the Vietnam War and the Watergate scandal—their fascination with impressions and images, and their disdain for history, complexity, and depth impress themselves on Sovietology, encouraging scholars to describe bits and pieces of events or processes, to seek out the unusual and exotic, and to avoid systematization, historical perspective, and comparison. Sovietology is especially prone to succumb to the media's blandishments as a result of its politicization by and close relationship with the state: just as the modern media tend to set much of the political agenda for the state, so, too, a politicized Sovietology is forced to draw on the media for much of its own agenda. Consequently, the media structure Sovietological perceptions of the Soviet Union as much as, if not more than, the profession's own attempts to penetrate the black box—and they are likely to continue to do so for some time. Recent events in the USSR and the way the media have brought them to our attention tend to confirm this interpretation. As any Soviet nationality expert can testify, there was always abundant evidence to suggest that the nationality question was critically important to the Soviet state.[24] And yet, it was only after the media discovered the non-Russians in 1987–1989 that mainstream Sovietology finally acknowledged that there was something to see in what its own subfield had been looking at for so many years.

In sum, Sovietology's prospects for escaping routine behavioralism's tentacles appear to be bleak. Besides the discipline's pedagogically and historically based theoretical underdevelopment, the state, the media, and, although decreasingly, the university will continue to reward doing research and to discourage, if not quite penalize, theory. Worse still, the information explosion brought about by *glasnost* is likely to impel Sovietologists to burrow even deeper into the mountains of data that Gorbachev, like the Prophet, has caused to come to them.[25] Because the system of environmental incentives and disincentives is unlikely to change dramatically, transcending routine behavioralism and reintegrating Sovietology into political science can be accomplished only by a collective act of will on the part of Sovietologists. As the pressure to publish or perish subsides, pedagogical reform—a field of endeavor wholly within Sovietologists' control—becomes imperative. Training in theory must come to supplement Soviet area studies: there is simply no other way to break routine behavioralism's stranglehold on the profession. Whether or not voluntarism will suffice to overcome the institutional sources of routine behavioralism and to restructure Sovietology is, of course, another question and one that I am inclined to answer negatively.

One thing, however, is quite clear. If Sovietology does *not* abandon routine behavioralism, it will eventually approach an intellectual dead end. In a word, Sovietology will face a "crisis"—a condition on the successful resolution of which Sovietology's survival as a scholarly discipline will depend.[26] The reason for so dire an outlook is that routine behavioralism is, quite simply, untenable. A nontheoretical Sovietology is not only impossible but also self-defeating. For better or for worse theory represents a form of intellectual endeavor that cannot be rejected, overcome, avoided, or ignored.

Whether we want it to or not, theory envelops Sovietology in two related ways. First and basically, theory suffuses the language and concepts we use, because no words exist independent of the variety of meanings attached to them. To use terms is to accept or to reject their connotations. To string terms together is to enmesh them in a connotational web that bears close resemblance to a theory. Indeed, Vernon Van Dyke defines a theory as nothing more complicated than a "series of concepts which are interrelated in a series of propositions."[27] To define a concept—to state what it is and what it is not—is to distinguish it from related concepts and thus to suggest how sets of concepts "hang together." As I argue later, such hanging together of concepts is rudimentary theory.

Facts, to be sure, are as necessary for understanding as theory, but routine behavioralism has two of them quite wrong. Contrary to what routine behavioralism would have us believe, intelligent appraisals of events, personages, and developments cannot possibly demand possession of all the data on these subjects, as the quantity of data that impinge on anything or anybody is literally infinite. The problem of data is doubly difficult in Soviet studies because of the relative paucity and unreliability of pre-1987 sources. Except for the Smolensk materials and a smattering of other documents, until recently scholars had no direct and unimpeded access to Soviet archives. In addition, for most of the USSR's history, Soviet evidence, like reflections in Socrates' parable of the cave, was several times removed from the purportedly objective reality: it was filtered, screened, selected, and even misrepresented. Reliability of data is still a problem, and even Soviet scholars question the accuracy of their country's statistics. Scholarly techniques can help overcome these limitations, but they should not blind us to the fact that, by applying such techniques, we—like Heisenberg—are interpreting data as well as distorting them. Indeed, if we were to be as rigorous about evidence as routine behavioralists insist, we would have to throw up our hands in despair and abandon the profession.

Paucity and unreliability of data, while severe limitations on behavioral Sovietology, are not really the central issue. More important is the second fact that routine behavioralism, like its more worthy predecessor, behavioralism, obscures: that understanding actually precedes the collection of data and the ordering of facts. Stephen Gaukroger's comments on this subject are worth quoting at some length:

> Observation is simply not possible without some kind of conceptualization. When we observe something we observe it as being something of a certain kind. This identification is dependent on some conceptualization, some classification. No demonstrative reference could be successful unless there were some shared principles of classification. For example, if I am asked to count the number of items in a certain area, I must restrict myself to a single system of classification—if I am counting the number of things in a room I cannot include a chair, wood, legs, molecules and oblong shapes in the same total. Thus observation is necessarily a conceptual activity insofar as it involves a system of classification and criteria by which things of a certain class are identified as being such, and thereby differentiated from other things of that class and from things of other classes.[28]

If, then, we want to understand Soviet politics, where do we start? By carefully reading the New York City telephone directory? The Moscow directory? Of course not. Why? Because our theoretical inclinations tell us that these are nonfacts and that we should be looking for real facts in, say, *Pravda* or *Izvestiia*. How do we know that a speech by Gorbachev is a fact we should consider? Because we are already working on the assumption that general secretaries are important personalities in the Soviet political process.

Conceptualization not only precedes observation but also imparts meaning to the things observed. Indeed, data—or the jumbled and random impressions that our senses are exposed to—become meaningful facts only after they have been interpreted; in fact, raw data acquire meaning only if a theoretical or conceptual framework assigns meaning and "factness" to them. Contrary to Francis Bacon and the inductivists, data do not generate understanding; indeed, on their own, sense impressions are quite meaningless. As Sir Karl Popper has persuasively argued, we cannot logically make the jump from individual observations or from individual pieces of data to some generalization. No matter how many white swans we see, we cannot conclude that all swans are white. As generalizations, therefore, theories cannot be derived from data, even if we were to assume—incorrectly, I believe—that data can be apprehended without the mediation of human perception.[29]

Consider Alexander Rabinowitch's excellent book, *The Bolsheviks Come to Power,* which wants "to let the facts speak for themselves."[30] In violation of Popper's injunction, Rabinowitch jumps to the conclusion that Lenin's supporters were not the unified, disciplined Leninist party of traditional studies, because the existence of many disorganized Bolsheviks must mean that the Bolsheviks were disorganized. Even if this conclusion, which is a classic example of the composition fallacy, were justified, critics could rightfully reply that the Bolsheviks were still better unified, better disciplined, and more Leninist than any other party, and that that fact made the difference.[31] At the root of the disagreement is not the data—after all, both Rabinowitch and his critics "know" what happened in 1917—or the methodological error Rabinowitch commits, but the interpretive framework used by both sides of the debate. Revisionists, such as Rabinowitch, implicitly prefer to think that elites play an incidental role in revolutions; traditionalists hold that elites are indispensable. Which perspective is correct is beside the point for my argument: namely, that only a perspective *of some kind* can give meaning to data.

The following example may also be illustrative. Generally speaking, if we want to show that some local phenomenon, X, is systemically significant, we do one of two things. Either we claim that some other phenomenon, which is demonstrably significant, is somehow a measure of X, or we claim that localized evidence for X is generalizable. As an example of the first technique, we might argue—as Sheila Fitzpatrick does—that widespread social mobility in the USSR during the 1930s, which is demonstrable, is evidence of regime support, which is harder to get at.[32] As an example of the second technique, we might argue, as J. Arch Getty does, that data from the Smolensk Archive are meaningful for other oblasts as well.[33]

Strictly speaking, both conclusions are insupportable. Evidence of social mobility is evidence of social mobility and nothing else; Smolensk data may tell us a lot about Smolensk, but not, *ipso facto,* about Tashkent or Kiev oblasts. Here again the jump from specific evidence to generalization requires some preexisting theoretical perspective on why social mobility translates into systemic support and why Smolensk is just a typical Soviet oblast. In the latter case, of course, even a persuasive conceptual connection cannot establish an unbreakable empirical tie between Smolensk data and the entire USSR. Clifford Geertz's judgment is even harsher:

> The Jonesville-is-America writ small (or America-is-Jonesville writ large) fallacy is so obviously one that the only thing that needs explanation is how people have managed to believe it and expected others to believe it. The notion that one can find the essence of national societies, civilizations, great religions, or whatever summed up and simplified in so-called "typical" small towns and villages is palpable nonsense. What one finds in small towns and villages is (alas) small-town or village life.[34]

Routine behavioralism is, therefore, manifestly counterproductive. It may dovetail nicely with the research inclinations of Sovietologists, but it decidedly does not contribute to or enhance our understanding of the Soviet Union, and it will do so even less as Soviet data increase in number and reliability. Instead, routine behavioralism drives Sovietology into a self-delusionary and self-destructive position. On the one hand, Sovietology's infatuation with trees can never help it apprehend the forest; on the other hand, its rejection of theory pushes it relentlessly into the role of servant of the state or, heaven forbid, of the media. To be incapable of grasping the USSR is bad enough; to lose one's scholarly soul to a wholly unworthy temptor is, I suggest, intolerable. If so, there is no alternative to marrying Sovietology to theory, to reintegrating it into political science.

Were the quest for theory like the ascent to a Platonic source of light, all political scientists long since would have become theorists. Alas, finding a philosopher king may be impossible, not because there are no candidates for the role, but because there are too many, and all of them have equally good credentials. The conundrum is all too familiar: theoretically curious political scientists turn to their colleagues in philosophy for the answers, only to discover that they, too, disagree violently. And if the forms elude even those who claim to know them best, then, what are mere political scientists to do? Far too many scholars fall into despondence, abandon their theoretical ambitions, and immerse themselves in area studies. There is another, somewhat more hopeful, response. If the multiplicity of philosopher kings is regarded as an inevitable epistemological condition of the social sciences, then it permits us to seek guidance from all quarters and undertake the upward journey on our own, as completely autonomous—though, admittedly, thoroughly terrified— agents. It is a condition of which Immanuel Kant would have been proud.

What, then, does theoretical enlightenment entail? Let us start our ascent by considering three definitions of theory.[35] Giovanni Sartori defines it as a "body of systematically related generalizations of explanatory value."[36] George Caspar Homans says that a "theory consists of a cluster of deductive systems."[37] Johan Galtung's defini- tion is the most formal: "A *theory, T,* is a structure (H, I) where H is a set of hypotheses and I is a relation in H called 'implication' or 'deductibility' so that H is weakly connected by I."[38] The terminol- ogy is different, but all three definitions suggest that theories are coherent sets of logically related statements that purport to explain something. Grand, middle-range, and low-level theories differ not in their degree of logical coherence or explanatory structure, but in the level of generalization at which their explanations aim. Thus, to take an example, although theories of mass movements are grander than theories of particular kinds of mass movements, which in turn are grander than low-level theories of particular mass movements—all are theories.

How, then, are theories structured and how do they explain what they claim to explain? Stephen Gaukroger dissects theories—or "ex- planatory structures," as he calls them—into four intimately related, mutually dependent, and equally important parts. Explanatory struc- tures, according to Gaukroger, consist of an ontology, "that primary structured set of kinds of entity in terms of which explanations can be given in that discourse," or what other scholars call axioms, principles, or assumptions; a "domain of evidence," which is the "set of those phenomena which could confirm, establish or refute pur- ported explanations"; a system of concepts that link "the ontology of a discourse to its evidential domain" and which are "peculiar to that discourse"; and a "proof structure which circumscribes the class of valid and invalid consequences and derivation relations which may hold between any statements in the discourse."[39]

Ontologies are intuitively derived premises that form what Imre Lakatos calls the "hard core" of a theory.[40] They cannot be proven; they are neither right nor wrong, correct or incorrect: they simply are taken for granted.[41] The parallel postulate in geometry, which asserts that only one line going through some point can be parallel to another line, is a typical example of such an unprovable assump- tion. A similar assumption in political science might be that human beings are selfish, altruistic, rational, irrational, and so on. Naturally, the assumptions that constitute an ontology should not be an arbi- trarily arranged hodge-podge. Instead, as Sir Karl Popper notes, the "system of axioms must be free from contradiction, . . . independent, i.e., it must not contain any axiom deducible from the remaining axioms," and sufficient and necessary for the "deduction of all statements belonging to the theory which is to be axiomatized."[42]

The second and third parts of theories consist of concepts and the evidential domain within which we expect the theory to hold. Sartori defines *concept* as "the basic unit of thinking. It can be said that we have a concept of A (or of A-ness) when we are able to distinguish A from whatever is not-A."[43] Walter Carlsnaes agrees: concepts "are not linguistic expressions or classifications but abstract constructions pointed to or symbolized by terms or expressions." A concept conveys an "abstract property shared by some substances and not by others."[44] It follows from both definitions that poorly defined concepts can but result in unfocused thinking. But poorly defined concepts have this unfortunate consequence only because lack of definitional precision precludes binding concepts to the ontological foundations of the theory. As definitional precision is possible only on the basis of the axioms, assumptions, and premises underlying a theory, lack of precision necessarily results in a thoroughly disjointed, indeed an incoherent, theory. No less important, however, evidential domains are to concepts as concepts are to ontologies. The conceptual framework underpinning a theory generates those facts that the theory will count as relevant evidence and eliminates problematic data from consideration as evidence by treating them as nonfacts. As I argued earlier, theory chooses the facts it wants, and it does so by means of the exclusionary power of its concepts. Gaukroger's claim, that "a physical phenomenon is such if and only if it is the referent of a concept specifying what 'physical phenomena' are,"[45] gets to the heart of the incestuous relationship between concepts and evidence.

Finally, proof structures combine the elements of a theory into a coherent and meaningful whole by providing them with internal logical consistency and by determining, in Gaukroger's words, "what kinds of inference are valid and under what conditions." Such a structure "provides the constraints on the formal relations between the concepts of a discourse, and hence on the statements produced in that discourse."[46] Most important for our purposes, proof structures detail the "initial conditions"—x, y, z—that must be present for a theory—If A, then B—to hold.[47] Without specification of these conditions, theories will always hover above the empirical domains they claim to address.

What should strike us immediately in considering these four elements is that they are not slapped together in a haphazard way. Quite the contrary, if a theory is well crafted, its elements will fit tightly because they will have been chosen, modified, and adjusted to fit tightly. But if well-crafted theories are human constructs that can explain only what they purport to explain, then it is impossible to tell whether or not social scientists paint bull's-eyes around gun shots or actually shoot at the targets. Galtung's proposition—"*If the hypothesis fits, then it fits;* and if the degree of confirmation is maximum, then so much the better"[48]—goes still further, even suggesting that, contrary to our expectations, the better a theory, the *less* susceptible it is to refutation. Thomas Spragens takes the argument to its logical conclusion, by speaking of the "inescapable ultimate circularity of all human thought—a circularity which can be repressed only by confining inquiry to proximate questions and denying the dependence of these proximate questions upon irreducible presuppositions . . ." Indeed, Spragens finds that "because epistemology is inherently reflexive—that is, it is thought about thought, to the point of infinite regress—it can finally rest only upon self-confessed circularity which will be 'paradoxical' or upon an affirmation of certainty which will be dogmatic. There are no other alternatives." Although Spragens suggests that the "choice between these two ultimate paradigms must itself be a matter of personal judgment," he prefers the "former alternative, self-confessed paradox . . . because it incorporates and accepts its own contingency. As Robert Merton has suggested, this justification of knowledge resembles Munchhausen's feat of extricating himself from a swamp by pulling on his own whiskers. But the alternative resembles standing on thin air, a tenuous basis for laughing at Munchhausen's efforts."[49]

To acknowledge the validity of Spragens' circularity thesis, or what W.V. Quine calls "holism,"[50] is to accept several far-reaching epistemological positions. First, the truth value and meaning of theoretical statements have no sense outside of some theory. Because we cannot apprehend the world in a manner that is unmediated by mental processes, truth and meaning are immanent qualities of theoretical understanding and have no independent ontological reality of their own.[51] Second, because the specific meaning of given concepts is contingent on the theoretical framework of which the concepts are an organic part, concepts can never have only one divinely ordained meaning. Indeed, Quine and his interpreter Paul A. Roth go so far as to argue that there is "no objective basis that uniquely settles questions concerning what a given utterance means."[52] As translation is indeterminate, we can never quite fathom "what the native said." Third, despite our certainty that an objective world exists, there can be no philosophical certainty that what we purport to observe is, in fact, what is. Thus, the facts that we claim as evidence for or against a theory are facts and are therefore evidence only because the theory acknowledges them as such. Lest this seem to be a recipe for anarchy, it is important to keep in mind that the data that enter the pool of potentially usable evidence acquire factness as a result not of individual whim, but of an intersubjective consensus that is formed on the basis of a little understood interaction between commonly held theoretical frameworks and the objective world.[53] And fourth, because facts are inextricably bound to intuitively derived conceptual frameworks, the fact-value distinction necessarily breaks down and normative considerations automatically become an integral part of all social science theorizing.[54]

If we accept these positions—and I stress that there is no law telling us to do so—we may be inclined to draw additional theoretical consequences. The least controversial such consequence concerns the explanation-interpretation dispute. Adherents of explanation, whose work is variously referred to as empiricist, positivist, and scientistic, claim that the social sciences should utilize the methods of the natural sciences. Supporters of interpretation reject the natural sciences as their *Vorbild*. As an ideal type, explanation looks at many cases by comparing only certain salient variables largely without reference to the concrete environmental and historical conditions that molded those features or to the entities into which they are developing. Interpretation, on the other hand, focuses on specific units of analysis and attempts to understand the actors involved in terms of the entire concatenation of factors embedded in the life of some society or country. Galtung only slightly overdraws the difference between these two ideal types by suggesting that explanation deals with space and interpretation with time.[55]

Holism breaks down any hard and fast distinction between these two approaches. By bridging the distance between subjective perceptions and objective facts, holism undermines positivism's pretensions to the status of a hard science. And by emptying concepts of any one given meaning, circularity explodes interpretation's hopes of attaining a genuine *Verstehen* of foreign thought systems, one that would be untainted by our own perceptual inclinations. In this sense, Jack Snyder's effort at reconciling the two approaches, although admirable, can be criticized for being premised on the view that they are, after all, distinct.[56] Far more in line with Quine, Roth, and Spragens is Douglas Chalmers, who argues that explanation and interpretation are not only complementary, but actually two sides of one coin: "Theory in the social sciences is clearly not one or the other. It is not a pure model of the sort of theory found in the natural sciences, nor is it purely a matter of understanding or interpretation. The social sciences appear to be the arena in which explanation and interpretation come together."[57] Such "interpretive frameworks" combine elements of natural science with interpretive historical methods and values in a manner that, willy-nilly, appears to inform the theoretical perspectives of both those who insist on explanation and those who prefer interpretation.

The second, more disturbing consequence of circularity and holism is, as Chalmers suggests, that political science and politics, just like facts and values, definitely overlap.[58] At some level, political science agendas are political agendas, and it would be self-delusionary to pretend otherwise. Naturally, as Spragens points out, political science and politics are not identical: "The old disjunction between thought and action may have been overdrawn at times, but it remains true that a commitment to a theoretical paradigm in the service of truth is not the same as a commitment to a partisan program in the service of particular political goals." Although "political science obviously has bearing upon political action" and "men act upon the basis of what they believe reality to be," the point is that "no finite political act can legitimately claim the sanction of political science, first, because of the ineluctable element of contingency within scientific knowledge itself and, second, because of the equally inescapable slippage between the judgment that such-and-such is true and the judgment that thus-and-so should be done, even where the normative component of truth is recognized."[59] Although we cannot escape Mannheim's paradox, we can strive to construct our theories in a manner that, while inevitably ideological in his sense, continues to differentiate between politically inspired constructs and political programs.

Third, and most distressing perhaps, theoretical holism and conceptual contingency force us to the conclusion that theoretical pluralism, or "theoretical anarchism" in Paul Feyerabend's words, is an inescapable condition of the social sciences.[60] That is, it is perfectly normal—and not an aberration caused by the truculence of social scientists—that there should be many competing theories of reality. There is no one correct theory, and to think otherwise is to engage in what Chalmers calls totalitarian thinking.[61] Once we accept this proposition, however, we are forced to realize that, other things being equal, there can be no intrinsically theoretical reason for accepting or not accepting, developing or not developing any one well-crafted theoretical framework as opposed to another. The choice is ours, and making it appears to require a leap of faith—which is to say that our choice of theories, interpretive frameworks, theoretical discourses, and the like is contingent on ourselves: on our value orientations, political beliefs, research interests, and institutional affiliations.

Theoretical pluralism—or, for that matter, theoretical anarchism— is decidedly not the same as anarchy and rampant relativism. There are very sensible criteria for distinguishing better theories from worse ones, so that not every imaginable theoretical framework need be taken equally seriously by scholars. The first, most obvious, and probably most important such criterion, one that I intimated above, is that the parts of a theory must fit. We can judge axioms and concepts for internal consistency, clarity, and parsimony. We can also ask whether ontologies, concepts, and evidential domains cohere as they should for a theory to be well crafted. Of course, although such tests will separate the wheat from the chaff, they will not enable us to differentiate among several well-constructed theories.

A second criterion for evaluating theories is that they actually explain what they claim to be able to explain. It seems indisputable that theories that generally pass tests should be retained, while those that consistently fail should be discarded. But how are we to falsify theories? Many social scientists believe that they confront theories with objective facts: we may dismiss this approach for being at odds with the view of facts expressed above.[62] Far more relevant is the argument of Ernst Nagel and Popper, who believe that "basic statements" or "experimental laws" about reality, which are derived from other, commonly accepted theories and therefore serve as conventions, may be used as measuring rods.[63] There is much to be said for this view, but, as even the inductively inclined Galtung concludes, "it is difficult to falsify a theory; even if it looks easy according to *modus tollens*," which is the essence of Nagel and Popper's scheme.[64] The tight fit between ontology, concepts, domain of evidence, and proof structure will always make it possible to save a Popperian theory by going up or down its edifice and making internally consistent adjustments within any or all of its levels in a manner spelled out nicely by Quine:

> Any statement can be held true come what may, if we make drastic enough adjustments elsewhere in the system. Even a statement very close to the [experiential] periphery can be held true in the face of recalcitrant experience by pleading hallucination or by amending certain statements of the kind called logical laws. Conversely, by the same token, no statement is immune to revision. Revision even of the logical law of the excluded middle has been proposed as a means of simplifying quantum mechanics; and what difference is there in principle between such a shift and the shift whereby Kepler superseded Ptolemy, or Einstein, Newton, or Darwin, Aristotle?[65]

Although Quine may be right to suggest that all but the most incompetent kind of theories will resist the falsification Nagel and Popper envision, the process of saving a theory by absorbing recalcitrant evidence via changes in concepts, proof structure, axioms, or evidential domain may so complicate the theory as to undermine its fit—our first criterion for evaluating theories—and, thus, to make it vulnerable to attack by Occam's Razor. Lakatos makes just this point when he argues that research programs should be considered degenerative, and therefore worse, if changes in the "soft core" of concepts, hypotheses, and so on outweigh the additional empirical content that they—the changes—can account for.

In his own, non-Popperian approach to falsification, Lakatos insists that

> a scientific theory T [is] falsified if and only if another theory T' has been proposed with the following characteristics: (1) T' has excess empirical content over T: that is, it predicts *novel* facts, that is, facts

improbable in the light of, or even forbidden by, T; (2) T' explains the previous success of T, that is, all the unrefuted content of T is contained (within the limits of observational error) in the content of T'; and (3) some of the excess content of T' is corroborated.[66]

Strictly speaking, according to Lakatos, theories are not so much tested as their empirical contents are compared. The procedure seems reasonable, but, as with Popper's version of falsification, the verdict on Lakatos' is mixed. It is easy to argue that, other things being equal, a theory the empirical content of which is greater than that of another theory ($n + 1$ as opposed to n) must be judged preferable. Difficulties arise when we drop the *ceteris paribus* clause and compare two theories with even slightly different ontologies, conceptual frameworks, and evidential domains: holism suggests that such theories are incommensurable. Although Lakatos' advice is helpful in eliminating contenders within larger theoretical families, it does not tell us how to resolve the competition among several well-crafted theories with different paradigmatic foundations.

Evidently, fit and falsification can only reduce the number of candidates for theoretical status, whereas those theories that fit tightly and resist falsification—and we know from Quine's underdetermination thesis that there always will be such theories[67]—must be judged equally sturdy and strong competitors. How, then, do we account for the fact that some theories rise, others fall, and still others are ignored? What accounts for the Kuhnian-like paradigm changes so characteristic of the social sciences in general and of political science in particular? As with Sovietology, contextual reasons, and not intratheoretical ones, appear to play a decisive role.[68] Most important perhaps, the value at any time of a theory seems to be a function of its acceptance or rejection by the community of scholars at large. "Theories," writes Chalmers, "and in particular, interpretive frameworks are tested in debate and not in the laboratory or through statistical analysis."[69] In a word, the popularity or unpopularity of good theories is determined by the value orientations of the scholars who judge them. For instance, it is difficult to explain the immense popularity of Theda Skocpol's theoretically vulnerable work, *States and Social Revolutions*, without reference to her skillful utilization of "the state" at a time when all political scientists appear to be "bringing the concept back in."[70]

Although a value-based procedure such as this obviously has certain safeguards built into it—the integrity of one's colleagues, their multitude, their different perspectives and values, and their competence, all of which militate against facile acceptance or rejection of some fashionable notion—it also opens a Pandora's box of potential, and sometimes very real, dangers. We need not accept Antonio Gramsci's notion of cultural hegemony to understand that scholarly consensus can often be a deadly thing. With regard to Sovietology, for example, both the totalitarian paradigm of the 1950s and the far more deeply entrenched totalitarianism-bashing of the 1970s and 1980s have stultified the field and prevented a multiplicity of views from arising—not because ideological hegemony necessarily suppresses alternative viewpoints in some quasi-coercive manner, but primarily because it excludes certain intellectual options from consideration by scholars and citizens alike.[71] Peter Bachrach and Morton Baratz's term, "nondecisions," refers to just that: the field of possible intellectual and political endeavor that is defined *a priori* as uninteresting or wrong.[72]

The above view suggests that the circulation of social science theories is probably a function of four factors. First is the way in which generational conflict and the tenure process interact. Junior scholars question given assumptions because they are junior and because the "publish or perish" syndrome demands a certain degree of originality; their perspectives become accepted as the conventional wisdom once they assume positions of influence in the academic world; in turn, their children question their hegemony, rediscover their grandparents, and so the cycle continues.[73]

Second, and no less important, the political, socioeconomic, and cultural environment—as mediated by the media—directly affects scholars' perceptions of the topicality, meaningfulness, and utility of theories. Marxism, for example, seems more compelling during times of intense group conflict, as in the 1960s; the pluralist framework appears to work better in times of social peace, as in the 1950s. The modernization approach foundered in the 1960s, when democracies were breaking down in all parts of the world, and seemed far more compelling in the 1980s, when numerous transitions to democracy occurred in rapidly modernizing countries.[74]

Third, political inclinations clearly do matter. Theories that address inconvenient questions and provide unpalatable answers tend to be ignored, while those that confirm political expectations tend to be accepted. When political pluralism is the norm within a scholarly community, such tendencies are not necessarily disturbing. They become so only if ideological hegemony maintains and theoretical challengers are discarded merely for being politically aberrant. The reasons for the emergence and persistence of ideological hegemony need not concern us here, but they appear to be related to generational change, perceptions of relevance, and, last but not least, the political environment in general and the academy's status position in it and relationship with it in particular.

Finally, I venture to suggest that the leading theories will tend to be the theories of the leading scholars. Just as Karl Marx argued that the "ruling ideas are the ideas of the ruling class,"[75] so, too, we may expect that the views, ideas, and theories of those scholars who occupy powerful or influential positions within the scholarly community and/or in the world at large will tend to be accorded greatest respectability and be subjected to the most gingerly of criticism. The obverse of this proposition is that the theories of less influential scholars will be most susceptible to exaggerated criticism by colleagues seeking to protect their academic flanks from possible rivals.

Our theoretical excursion is complete, and it has important methodological implications for Sovietology. The first is that Sovietologists should disabuse themselves of the totalitarian mentality they so decry in their object of study and accept the existence of a plurality of politically inspired perspectives on Soviet politics. Because all well-crafted theories are valid interpretations of Soviet reality, Sovietologists must understand that no one framework dare ever dominate the field. Just as the earlier hegemony of totalitarianism was counterproductive, so, too, the present aversion to anything that smacks of totalitarianism is surely misguided, especially when scholars of Anthony Giddens' calibre can write—in 1987 no less!—that they "consider Friedrich's concept of totalitarianism to be accurate and useful."[76]

A corollary of this conclusion is that policy advice is probably a self-defeating undertaking. Because no truth is true outside of some theoretical framework, theoretically sensitive scholars cannot provide policy makers with "objective" analysis of the sort that policy makers claim to want. The question of what states should do can be answered only provisionally: everything depends on the premises and concepts that one employs to provide an answer. We cannot suggest a line if all we can do is move in circles. And as there is no view the correctness of which is independent of the implicit or explicit theory one employs to find it, states and scholars and, for that matter, the media and scholars have little to say to each other— unless, of course, scholars have special political programs that they wish to pursue.

Although theoretical anarchism should be a liberating scholarly condition, it has the potential to create anarchy in Sovietology by reinforcing its atheoretical pretensions. To avoid this possibility, it is necessary that Sovietology adopt polemical restraint, conceptual self-discipline, and comparative vision—a tall order, if there ever was one. Fundamentally, accepting that theories, politics, and values are inextricably related means acknowledging the inevitability of passionate debate and, therefore, of the absolute necessity of civility. The ongoing controversy over the 1930s is a case in point. Revisionist social historians are not just proffering what they consider to be a more realistic view of the Soviet Union; they are also challenging the strongly felt values of generations of scholars and nonscholars. From the perspective of their detractors, the revisionists are doing nothing less than whitewashing Stalin and his crimes by declaring that no one was responsible for much that went on in the 1930s and 1940s and that these events, be they the famine of 1932–1933 or the Great Terror, were not so terrible as traditionalists and survivors insist they were. Revisionists may or may not be right, but they should understand that, from the traditionalist perspective, their arguments are the moral equivalent of attempts at denying the Holocaust. As a result, the traditionalist-revisionist controversy is inevitably passionate, because it is fundamentally moral. Because there is no escaping this dilemma, it behooves all scholars to refrain from mudslinging and to realize what issues are ultimately at stake.[77]

One way of acquiring greater civility is to pay closer attention to Sartori's insistence on conceptual clarity. Much confusion and infighting could be avoided if theoretically disinclined Sovietologists were to be more careful about the concepts they employ, wittingly or unwittingly. Indeed, I submit that most Sovietological debates only appear to involve differences of opinion: in reality, what is most often involved is radically different intensions and extensions of common terms. Conceptual clarity not only enhances intersubjectivity and understanding, but is also a precondition of intelligent debate. Sloppy concepts reflect sloppy thinking, and both are incompatible with intelligent theorizing, which, as I argued earlier, should be the ultimate object of Sovietology in the first place.[78]

Finally, comparison is critical as a control on flights of the Sovietological imagination. To quote C. Wright Mills: "Comparisons are required in order to understand what may be the essential conditions of whatever we are trying to understand, whether forms of slavery or specific meanings of crime, types of family or peasant communities or collective farms. We must observe whatever we are interested in under a variety of circumstances. Otherwise we are limited to flat description"—or, I would add, to undisciplined theorizing.[79] Comparison entails going outside the Soviet experience, thereby extending one's evidential domain and sharpening one's concepts. Without comparison, Sovietology will not only remain trapped in routine behavioralism, but it will be very difficult for it to accept and live with a theoretically plural world. Fortunately, unlike most other area specialists, Sovietologists can take a shortcut to comparison and, thus, to disciplined theory via the nationality question, the study of which represents comparative politics *par excellence*. Incorporating the non-Russians into Soviet studies would not only expand the field's empirical scope, but also transform what I have elsewhere termed "Sovietology in one country" into genuine political science.[80]

Naturally, my conclusions can resolve neither the theoretical dilemmas faced by the social sciences nor the existential dilemmas of Sovietology. All they can do is suggest what I believe to be a creative, challenging, and frightfully uncertain way of engaging in scholarship, while retaining one's sense of values and political commitments. That is, political science and Sovietology should draw on the Muses of art and science for inspiration, take a deep breath, and hope for the best. Catullus' predicament is inescapable.

NOTES

1. Throughout this study, the term *Sovietology* designates the study of Soviet domestic politics by political scientists and, where relevant, historians in the United States. I am not concerned with Soviet foreign policy or with demography, geography, and economics. Confining my enquiry to scholarly developments in the United States is valid, because the American versions of Sovietology and political science have dominated both fields since World War II, so that the connections, or lack thereof, between Sovietology and political science may be best comprehended in the American setting.

2. On the "comparative communism" debate, see John H. Kautsky, "Comparative Communism Versus Comparative Politics," and S.N. Eisenstadt, "Change in Communist Systems and the Comparative Analysis of Modern Societies"; Rudolf L. Tökés, "Comparative Communism."

3. See Alfred G. Meyer, *The Soviet Political System;* H. Gordon Skilling and Franklyn Griffiths, *Interest Groups in Soviet Politics;* J.M. Montias, "Modernization in Communist Countries"; Robert C. Tucker, "Communist Revolutions, National Cultures, and the Divided Nation."

4. Joseph LaPalombara, "Monoliths or Plural Systems," p. 314.

5. Lawrence C. Mayer, *Redefining Comparative Politics: Promise Versus Performance,* pp. 234–68. Who are the "best Sovietologists"? As a rational actor who prefers to maximize utility *and* minimize risk, I suggest that readers answer this question for themselves.

6. See Roger Kanet, *The Behavioral Revolution and Communist Studies,* p. 2.

7. Jacques Barzun, "Doing Research—Should the Sport Be Regulated?" Of course, Sovietologists are not the only scholars who suffer from this affliction. Gore Vidal has written of "squirrel scholars," a somewhat harsh term for the type of academic who feels impelled to collect for the sake of collecting, a tendency that is all too manifest in the contemporary vogue for writing biographies of no fewer than one thousand pages.

8. Frederic J. Fleron, Jr., "Soviet Area Studies and the Social Sciences," pp. 313–17.

9. Thus, in 1909, James Bryce, the American Political Science Association's fourth president, "called upon his colleagues to 'stick close to the facts.' Above all, he said, researchers should avoid losing themselves in 'abstractions,' meaning that the time had come to abandon the traditional search for wisdom on matters such as 'sovereignty,' 'law,' or the 'state,' via 'efforts of thought' and 'the methods of metaphysics.' In the era of science, or so it seemed to Bryce, more empirical research was needed, to see 'what forms the state has taken and which have proved best, what powers governments have enjoyed and how those powers have worked.' Bryce did not advocate a complete disregard for 'philosophical generalizations' about politics, but he did strongly insist that political inquiry needed a new approach to its subject, and that such generalizations would be justifiable only after the thorough-

going examination of facts which political science could provide" (David M. Ricci, *The Tragedy of Political Science,* p. 67).

10. Paul Hollander, *Political Pilgrims.*

11. Walter Laqueur, "In Search of Russia," p. 44.

12. Sidney and Beatrice Webb, *Soviet Communism: A New Civilization.*

13. Consider the bizarre Shul'gin affair, as depicted by Roland Gaucher in *Opposition in the USSR: 1917–1967,* p. 147.

14. See Alexander J. Motyl, "Bringing the USSR Back In: Comparative Research Agendas and the Necessity of a Totalitarian Type," unpublished paper, 1988.

15. Consider the following statement by Columbia University's Presidential Commission on the Future of the University: "Because it represents the creation of knowledge and extends the influence and activity of the university beyond its walls, the publication of important and original work is the best, and indispensable, measure of the productivity of both the junior and senior faculty of a research university and of how the university itself is known and judged. Publications provide the primary evidence of the quality of individuals and problems, particularly when they appear in influential refereed journals or take the form of books and monographs under a distinguished imprint. Reviews by professional peers and prizes for outstanding works in a given field or category provide further external evidence. In some fields the number of citations to original work is an important indicator. The writing of a widely-used textbook can add to professional standing as well as to visibility. A long publication list is not synonymous with quality, but at least it indicates drive and activity" (*Strategies of Renewal: Report of the President's Commission on the Future of the University* [New York: Columbia University, May 1987], pp. 129–30).

16. Ricci, pp. 221–22.

17. Laqueur, "In Search of Russia," p. 44.

18. See John N. Hazard, *Recollections of a Pioneering Sovietologist.*

19. See Arnold Buchholz, *Soviet and East European Studies in the International Framework,* p. 11–31.

20. Stephen F. Cohen, *Rethinking the Soviet Experience,* p. 12.

21. Ibid., pp. 11–12.

22. Surely, there is no logical reason why moral condemnation of the USSR should imply acceptance of a conservative agenda. That it has done so over time is due to the peculiar nature of American politics and not to any logical connection between opposition to Stalinism and conservatism.

23. See L.G. Ionin, ". . . I vozzovet proshedshee (razmyshleniia sotsiologa o novom fil'me T. Abuladze)."

24. See Alexander J. Motyl, "'Sovietology in One Country'."

25. Harley Balzer, "Can We Survive Glasnost?," pp. 1–2.

26. On the conceptual confusion surrounding the term crisis, see Alexander J. Motyl, "Reassessing the Soviet Crisis."

27. Vernon Van Dyke, *Political Science: A Philosophical Analysis,* p. 96.

28. Stephen Gaukroger, *Explanatory Structures,* p. 45.

29. How, then, are theories generated? Popper's comments regarding ideas are instructive: "There is no such thing as a logical method of having new ideas, or a logical reconstruction of this process. My view may be expressed by saying that every discovery contains 'an irrational element,' or 'a creative intuition,' in Bergson's sense. In a similar way Einstein speaks of the 'search

for those highly universal laws . . . from which a picture of the world can be obtained by pure deduction. There is no logical path,' he says, 'leading us to these . . . laws. They can only be reached by intuition, based upon something like an intellectual love (*Einfühlung*) of the objects of experience'" (Karl Popper, *The Logic of Scientific Discovery*, p. 32).

30. Alexander Rabinowitch, *The Bolsheviks Come to Power*, p. xxi.

31. For example, see John L.H. Keep, *The Russian Revolution: A Study in Mass Mobilization*.

32. Sheila Fitzpatrick, *The Russian Revolution: 1917–1932*.

33. J. Arch Getty, *Origins of the Great Purges*.

34. Clifford Geertz, *The Interpretation of Cultures*, pp. 21–22.

35. Throughout this chapter I am concerned only with social science theory. I draw on philosophers of science when what they say of natural science theory may also apply to social science theory, but I make no pretense of addressing the theoretical issues of interest to natural scientists.

36. Giovanni Sartori, "Guidelines for Concept Analysis," in *Social Science Concepts*, p. 84.

37. George Caspar Homans, "Contemporary Theory in Sociology," p. 53.

38. Johan Galtung, *Theory and Methods of Social Research*, p. 451.

39. Gaukroger, *Explanatory Structures*, pp. 39, 14, 68, 15.

40. Imre Lakatos, "Falsification and the Methodology of Scientific Research Programmes," in *Criticism and the Growth of Knowledge*.

41. Sovietologists are notoriously prone to miss this point. It seems that every second review in professional journals tediously disputes some book's premises as "false," "incorrect," "questionable," or "debatable."

42. Popper, *The Logic of Scientific Discovery*, pp. 71–72.

43. Sartori, p. 74.

44. Walter Carlsnaes, *The Concept of Ideology and Political Analysis*, p. 5.

45. Gaukroger, p. 244.

46. Ibid., pp. 77, 74.

47. Ernst Nagel, *The Structure of Science*, p. 31. Here, again, Sovietologists are inclined to ignore the importance of initial conditions and to assume that a theory that may have held under, say, Brezhnevite conditions is proven "wrong" under Gorbachevian ones.

48. Galtung, p. 334.

49. Thomas A. Spragens, Jr., *The Dilemma of Contemporary Political Theory*, p. 155.

50. W.V. Quine, *Theories and Things*, pp. 71–72.

51. Paul A. Roth, *Meaning and Method in the Social Sciences*, p. 19.

52. Ibid., pp. 4–8.

53. Ibid., pp. 44–72.

54. See, for example, Ronald H. Chilcote, *Theories of Comparative Politics*.

55. Galtung, pp. 23–25.

56. Jack Snyder, "Richness, Rigor, and Relevance in the Study of Soviet Foreign Policy"; "Science and Sovietology: Bridging the Methods Gap in Soviet Foreign Policy Studies."

57. More specifically, according to Chalmers, all such "interpretive frameworks" consist of a "macro-theory" based on a conceptual and historical macrostructure, valued dimensions, and explanations of structural change; a "problematic" that identifies crises, problems, tensions, or contradictions within the macrostructure; and a "model of explaining and interpreting the

significance of particular events." (Douglas A. Chalmers, "Interpretive Frameworks," pp. 29, 31.)

58. Ibid., p. 56.

59. Spragens, pp. 165–66.

60. See Paul Feyerabend, *Against Method.*

61. Chalmers, p. 45.

62. See Alan C. Isaak, *Scope and Methods of Political Science.*

63. Nagel, pp. 79–88.

64. Galtung, p. 458. *Modus tolens* is the "argument that if a conditional statement is true but its consequent is false, then its antecedent is false, e.g., 'If this, then that. But not that. Therefore not this'." (A.R. Lacey, *A Dictionary of Philosophy,* p. 137.)

65. W.V. Quine, *From a Logical Point of View,* p. 43, as quoted in Galtung, p. 458.

66. Lakatos, p. 116. For a discussion of Lakatos' approach to theory-building, see Terence Ball, "From Paradigms to Research Programs."

67. Quine, *Theories and Things,* pp. 24–30; Roth, p. 7.

68. Thomas S. Kuhn, *The Structure of Scientific Revolutions.*

69. Chalmers, p. 51.

70. Theda Skocpol, *States and Social Revolutions;* Peter B. Evans et al., *Bringing the State Back In.*

71. On the utility of the totalitarianism concept, see Giovanni Sartori, "Soviet Studies: A Scheme for Analysis"; Edward W. Walker, "Totalitarianism, Comparative Politics, and Sovietology."

72. Peter Bachrach and Morton Baratz, "Decisions and Nondecisions."

73. See Alfred G. Meyer, "Coming to Terms with the Past . . . And with One's Older Colleagues."

74. For example, see Jerry F. Hough, *Russia and the West.*

75. Karl Marx, "The German Ideology," in Robert C. Tucker, *The Marx-Engels Reader,* p. 172.

76. Anthony Giddens, *The Nation-State and Violence,* p. 301.

77. The following comments, by prominent scholars whose names—mercifully—will go unmentioned, illustrate exactly the lack of civility I have in mind: (1) "I doubt he [a scholar whose academic interests the scholar disagrees with] could have gotten a real academic job. . . . If he hadn't hopped on this political cause, he would be running research for a bank, or running an export-import business." (2) "This [Robert Conquest's book, *Harvest of Sorrow*] is crap, rubbish." ("In Search of a Soviet Holocaust: A 55-Year-Old Famine Feeds the Right," in *The Village Voice,* January 12, 1988, pp. 31–32.) The ultimate irony is, of course, that some of Conquest's work on the famine and the terror currently is being published by the Soviets.

78. Fleron, "Soviet Area Studies and the Social Sciences."

79. C. Wright Mills, *The Sociological Imagination,* p. 147.

80. Motyl, "'Sovietology in One Country'."

BIBLIOGRAPHY

Bachrach, Peter and Morton Baratz. "Decisions and Nondecisions: An Analytical Framework." *American Political Science Review* (September 1963), 57 (3): 632–42.

Balzer, Harley. "Can We Survive Glasnost?" *AAASS Newsletter* (January 1989), 29 (1): 1–2.

Barzun, Jacques. "Doing Research—Should the Sport Be Regulated?" *Columbia* (February 1987), 12 (4): 18–22.

Buchholz, Arnold, ed. *Soviet and East European Studies in the International Framework: Organization, Financing and Political Relevance* (Dobbs Ferry, NY: Transnational, 1982).

Carlsnaes, Walter. *The Concept of Ideology and Political Analysis* (Westport, CT: Greenwood Press, 1981).

Chalmers, Douglas A. "Interpretive Frameworks: A Structure of Theory in Political Science." Unpublished paper, 1987.

Chilcote, Ronald H. *Theories of Comparative Politics: The Search for a Paradigm* (Boulder, CO: Westview, 1981).

Cohen, Stephen F. *Rethinking the Soviet Experience: Politics and History Since 1917* (New York: Oxford University Press, 1985).

Eisenstadt, S.N. "Change in Communist Systems and the Comparative Analysis of Modern Societies." *Studies in Comparative Communism* (Spring/Summer 1973), 6 (1–2): 171–83.

Evans, Peter B. et al., eds. *Bringing the State Back In* (Cambridge: Cambridge University Press, 1985).

Feyerabend, Paul. *Against Method* (London: Verso, 1988).

Fitzpatrick, Sheila. *The Russian Revolution, 1917–1932* (Oxford: Oxford University Press, 1984).

Fleron, Frederic J., Jr., ed. *Communist Studies and the Social Sciences* (Chicago, IL: Rand McNally, 1969).

Fleron, Frederic J., Jr. "Soviet Area Studies and the Social Sciences: Some Methodological Problems in Communist Studies." *Soviet Studies* (January 1968), 20 (3): 313–39.

Galtung, Johan. *Theory and Methods of Social Research* (New York: Columbia University Press, 1969).

Gaucher, Roland. *Opposition in the USSR, 1917–1967* (New York: Funk & Wagnalls, 1969).

Gaukroger, Stephen. *Explanatory Structures* (Hassocks, Sussex: Harvester Press, 1978).

Geertz, Clifford. *The Interpretation of Cultures* (New York: Basic Books, 1973).

Getty, J. Arch. *Origins of the Great Purges: The Soviet Communist Party Reconsidered, 1933–1938* (Cambridge: Cambridge University Press, 1985).

Giddens, Anthony. *The Nation-State and Violence* (Berkeley, CA: University of California Press, 1987).

Hazard, John N. *Recollections of a Pioneering Sovietologist* (New York: Oceana, 1984).

Hollander, Paul. *Political Pilgrims: Travels of Western Intellectuals to the Soviet Union, China, and Cuba* (New York: Harper & Row, 1983).

Homans, George Caspar. "Contemporary Theory in Sociology." In Norman K. Denzin, ed., *Sociological Methods* (Chicago, IL: Aldine, 1970), pp. 51–69.

Hough, Jerry F. *Russia and the West: Gorbachev and the Politics of Reform* (New York: Simon & Schuster, 1988).

Ionin, L.G. ". . . I vozzovet proshedshee (razmyshleniia sotsiologa o novom fil'me T. Abuladze)." *Sotsiologicheskie issledovaniia* (May–June 1987), no. 3, pp. 62–72.

Isaak, Alan C. *Scope and Methods of Political Science* (Homewood, IL: Dorsey Press, 1985).

Kanet, Roger E., ed. *The Behavioral Revolution and Communist Studies* (New York: Free Press, 1971).

Kautsky, John H. "Comparative Communism Versus Comparative Politics." *Studies in Comparative Communism* (Spring/Summer 1973), 6 (1–2): 135–70.

Keep, John L.H. *The Russian Revolution: A Study in Mass Mobilization* (New York: Norton, 1976).

Kuhn, Thomas S. *The Structure of Scientific Revolutions*, 2nd ed. (Chicago, IL: University of Chicago Press, 1970).

Lacey, A.R. *A Dictionary of Philosophy* (New York: Scribner's, 1976).

Lakatos, Imre. "Falsification and the Methodology of Scientific Research Programmes." In Imre Lakatos and Alan Musgrave, eds., *Criticism and the Growth of Knowledge* (Cambridge: Cambridge University Press, 1970), pp. 91–196.

LaPalombara, Joseph. "Monoliths or Plural Systems: Through Conceptual Lens Darkly." *Studies in Comparative Communism* (Autumn 1975), 8 (3): 305–32.

Laqueur, Walter. "In Search of Russia." *Survey* (January 1964), no. 50, pp. 41–52.

Mayer, Lawrence C. *Redefining Comparative Politics: Promise Versus Performance* (Newbury Park, CA: Sage, 1989).

Meyer, Alfred G. "Coming to Terms with the Past . . . And with One's Older Colleagues." *The Russian Review* (October 1986), 45 (4): 401–08.

_____. *The Soviet Political System* (New York: Random House, 1965).

Mills, C. Wright. *The Sociological Imagination* (London: Oxford University Press, 1959).

Montias, J.M. "Modernization in Communist Countries: Some Questions of Methodology." *Studies in Comparative Communism* (Winter 1972), 5 (4): 413–27.

Motyl, Alexander J. "Reassessing the Soviet Crisis: Big Problems, Muddling Through, Business as Usual." *Political Science Quarterly* (Summer 1989), 104 (2): 269–80.

_____. "'Sovietology in One Country' or Comparative Nationality Studies?" *Slavic Review* (Spring 1989), 48 (1): 83–88.

Nagel, Ernst. *The Structure of Science: Problems in the Logic of Scientific Explanation*, 2nd ed. (Indianapolis, IN: Hackett, 1977).

Popper, Karl. *The Logic of Scientific Discovery* (New York: Harper & Row, 1965).

Quine, W.V. *From a Logical Point of View* (Cambridge, MA: Harvard University Press, 1953).

_____. *Theories and Things* (Cambridge, MA: Belknap Press, 1981).

Rabinowitch, Alexander. *The Bolsheviks Come to Power* (New York: Norton, 1976).

Ricci, David M. *The Tragedy of Political Science: Politics, Scholarship, and Democracy* (New Haven, CT: Yale University Press, 1984).

Roth, Paul A. *Meaning and Method in the Social Sciences* (Ithaca, NY: Cornell University Press, 1987).

Sartori, Giovanni, ed. *Social Science Concepts* (Beverly Hills, CA: Sage, 1984).

Sartori, Giovanni. "Soviet Studies: A Scheme for Analysis." Unpublished paper, February 1988.

Skilling, H. Gordon and Franklyn Griffiths, eds. *Interest Groups in Soviet Politics* (Princeton, NJ: Princeton University Press, 1971).

Skocpol, Theda. *States and Social Revolutions* (Cambridge: Cambridge University Press, 1979).

Snyder, Jack. "Richness, Rigor, and Relevance in the Study of Soviet Foreign Policy." *International Security* (Winter 1984/1985), 9 (3): 89–108.

_____. "Science and Sovietology: Bridging the Methods Gap in Soviet Foreign Policy Studies." *World Politics* (January 1988), 40 (2): 169–93.

Spragens, Thomas A., Jr. *The Dilemma of Contemporary Political Theory* (New York: Dunellen, 1973).

Tökés, Rudolf L. "Introduction: Comparative Communism: The Elusive Target." *Studies in Comparative Communism* (Autumn 1975), 8 (3): 211–29.

Tucker, Robert C. "Communist Revolutions, National Cultures, and the Divided Nation." *Studies in Comparative Communism* (Autumn 1974), 7 (3): 235–45.

Tucker, Robert C., ed. *The Marx-Engels Reader*, 2nd ed. (New York: Norton, 1972).

Van Dyke, Vernon. *Political Science. A Philosophical Analysis* (Stanford, CA: Stanford University Press, 1960).

Walker, Edward W. "Totalitarianism, Comparative Politics, and Sovietology." Unpublished paper, March 1988.

Webb, Sidney and Beatrice Webb. *Soviet Communism: A New Civilization* (New York: Scribner's, 1936).

4

SCIENCE AND SOVIETOLOGY:

Bridging the Methods Gap in Soviet Foreign Policy Studies

Everyone is in favor of greater scholarly rigor, but people define rigor in seemingly antithetical ways. Two methodological cultures, positivism and holism, coexist uneasily in the social sciences. For "logical positivists," rigor means deducing an "if, then" hypothesis from a general theory, and testing whether the predicted relationship holds true over a set of cases in which the influence of extraneous factors is held constant. Holism is more eclectic in its methods; for most holists, rigor means reconstructing the meaning of an action in the subject's own terms, and interpreting it in light of a richly detailed cultural, social, and historical context. Thus, positivists usually seek objective causes; holists typically explain behavior through the prism of the actor's subjective understanding. Positivists trace patterns across many cases, setting context aside by holding it constant; holists trace patterns within cases, exploring connections between context and action.[1]

Underlying these different approaches to scholarly method are different assumptions about the nature of reality. Holists see a world of great complexity and interrelatedness. In any situation, many independent elements interact in complex ways to shape the ideas and actions of actors. Artificial attempts to focus on some small number of factors and relationships, which could be compared across cases, only hinder understanding. Emphasis is placed on the unique aspects of each situation, not on superficial or partial similarities across situations. Consequently, theories designed to illuminate more than one case must be rich, open-ended check-lists, not deductive, narrow-beam searchlights. Some holists even take the position that objective reality is so complex, diverse, and unknowable that only subjective (or "intersubjective") dialogues about reality can be profitably studied.

105

Positivists, on the other hand, believe that the analytical convenience of simplification is legitimate because it can be shown empirically that some factors are more important than others. Complex
interactions between some important variables may occur, but everything is not inextricably related to everything else. Even "unique"
situations are not considered to be *sui generis,* but rare types whose
differences from other cases can be described in general terms. Moreover, when positivists look at whole systems, they assume that
relationships among the parts can be explained in terms of some
relatively simple and regular structural effects.

The relationship between positivism and holism is especially important for Soviet foreign policy studies. In that field, as in area
studies more generally, a scholar's regionalist culture pulls him toward holism, while his disciplinary culture of political science pulls
him toward positivism. In this conflict of cultural and institutional
cross-pressures, it is important to find some firm intellectual ground
on which methodological choices can be based.

The distance between positivism and holism is not as great as it
appears. Each captures a valuable truth, and the two work best in
conjunction. Positivism—and in particular its driving engine, deductive theory—poses questions in a way that clarifies arguments, facilitates testing, and directs research to ripe, important questions.
Holism, on the other hand, reminds us that in the Soviet field causal
generalizations that hold true 60 percent of the time are not the
ultimate goal of research. Rather, such generalizations must contribute to understanding in full contextual detail the one particular case
that we care most about—the present. Moreover, reconstructing the
Soviets' thinking may sometimes be easier than understanding the
underlying causes of their behavior, and just as valuable in guiding
policy choices.

The benefits of positivism and holism can often be captured simultaneously by recasting holist interpretations in deductive, causal
terms. A holist's "context" can in most cases be translated into the
positivist's "causal variables." Even when holist explanations deal
with ends and means rather than with causes, they can often be
sharpened by expressing them in deductive terms.

Most Sovietologists are already using a method that combines the
reconstruction of Soviet thinking with a complex causal explanation
of behavior. In executing this method, however, positivist rules for
stating and testing causal arguments are often ignored. As a result,
debates go in circles and irrelevant evidence piles up. The most
urgent need in the field of Soviet foreign policy today is to reformulate research questions in terms of deductive arguments, but
without sacrificing the sound holist traditions of the discipline.

In an earlier article on a similar theme, I laid out the logic of
positivist testing procedures, paying only brief attention to the cen-

tral role of deductive theory in the positivist approach; I was similarly brief on the compatibility of positivism and holism.[2] The present essay will focus on those more basic questions as they relate to Soviet foreign policy studies. Its sections will focus on (1) what positivism is, and the role of deductive theory in it; (2) what holism is, and its relation to positivism; (3) the shortcomings of holism; (4) the use of deductive theory to repair holism's shortcomings and, more generally, to set a research agenda for the field; (5) the shortcomings of positivism; and (6) the use of hybrid methods to repair the shortcomings of positivism. Illustrations will show the value of deductive theory in addressing some of the major questions of the field, including Soviet views on the political implications of military imbalances and the domestic sources of Soviet expansionism. These and other illustrations will be drawn from some of the best secondary works in the field.

I. POSITIVISM

Explanation and testing in the positivist framework can be summarized in terms of five elements, the most central one being deductive theory.[3]

A. Causal Generalization

Positivists state their hypotheses in the form of "if, then" generalizations. They seek to explain individual events by identifying "if, then" generalizations, or covering laws, that match the patterns of those events. For example, a hypothesis in the literature of international politics posits that, if offense becomes easier, then international conflict will increase.[4] Thus, one explanation for the origins of the cold war could be that the fluid political situation in Europe after Germany's defeat made offensive tactics advantageous, both for opportunistic and security purposes. The converse suggests that if offense becomes more difficult, then conflict will diminish. Thus, one explanation for the rise of detente in Europe is that the Berlin crisis of 1958–1961 showed it was easier to defend the status quo than to change it.

B. Operational Definitions of Variables

The terms of the hypothesis, including causes and consequences, must be clearly defined to minimize disagreements about the classification of particular cases. For example, definitions of offensive advantage and defensive advantage must be clear enough so that a researcher can decide into which category his case falls.[5]

C. Covariation

Testing must show that offensive advantage correlates with increased conflict, and that defensive advantage correlates with decreased conflict.

D. Controlled Comparison

Testing focuses on cases in which competing hypotheses make opposite predictions. For example, it might be argued that international conflict is caused not by offensive advantage but by domestic political pathologies that promote expansionism. If so, offensive advantage might be spuriously related to increased conflict, because domestically motivated expansionists work to create offensive capabilities. In order to disentangle the effects of the two putative causes, the researcher looks for cases where there is an offensive advantage but no domestic motivation to expand, and for causes where there is a defensive advantage but high domestic motivation to expand.[6]

E. Deductive Theory

Just as "if, then" generalizations at a low level of abstraction act as covering laws that explain individual events, so too generalizations at higher levels of abstraction explain the covering laws. For example, the hypothesis that offensive advantage causes conflict even among status quo powers is just one application of the more general Prisoners' Dilemma theorem in game theory.[7] According to a strictly mathematical proof, rational players in a single-play Prisoners' Dilemma, by the logic of their situation, are constrained to compete even though they end up worse off than if they had cooperated. Offensive advantage increases the incentive for competitive play by magnifying the gains that arise from exploiting one-sided cooperation in a single play of the game, and by magnifying the losses that arise from being exploited. If international politics is like a Prisoners' Dilemma, and if offensive advantage makes it resemble a single-play contest, then, by logical deduction, offensive advantage should promote conflict.

Deductive theory is the predictive engine that drives the positivist method as a whole. It generates "if, then" hypotheses, which in turn generate testable predictions in specific cases. As a result, the implications of arguments are made clearer when they are expressed as theoretical deductions, and tests for them are easier to think up.

II. HOLISM

In a study of Soviet views on the role of military power in international politics, Robert Legvold has reiterated the main tenets of the holistic position: understanding behavior in terms of the actor's own frame of reference, and explaining it by placing it in a rich context. Thus, "the student of politics who looks only at patterns of behavior but leaves out the meanings that actors give to their own and to each other's conduct turns into a specialist of shadows."[8] Analyzing another culture's approach to strategic thought in terms of one's own theories (in this case, Thomas Schelling's ideas about the "diplomacy of violence") introduces an ethnocentric bias that hinders understanding. Moreover, "Soviet thoughts about semiabstractions, like the functioning of force in contemporary international politics, are but a fragment of the larger issue." They must be understood in the larger context of Soviet goals and fears, the broader Soviet worldview, and the international environment in which the Soviets calculate. Understanding also requires distinguishing among different contexts in which the question arises: using force, deterring the use of force, indirectly influencing diplomatic trends, and so forth.[9] Empathy and context-dependent nuances of meaning are the watchwords of this approach.

Though the general epistemological stance of holism is quite clearly articulated, its methodological prescriptions rarely are. In part, this reflects a conscious choice to avoid imposing *a priori* concepts and approaches, and a preference to be guided *ad hoc* by the data of the particular case. Still, Sovietologists, like anthropologists setting out to do fieldwork, like to bring along a checklist of questions to think about. These initial concepts or theories are usually designed to be flexible and nondeductive so that they adjust to fit the case rather than force it into a Procrustean bed.[10]

In the Soviet field, the clearest exposition of this method is the framework that Marshall Shulman used in his study of Stalin's foreign policy and his attempt to think through contemporary Soviet arms-control policy while he served in the Carter administration.[11] The method is roughly as follows: Prepare a chart arraying the major domestic and international developments impinging on Soviet calculations; track these developments over the period to be studied, along with the development of Soviet statements and actions; and reconstruct a plausible line of Soviet reasoning that could have led to those actions, using a background knowledge of Soviet history and politics for guidance. The objective international setting and the peculiarly Soviet way of looking at it are both included.

In this style of analysis, positivist and holist elements are mixed. At one level, situational constraints and deep structural effects of history and the social system are treated like *causes,* in a basically positivist fashion. Thus, the Soviets behave a certain way "because of" the effects of these variables. However, these causal inputs are integrated through an analysis of the Soviets' *reasons* for pursuing certain ends with certain means, in a holist fashion. Thus, the Soviets' subjective perspective leads them to behave in a particular way "in order to" achieve certain goals.

There is nothing in this method that bars the development of a general thesis from which testable hypotheses can be derived. When this occurs, it comes close to replicating the positivist method. In *Stalin's Foreign Policy Reappraised,* for example, Shulman adopted what amounts to a rational-choice theory of Soviet international behavior, arguing for "the largely rational responsiveness of Soviet policy to changes in the world environment, and particularly to changes in power relationships." According to this case study, the Soviet leadership by 1949 began to recognize the counterproductive effects of its confrontational policies, decided that adverse trends in both the socialist and capitalist camp dictated the need for a breathing spell, and consequently moved toward a policy of peaceful coexistence in order to demobilize the opposing bloc.[12]

From this rational-choice theory, Shulman deduced testable "if, then" hypotheses—some explicit and some implicit. One is that the Soviets are less confrontational when the balance of power is against them in the short run and favors them in the long run. Another is that the Soviets are more confrontational in situations of offensive advantage (e.g., when the status quo is fluid) than in situations of defensive advantage (e.g., when militancy is seen to unify opponents, when peace propaganda sells better than revolutionary appeals).[13]

Because of the emphasis on the interaction of multiple factors in chronological context, however, effects of the individual variables, such as the balance of power, are not fully tested as separate hypotheses.[14] From a positivist standpoint, this leads to some puzzles in the course of the narrative. Weakness and fear sometimes appear as motives for restraint; at other times they serve as rationalizations for militancy—as in Zhdanov's response to the Marshall Plan and in Molotov's reasons for retaining the confrontational line even after the Berlin crisis.[15] Likewise, the strength of socialism sometimes appears as an argument for militancy, sometimes as an argument for the feasibility of peaceful coexistence.[16] These apparent anomalies do not stand out in the chronological narrative because they are plausibly integrated into reconstructions of how a whole range of incentives came together to shape Soviet thinking.

This might lead a positivist to question whether the balance of power really was the key factor in Soviet policy—or indeed, whether it had any systematic effect at all. Perhaps the relative advantages of offense and defense determined Soviet policy, and not the current or prospective balance of power. Or perhaps the effect of these two factors varies, depending on the aggressiveness of the opponent. To test this, the positivist might want to set up a chart with eight boxes, think through the logic of all the permutations, and look for cases to test each one.

To the holist, such testing might seem beside the point, since the main thing is to demonstrate the validity of the general thesis about the rational responsiveness of Soviet policy, not to produce law-like statements about the effects of separate variables. Once he knows that the Soviets are rationally responsive to their environment, he can interpret their moves in specific contexts *ad hoc.* In this view, to be valid, laws would have to be so complex, qualified, and cumbersome that they would offer no advantage over *ad hoc* reconstruction.

To the positivist, the basis for the larger generalization is shaky without the separate testing of the effects of individual variables. Unless a close connection between specific incentives and specific policies is shown, there is a possibility that Soviet policy is not based on rational calculations, but on a rote response to the failure of the previous policy. It makes a great deal of difference whether the Soviets are rationally reacting to specific geopolitical incentives or whether they are cybernetically alternating between stereotyped policies of militancy and lulling.[17] Indeed, Shulman identifies two patterns of Soviet learning: a cyclical alternation between confrontational "left" and nonconfrontational "right" tactics, which seems to be cybernetic, and a secular shift to the right which may be a rational response to a secular decline in revolutionary opportunities.[18] It might also be caused, however, by factors such as the evolution of the Soviet political system. A recasting of these questions in terms of explicitly competing theories and deducing testable "if, then" hypotheses from them could open up a fresh line of research, building on Shulman's ideas and leading to practical conclusions about how the Soviets learn in response to U.S. behavior.

In short, some forms of holism are not far from positivism in their implicit use of deductive theory and "if, then" hypotheses. In such cases, it may be quite easy to recast the holist argument in terms of explicit, deductive theory. Holism may be farther from positivism, however, in its reluctance to test the effects of individual variables in controlled contexts. Problems arise when the deductive links in a theory are left implicit and when multiple causes are examined all at once.

III. SOME SHORTCOMINGS OF HOLISM

The lax attitude of holism toward deductive logic leads to two errors. The first is that its predictions tend to be logically underdetermined. Causal assertions are made without showing why the same stimulus could not just as easily have led to the opposite consequences. The second error is that holistic explanations after the fact tend to be logically overdetermined. Several independent factors are indiscriminately listed as the joint causes of an action, even though any one of them might have been sufficient to cause it. This shortcoming is serious in cases where different causes might have different policy implications for the West. Closer attention to the deductive logic of arguments can help to avoid these problems.

A. Predictive Underdetermination

Harry Gelman's argument about the role of Soviet leadership politics in promoting an opportunistic, expansionist approach to detente illustrates the problem of logical underdetermination.[19] Gelman's book is a good example of eclectic holism, integrating causal explanations with the reconstruction of Soviet ends/means calculations. Despite some logical loose strands, it offers the best available account of the domestic politics of foreign policy in the Brezhnev period; if reinterpreted in the light of rational-choice theories of logrolling, it constitutes a significant theoretical advance as well.

Gelman offers three kinds of causal factors to account for the Soviet Union's tendency toward opportunistic expansion and for variations in its intensity. The first—not an argument that is distinctive to Gelman—focuses on the balance of costs, risks, and opportunities present in the international environment. The second is an endemic "attacking compulsion" rooted in the deep structure of the Leninist political culture and operational code. Gelman does not advance direct evidence for this proposition aside from its general plausibility in light of the obvious facts of Soviet expansionism. As such, it functions as a kind of residual, explaining what cannot be explained in any other way.

The third line of explanation rests on consensus building and leadership politics. Though the narrative sounds persuasive, Gelman never makes clear why consensus building produces an expansionist result rather than the opposite. His historical reconstruction holds that,

> since Brezhnev was confronted simultaneously with temptation (Podgornyy's assumption of a vulnerable political stance [in favor of restraint on defense spending]), positive incentives (the political rewards waiting in the form of support from the military and Suslov), and competition (the extreme rhetoric Shelepin offered the military and the ideologues), his reaction was a foregone conclusion.[20]

But why was it a foregone conclusion? Couldn't this whole formulation be turned on its head: temptation in the form of the vulnerability of Shelepin and the military, due to their reckless rhetoric and opposition to obviously beneficial arms restraint; positive incentives in the form of Podgornyy's support; competition in the form of Kosygin's budgetary alliance with Podgornyy—leading to international retrenchment? It didn't work out this way, but why?

The simplest explanation would be that elite groups and institutions with an interest in expansion (Gelman cites the military and the Central Committee's International Department) became disproportionately powerful in the Brezhnev years. That, however, begs the questions of where their power came from, and why it increased in this period. Moreover, Gelman's own account emphasizes that the rising power of these groups was as much a result or a concomitant of the expansionist consensus as a cause of it. The basic levers of power, Gelman argues, remained in the hands of the Politburo, above the level of institutional interests.[21]

Another explanation (which Gelman does not explicitly advance) would argue, along with George Breslauer, that the process of logrolling and consensus building in itself tends to produce "taut," overcommitted policies.[22] Gelman's evidence, reinterpreted in light of this theory, suggests that Brezhnev succeeded politically because he devised a policy of expansionist detente that promised to reconcile an arms build-up for the military, expansion into the third world for the ideologues, and increased technology transfer to co-opt Kosygin's domestic economic issue. For this line of argument, it need not be true that expansionist interests were more powerful than anti-expansionist interests. Rather, in a system where each interest gets what it wants most, expansion will result as long as *any* veto groups have an interest in it. That is a straightforward deduction from rational-choice theories of logrolling.[23]

Lacking this theoretical element, however, Gelman is unable to explain the expansionist character of the coalition in terms of domestic political dynamics alone. Consequently, he resorts to the notion of an "attacking compulsion": for reasons rooted in the deep cognitive structures of Leninists, it is political death to be considered, as Podgornyy was, "unacceptably 'soft'."[24] If that is true, an entirely different research design is indicated. Domestic politics, the area in which Gelman carried out most of his original research, "becomes all product and is not at all productive."[25] If the "attacking compulsion" is really the key to the explanation, then it would have been better to look for propositions and tests focusing on the origin, structure, and evolution of belief systems. Alternatively, Gelman could have stayed with the domestic focus while recasting and sharpening his hypothesis with the help of rational-choice logrolling theory.

B. Explanatory Overdetermination

As if to compensate for arguments that are loose enough to predict any outcome and its opposite, holists tend toward explanatory overkill, piling up any number of logically unrelated or logically contradictory reasons for an occurrence. It is true that a variety of unrelated factors may sometimes come together to produce an outcome or a decision, but psychologists tell us that decisions are often taken on the basis of one salient consideration, and that multiple rationales are invented later.[26] When each of several candidate explanations implies a different policy prescription, it is especially important to distinguish which of them are really operating and which are spurious.

An example is provided by explanations that consider aggressiveness in Soviet foreign policy to be rooted in the totalitarian origins of the political system. This argument is often invoked without supplying any logical connection at all, relying on the analogy to Nazi Germany for persuasiveness. At other times, a whole list of reasons is supplied: (1) totalitarians take their ideology seriously; (2) their political style requires either total control or total conflict; (3) they manufacture foreign threats and successes abroad to shore up their tenuous legitimacy; and, more subtly, (4) real pressures of international competition force the leader of a backward state to use domestic repression and militant appeals to mobilize his inefficient society.[27]

Each of these explanations is logically distinct. There is no reason to believe that if one of them is true, the rest are true also. Moreover, each of them seems to imply a different strategy for the opponent: (1) firm deterrence while waiting for the totalitarians' ideology to atrophy; (2) subversion to change their political system; (3) symbolic international agreements to replace symbolic conflict as the basis for their domestic legitimacy; and (4) an easing of external pressure to reduce the need for internal repression. Since some of these policies are opposites, lumping these explanations together indiscriminately, in typical holist fashion, would destroy their practical value. Logically independent explanations need to be disentangled and tested separately, in positivist fashion.

In short, holist studies of Soviet foreign policy often include causal arguments as part of their interpretation. Typically, these arguments suffer from the errors of predictive underdetermination and explanatory overdetermination. Such problems can be corrected by recasting the arguments in terms of deductive theory and by adopting positivist testing procedures. In the examples cited above, this could be accomplished through relatively small adjustments to the original holist argument. The intervention of deductive theory can also transform a holist debate in a more fundamental way, refocusing its arguments and establishing an entirely new research agenda.

IV. TRANSFORMING A RESEARCH AGENDA BY MEANS OF DEDUCTIVE THEORY

Deductive theory can do much more than just clean up the loose ends of holist arguments. At its best, it can reformulate the questions asked in academic and policy debates, clarify the branchpoints where contending arguments diverge, and reorient research toward more decisive tests. Beyond this, a deductive theory can turn diverse, narrowly focused studies into contributions toward a unified research program. Historians of science have found that the take-off point for most disciplines comes when work is focused on a stable core of explanatory goals that are expressed as a set of deductively interrelated puzzles.[28] One of the main barriers to progress in the field of Soviet foreign policy is the absence of this kind of research program that would provide direction to its work.

In recent years, the discipline of international politics has been making considerable progress toward defining a coherent, productive, yet flexible and relatively pluralistic research program. Though this field is hardly a perfect model for emulation, it is normal in science for the more applied fields to borrow ideas and approaches from the more basic, more theoretical field that is most closely related to it. Thus, it is natural for Soviet foreign policy studies to look to the discipline of international politics for guidance in setting an agenda for research.

One of the core aspirations of the field of international politics is to explain outcomes on the two game-theory dimensions of cooperation/conflict and win/lose—especially counterintuitive outcomes produced by the perverse effects of international anarchy. From this core explanatory goal and rational-choice base, puzzle-solving activity radiates outward in a variety of directions toward systems theory, deterrence theory, bargaining theory, regime theory, theories about the effects of anarchical competition on domestic structure, and theories about adjustments needed in rational-choice models to take into account systematic psychological biases.[29] This is a rich and diverse agenda, which unites the security and political economy subfields and even accommodates nonpositivist offshoots.[30] Despite this diversity, the research program hangs together because of its core puzzles and common intellectual style, much of which can be traced back to Thomas Schelling.

If this research agenda is applied to the Soviet field, it offers some advantages and some potential disadvantages. To demonstrate the advantages, an extended example will show how Schelling's theoretical insights can be used to restructure the Garthoff-Pipes debate on Soviet attitudes regarding nuclear deterrence by clarifying the opposing arguments, proposing new empirical tests, and pointing toward a broad agenda for further research. In a subsequent section, I will discuss the potential disadvantages of importing a deductive research program of this kind into the Soviet field: its ethnocentrism, its monolithic character, and the questionable applicability of the special skills of Sovietologists to the research program it proposes.

The disagreement between Raymond Garthoff and Richard Pipes over Soviet attitudes on the nature of nuclear deterrence has been one of the most lively and consequential debates in research on Soviet military strategy.[31] In essence, Garthoff contends that the Soviets accept the inexorability of a deterrent relationship based on mutual assured destruction, though they retain the vestiges of a war-fighting doctrine and force posture in case deterrence fails. Pipes avers that the Soviets seek a war-winning capability, though they are resigned temporarily to its infeasibility. When the debate is formulated in this way, it is unclear what evidence might constitute a test of the two views. Garthoff could explain the war-fighting capability of the SS-18 as a hedge against the failure of deterrence, while Pipes could explain the ABM Treaty as a temporary expedient. War-fighting statements in the military press could be explained as reflecting only the military-technical level of doctrine, while politicians' renunciation of nuclear first-use and the possibility of victory in nuclear war could be explained as eyewash for the West.

As a result of this impasse, empirical research has moved on to narrower, more concrete questions such as Soviet force posture and doctrine for a major conventional war in Europe. The Garthoff-Pipes debate is hard to escape, however, because the question of what deters nuclear escalation is central to interpreting Soviet conventional strategy. Do the Soviets believe that mutual vulnerability will deter both sides from nuclear use regardless of the nuclear balance, or do they believe that superiority in nuclear war-fighting capability is needed to prevent NATO from escalating? The answer to this question has profound implications for the choice of forces to deter a Soviet conventional offensive, the strength of Soviet inclinations to preempt, and the interpretation of Soviet diplomatic and arms-control motivations.

Because the Garthoff-Pipes debate, in one guise or another, cannot be avoided, perhaps it can be reformulated in ways that make it more amenable to testing. To produce findings that cannot be easily explained away, the testing strategy should focus on evidence that is unambiguously at the political level of doctrine, and on behavior that is too important to be used for the purposes of disinformation. Only Soviet crisis diplomacy and coercive bargaining meet these criteria. But exactly what predictions should follow from the views of Garthoff and Pipes in such circumstances? Here is where Schelling's help is essential in clarifying arguments and deducing empirical hypotheses.

Schelling and other games theorists have argued that, under conditions of mutual assured destruction, the outcome of coercive diplomacy depends not on who is stronger (since the ability to punish is absolute), but on who is more willing to run risks and who bears the onus of the last clear chance to avoid disastrous escalation.[32] From this logic of the game of Chicken, Robert Jervis has deduced the corollary that, in most situations, nuclear weapons give a double advantage to the defender of the status quo.[33] First, defenders will be more willing to run risks, since people usually value what they have more than what they covet. Second, the onus of the last clear chance to avoid the risk of uncontrolled escalation normally weighs more heavily on the side trying to change the status quo. That is why Schelling found deterrence to be easier than compellence. He added, however, that this is less true when there is uncertainty about who has the last clear chance, or when clever tactics can shift it to the opponent.

These deductions help to clarify the Garthoff-Pipes dispute and to devise tests that would determine which side is right. If the view that the Soviets accept the implications of the mutual deterrent relationship means anything, it should mean that Soviet coercive bargaining behavior fits Schelling's pattern. That is, the Soviets are predicted to stand firm when the balance of motivation favors them (in particular when defending the status quo), and to be extremely cautious in trying to change the status quo by force. Nonetheless, we would expect them to try to manipulate the last clear chance and to take advantage of ambiguities in the status quo in order to make limited gains. Assuming that both sides have at least minimum assured destruction capabilities, the balance of nuclear capabilities should *not* correlate strongly with Soviet behavior. Moreover, the more strongly the Soviets share Schelling's view that the function of conventional combat is to generate the risk of escalation,[34] the less strongly Soviet behavior will be shaped by the local balance of conventional forces.

Pipes should make the opposite predictions. He believes that Soviet strategic calculation "always involves matters of relative not absolute advantage."[35] Even if both players are Chicken, to use Schelling's categories, relative war-fighting disparities make some players more Chicken than others. Following this logic, Soviet coercive diplomacy should not be decisively driven by the balance of motivations in a particular case, nor should it distinguish strongly between defending the status quo and changing it, or between deterrence and compellence. Rather, the Soviets are predicted to stand firm when they enjoy dominance in nuclear war-fighting capabilities and/or a local conventional preponderance, and to give in when their war-fighting capabilities are weaker than those of their opponents. Rather than manipulating the last clear chance, the Soviets' coercive bargaining tactics are predicted to focus on demonstrating their ability to deploy or alert a superior war-fighting force.

With these deductions in hand, tests bearing on the Garthoff-Pipes debate are easy to devise and to carry out. In fact, an existing analysis of Soviet naval diplomacy by James McConnell comes close to being a test of Schelling's theory, and thus of the Garthoff-Pipes debate, though he did not conceive of it as such.[36] McConnell's tests illustrate many of the procedures used in positivist comparative methods, but they also reveal some of positivism's pitfalls.

A. Covariation

McConnell tests for covariation between the defense of the status quo and the achievement of one's aims in coercive diplomacy. He finds that the two correlate in the vast majority of his cases; but this result is marred by his *ad hoc* approach to determining what the status quo is and who is defending it. In a few cases, the judgment of who was the defender in a showdown seems to be influenced by who was the winner.[37]

B. Alternative Explanations

McConnell also tests for covariation between the military balance and success in coercive diplomacy—a relationship that Pipes would predict to be a strong one. McConnell does not explicitly discuss the nuclear balance; if he had, he would have found no correlation over the 1967–1976 period that he examined.[38] Instead, he focuses on the local naval balance, finding little correlation between it and the outcome. In most cases of naval confrontation on the high seas, the superpowers simply matched each other's deployment, each carrier task force calling forth a comparable anti-carrier force.[39] Regardless of the ships available for further reinforcement, deployment races to achieve local superiority failed to occur, implying that the superpowers viewed the purpose of the forces not as war-fighting, but as a token of commitment and risk-taking.

C. Crucial Cases

McConnell looks for crucial cases that stack up all other alleged explanations against the status quo explanation. Enclaves within the opponent's sphere of interest, such as Berlin and Cuba, are cases of this type, in which the balance of local capability and the balance of strategic interests (apart from the reputational interest in defending the status quo) work against the survival of such enclaves.[40] The fact that they do survive against challenges means that McConnell and Schelling pass a hard test.

D. Process Tracing

Schelling's predictions concern not only outcomes, but also tactics and process; so these too can be the basis for corroborative tests. Schelling expects that players will try to manipulate the status quo and the "last clear chance" to their advantage. McConnell offers some illustrations of the Soviets' use of such tactics. For example, during the Angolan civil war, there was no stable status quo, so outsiders were relatively free to jockey for advantage. In doing so, the Soviets counted on using the freedom of the seas (a kind of normative status quo or, for Schelling, an escalation threshold) to protect the movement of Cuban troops through seas dominated by the U.S. Navy.[41]

E. Deviant Cases

McConnell seeks out deviant cases in order to refine his hypothesis. The Middle East wars, for example, show that the bargaining advantage of the defender extends only to the protection of a client's core areas and not to peripheral aspects of the status quo, such as desert frontiers.[42] This raises the question of how to distinguish progressive refinements of a theory from *ad hoc* rationalization to excuse its degeneration. The general rule is that refinements are progressive if they help explain many cases rather than just one, and if they suggest ways to apply the theory to new questions.

To sum up, the Schelling/McConnell example shows that recasting holist debates in positivist terms can help to clarify arguments and make them more amenable to testing. It also sets in motion a self-sustaining program of research, involving the analysis of deviant cases, the refinement of the original hypothesis, and the tracing of the implications of the theory into new areas. In this case, for example, an important extension of the theory might examine what happens under conditions in which conflict is predicted to be greatest—in cases where the status quo is ambiguous or where both sides believe they are defending it.[43] Research might address the causes and consequences of such situations, how the Soviets behave in them, and what tactics have proved safe and effective in confronting such dilemmas.

This theory-driven research program can also suggest questions for holist scholars engaged in the detailed reconstruction of Soviet perceptions and calculations in individual cases. Direct evidence of Soviet thinking could be important for corroborating or refuting McConnell's interpretation of his cases, for example. Schelling himself uses a number of Khrushchev quotations to illustrate his tactical theories. In one partially apocryphal example, Khrushchev is said to have remarked that Berlin was not worth a war, but his Western interlocutor reminded him that this shared risk was a two-edged sword. Khrushchev, as if coached by Schelling, replied that "you are the ones that have to cross a frontier"—thereby showing that he did think in terms of the manipulation of shared risk as well as the manipulation of the status quo as a means to pass the onus of the last clear chance to the opponent.[44] Sovietological scholarship producing this kind of evidence would nicely complement multi-case analyses of overt behavior by specialists in international relations.

More generally, the game-theoretic perspective opens up a variety of questions for the area-studies scholar. Though simplified versions of game theory assume a generic rational player, the character and tactical style of the player can be treated as a variable in the theory.

In Chicken games, for example, Schelling argued for surrendering the initiative by means of irrevocable preemptive defection, but Nathan Leites's Bolshevik chooses to probe cautiously and to retain the last clear chance to avoid disaster.[45] The work of Sovietologists on such questions is likely to be better focused and more useful if they use game theory to shape the questions they ask.

In short, deductive theory can undoubtedly be used to reformulate holist debates and direct the work of holist scholars. Certain obvious benefits would result, but at what cost? Because of some of the shortcomings and limitations of positivism, caution must be exercised against completely subsuming holist research under a monistic program of positivist research.

V. SHORTCOMINGS AND LIMITATIONS OF POSITIVISM

Three objections may be raised to the use of positivist international relations theory to reformulate the research agenda of the field of Soviet foreign policy: the question of ethnocentrism, inherent problems of implementing the positivist method in the social sphere, and the danger of adopting any single approach.

A. Ethnocentrism

In order to minimize the danger of ethnocentrism, holists suggest analyzing the Soviets' behavior in terms of the Soviets' own categories and concepts. Certainly one way of testing an interpretation of Soviet behavior is to find out whether the Soviets share it. That has its limits, however. Robert Legvold, in his study of Soviet attitudes toward military power, starts with the Soviet literature, but then adds distinctions and concepts that are entirely his own. The question, then, is not whether Western ideas are admissible, but when and with what safeguards they are introduced.

In view of these criteria, does the imposition of Schelling's categories on Soviet behavior constitute unchecked, unvarnished ethnocentrism? Schelling's ideas, like those of Clausewitz, were produced by particular historical experiences in a particular social setting. Both transcend that setting, however, by virtue of their high degree of abstraction, their deductive clarity, and their susceptibility to empirical refutation. Using Western concepts like "escalation dominance" in an *ad hoc* manner to describe Soviet thinking is surely ethnocentrism, but using Schelling's theory self-consciously as a guide for careful testing is not. How could a science make any headway if it were forbidden to use ideas that it had thought up itself?

B. Inherent Flaws in Positivist Testing Procedures

A more fundamental objection is that positivism, at least in the social sciences, is unable to fulfill its promise to carry out conclusive tests. McConnell's tests, for example, are not fully satisfying because he does not offer a reliable definition of the status quo, such that any two researchers would always agree on who was defending it and who was challenging it in a given case. As a consequence, deciding whether a case supports or contradicts his hypothesis involves a partly subjective, *ad hoc* judgment.

Though it is possible that more precise measures could have reduced arbitrariness, nonpositivist philosophers of science contend that the underlying problem is inherent: in their view, the variables in social theories do not closely correspond to hard observables in nature. The variables exist only as conventions, either as a linguistic custom of the people under study or as a category imposed by the scientist. Several consequences thus undermine the positivist method. First, most of the phenomena that social scientists find interesting will be difficult to measure. Second, measurements must either be subjective or rely on highly artificial protocols that measure a variable only indirectly. Third, the scientist is allowed a degree of arbitrariness in deciding whether cases fit his theory and, if they do not, whether the theory or the measurement procedures are at fault. Under these conditions, "objectivity" can at best mean agreement among subjective observers, each of whom brings biases and preconceptions to the task of observation.[46]

William Zimmerman and Robert Axelrod's quantitative study of the lessons that Soviet commentators drew from the Vietnam War illustrates some of these difficulties.[47] In testing the hypothesis that different Soviet press organs serve as forums for the articulation of "left" and "right" opinions in foreign policy debates, these authors first classify press statements on the lessons of Vietnam as either left or right, using well-articulated criteria and requiring agreement among multiple coders. They then show that press organs vary on the left/right spectrum, with differences across various newspapers and journals that were, for the most part, just barely significant by conventional statistical standards. Despite the extreme care taken in measuring left and right lessons, residual ambiguities in the research design make it difficult to judge whether the results support or contradict the hypothesis.

One view might be that these results impressively confirm the existence of pluralistic press debates, on the grounds that the findings would have been even stronger if sharper concepts and better measures had been used. Because the operational definitions of left and right failed to capture logically coherent and mutually exclusive belief systems, correlations were watered down by extraneous, random data. On some of the dimensions measured, the left/right dichotomy is clear: for example, the sharp contrast between the left assertion that "the aggressive essence of imperialism is unchanged" with the right view that "realistically thinking circles of the capitalist states have become increasingly conscious of the necessity for peaceful coexistence." But the connection between this and dichotomies that are less stark seems problematic. Compare, for example, the allegedly left statement that "the patriots of South Vietnam will surmount all the obstacles in the path to the complete triumph of their just cause" with the allegedly right statement that "there is no force that could turn back developments in South Vietnam."[48] In short, debate on the general left/right dimension surfaces in the data even though some murky conceptual distinctions and operational measures tend to blur it.

In an opposite view, the findings tend to refute the hypothesis, since the small variations across different press organs could easily have been caused by differences in propaganda strategy or institutional function. For example, Zimmerman and Axelrod note,

> We treated as leftist those statements that emphasized the role of military aid to Vietnam and the significance of military and political doctrine in the North Vietnamese victory; as rightist those statements that stressed economic and material support.[49]

By this coding rule, a military newspaper could be expected to wind up on "the left" simply by devoting disproportionate space to issues within its own functional purview or by targeting "lessons" considered appropriate for its distinctive readership.

In short, all the inherent difficulties of positivism seem to show up in this example. In order to test a hypothesis whose variables do not closely correspond to hard facts in nature, cases must be classified either by partially subjective judgments or by indirect, artificial measures. When subjectivity is permitted, researchers tend to see what they want to see; when indirect measures are concocted, there is a tendency to get weak correlations. And when that happens, it is unclear whether the fault lies with the measures or with the theory.

Defenders of positivism, however, could argue that the solution lies in tightening up the sources of ambiguity: control for alternative explanations, develop logically tighter ideal types for the left and right syndromes, and throw out ambiguous dimensions that water down the findings. Only then—if the hypothesis continued to produce weak correlations across a shrinking range of successful applications—would we know that the research program based on that theory was degenerating. Although an evaluation of the results of any particular test may involve subjective judgments, objective criteria can be applied to appraising the long-run outcome of a whole research program.[50]

Though positivism can answer its critics in principle, in practice there are limitations to what can be expected from the use of positivist methods in the social sciences. Positivism is like democracy—the worst system except for all the rest. Because of its limitations, however, it makes sense to use other methods to cross-check its findings and to provide alternative guides when it falters.

C. The Dangers of Monolithic Dogmatism

Academic strategy, like military strategy, must avoid the equal dangers of dogmatic attachment to a single doctrine and of aimless activity in the absence of any doctrine at all. Though the game-theoretic, rational-choice traditions of the field of international politics are flexible enough to encompass a variety of opinions and approaches, the exclusive adoption of any theoretical stance will tend to focus attention on some new ideas and blinker it toward others. For this reason, it is healthy for some proportion of the research to be conducted outside the dominant paradigm. In the Soviet field, research driven by international relations theory should be supplemented by research on ideas that emerge more directly from the data. Even in the latter case, however, positivism can play a role in increasing the payoff from the work.

VI. HYBRID METHODS

Some holist arguments are causal, staying close to the Soviets' categories and tending toward complex, case-specific explanations. Other holist arguments are reconstructions of Soviet ends/means calculations, interpreting Soviet behavior in terms of what it was trying to achieve. In arguments of both types, positivist methods and deductive thinking can be usefully applied without undercutting the distinctive character of the holistic approach.

A. Recasting Causal Arguments

In the study cited earlier, Robert Legvold argues that the Soviets evaluate the utility of military power according to different criteria in different contexts. He quotes Vasilii Kulish as saying that the effectiveness of military power is "determined not only by the forces themselves," but "depends upon the specific international-political situation." Kulish then goes on to muse about the "complicated interlacing" of national interests, political constraints on the use of force, the strength of the national liberation movement, and so forth.[51] In testing whether the Soviets actually behave in accordance with these notions, however, the "complicated interlacing" of putative causes can only be the final step in a systematic process. The first step is to make a list of "contexts" or characteristics of "international-political situations." Such a list might include Legvold's own distinction among peace, crisis, and war situations, as well as items from Kulish's list. These are the independent variables. The next step is to offer a hypothesis about how the Soviets view the utility of military superiority in each of these contexts. For example, one hypothesis might be that superiority is useful in preventing NATO escalation in the context of an ongoing war, but that it has no value for supporting progressive change in peacetime. What counts in that context is whether strong national liberation movements can achieve gains on their own initiative—which strategic parity will suffice to defend. Subsequent steps would carry out the usual kinds of positivist testing across a varied range of behavioral and verbal evidence. Only at the final stage could there be complicated interlacing of the hypotheses—for example, by specifying which conditions were necessary or sufficient conditions for certain outcomes, how the interaction of two variables might change their effects, and so forth.

If a large number of variables must be considered simultaneously, this procedure will become too cumbersome. In that event, it may be necessary to step back and look for a few "taproot" causes, like bipolarity or nuclear weapons technology, which exert their effects simultaneously and systematically on a lot of seemingly independent variables.

B. Deductive Reconstruction of Soviet Ends/Means Calculations

Michael MccGwire's analysis of Soviet military policy in terms of a changing set of military objectives shows how a Sovietologist can use deductive logic and positivist testing procedures to reconstruct Soviet aims and strategies.[52] MccGwire argues that around December 1966, a decision was taken to change the objective of Soviet military strategy in a world war from "do not lose the war" to "avoid the nuclear devastation of Russia,"—a shift that reflected the new belief that a war might be kept limited. He proceeds to deduce a set of specific missions, doctrines, force structures, and organizational structures that would logically follow from those general objectives.

At this point, MccGwire is ready to carry out a number of tests based on the predictions that flow from his deductive model and his tentative identification of a decision period in late 1966. In the jargon of social science, he is carrying out cross-sectional and lagged time-series tests of covariation. The cross-sectional tests involve checking whether his predictions are borne out—not only, say, in the area of doctrinal writings, but also in the areas of force posture and arms control. The time-series test is a before-and-after check to show that the hypothesized changes in higher-level objectives correspond to observed changes in doctrine and force posture, with adjustment for necessary lead times. In carrying out these before-and-after tests, MccGwire tries to hold constant as many perturbing factors as he can. Therefore, in reading the Soviet press to establish the date of the decision to pursue a conventional option in Europe, he compares relevant passages in back-to-back editions of the same authoritative book, one signed to press just before the presumed decision, the other after.

In short, MccGwire's theory is holistic in the sense that it explains various parts of Soviet policy in terms of their relation to a larger whole that gives them meaning. It is also holistic in paying more attention to reconstructing Soviet perspectives and calculations than to discovering their underlying causes. Nonetheless, he constructs and tests his deductive argument according to standard positivist procedures.

CONCLUSION

Both positivism and holism can make valuable contributions to the study of Soviet foreign policy. Positivist theories, borrowed in part from the field of international politics, can provide sharp, testable arguments and a fertile research agenda. Holism can provide the means to harness positivist generalizations in a detailed understanding of particular cases, including the present.

Far from being incompatible, holism and positivism can often work synergistically. Holists, while taking up questions appropriate to their particular skills, can use positivist theories to shape their research agenda. Even when they pursue research questions suggested mainly by their own data, holists can use deductive logic and positivist methods to help structure their work.

Despite this complementarity, some irreducible disagreements between the practitioners of holist and positivist methods are likely to persist. Differing attitudes about such issues as simplification, generalization, and empathy are rooted in different views of the nature of reality and of the purposes that knowledge is meant to serve. However, because the implicit stance of most Sovietologists lies not at the extremes of this dichotomy but in the middle, the complementary use of both approaches will be compatible with these scholars' assumptions about the natural order of social life.

In the past, the positivist side of Soviet foreign policy studies has remained underdeveloped. In the present, therefore, the most pressing task is to use the opportunity presented by recent developments in international-relations theory to correct that weakness, and to do this in a way that leaves the old virtues of the field's nonpositivist traditions intact. Together, these complementary research strategies can sharpen old debates, spark new ones, and generally put scholarly discourse in the Soviet field on a livelier, sounder footing.

NOTES

The present article is based on a report prepared for the Subcommittee on Soviet Foreign Policy of the Joint Committee on Soviet Studies of the Social Science Research Council and the American Council of Learned Societies; the views expressed do not necessarily reflect the views of the subcommittee or its members. Douglas Blum, Richard Herrmann, Theodore Hopf, Robert Jervis, Friedrich Kratochwil, Robert Legvold, Cynthia Roberts, and Marshall Shulman have offered helpful suggestions and criticisms.

1. These are ideal types. Real scholars often use both approaches in varying combinations or proportions. For example, some positivist scholars, like Kenneth Waltz, look at whole systems or, like Robert Jervis, try to explain the subjective understandings of actors. Despite these qualifications, I would contend that the above distinctions capture the most important lines of epistemological cleavage. The term "holism" is unsatisfactory, but alternatives like "traditionalism" or "non-positivism" are even more problematic. For further discussion, see Paul Diesing, *Patterns of Discovery in the Social Sciences* (New York: Aldine, 1971), and Donald Polkinghorne, *Methodology for the Human Sciences* (Albany: State University of New York Press, 1983).

2. Jack Snyder, "Richness, Rigor, and Relevance in the Study of Soviet Foreign Policy," *International Security* 9 (Winter 1984--1985), pp. 89--108.

3. For elaboration and qualifications, see Snyder (fn. 2) and Diesing (fn. 1).

4. Robert Jervis, "Cooperation Under the Security Dilemma," *World Politics* 30 (January 1978), pp. 167–214.

5. Jack S. Levy, "The Offensive/Defensive Balance of Military Technology: A Theoretical and Historical Analysis," *International Studies Quarterly* 28 (Summer 1984), pp. 219–38.

6. Robert Jervis, *Perception and Misperception in International Politics* (Princeton, NJ: Princeton University Press, 1976), chap. 6, illustrates how to detect spurious causal inferences.

7. Jervis (fn. 4).

8. Robert Legvold, "Military Power in International Politics: Soviet Doctrine on Its Centrality and Instrumentality," in Uwe Nerlich, ed., *Soviet Power and Western Negotiating Strategies* (Cambridge, MA: Ballinger, 1983), p. 124, quoting Stanley Hoffmann, "Perception, Reality, and the Franco-American Conflict," *Journal of International Affairs* 21, 1 (1967), p. 57.

9. Legvold (fn. 8), pp. 125, 123, and passim. I will return to Legvold's study in order to suggest how it might be recast in positivist terms.

10. Diesing (fn. 1).

11. Marshall Shulman, *Stalin's Foreign Policy Reappraised* (New York: Atheneum, 1969); Strobe Talbott, *Endgame* (New York: Harper Colophon, 1980), p. 80.

12. Shulman (fn. 11), pp. 3, 50, 259, and passim.

13. Ibid., pp. 8, 14, 123, and passim.

14. Ibid., p. 8, comes close to doing this, citing a few instances of Soviet attempts to buy time during periods of weakness.

15. On Zhdanov and Molotov, see ibid., pp. 14–15, 117–18. Suslov's militancy, however, is linked to the argument that the correlation of forces was turning in favor of socialism; see ibid., p. 119.

16. See especially the discussion of Malenkov, ibid., pp. 111–17.

17. On cybernetic decision making and how it differs from analytic rationality, see John Steinbruner, *The Cybernetic Theory of Decision* (Princeton, NJ: Princeton University Press, 1974).

18. Shulman (fn. 11), pp. 3–9, 263–71.

19. Gelman, *The Brezhnev Politburo and the Decline of Detente* (Ithaca, NY: Cornell University Press, 1984). On the problem of *a priori* underdetermination and *a posteriori* overdetermination, see James Kurth, "United States Foreign Policy and Latin American Military Rule," in Phillippe Schmitter, ed., *Military Rule in Latin America* (Beverly Hills, CA: Sage, 1973), pp. 244–322.

20. Ibid., p. 83.

21. Ibid., pp. 46, 52–58.

22. George Breslauer, *Khrushchev and Brezhnev as Leaders* (London: Allen & Unwin, 1982), conclusion, esp. pp. 280, 284–90.

23. William H. Riker and Steven J. Brams, "The Paradox of Vote Trading," *American Political Science Review* 67 (December 1973), pp. 1235–47.

24. Gelman (fn. 19), p. 73; also pp. 79, 90, 114.

25. Kenneth Waltz, *Theory of International Politics* (Reading, MA: Addison-Wesley, 1979), p. 50, used this phrase to characterize earlier systems theories.

26. Jervis (fn. 6), pp. 128–42.

27. The last hypothesis, omitted in most accounts of the links between totalitarianism and foreign policy, is based on Alexander Gerschenkron, *Economic Backwardness in Historical Perspective* (Cambridge, MA: Belknap, 1962). For other arguments, see Carl Friedrich and Zbigniew Brzezinski, *Totalitarian Dictatorship and Autocracy* (Cambridge, MA: Harvard University Press, 1956), and Zbigniew Brzezinski, *Ideology and Power in Soviet Politics* (New York: Praeger, 1962).

28. See Stephen Toulmin, *Human Understanding* (Princeton, NJ: Princeton University Press, 1972).

29. A recent example of work done in this tradition is the special issue of *World Politics* 38 (October 1985), also published as *Cooperation Under Anarchy*, Kenneth A. Oye, ed. (Princeton, NJ: Princeton University Press, 1985).

30. See, for example, Friedrich Kratochwil and John Ruggie, "International Organization: A State of the Art on an Art of the State," *International Organization* 40 (Fall 1986).

31. "A Garthoff-Pipes Debate on Soviet Strategic Doctrine," *Strategic Review* 10 (Fall 1982), pp. 36–63.

32. Thomas C. Schelling, *Arms and Influence* (New Haven, CT: Yale University Press, 1966), chaps. 2 and 3; Schelling, *The Strategy of Conflict* (London: Oxford University Press, 1960), chap. 2.

33. Jervis, "Why Nuclear Superiority Doesn't Matter," *Political Science Quarterly* 94 (Winter 1979–1980), pp. 617–33.

34. Schelling (fn. 32, 1966), p. 106.

35. *Strategic Review* (fn. 31), p. 57.

36. James M. McConnell, "The 'Rules of the Game': A Theory on the Practice of Superpower Naval Diplomacy," in Bradford Dismukes and James McConnell, eds., *Soviet Naval Diplomacy* (New York: Pergamon, 1979).

37. For example, the argument (ibid., pp. 265–66) that the United States was the defender in the mining of Haiphong Harbor, though not unreasonable, makes use of *ad hoc* criteria that place more weight on American statements linking the action to the defense of South Vietnam than on the *prima facie* offensive character of U.S. behavior.

38. See also Barry Blechman and Stephen Kaplan, *Force Without War* (Washington, DC: The Brookings Institution, 1978), pp. 127–29.

39. For this point, and qualifications to it, see McConnell (fn. 36), p. 244.

40. Ibid., pp. 247–48.

41. Ibid., p. 265.

42. McConnell's own conclusions from these cases are somewhat more complex. See ibid., pp. 246, 267–76.

43. Richard K. Betts, "Elusive Equivalence: The Political and Military Meaning of the Nuclear Balance," in Samuel P. Huntington, *The Strategic Imperative* (Cambridge, MA: Ballinger, 1982), p. 108, draws attention to this question. See also Richard Betts, *Nuclear Blackmail and Nuclear Balance* (Washington, DC: The Brookings Institution, 1987), which carries out detailed, sophisticated tests similar to those described above.

44. Schelling (fn. 32, 1966), pp. 46–47. This vignette seems to be a conflation of several Khrushchev remarks. For an example of the invocation of uncontrollable risk, see Robert Slusser, *The Berlin Crisis of 1961* (Baltimore, MD: The Johns Hopkins University Press, 1973), pp. 98–99; for asymmetry in motivation, Hannes Adomeit, *Soviet Risk-Taking and Crisis Behavior* (London: Allen & Unwin, 1982), p. 207, and Jack Schick, *The Berlin Crisis, 1958–1962* (Philadelphia, PA: University of Pennsylvania Press, 1971), p. 178; for the onus of the last clear chance, Strobe Talbott, ed., *Khrushchev Remembers: The Last Testament* (New York: Bantam, 1974), p. 575. For more examples and for some qualifications to this view, see Hope Harrison, "Was Khrushchev a Student of Thomas Schelling?: Khrushchev's Coercive Diplomacy in the 1958–1961 Berlin Crisis," unpub. (Harriman Institute, Columbia University, 1987).

45. Nathan Leites, *A Study of Bolshevism* (Glencoe, IL: Free Press, 1953); Alexander George, "The 'Operational Code': A Neglected Approach to the Study of Political Leaders and Decision-Making," in Erik Hoffmann and Frederic Fleron, eds., *The Conduct of Soviet Foreign Policy*, 2nd ed. (New York: Aldine, 1980), pp. 191–212.

46. Polkinghorne (fn. 1), p. 107, and passim.

47. William Zimmerman and Robert Axelrod, "The 'Lessons' of Vietnam and Soviet Foreign Policy," *World Politics* 34 (October 1981), pp. 1–24.

48. Ibid., pp. 10–11.

49. Ibid., p. 8.

50. Polkinghorne (fn. 1), pp. 117–18; Imre Lakatos, "Falsification and the Methodology of Scientific Research Programmes," in Imre Lakatos and Alan Musgrave, *Criticism and the Growth of Knowledge: Proceedings of the International Colloquium in the Philosophy of Science, London, 1965,* Vol. IV (Cambridge, MA: Cambridge University Press, 1970).

51. Legvold (fn. 8), p. 131.

52. Michael MccGwire, *Military Objectives in Soviet Foreign Policy* (Washington, DC: The Brookings Institution, 1987).

5

THE USES AND ABUSES
OF RUSSIAN HISTORY

THE PROBLEM

It is a commonplace that historians, or would-be historians, all too often become politicians and generals shaping and reshaping the historical record to score points, clinch arguments, and advance their own solutions and nostrums. The history of Russia has surely been no exception to this pattern. Russian historians have written their self-serving patriotic versions from medieval times to the present day, and foreign scholars, journalists, and statesmen have used both fact and fiction to make their case and have perpetuated a centuries-long legacy of forgeries and fabrications.

The uses and abuses to which the ostensible record of the Russian past can be put deserve a more comprehensive examination than can be attempted here. This chapter focuses only on the current effort to make Russian history a tool for partisan argument in policymaking in the United States. Not that such an endeavor is the exclusive preserve of any one orientation: If there are some whose reading of the past leads them to conclude that the values and purposes of the Russians are and will remain incompatible with those of the civilized West, there are also others who find the key to Soviet behavior abroad in the fear engendered by memory of a millennium of invasions and incursions from abroad—a view that sees Moscow's policy as a defensive response to this trauma. Both of these arguments are woefully wide of the mark.

In recent years an unprecedented upsurge of efforts to "explain" the Soviet present in terms of continuities from the Russian past has stressed the unique or exceptional features of that past. Several circumstances have contributed to this increasingly widespread trend.

In the search for master keys to Soviet behavior, the two "leading" earlier hypotheses—Communist ideology and the totalitarian model—have come to be recognized as unsatisfactory at best. The continuity of Russian history has seemed to provide a simple and plausible alternative.

If in earlier days the Bolsheviks as well as their opponents stressed the gulf that separated "traditional Russia" from the Soviet regime, over time public Soviet attitudes toward Russian history changed dramatically, and many observers reacted against the initial disjunction by erasing the caesura represented by 1917.

Western social science in the 1970s saw an upsurge of interest in "political culture" and social history. It is natural that, to the extent that group norms and attitudes can be studied, interest in (and the seeming relevance of) traditional Russia should have reemerged.

But to all these legitimate and natural contributing reasons, which are welcome in a healthy climate of scholarly diversity, one more reason needs to be added—a strictly political one. The stress on distinctive and unchanging (and presumably unchangeable) characteristics of Russian history has appealed to, and has been particularly compatible with the views of, those who see the Soviet regime as beyond the pale and perhaps beyond redemption. Some of the most vociferous affirmations of historical determinism, which sees the Soviet system as an extrapolation of the Russian past (at times accompanied by the view that "every nation gets the government it deserves"), have come from persons espousing the most militant and anti-Soviet positions.[1]

It must be recognized that there is indeed a suggestive seductiveness in the familiar parallels between Ivan the Dread, Peter the Great, and Stalin; between the *okhrana* and the KGB; in the attitudes of old and new Russia toward Poland; in the well-nigh unchallenged acceptance of autocratic government at various times in the tsarist as well as in the Soviet eras. To point to such similarities and seeming continuities, however, is not to answer the questions before us: it is merely to raise them.

CONTINUITY AND DETERMINISM

Let us assume for the moment that the image of Russia, as offered in the "hard-line historiography" (the apt term is James Cracraft's),[2] is substantially accurate. It depicts a Russia isolated from the West since the Church schism, with an elite influenced by the Byzantine legacy, a culture forcibly subjected to centuries of the "Tatar yoke," a country deprived of Renaissance and Reformation, with an arbitrary regime based on "patrimonial" rights, mixing property with political authority, instituting slavery and serfdom, denying groups and individuals what in the West came to be accepted as civil rights, generating a rapidly growing bureaucratic machine and armed force, and possessed by a relentless drive to expand abroad, combining cunning and suspicion, intolerance and xenophobia. If we view the present as the product of heredity and environment, that past cannot be ignored. In fact, the "hard-line historiographers" posit a powerful determinism in projecting the past forward to our days and beyond.

The first thing to note with regard to what David Hackett Fischer has called the "fallacy of presumptive continuity,"[3] is our methodological poverty: Surprising as it may appear at first glance, we have simply no technique by which to test whether event E' and a later event E" are continuous manifestations of the same phenomenon (or products of the same motivation) or are autonomous events. (This also implies that neither hypothesis can be conclusively falsified.) To be sure, there is a good deal of commonsense plausibility in the view that, say, the Russian peasants' drinking, or their beating their wives, both before and after the 1917 Revolution represents a "continuity"; but it is far more debatable whether the Soviet invasion of Afghanistan in 1979 was an extension of the Russian drive into that country begun a century earlier; or whether the treatment of Pasternak and Sakharov was essentially the same as that accorded Chaadaev and Tolstoy under the tsars. Such assertions require a scholarly judgment necessarily based on selective use of historical evidence, with all the attendant dangers against which scholars have often warned.[4]

In his *The Whig Interpretation of History* Herbert Butterfield was setting criteria relevant to our discussion. "The chief aim of the historian," he wrote, "is the elucidation of the unlikenesses between past and present. . . . It is not for him to stress and magnify the similarities between one age and another. . . . Rather it is to work to destroy those very analogies which we imagined to exist."[5] The historian "can draw lines through certain events . . . and if he is not careful he begins to forget that this line is merely a mental trick of his; he comes to imagine that it represents something like a line of causation."[6] Butterfield warned against reading the present back into the past by discovering a "false continuity" that is the result of selecting out those events and trends which reinforce the author's thesis and omitting the rest, "remov[ing] the most troublesome elements in the complexity."[7]

Gordon A. Craig, past president of the American Historical Association, warned not long ago in regard to German history that "too great a desire to prove continuity leads to a tendency to ignore nuances and to confuse chance likenesses and similarities of formulation with identity in essence."[8] Indeed, the attempts to trace the sources of Hitlerism back to the Reformation and beyond are not unlike the attempts described in this paper in regard to the Soviet era. Similarly, in regard to China, Benjamin Schwartz has argued that the heritage of Imperial China was so "fundamentally undermined in the twentieth century" that "we should be extremely skeptical of assertions that assign it greater causal weight in explaining present or future Chinese policies."[9] "One of the aims of sound historical education," remarked Sir Lewis Namier, "must be to wean men from expecting automatic repetition and from juggling with uncorrelated precedents and analogies."[10] And in a recent essay entitled, "Is History a Guide to the Future?" Barbara Tuchman concludes, "In the absence of dependable recurring circumstances, too much confidence cannot be placed on the lessons of history." Her examples, she finds, demonstrate two things: "one, that man fails to profit from the lessons of history because his prejudgments prevent him from drawing the indicated conclusions; and, two, that history will often capriciously take a different direction than in which her lessons point."[11]

Thus cautioned, we might also reflect on the characteristic fate of "political cultures." This is not the occasion to examine the content and scope of that concept, both useful and dangerous;[12] but however described and defined, "political culture" cannot be seen to be unchanging. If it were, the entire notion of political socialization would be absurd, for—surely in Communist systems—political socialization hinges on the alteration of prior norms and political values. Far better then to recognize the formidable body of evidence that, whatever the particular cultural traits of a given society, the process of socioeconomic modernization tends to lessen the specific weight and the saliency of traditional culture. It is typically marked by the uprooting of large groups from the traditional environment in the course of wholesale urbanization, by a change of occupations and of reference groups, by greater exposure to mass communications and access to new sources of information, by greater interaction with the world abroad, and by an attenuation of traditional attachments. There is good evidence that this tends to make for the emergence of commonalities across cultures at the expense of particular traditional values and attitudes.[13] As Dietrich Geyer reminds us, moreover, in the Russian case it is scarcely possible to argue both the operational importance of traditional popular culture and national character in the Soviet era *and also* to insist on the utter divorce of the Kremlin's masters from the rank and file and their yearnings and anxieties.[14]

Do we need to invoke the Tatars, the Time of Troubles, Pugachev, Pobedonostsev, or the village commune to understand current Soviet policies and attitudes? Although perhaps not in all instances a safe guide to the choice of explanatory variables, in case of doubt a sound rule would be to opt first of all for parsimony in causality, rather than for more devious, remote, complex, or overdetermined alternatives. Indeed, in regard to other societies this seems to be done without dispute. Who would refer to Savonarola, Cromwell, or Robespierre, or to the War of the Roses, the Huguenots, and the Treaty of Campoformio to explain the contemporary behavior of Italians, British, or French? And although there may well be a traditional component, say, in the Soviet inclination toward excessive secrecy, there are also perfectly rational explanations why Stalin (and, to a lesser extent, his successors) chose to conceal much of what was going on in the USSR from foreign eyes and ears.[15]

All these injunctions together argue that, even if we accept the accuracy of the hard-line determinists' accounts of Russian history, we would be well advised against a mindless extrapolation from the past into the future. With a similar deterministic bias a Parisian in the 1780s, prior to the capture of the Bastille, would have argued that French political culture was authoritarian and permitted no democratic or republican traits. Political scientists and journalists writing about Germany and Japan, prior to 1945, did indeed often— and erroneously—deny the possibility of a significant change in political behavior and institutions, given the dominant and presumably persistent political cultures in these two countries. It behooves us then to allow for some doubt and some humility in our projections and to beware of erecting a mental wall against the possibility of future change.

RUSSIA: HOW UNCHANGING? HOW UNIQUE?

But is the version of Russian history propounded by the continuity school factually and analytically accurate, and are its representatives drawing proper inferences from it? This is a subject that has often invited intense and bitter controversy, and surely this paper cannot go through the whole problematic alphabet, from aggression to xenophobia, that this question conjures up. Suffice it to look at a few relevant points.

If Mackenzie Wallace and the elder George Kennan had revealing insights into Russian life, other Western travelers—often ignorant of the language and the country—in that long roster from Herberstein and Fletcher to Custine and Haxthausen and beyond, produced accounts no more reliable than the wild reports of travelers in early America about the red man and his habits, or the dispatches from the first visitors to Cathay and Cipangu. Now it may well be that Russia was (as an English traveler reported) inhabited by a people "ignorant, superstitious, cunning, brutal, barbarous, dirty, and mean";[16] that the tsarist regime amounted to an autocracy atop a "garrison state" (albeit a garrison state with a Tolstoy, a Nijinsky, and a Mendeleyev), marked by an absence of civil rights, a lack of constraints on the *samoderzhavie* (autocracy), and riddled with abuse and corruption that only a Solzhenitsyn would deny. The question is what all this adds up to. Richard Pipes ends his account of *Russia Under the Old Regime* in 1880—not because the years from 1880 to 1917 cannot be made to fit his thesis, he tells us, but because by then Russia had assumed the contours of a bureaucratic police regime that it has ostensibly been ever since. To be sure, this requires ignoring much of what occurred in the early years of the twentieth century. In this light not only 1905 but 1917 becomes a mere detail: The Soviet takeover is the only possible outcome of the February Revolution (the hard-liners must thus agree with Soviet historiography on the inevitability of the event), and if the handful of Bolsheviks had not existed, they would have had to be invented.[17]

Actually, of course, the events of 1917 can be fruitfully examined in the framework of comparative history (as well as comparative revolutions). Then we discover that a good deal of the alleged Russian uniqueness fades once the Russian experience is compared with that of other societies. Thus—citing almost at random—J.H. Plumb reminds us "In the seventeenth century Englishmen killed, tortured, and executed each other for political beliefs; they sacked towns and brutalized the countryside. They were subjected to conspiracy, plot, and invasion. . . ."[18] It would be easy to document the brutality of the Thirty Years' War or the insensitivity of Europe's crowned heads to popular aspirations. As for the misery of the countryside, prior to modernization and the emergence of a sense of citizenship, we need go no further than Eugen Weber's *Peasants into Frenchmen*.[19] Like Russia, India and Japan failed to experience the Renaissance—without therefore having turned to Bolshevism. Tsarist officialdom deserves careful comparison with others, such as the Prussian or the Swedish. Neither serfdom nor autocracy, neither a service nobility nor borrowing from more technologically advanced societies was peculiarly Russian. And if the autocracy finally decayed in St. Petersburg, so it did of course in the Ottoman Empire and under the Habsburgs and Hohenzollerns, too. True, much of what developed in Russia came with a substantial time lag and often did have a particular Russian stamp to it: There is truth in Henry L. Roberts' formula that, by comparison with the European West, Russia often seemed both "related and belated"[20]—but surely not unique.

It is in such comparisons that selectivity of information becomes crucial, for the historian can stack the deck either way. If there was (let us call it) a Slavophile tradition that stressed and cherished the distinctiveness of Russia, there were also the Westernizers who saw salvation in modernization. For every "tradition" we can find a countertradition, for every Dostoyevsky there was a Turgenev, and if the anti-Western animus runs like a thread through Berdiaev to Solzhenitsyn, the opposite thread links ancient Novgorod, the *veche*, Miliukov, the Constituent Assembly, and Andrei Sakharov. If before the twentieth century there was little evidence of institutionalized pluralism in Russian political life, the emergence of political parties, partisan journals and newspapers, and the vigorous public life of the last fifteen years of the monarchy—along with economic development—testify to the fact that the gap between Russia and the more developed countries was shrinking fast.

The view that the Soviet Union inherited a tradition encompassing a highly centralized government, a command economy, and a large bureaucracy, is challenged by S. Frederick Starr, who writes:

> It need hardly be said that this is a highly selective characterization of Russia's political heritage. One might suggest, for example, that Russia has suffered as much from undergovernment as from overgovernment; that its undermanned elites have ruled as much by default as by design; or that centralization has existed more as an ideal than as a functioning reality.[21]

Perhaps the area where the continuity thesis has been applied with greatest abandon relates to Russian (and Soviet) foreign affairs. As Geyer states in his skillful review of the historiographic arguments, those stressing continuity in foreign policy have focused on three aspects: (1) imperial interests and expansionist tendencies abroad; (2) autocratic or dictatorial rule in Russia as the basis of decisionmaking; (3) attitudes toward the outside world, in substance a part of the "national character." The first of these is the primary question at issue for our purposes. What the similarity in the locus of Russian expansion before and after 1917 illustrates, Geyer correctly points out, be it Poland, Finland, Manchuria, or Northern Iran, is the "continuity of geography," but not necessarily the continuity of perceived interests or objectives. To be sure, a recital of tsarist and Soviet interests in neighboring areas, from the Balkans to Korea, is at least suggestive, but a closer look leads to the conclusion that not only the international context but also the definition of interests has radically changed.[22]

As for that recurrent reference to Russian messianism, it remains to be shown that it actually motivated any policymakers. There is no obvious evidence to support the view that any Muscovite prince went to battle in pursuit of the tenet of the Third Rome or that Panslavism—rather than creating a political climate around the court and in high society—actually prompted the tsar or his minister to take action in the Balkans. No doubt the verbiage was there— just as the "pragmatic" United States easily generated a concept of manifest destiny or European empires rationalized their colonial conquests as the "white man's burden."

Some familiar clichés—such as the perennial "urge to the sea" or the search for warm-water ports—that are so often used to "explain" Soviet policy, simply do not stand up. Neither Central Europe nor Central Asia fits these formulae; and when Yermak crossed the Urals, he could scarcely have known that there was a Pacific Ocean at the other end of Siberia. In any event, in the age of jets and ICBMs,

warm-water ports have shrunk considerably in priority or importance.[23]

Nor does the historical record bear out the notion of a grand
design or master plan of Russian imperial expansion. As Michael
Karpovich put it, it amounted to the pursuit of "concrete aims
unconnected by any general idea." Indeed, there was no sense of any
national interest underlying the process, and at times the drive to
the south and east resulted from decisions by local commanders
acting without prior sanction from St. Petersburg.[24]

The discontinuity of objectives is particularly clear in regard to
the Middle East. Whereas the tsar's court was, in the nineteenth
century, concerned to keep the Holy Places out of the hands of the
infidels, the Soviet authorities can hardly be said to have shared this
worry. And if a century ago St. Petersburg wanted to assure the
safety of Russian grain exports to the West going from Black Sea
ports to the Mediterranean, Moscow today would look with nostalgia
upon an era in which Russia had grain to spare for export abroad.[25]

My point is neither to argue that there have not been significant
continuities and similarities over time; nor is it to claim that there
were no significant differences between Russian and other foreign
policies. The question is whether the burden of these constants
outweighs the impact of change, and whether these differences between Russia and other societies were so fundamental and enduring—in particular, in foreign policy, as in the hard-liners' point of
view—as to set it apart as unique and essentially beyond any prospect of repair.

For that is what the curious linkage between hard-line historiography and hard-line politics now suggests. It is well illustrated in
the writings of Colin Gray (but could be shown to apply equally to
the writings of others of substantially similar political orientation).
A paper coauthored by Gray examines "the extent to which the
Soviet Union has adopted tsarist Russia's imperial ambitions, attitudes and style" and, more broadly, "the influence of the imperial
factor on Soviet strategy."[26] If most of the historical argument is
familiar, its congruence with its political counterpart is striking:

> Save as a tactical ploy the Soviet Union cannot endorse a concept of
> stability in the relations between socialist and nonsocialist states. Richard
> Pipes almost certainly is correct when he argues that Marxism-Leninism
> became the state ideology in Russia because the grosser features of that
> ideology, and the practices that they legitimized, fit so well a Russian
> national political character marked by cunning, brutality, and submis-
> siveness.

This leads Gray to reject the possibility of successfully dealing with
the Soviet Union. As he puts it, "It is virtually self-evident that
Soviet strategic culture precludes the negotiation route to enhanced

stability." The answer is nuclear warfare as a realistic choice: "A stable strategic balance, in US/NATO perspective, is one that would permit the United States [among other things] to initiate central strategic nuclear employment in expectation of gain."[27] Despite the quaint terminology, the meaning—a first strike—is clear.

There are several related elements that recur frequently as part of the same hard-line syndrome, including the repeated conjunction of some or all of the following elements: (1) assertions of historical determinism; (2) advocacy of militant strategic options; (3) the alleged "militarization" of Soviet society; (4) the denial of diversity and politics at the apex of the Soviet system; and at times (5) stress on the role of non-Russian nationalities of the Soviet Union as a cause of both militarization and expansionism.[28]

THE LIMITS OF HISTORY

Of course, there are continuities in Russian history. They may well be strongest in the areas of social and economic history and in regard to popular attitudes and values. The attitude toward authority and the state is a likely candidate for significant continuity. The axiomatic acceptance of a powerful centralized state—although by no means unusual—does contrast strikingly with the characteristic American suspicion of government, regulation, and politicians. The role of the state as the principal source and instrument of change, as well as its paternalistic function as dispenser of welfare, have "objective" historical causes. The paucity of secondary, voluntary associations mediating between state and individual has been remarked upon more than once. Even if that too had begun to change before 1917, it may be viewed as another part of the legacy inherited by the Bolshevik era. The weakness of individualism, the frailty of representative institutions at the national level, the absence of the values and forms of a *Rechtsstaat*—these are but a few of the prerevolutionary trends that have indeed affected the Soviet era. In all likelihood, prejudices, stereotypes, and customs of all sorts have persisted as well.[29]

The question is what weight to attach to them. In all likelihood the love/hate relationship one finds in Russian attitudes toward the "advanced" West is none too different from the ambivalence toward the West found in India, Nigeria, or Japan. Many aspects of the critical attitude toward "bourgeois" norms and values may resemble those found both in "Cherry Orchards" and *barrios* the world over. The personalized attachment to the ruler—to the *batiushka-tsar'*—is a common trait in less-developed societies. Autocracy, bureaucracy, red tape, and military necessity have their many analogs over time and space. Russification too has its counterparts in other societies where the dominant ethnic, linguistic, or cultural group imposes its hegemony, with varying degrees of coercion and success.

No doubt, there remain peculiar features that contribute to the operational code of the Soviet decision-making elite. Some of its traits may be repugnant to US observers or travelers.[30] Yet none of this validates the gloomy verdict of predestination that the hard-line historiographers seek to pronounce.[31] If this should have been apparent throughout the post-Stalin years, it has surely been dramatized by the events of the Gorbachev era.

*   *   *

Historians must know not only the uses of history but also its limits. The future can never be assumed to be a replica, or an extrapolation, of the past: If it were, history as a subject of study might indeed be as boring as some of our students allege. To the earlier saying that history does not repeat itself, historians do, one may now add the remark of Sidney Hook: "Those who always remember the past often don't know when it's over." For this observer at least, there is no more validity in historical determinism than in economic or technological determinism.

There is ample room—indeed, there is need—for honest and profound differences among scholars. Especially in an area as vague and vast as this one, and as difficult to investigate, disagreements are both natural and healthy. What is lamentable is the use and abuse of the historical record to serve partisan political ends.

We have all damned Soviet historiography for rewriting the past in accordance with the changing demands of the political authorities. Professional integrity requires the application of similar standards among ourselves. In condemning those in the Soviet Union who would let history be made into a tool of politics, we must guard against those among us who, intentionally or otherwise, would likewise tailor history to suit their political needs.

NOTES

1. These include several prominent appointees of the Reagan administration, such as Richard Pipes (who in 1981–1982 served on the National Security Council staff), Edward Rowney (US negotiator in the arms control talks with the Soviet Union), and William Odom (director of the National Security Agency).

This general approach has been stressed, in the past, by a number of East European historians. Cf. Jan Kucharzewski, *Od bialego caratu do czerwonego,* 7 vols. (Warsaw: Wydaw. im Mianowskiego, 1923–1935), and *The Origins of Modern Russia,* abridged trans. (New York: Polish Institute, 1948); and Tibor Szamuely, *The Russian Tradition* (New York: McGraw-Hill, 1974). In different versions it has also been popular with publicists of the latest Soviet emigration (e.g., Boris Shragin and Alexander Yanov).

2. James Cracraft, "The Soviet Union: From the Russian Past to the Soviet Present," *Bulletin of the Atomic Scientists* (January 1982), pp. 8–12.

3. David Hackett Fischer, *Historians' Fallacies: Toward a Logic of Historical Thought* (New York: Harper & Row, 1970), p. 154. He also pillories "the fallacy of prediction by analogy" (p. 357). It is scarcely necessary to warn against the familiar trap of *post hoc propter hoc.*

4. For a sophisticated discussion of the whole problem, see Alexander Gerschenkron, "On the Concept of Continuity in History," in his *Continuity in History* (Cambridge, MA: Harvard University Press, 1968), pp. 11–39.

5. (London: Bell, 1931), pp. 10 ff.

6. In the words of Gerschenkron ("On the Concept of Continuity in History," p. 38), "At all times and in all cases, continuity must be regarded as a tool forged by the historian rather than as something inherently and invariantly contained in the historical matter. To say continuity means to formulate a question or a set of questions and to address it to the material."

7. Cf. Dimitri Obolensky's comment "There is much in contemporary Russia that seems unfamiliar and puzzling to the modern Western observer . . . and so, wishing to understand the origin and meaning of these strange phantoms, he is tempted to single out those which appear to him most striking and to trace them back as far as possible into Russia's past history. . . . He will be inclined to conclude that the similarity is proof of historical filiation." (D. Obolensky, "Russia's Byzantine Heritage," *Oxford Slavonic Papers* 1 [1950], pp. 37 ff.)

8. *American Historical Review* (April 1976), p. 403.

9. Benjamin Schwartz, "The Chinese Perception of World Order, Past and Present," in John K. Fairbank, ed., *The Chinese World Order* (Cambridge, MA: Harvard University Press, 1968), p. 284.

10. Sir Lewis Namier, "History and Political Culture," in Fritz Stern, ed., *The Varieties of History* (New York: Meridian Books, 1956), p. 377.

11. Barbara W. Tuchman, *Practicing History* (New York: Knopf, 1981), pp. 249, 251. This tallies with H.A.L. Fisher's conclusion that time and again historians, after searching for laws and patterns, recognize "the play of the contingent and the unforeseen." See also Ernest R. May, *"Lessons" of the Past: The Use and Misuse of History in American Foreign Policy* (New York: Oxford University Press, 1973).

12. For some of the relevant debate, especially in regard to Russia, see Archie Brown, "Introduction," to Brown and Jack Grey, eds., *Political Culture and Political Change in Communist States* (New York: Holmes and Meier, 1977) and the literature cited there. The writings of Robert C. Tucker, Stephen White, and Frederick C. Barghoorn illustrate significant attempts to apply the concept to the Soviet experience. An important theoretical contribution is Kenneth Jowitt, "An Organizational Approach to the Study of Political Culture in Marxist-Leninist Systems," *American Political Science Review* 68, no. 3 (September 1974), pp. 1171–91. I am not here concerned with the interesting and rather deviant views on the subject by Robert C. Tucker and Zbigniew Brzezinski. (See Brzezinski's "Soviet Politics: From the Future to the Past?" in Paul Cocks et al., eds., *The Dynamics of Soviet Politics* [Cambridge, MA: Harvard University Press, 1976], pp. 337–51.)

13. See in particular Alex Inkeles, "The Modernization of Man in Socialist and Nonsocialist Countries," in Mark Field, ed., *Social Consequences of Modernization in Communist Societies* (Baltimore, MD: Johns Hopkins Press, 1976), pp. 50–69; and Alex Inkeles and David Smith, *Becoming Modern* (Cambridge, MA: Harvard University Press, 1974). See also Richard Fagen, *The Transformation of Political Culture in Cuba* (Stanford, CA: Stanford University Press, 1969). The argument is not meant to challenge either the survival and indeed frequent revival of traditional culture at a later stage, or the different ways in which traditional culture may impede or assist modernization in different settings.

14. Dietrich Geyer, ed., *Osteuropa-Handbuch: Sowjetunion Aussenpolitik 1917–1955* (Cologne: Ohlau Verlag, 1972), pp. 16–19.

15. Cf. Werner Hahn, "The Mainsprings of Soviet Secrecy," *Orbis* 7, no. 4 (1974), and Alexander Dallin, *The Soviet Union, Arms Control and Disarmament* (New York: Praeger, 1964), Chapter 10.

16. Cited in Ann Kleimola, "Muscovy Redux," *Russian History* 4, no. 1 (1977), p. 23. See Lloyd E. Berry and Robert O. Crummey, eds., *Rude and Barbarous Kingdom* (Madison, WI: University of Wisconsin Press, 1968).

17. For an articulate expression of differences on this issue, see the exchange between Richard Hellie, Ann Kleimola, James Cracraft, and Richard Wortman, in *Russian History* 4, no. 1 (1977), pp. 1–41.

18. J.H. Plumb, *The Growth of Political Stability in England, 1675–1725* (London: Macmillan, 1967), p. xviii.

19. (Stanford, CA: Stanford University Press, 1977).

20. See Henry L. Roberts, "Russia and the West: A Comparison and Contrast," *Slavic Review* 23, no. 1 (March 1964), pp. 1–12. Cracraft reminds the reader that "the larger historical field against which Russia is more properly studied is surely that of Western Asia, the Balkans, Central and the rest of Eastern Europe, where often similar conditions produced often similar results, including in modern times more or less imitative cultures, bureaucratic absolutism, agrarian forced labor, virulent nationalism, acquiescent church hierarchies, alienated intellectuals, and the active, interventionist, regulatory *Polizeistaat. . . ."* (*Russian History* 4, no. 1 [1977], p. 33).

21. US Senate, Committee on Foreign Relations, *Perceptions: Relations Between the United States and the Soviet Union* (Washington, DC: Government Printing Office, 1979), p. 65.

22. Geyer, *Osteuropa-Handbuch,* pp. 2–15.

23. An exception to this generalization must be made for those instances in which a Soviet policymaker believes that such a continuity exists and acts on this belief. If true, this was the case with Stalin in regard to Korea, as analyzed by Robert Slusser, in Yunosuke Nagai et al., eds., *The Origins of the Cold War in Asia* (New York: Columbia University Press, 1977).

24. This point is reinforced by Muriel Atkin's conclusion regarding tsarist policy toward Iran: "Russian expansion in this part of Asia, for all its momentous consequences, was more the product of accident than of a carefully considered master-plan." It is true, she finds, that Russia was consciously imitating a Western colonialist approach: Not only would colonies make Russia rich; they would also make her look great and civilized like the empires of the West. (Muriel Atkin, *Russia and Iran, 1780–1828* [Minneapolis, MN: University of Minnesota Press, 1980], pp. 162–63.) I owe this reference to Cracraft, "The Soviet Union," p. 12. See also Michael Karpovich, "Russian Imperialism or Communist

Aggression?" in Alexander Dallin, ed., *Soviet Conduct in World Affairs* (New York: Columbia University Press, 1960), pp. 186–95.

25. For a macrocomparison of the course of empires, which reaches substantially similar conclusions about Russia's conforming to the patterns typical for big-power expansion, see George Liska, *Russia and the Road to Appeasement* (Baltimore, MD: Johns Hopkins Press, 1982), pp. 18, 51.

26. Rebecca V. Strode and Colin Gray, "The Imperial Dimension of Soviet Military Power," *Problems of Communism,* November–December 1981.

27. Colin S. Gray, "Strategic Stability Reconsidered," *Daedalus,* Fall 1980, pp. 142, 150–51. See also Colin S. Gray and Keith B. Payne, "Victory is Possible," *Foreign Policy,* no. 39 (Summer 1980), pp. 14–27, on nuclear war; and Colin Gray, "Nuclear Strategy: The Case for a Theory of Victory," *International Security,* Summer 1979. For an able rebuttal of Gray's views, see the first UCLA Distinguished Lecture in honor of Bernard Brodie: Michael Howard, "On Fighting a Nuclear War," *ACIS Working Paper,* no. 31 (January 1981). Gray is a member of the US Government's General Advisory Committee on Arms Control and Disarmament.

28. See, e.g., William Odom, "A Dissenting View of the Group Approach to Soviet Politics," *World Politics,* July 1976; Odom, "The Militarization of Soviet Society," *Problems of Communism,* September–October 1976; and Odom, "Whither the Soviet System?" *Washington Quarterly* 4, no. 2 (Spring 1981).

29. A substantial part of the more-sophisticated observation of continuities turns out to be precisely in the area of attitudes. See, e.g., Hedrick Smith, *The Russians* (New York: Quadrangle, 1976); Edward L. Keenan, "Muscovite Political Folkways," *The Russian Review* 45 (1986), pp. 115–81. For a brief discussion of "continuities" shaping Russian economic development, see William L. Blackwell, *The Industrialization of Russia,* 2nd ed. (Arlington Heights, IL: Harlan Davidson, 1982), Chapter 5.

30. As a senior US arms control negotiator concludes, "The main lesson to learn is that the Russians are, as the Marquis de Custine pointed out 150 years ago, of a different culture from us. We spring from different roots and do not share a common heritage. My six and one-half years at the negotiating table taught me two fundamental lessons. First, that the Soviets are still Russians. Second, that they are more unlike us than like us." (Edward L. Rowney, "The Soviets Are Still Russians," *Survey,* 111 [25:2] [Spring 1980], p. 9.)

31. For a survey of Western perspectives on the possibilities of change in the Soviet system prior to the Gorbachev era, see M. Kamil Dziewanowski, "The Future of Soviet Russia in Western Sovietology," *Co-Existence* 19, no. 1 (April 1982), pp. 93–114.

6

HISTORICAL CONSCIOUSNESS AND THE INCORPORATION OF THE SOVIET PAST

Anti-Sovietism is faddish these days. This profoundly negative evaluation of historical experience is hardly surprising given the well-documented economic turmoil and the painful process of political reform in the Soviet Union.[1] This negative evaluation is, however, grossly overstated.

The virulent anti-Sovietism of Western observers draws sustenance from a wildly radical and poorly considered rejection of the totality of the Soviet experiment on the part of observers within the Soviet Union. Such thinkers as the economist Vasiliy Selyunin, the philosopher Aleksandr Tsipko, and the film director Stanislav Govorukhin have outdone each other in denying the validity of any part of the Soviet past. Reinforcement of this trend comes from the recent publication of Aleksandr Solzhenitsyn's works in the Soviet Union, as well as from the translation and publication of such examples of Western cold-war historiography as Robert Conquest's *The Great Terror* and Richard Pipes's *The Russian Revolution*. Like waves in harmonic resonance, the condemnatory currents from within and outside of the Soviet Union are giving rise to ever higher peaks of anti-Sovietism.[2] As a result, there is enormous pressure on Soviet studies, broadly conceived, to participate in this baby-with-the-bathwater discarding of Soviet history.[3]

The practice of denying a significant component of their national life experience is itself an important part of the Russians' past, but it is a part which they very much need to transcend, and it is certainly not one in which the West needs to participate. On the contrary, the Russians, and other Soviet peoples to equal or greater degrees,[4] have a pressing need to incorporate the shadows and light of all aspects of their histories in a single general composition acceptable to the national eye.

Western Russian/Soviet studies—as a corporate body interested in and affected by, but not directly immersed in, the current trauma—

145

could assist in this constructive task. Through an interdisciplinary "intellectual Marshall Plan," we stand to gain a great deal ourselves by way of enormously enriched theoretical perspectives and interpretive approaches for our own disciplines. By helping the peoples of the former Soviet Union gain an historically grounded, critically constructive perspective on their own past, we will profit from the insights and interpretive frameworks generated by a solidly based native Soviet studies community. At the same time, the depoliticization of Western Soviet studies will free us from some of the constraints of our own Left-Right debate and allow us to pursue interesting new questions.

It was often the case in Russian history, however, that promising potentialities went undeveloped because the social base supporting them was too narrow. Therefore, it will not be enough to foster a nuanced view of the past only among the more highly educated strata of the population. There is still a very real possibility of the re-emergence of the phenomenon of two Russias—the Russia of the more educated and intellectually developed groups and the Russia of the common people. If all efforts at developing a balanced historical vision center solely on the educated elite, the common people will be left with an anti-historical, politically authoritarian tradition. It will hardly be surprising, then, if, excluded and ignored, they support the kind of authoritarian, anti-intellectual policies characteristic of much of the Soviet period.

Relying, however, on the central themes of the three books under review here—Richard Stites's stress on the need for positive utopias in *Revolutionary Dreams: Utopian Visions and Experimental Life in the Russian Revolution* (Oxford: Oxford University Press, 1988), the social divisions in late imperial Russia that Marshall Shatz elucidates in *Jan Waclaw Machajski: A Radical Critic of the Russian Intelligentsia and Socialism* (Pittsburgh, PA: University of Pittsburgh Press, 1989), and Aleksandr A. Bogdanov's systemic approach with its heavy emphasis on culture, which Zenovia Sochor treats in *Revolution and Culture: The Bogdanov-Lenin Controversy* (Ithaca, NY: Cornell University Press, 1988)—we can fashion an alternative way, both more positive and more inclusive, of visualizing the pasts of the peoples, Russian and non-Russian, of the former Soviet Union. By pursuing this goal, all of those who support and benefit from the current intellectual ferment can help to ensure that the "broad popular masses" are not excluded from this enterprise. Otherwise, one of the most important lessons of Russian history will have been missed, and the whole effort may well prove to have been for naught.

It is a very good time to be a Russian and Soviet specialist. Interest in things Soviet has seldom been as great, and the public profile of Soviet analysts, many of whom are frequent commentators in the media, is at an unprecedentedly high level. Long gone are the sunset years of Leonid Brezhnev and company, when there was minimal general interest and one had almost to justify one's serious intellectual involvement in the subject. Today, there is a fascination among the general public with *le monde russe et soviétique,* which has elevated the status of the profession. However, this heightened stature masks the very real, inherent threat that the profession will lose its equilibrium in the quest for contemporaneity. Defining ourselves exclusively in terms of immediacy and currency will do serious long-term damage to our profession.[5]

Fortunately, this is not the only possibility in the present situation for those who have chosen "Sovietology as a vocation."[6] In fact, far from it. Many elements are in place to make this an era to rival in importance the two most significant previous phases in the development of Western Soviet studies: the postwar *Grundzeit* and the revisionist *Historikerstreit* of the 1960s. For one thing, despite the dangers of a focus on current events, the field does stand to be re-energized by the enormous changes now taking place in the Soviet Union. Such changes will also attract bright new minds to the field.[7] Another avenue to theoretical and interpretive renewal is via access to important new sources and databases. Soviet archivists and librarians have welcomed the opportunity to work in a less constricted and more cooperative manner with foreign scholars. While we still await the appearance of significant documentary publications from their archival *fondy,* there has been a meaningful opening up of new archival troves.[8] It is to be hoped that the *glasnost'* of *Glavarkhiv* will develop apace and along with it our various disciplines.

Together with these straws in the present-day winds of change, there is another incipient development with incalculable significance for Soviet studies—the emergence of *Soviet* Soviet studies as a legitimate, respectable enterprise.[9] It is an historical anomaly that generally speaking, the most interesting, insightful, and worthwhile studies of the Soviet Union in the fields of sociology, anthropology, economics, legal studies, political science, and so on—and to a certain extent in the field of Russian history—have originated outside of the Soviet Union. To be sure, it is not unknown for foreign scholars to pioneer and excel in the study of another society. To take a case from Russian history, in the second half of the nineteenth century and up to 1917, certain Russian historians, clearly responding to problems of the day in tsarist society, produced a series of studies of *ancien régime* and revolutionary France, many of which were ground-breaking efforts that surpassed the investigations of the French themselves. But the so-called *école russe* did not dominate French historical study. It is not that Sovietology as we have known it has partially or temporarily fallen under the sway of non-Soviets; the very field itself is the creation of non-Soviets. For too long, the entire interdisciplinary effort has proceeded without a healthy Soviet scholarly community to challenge and invigorate its precepts and its interpretations.[10] Happily, that is changing.

These developments in Soviet studies are not occurring in a political vacuum. They have taken place during a time of vigorous popular reaction against both the communist system and the current situation to which that system has given rise. This reaction entails a rejection of nearly the entire Soviet experience.[11] Among a broad cross section of the populace, this defense mechanism against the "terror of history" has taken on the form of a temporal version of *russkaya chekharda* or leap-frog. Jumping over the Soviet era, many people look back to the tsarist era and to a monarchism dusted off and polished up a bit, or at least they partake of a certain nostalgia for the old regime.[12]

The selective rejection of the past is a well-developed Russian tradition. In ancient times, Russian peasants practiced the slash-and-burn method of agriculture: after a few years of farming the same piece of land to exhaustion, they moved to new lands, clearing them by the simple expedient of burning off the forest and underbrush, thereby fertilizing the soil with the ash. This experience (extending, arguably, right up to the present) left an important legacy; it engendered in the Russian people an extensive and expansive approach to problems, as opposed to an intensive, internal one.[13] And this is precisely the way many Russians go about formulating their view of history—bundling up a few treasured items, abandoning their roots, and torching that which they do not want in their new environment. From time to time, they return to the original piece of historical ground to try to work it again. Equally important, the very nature of their history has encouraged this tendency; much of it one would rather not have to remember.

This same tendency was also quite pronounced both within the government and within Alexander Herzen's "other" Russia—the Russia of the educated elite. The Russian government has both participated in and contributed enormously to this attitude of rejectionism, partly as a result of the callousness of many of its policies, which the general populace passively repudiates through its approach to history, and partly in its abrupt reversals of policy. Rejectionism is not only evident in Peter the Great's chopping of beards from boyars' faces and smashing of icons, both physical and mental. One also recalls the relative abruptness of the decision to emancipate the serfs, the suddenness of the Stolypin reforms after much official oscillation, the thunderbolt of Nicholas's abdication, the New Economic Policy, collectivization, and so on. The overall result is that one of the enduring problems of the Russians' *Weltanschauung* is their inability to reconcile in one synthetic and synergistic whole the entire spectrum of their historical experience.

When members of the intelligentsia attempted to resolve the complicated issue of the Russian past, they too placed a negative valuation on whole stretches of their history. In the Solov'yevian historical tradition,[14] Russian history could be said to have begun only with Peter, that is, roughly in 1700. The Slavophiles in a sense offered the photographic negative of this picture, arguing that Peter and his fledglings created a deracinated, ahistorical monstrosity that violated the historically developed (yet, somehow, ahistorically created) Russian character. For them, history ended with Peter the Great.

Herzen's creative contribution to Russian social thought was to meld the Western, Enlightenment-based ideal of socialism with the Russian folk "socialism" of the commune. In practice, then, he—and the populists who built on this idea—accepted the Western intellectual legacy of Peter and rejected all the rest "in the name of the people."

The Russian Marxists, of course, worked for the final eradication of the Russian pasts, both "feudal" and "bourgeois," and the anarchists—representatives of one of the most important currents within Russian social and political thought—repudiated almost all historically developed political structures and practices. The incomplete incorporation of the Russians' historical experience did not allow them a Nietzschean escape from the dead weight of a useless legacy,[15] but rather left them with only partial solutions to enormously complex problems.

In order to move forward and to deal in a truly effective manner with the challenges facing the country, the Soviet people must encompass the past, not exclude it, as the current "totalitarian" anti-Sovietism would have it do.[16] No long-term resolution of this problem will emerge as long as the Bolshevik Revolution of 1917 is written off simply as an aberrant historical eruption and the Soviet era as an historical interruption. In point of fact, not only the period from 1917 to the present is being erased from historical memory, but the years 1914 to 1917 are also being omitted. Thus, the nostalgia for the old regime is of an antebellum variety.[17] This is important, not for the purposes of casting blame, but for establishing historical balance. With the issue of the tsarist government's entry into World War I eliminated from consideration, it is possible to cast too rosy a light on the prewar years and to see the Civil War as merely blood-thirsty and inhuman. In fact, the horror—both White and Red—of the Civil War grew directly out of the organized insanity of World War I.[18]

Systems theory offers one set of analytical tools for the reconceptualization of late imperial history and Soviet history together as a series of efforts to rebalance an out-of-kilter mechanism. This theory conceives of a system as "a complex of interdependencies between

parts, components, and processes that involves discernible regularities of relationship. . . ."[19] Change and adjustment are natural re-
alignments of a system, which has "a tendency toward a state of
equilibrium, i.e., the system tends to maintain itself through various
processes whenever it is disturbed, either from within or without
its boundaries."[20]

One real disadvantage of the systems approach is that it tends to
make any system seem "functional"—no matter how inequitable or
inhumane that system is.[21] It is also quite easy to fail to discern the
true nature of internal adjusting mechanisms by regarding them as
a normal part of any social system, so that the action of the police
can become routinized as mere law enforcement, ignoring elements
of the forcible maintenance of privileges based on gender, class,
ethnicity, race, religion, or other factors.

On the other hand, systems theory enables one to see all parts of
the whole in an interconnected fashion. That is also, after all, one
of the enduring strengths of Marxism, and it seems in some ways
fitting and natural that as Zenovia Sochor details for us in her study
of the Bogdanov-Lenin controversy, one of the pioneers of systems
theory was a rogue Russian Marxist, Aleksandr A. Bogdanov. Bogdanov was an early member of the social democratic movement in
Russia and a close collaborator of Lenin's in the early years of
Bolshevism. Bogdanov later broke with Lenin, vigorously contesting
certain of the Bolshevik leader's political, ideological, and intellectual
positions.[22]

Differences over the nature of the base-superstructure linkage
served as the starting point for the heated and prolonged theoretical
struggle between Bogdanov and Lenin. One of the weaker systemic
linkages in Marxist theory is that which is supposed to exist between
base and superstructure. In its Leninist variant, this linkage became
rather crude and automatic. Indeed, many of Lenin's more murderous
and vindictive policies can be seen as attempts to inflame class
hatred with the aim of sealing an identification of social position
and class values.

By contrast, Bogdanov's approach had two interrelated elements
to recommend it. First, he reduced Marxism's emphasis on conscious
exploitation of one class by another, shifting the focus to the system
itself. Second, this shift in focus enabled Bogdanov to view the lower
classes less heroically and more realistically and to comprehend the
distorting impact that their harsh class and social experience had
had on their perspectives. As a result, he understood that the working class would not automatically embody the humane values expected under socialism. Bogdanov therefore argued that the social
democratic movement ought to take on a much more rigorous edu-
cative mission to offset the negative life lessons of poverty and
brutality to which the lower classes were routinely exposed. Unfor-

tunately and perhaps ineluctably, this more nuanced and more comprehensive effort was not pursued to much purpose, losing out to the more immediately pragmatic and power-oriented policies of Lenin.

We need to take a cue from Bogdanov and analyze the current situation in the Soviet Union from a systems perspective with a strong emphasis on culture. We can thus envision the upheavals of the first years of this century, the war years, and the entire Soviet period as a prolonged systemic adjustment on the part of the Russian socio-political order to the massive socio-economic transformations initiated in Europe and affecting the entire world in socio-economic, political, and military terms. This formulation of the problem allows us to transcend the constricting categories of the past. Hence, there is no need to demonize either the tsarist elite, which failed to steer the country through the necessary changes in the prewar years, or the Soviet elite, whose leadership has of late come up so short. Instead, we ought to look for the limiting factors that contributed to their joint downfall.

While shifting the focus away from the elites, we can also move away from the view of the noble *narod*. In Bogdanovite terms, we can begin to see that however unfortunate—and however much a result of factors beyond its control—the Soviet populace, as the product of an unhealthy social order, could scarcely have avoided some disfiguring scars stemming from its experiences. For example, violence was one of the distinguishing features of tsarist society.[23] And yet, there is no general study of the role of violence in that society. Enormously magnified by the brutalizing experience of World War I, this is one of the central components of the social basis of Stalinism. It remains unexplored, I suspect, because those most likely to do this sort of socio-historical study are ideologically on the Left, and for them this is too much like blaming the victim.[24] Furthermore, there is probably a reluctance to contribute to the reigning anti-Sovietism and anti-Russianism in American society.[25] Viewing the whole systemically, however, and in a *durée un peu plus longue,* frees us to examine vital questions outside of any planned economy of blame or exoneration. This approach, combined with the critical perspectives flashing forth from an emerging and energized community of native Soviet analysts, makes it all the more likely that Western, and especially American, Sovietologists can break free from the intellectually inhibiting constraints that I discussed above.

In this vein, we can answer the question "What was the revolution about?"[26] by depicting the painful transformation of a poorly educated, peasant society dominated by a Russian elite into a relatively modern, urbanized society with multiple centers of ethnic consciousness and political representation. Hence, although innumerable problems remain, the Russian and Soviet social organization and polity may be in a position for the first time in their history to create a democratic order in which the individual—every individual and not just the socio-political elite and the well-educated—is respected.

As argued above, the systems approach considers modern Russian/Soviet society to be in a state of systemic disequilibrium that is in the process of stabilizing. An enduring equilibrium requires incorporation of a nation's historical experience, because the past contains so much that is necessary for a successful resolution of present problems. For example, people throughout the Soviet Union have a great need at present for human hope and vitality. They can find a model for these ideals in the thought of the leftist utopians of the late imperial period. However, these visionaries, who in their own day were assailed by the neo-Kantian intellectuals of the *Vekhi* movement,[27] are castigated these days as proto-Stalinists.[28] Reevaluating this aspect of the Russians' historical experience would legitimate the rehabilitation of the leftist intelligentsia, which for all its faults, contained people of good conscience and insight (such as Bogdanov) who were attempting to deal with an impossible situation.

Catherine II also criticized the utopianism of a "leftist *intelligent*" when she dismissed the reform projects proposed by the philosophe Denis Diderot, saying that he wrote on paper while she had to write on human flesh. Those ready to ostracize historically and morally the leftist "utopian" intelligentsia must bear in mind that the majority of them—hoping to help humanity—wrote projects intended for paper, not flesh, and that in many instances a much larger project was ultimately written, against their will and sometimes on their own flesh.

If the leftist intelligentsia and the utopians were attacked (and are being attacked) by other members of the intelligentsia, they were also under assault from below, an assault thoroughly investigated by Marshall Shatz in his book on Jan Waclaw Machajski. It is vital to keep constantly in mind the legacy of class chasms—and of the hatred they engendered. This hatred took on many forms, one of the starkest of which was "Makhayevism." In the summer of 1920, the historian Nikolay Ivanovich Kareyev gave a public talk in the countryside "on the life and activity of Marx." During the course of his talk, a note was sent to him by a member of the audience accusing him of concealing "the conspiracy by which the whole intelligentsia was with tsarism against the *narod*."[29] Consciously or not, this was a manifestation of Makhayevism, which understood the activity of the leftist intelligentsia as an attempt to use the people to make a revolution from which the intelligentsia itself would benefit. "The result," in Shatz's words, "was the first systematic theory of socialism as the ideology not of the proletariat but of a new class of aspiring rulers" (p. 41). This social philosophy—based as it was on a suspicion of the *beloruchki* (the "white hands") or, as Machajski came to represent them, everyone with a diploma—also rejected any collaboration or cooperation between classes.

Condemnation of the leftist intelligentsia from below together with the attack on it by the non-leftist intelligentsia (indeed, *Vekhi* was even sardonically characterized as "Makhayevism from above" [cited in Shatz, p. 143]) typified the lack of social cohesion in late tsarist society. Makhayevism was not a major intellectual current, but it speaks to the enduring problem of the distance between those with specialized knowledge and those whose needs the knowledge is supposed to serve, a problem structurally rooted in the modern specialization of labor and of knowledge. This polarization contributed enormously to the consolidation of Stalinism, in which a bureaucratic, ultimately terroristic, apparatus substituted itself for a fragmented society as a social basis of the state.[30]

The Soviet experience has gone no small distance toward reducing those divisions within Soviet society, especially when compared with the situation in tsarist Russia, but contemporary circumstances threaten to revive them. Thus, another of the historical lessons that must be borne in mind in the current situation is an awareness that Makhayevism could reemerge if a legitimate democracy providing for the genuine social welfare and a popularly oriented educational and cultural system are not crafted.[31] This lesson is particularly important, since it is in vogue these days to cite the market as the deus ex machina that will extricate the Soviet system from its current dilemma. Whatever else the market does, it will exacerbate social divisions and, if left unchecked, could well contribute to a neo-Stalinist backlash.[32]

By reconceptualizing the Soviet era as part of a historical continuum with the tsarist experience, and viewing them together as a difficult path toward resolution of problems posed by the past and ultimately leading to a more balanced and healthy social formation, the peoples of the former Soviet Union can overcome the conceptual sterility of the present and gird themselves for the still difficult, but realizable, passage into the future.[33] But the peoples of the former Soviet Union still need a positive vision of the future. Utopia—the creative projection into the future—has not fared well in the Soviet Union, as a result of its identification with the anti-human excesses that have marred significant stretches of Soviet history. Utopia is currently, as Richard Stites tells us, "a term of bitter derision among Soviet dissidents and émigrés," equated with "an outdated and rickety system that is seen as false, hypocritical, and repressive" (p. 250). But a complete rejection of utopia leaves one with either "reality," however grim and uncomforting, or with some idealized version of the pre-Soviet past, a sort of conservative utopia.

The Russian and Soviet historical understanding thus requires an adaptive self-conception, a new myth, a *utopian* reconsolidation of the past.[34] It need not be a white-washing of the past. In this vein, one thinks of Richard Hofstadter's *The American Political Tradition*, which, even while revealing the less-than-positive aspects of important American political figures (for example, John C. Calhoun and Teddy Roosevelt), manages to affirm as dominant a tradition that is moral, humane, democratic, and popular. Something similar can be done for the Russo-Soviet political tradition by drawing on such figures as Boris Godunov, the Archpriest Avvakum, Tsaritsa Sophia and Prince Vasiliy Golitsyn, Empress Catherine and the Panin brothers, Speranskiy, Loris-Melikov, Bogdanov, Aleksandra Kollontay, Khrushchev, Kosygin, and Sakharov and Bonner, with Konstantin Pobedonostsev in Calhoun's negative role. This list is quickly devised and may seem trivial; the task itself and the overall agenda are not. Utopia must be refurbished in the form of some kind of positively critical myth that explains the torments of the past as part of the experience necessary to reach a stable, just social order.[35]

Moshe Lewin has suggested that the more forcefully and artificially one attempts to speed the course of change, the more of the past one retains.[36] Rather than force the Soviet experience into some Western Procrustean bed, the global community of scholars dedicated to the study of those societies that comprised the old Soviet Union could extricate from the Soviet and pre-Soviet pasts those elements from which the former Soviet peoples can fashion a more acceptable future. For example, as World War II demonstrated, for all their other failings, one thing that the communists did well was mobilize to face crisis situations. Is it possible that the communists' organizational expertise has prepared the former Soviet peoples for the current situation? Put more neutrally, what has been the impact of communist organizational approaches on the capacity of the Soviet peoples for self-organization? Along the same line, is it absolutely heretical to propose that Soviet nationality policy, with all of its violations of "socialist legality" and assaults on national rights, somehow contributed to the readiness with which various Soviet national groups responded to opportunities inherent in the present situation by helping forge national consciousness, means of national self-expression (written languages), modern national elites, and even practical political expertise? However one views these particular problems, the conclusion is the same: we must write through, and not write off or write out, the Soviet period.

The point is not simply that we cannot return to what existed before Lenin because of all the changes that have occurred. Horrible, unspeakable things happened under communism, but, ironically, it may have created some of the socio-political bases for democracy. The society emerging from the ashes of the Russian empire was not

See his contribution to *Vesna 89: Geografiya i anatomiya parlamentskikh vyborov* (Spring 89: Geography and the Anatomy of Parliamentary Elections), Moscow, Progress, 1990; and the collective effort by A.V. Berezkin, et al., "The Geography of the 1989 Elections of People's Deputies of the USSR (Preliminary Results)," *Soviet Geography* (Silver Spring, MD), October 1989, pp. 607–34.

10. This is not to say that the Soviet academic community has not produced works of enormous scholarship and erudition. However, taken as a whole, the community is not a healthy and vibrant one.

11. A ready example of this on the part of the government is the current Gorbachevian fashion of referring to the Brezhnev era as "the period of stagnation" (*period zastoya*).

12. In the beginning was the word. An instance of popular affirmation of the return to pre-Soviet times is the wave of "urban renewal"—the renaming of cities—going on at present. It is worth noting that the referendum to revive the name St. Petersburg carried by a narrow majority over both Leningrad and Petrograd. Some opposed the renaming because of the expense involved; others associated the name Leningrad with the heroic wartime defense; still others maintained simply enough that Leningrad was the name they had grown up with and St. Petersburg meant nothing to them. I know of no analysis of this vote in terms of social class, education, age group, etc. Such an investigation might reveal a great deal about the social locus of the rejection of the Soviet experience. However that may be, the majority of the population of the city voted to return to the prewar, tsarist name, and it has been so adopted. There are many other examples: Tver' (Kalinin) and Nizhnyy Novgorod (Gorkiy), to name just a couple.

13. Basing his ideas on the work of his teacher, S.M. Solov'yev, V.O. Klyuchevskiy emphasized the migratory nature of the Russian people. This propensity has not ended. In recent years, there has been a noticeable migration of Russians from non-Russian ethno-territories back to the heartland. See Lee Schwartz, "USSR Nationality Redistribution by Republic, 1979–1989," *Soviet Geography*, April 1991, p. 211.

14. The dominant view among the elite in Russia from at least the time of his death was that Peter the Great (1682–1725) created the modern Russian state and led the nation onto the stage of history by bringing it forcefully and inextricably into the European political order. This idea received further support from the powerful Hegelian intellectual currents swirling through Russia in the first half of the 19th century. Sergey Mikhailovich Solov'yev, in Nicholas Riasanovsky's considered opinion, "probably the greatest Russian historian of all time," was strongly influenced by these currents. See *The Image of Peter the Great in Russian History and Thought* (New York: Oxford University Press, 1985), p. 154. Still, as Riasanovsky makes clear, Solov'yev assessed Peter from a very mature historical perspective, reducing the sense that under Peter's tutelage Russia was led from "nonbeing to being." Ibid., p. 165. It is difficult to argue that Solov'yev treated pre-Petrine history ahistorically, since 13 volumes of his 29-volume *History of Russia from Most Ancient Times* deal with Russia to the time of Peter. Solov'yev did, however, consider Peter a genius and world-historical figure who led the people into the battle of Poltava, out of which "there was born for Europe, for the

common European life, a new great people; and not only one people: in the thunder of that battle, there was born an entire new race, the Slavic race, which had found for itself a worthy representative, with the aid of which it could rise to a mighty and glorious historical life. A new epoch dawned in European history." *Publichnyye chteniya o Petre Velikom* (Public Lectures on Peter the Great), Moscow, 1872, cited in ibid., p. 73. Many Russians missed Solov'yev's nuance and continued to view Russian history as beginning with Peter.

15. Nietzsche contended that an "excessive" concentration on the past inhibited human behavior. Concerned as he was with the free creative assertion of the individual existential agent, his approach was essentially ahistorical. Leaving aside the difficulties of this position, I find little that is free and self-defining in the Russian approaches discussed here. I do find an inadequate resolution of outstanding problems and issues. See Friedrich Nietzsche, *The Use and Abuse of History* (New York: Liberal Arts Press, 1949).

16. There are, of course, countercurrents in Russia. New historical journals are being planned and launched, documents published, and so on. In this way, the "blank spots" of the Soviet past are being filled in. Nor is this the exclusive territory of professional historians or even of the more educated strata. People whose family members perished or disappeared in the terror, united in the various *Memorial* organizations or acting on their own, are trying to uncover the truth about their relatives. This is an extraordinarily painful—and necessary—experience. The past cannot be denied. For the time being, however, each new finding will be like an exposé, further reinforcing the tendency to reject the entire Soviet experience.

17. For warnings about possible "blank spots" in the historical memories of some Eastern European peoples, see Jerzy Jedlicki, "The Revolutions of 1989: The Unbearable Burden of History," *Problems of Communism* (Washington, DC), July–August 1990, pp. 39–34, and the commentary by Roman Szporluk, "The Burden of History—Made Lighter by Geography?" ibid., pp. 45–48.

18. On the connection of the prewar political system, the Great Power status of Russia, and the decision to go to war, see Geoffrey Hosking, *The Russian Constitutional Experiment* (Cambridge, MA: Cambridge University Press, 1973); and Dietrich Geyer, *Russian Imperialism* (Leamington Spa: Berg, 1987).

19. Talcott Parsons, "Social Systems," Section II of "Systems Analysis," in David L. Sills, ed., *International Encyclopedia of the Social Sciences* (n.p.: The Macmillan Company and the Free Press, 1968, Vol. 15), p. 458.

20. William C. Mitchell, "Political Systems," Section III of "Systems Analysis," in ibid., p. 473.

21. In Parsons's words, "The cultural (pattern-maintenance) system centers on the institutionalization of cultural value patterns, which, at the general cultural level, may be regarded as moral." Parsons, loc. cit., p. 463.

22. An impressive body of literature on Bogdanov has sprung up in recent years. See Sochor, pp. 6–10, for a brief biography and discussion of the literature. Her bibliographical notes 9, 10, 11, and 18 are especially helpful. See also Alexander Vucinich, *Social Thought in Tsarist Russia: The Quest for*

a *General Science of Society, 1861–1917* (Chicago, IL: University of Chicago Press, 1976), esp. Ch. 8.

23. A convenient place to look for examples of the violence routinized in tsarist society, and for much more, is Reginald Zelnik's marvelous edition of the autobiography of the "Russian Bebel," Semeon Kanatchikov. See *A Radical Worker in Tsarist Russia: The Autobiography of Semeon Ivanovich Kanatchikov* (Stanford, CA: Stanford University Press, 1986).

24. Howard Zinn reminds us that "the lines are not always clear . . . the victims, themselves desperate and tainted with the culture that oppresses them, turn on other victims." On the other hand, while we should "try not to overlook the cruelties that victims inflict on one another as they are," in his powerful image, "jammed together in the boxcars of the system," we should also remember that "the cry of the poor is not always just, but if you don't listen to it, you will never know what justice is." Howard Zinn, *A People's History of the United States* (New York: Harper Perennial Edition, 1990), p. 10.

25. See the essay-review by Marc Raeff, "Consequences of Glasnost'," *Problems of Communism,* March–April 1990, pp. 105–08, in which he criticizes the latest edition of the Marquis de Custine's *Empire of the Czar: A Journey Through Eternal Russia,* with its distorted view of the Russians. That the publication of this bilious, tendentious text has been something of a cottage industry in American Soviet studies is indicative of our national anti-Russian prejudices.

26. Posed by Sheila Fitzpatrick in *The Russian Revolution* (Oxford: Oxford University Press, 1982).

27. The *Vekhi* movement was named after an anthology of articles by a number of prominent, like-thinking intellectuals—Nikolay Berdyayev and Peter Struve are the most famous—who broke with Marxism and the political Left and looked for renewal in spiritual values. See Marshall Shatz and Judith Zimmerman, trans. and eds., *"Vekhi* (Signposts): A Collection of Articles on the Russian Intelligentsia," *Canadian Slavic Papers* (Toronto), Summer 1968–Autumn 1971.

28. See especially the interesting, but flawed and slightly dangerous, work by the social philosopher Aleksandr S. Tsipko, *Is Stalinism Really Dead?* trans. from Russian by E.A. Tichina and S.V. Nikheev (San Francisco, CA: Harper, 1990). In fact, Tsipko is a latter-day Vekhist.

29. Cited by Vasiliy Pavlovich Zolotarev in "The Historian Nikolay Ivanovich Kareyev and his Memoirs *Prozhitoye i perezhitoye"* in N.I. Kareyev, *Prozhitoye i perezhitoye* (To Experience and to Suffer), (Leningrad, 1990), p. 29.

30. This is the major interpretive position of Moshe Lewin, "The Social Background of Stalinism," in Robert C. Tucker, ed., *Stalinism: Essays in Historical Interpretation* (New York: Norton, 1977), pp. 111–36.

31. A valuable and much overlooked book is James C. McClelland's *Autocrats and Academics: Education, Culture, and Society in Tsarist Russia* (Chicago, IL: University of Chicago Press, 1979). McClelland demonstrates the distorted, top-heavy nature of the tsarist educational system. Similar, if less extreme, difficulties trouble the contemporary American system, because of the university's emphasis on publication and research.

It may be the case in areas such as Central Asia, which is not noted for strong traditions of democratic government, that democracy will not be an essential aspect of a stable new system, so long as socio-economic and cultural-educational performance conform to the expectations of the various peoples.

32. As has been pointed out, "Markets neither came into existence spontaneously . . . nor are they sustained without the considerable force of state coercive and ideological apparatuses; nor have they proved capable of resolving major social and political dilemmas. . . . Furthermore, markets are not neutral in their social and economic consequences. . . ." Mark Von Hagen, "The Stalin Question," *The Nation* (New York), March 25, 1991, p. 286. See also Karl Polanyi, *The Great Transformation* (New York: Rinehart and Co., 1944), p. 140. Contesting the "liberal creed," Polany argues that "the free market was opened and kept open by an enormous increase in continuous, centrally organized, and controlled interventionism . . . the introduction of free markets, far from doing away with the need for control, regulation, and intervention, enormously increased their range." For his part, Eric Wolf demonstrates that the choice of entering the capitalist world market "was rarely free." Usually, "it was imposed by force, or by constraints stemming from market domination by powerful participants. Coercion or constraint . . . were of the essence of the process; they were not epiphenomena." Each region entering the "circuits of capital" "had to reorganize . . . to intensify capital growth, or else fall under the wheels of the chariot of progress." Eric R. Wolf, *Europe and the People Without History* (Berkeley, CA: University of California Press, 1982), p. 314.

33. The Russians are not unique in this matter. In a somewhat similar way, the French have had to work through the monarchist-republican-imperial conflict left to them as a legacy of their great revolution. In fact, many peoples with troubled historical experiences have difficulty reconciling all of them in a facile whole. The most instructive instance may be the German postwar case but the historiography of the Reconstruction era in the American South may also lend useful insights.

34. To a certain extent every national history is a myth. For the United States, that myth is generally triumphal and untroubled. Our classroom maps show the "Growth of United States"; our movement across the continent is expansion, not colonization. This movement is somehow natural, organic; its destiny is *manifest* for all to see. There are numerous painful socio-economic and political legacies of our past in contemporary America, yet the negative aspects of our past seem to fit quite comfortably beneath the bright beacon of our national self-image as Lady Liberty.

35. Using Hayden White's conception of history and its tasks, we should overturn the skepticism of the "ironic" mode in favor of a more positive mode of discourse. See Hayden White, *Metahistory: The Historical Imagination in Nineteenth-Century Europe* (Baltimore, MD: The Johns Hopkins University Press, 1973), p. 433.

36. "Incidentally, the peculiar factor of haste should be underlined and its influence explored. . . . It is worth venturing, quite tentatively, on the basis of the Soviet experience, the following maxim: The quicker you

break and change, the more of the old you re-create." Lewin, loc. cit., p. 126.

37. In a similar way, although Gorbachev is largely a superfluous man at present, it is essential to remember that the formation of the current constellation of social and political forces would have been unimaginable without him.

38. Something like this happened, in fact, in postwar Berlin, in the western sector of which libraries and even a university were opened with substantial financial backing as a means of making sure that democratic institutions could take root.

ALFRED G. MEYER

7

POLITICS AND METHODOLOGY
IN SOVIET STUDIES

It is safe to assert that every important event that has taken place
in the communist world within the last five years or so has come
as a surprise to the profession, i.e., to students of the USSR and its
client states. What does that say about the state of the art, and is
this failure to foresee current developments to be explained by political influence or political bias? I shall answer the last question
with a very much qualified "yes." Indeed, political attitudes have
tended to determine the profession's image of the Soviet Union; but
I shall argue also that our colleagues studying other areas of the
world have not fared much better. Politics and social life in general
are too complex and too unpredictable to lend themselves to rigorous
"scientific" analysis.

The study of foreign cultures is in itself implicitly political since
it always implies critical evaluation both of the culture being studied
and of one's own. The bias may be celebration or rejection of one's
own or the foreign culture or a mixture of attitudes. It may be well
hidden under the guise of a supposedly neutral set of concepts; but
it is likely to be there always.

Tacitus writing about Germanic tribes, Margaret Mead investigat-
ing the sex life of Samoan adolescents, or Lewis Morgan reporting
on the social life of the Iroquois of upstate New York—they all were,
in effect, holding up a moralizing mirror to their own societies.
Similarly, there is a long tradition in China studies which conveys
love for Chinese culture and admiration for the traditional bureaucracy of scholars and the incredible stability of the governmental
system. In a similar spirit, radical intellectuals in eighteenth century
France turned their eyes toward England and its admirable constitution; and in the nineteenth century German and Russian radicals,
among others, described the United States as a system in which
individual freedom and communal self-government had been established in exemplary fashion.

In the United States, the study of foreign areas has more often
than not had a very different bias, i.e. one of celebrating one's own

163

system. Due to its geographic position, its wealth in resources and its preoccupation with exploring and exploiting these resources, American scholarship had traditionally shown relatively little interest in learning about the world outside its own borders. The study of selected foreign areas became parts of regular college curricula only when political events made them a matter of public concern. Even that statement must be qualified: American involvement in World War I stifled rather than promoted German studies in the United States at least until the mid-1930s, and only after the National-Socialists had come to power did Germany become more interesting both to those who admired the new regime and those who loathed or feared it. Within academia, the latter predominated, primarily because of the large number of exiled scholars from Central Europe who came to the United States.

The study of Russia had traditionally been the study of an evil empire. Tsarism and the American way of life were seen as polar opposites. With the exception of the 1860s, when St. Petersburg sided with the North, Russia tended to have a very bad press in the United States. The radical *New York Tribune* may not have been representative of general public opinion; let me nonetheless quote from an article it published on April 12, 1853:

> These vital interests should render Great Britain the earnest and unyielding opponent of the Russian project of annexation and aggrandizement. . . . Having come this far on the way to universal empire, is it probable that this gigantic, swollen power will pause in its career?. . . . It would appear that the natural frontier of Russia runs from Danzig or perhaps Stettin to Trieste. And as sure as conquest and annexation follows annexation, so surely would the conquest of Turkey by Russia be only the prelude to the annexation of Hungary, Prussia, Galicia, and the ultimate realization of the Slavonic empire. . . . The arrest of the Russian schema of annexation is a matter of the highest moment. In this instance the interest of democracy and of England go hand in hand . . .

This was written for the *Tribune* by its then European correspondent, Karl Marx, but ghostwritten by Engels.

One of the many reasons why Americans were reluctant to have their country involved in World War I undoubtedly was their feeling of discomfort at the idea of being allied with the tsarist empire. That feeling changed into one of relief and rejoicing after the February revolution. To American observers, this seemed to be merely one more link in the long chain of popular revolts against monarchy and thus yet another confirmation of the political principles proclaimed by the American revolution. The October revolution quickly reversed this attitude. Having hailed revolutions throughout the nineteenth century, Americans now denounced this particular revolution. Having been the first government to recognize the Provisional Government, the United States became the last major power to establish diplomatic relations with the Soviet regime. Gordon S. Wood in a recent review explains this as a consistent application of previously held beliefs: Americans thought of their revolution as the model to which all other countries should conform, and of their political system as one which genuinely institutionalized democratic principles. This role as the beacon of progress and liberalization was now claimed by a novel kind of revolutionary regime:

> The Soviet Union threatened nothing less than the displacement of the United States from the vanguard of history. The Russians, not the Americans, now claimed to be pointing the way toward the future (and more alarming still, there were some Americans in the 1920s and 1930s who agreed with that claim). For the first time since 1776 Americans were faced with an alternative revolutionary ideology with Universalist aspirations equal to their own. This ideological threat . . . seemed to make all of America's heritage irrelevant . . .

For a wide range of reasons, socialist movements in the nineteenth century were weak in the United States, though around the turn of the century, in the McKinley era, socialism gained considerable strength. In 1912, Eugene Debs, running for the Presidency on the Socialist ticket, gathered an impressive portion of the vote.

After the October revolution, the Soviet regime generated a good deal of sympathetic interest among left-of-center people in the USA. By proclaiming itself to be a socialist system, it appeared to many as an alternative to the harshness and the inequities of capitalism. Moreover, progressives of diverse kinds were fascinated by the brave experiments undertaken in a broad array of avant-gardist ideas and practices in the 1920s, especially since some of these experiments seemed to practice what American progressives had preached. Soviet penology in the 1920s was inspired largely by American models such as the Concord (Massachusetts) reformatory. Soviet schools sought to put into practice American theories of progressive education. Welfare legislation, experimentation in the arts, family law, all seemed to conform to the ideals of American and European progressives. So did the proclamations concerning minority rights and religious freedom; and the Soviet system of government looked to many progressives like a democratic, participatory institution similar to a New England town meeting.

Once the Great Depression hit the United States, Soviet socialism appeared to many an alternative to capitalism worth taking seriously, while in the mid-1930s the Popular Front policy pursued by Moscow made the Soviet Union seem to be the most active and sincere opponent of fascism.

Sympathetic appraisals of these kinds found expression in numerous radical and progressive journals, but did not lead to the emergence of Russian or Soviet studies as a serious academic sub-field. Moreover, when during the Second World War the US War Department decided to provide intensive Russian language training to some selected enlisted men in the Army Specialized Training Program, the area courses that accompanied these language instructions dealt, not with the Soviet Union, but with Germany. The assumptions made by the managers of this program seem to have been that the war-time allies jointly would some day administer a defeated Germany and that we would be needed as interpreters or liaison personnel. I say "we" because I was one of the graduates of this program. Few if any of us in fact found occasions to use their newly acquired language skills. I myself was sent to a Military Intelligence training center to be trained as a prisoner-of-war interrogator, and eventually functioned as such with an infantry division in the German campaign. I found use for my knowledge of Russian only in occasional encounters with captured members of the Vlasov army or with Russians who had been deported to do forced labor in Germany. I used it "in the line of duty" once, when in late April, 1944, our division reached the left bank of the Elbe and linked up with our Soviet allies coming up to the other side. Our division commander gave a big party, and there I served as interpreter.

And so, in the Army Specialized Training Program we were taught Russian without being given the slightest information about Russia or the Soviet Union. Our basic text was *Simplified Russian Grammar* written by Bondar, an émigré whose vocabulary, including terms referring to political institutions, was pre-revolutionary, just as most of our instructors, hurriedly gathered from the émigré community of Boston, consisted primarily of former members of St. Petersburg high society. Meanwhile, some of our practice readings consisted of TASS communiques that spoke a very different language. The discrepancy was never noticed or discussed. I will leave it to others to speculate about the reason for this studious omission of all discussion of the USSR.

To my knowledge, the only research on the Soviet Union conducted during the war was done by a small team in the OSS headed by Geroid T. Robinson. Systematic Soviet studies within university settings began in the United States only in the late 1940s when the war-time alliance had given way to the cold war. Soviet studies began as studies of the enemy, the rival. A fellowship program on Russian studies, financed by the Rockefeller Foundation, was created at the Hoover Institution; the Russian Institute was set up at Columbia and, a bit later, the Russian Research Center at Harvard. The fact that the Russian Research Center from the very beginning included research fellows studying the communist parties of Poland, Czechoslovakia, and China indicates the political orientation of at least this one organization. Charles O'Connell in a recent doctoral dissertation has explored this political orientation and has also shown the degree to which the federal government was involved in sponsoring these beginnings.

Research in the field, in these early days, was conducted under burdensome political constraints, some of them imposed by the nature or practices of the Soviet system, others by the political winds then blowing in the United States.

Until the late 1950s, Western scholars simply were not permitted to enter the Soviet Union or any of its East European client states. Then the ban was lifted, however slowly and cautiously, not to say capriciously; and I am sure most readers are familiar with the enormous barriers that Western scholars faced when they tried to establish meaningful communications with colleagues, officials, or simply Soviet citizens. The accessibility of the system that has been made possible during the last five years is a change so total that an old-timer of my generation still finds it difficult to comprehend.

The hermetic isolation of the Soviet Union from Western visitors was aggravated by the scarcity and unreliability of printed information. Again, I surely need not list the many topics that until the era of *glasnost* were left undiscussed in the press and in the professional literature. Statistical data, demographic as well as economic, were scarce, unreliable, and at times misleading. The early efforts of the economists at the Russian Research Center were painstaking and painful attempts to translate opaque Soviet economic statistics into figures that would be meaningful to American specialists. Luckily, the Germans in their rapid advance toward Moscow had captured part of the 1940 economic plan, a top-secret document that contained some hard statistical data. Without that document, research on the Soviet economy would have remained far more speculative.

If I am not mistaken, the 1940 plan was part of the Communist Party archive captured by the Germans at Smolensk. The fact that this Smolensk archive was in American hands was for many years treated highly confidentially. It is good intelligence practice to keep the enemy in the dark concerning the amount of information we possess about him. And in order to conceal our sources of information from the enemy, we also conceal them from our own colleagues. Thus academic research took on some of the traits of military and political intelligence.

Given the inaccessibility of the area and the lack of reliable data, those in search of information on the Soviet Union had to rely very much on informants. Among these the most important ones were former members of communist parties, including some prominent former police or intelligence operatives from the USSR, as well as recent refugees from or non-returnees to the Soviet Union and Eastern Europe. In government organizations, their accounts were complemented by the information provided by former German diplomatic and intelligence personnel, such as the former counselor of the Germany Embassy in Moscow, Gustav Hilger, secretly spirited to the United States, who served as a consultant to the Department of State and, urged on by George Kennan and Charles Bohlen, wrote his memoirs with my assistance. I will have a few words to say further below about the value of these informants' contributions. Suffice it to say here they were deeply engaged in partisan politics and obviously had axes to grind.

Research on the Soviet Union was conducted in an atmosphere that was indeed highly charged with partisan politics—the politics of the cold war. The fascist powers having been defeated, Americans—from opinion makers and political leaders to the general citizenry—took it for granted that Marxism was a false and pernicious doctrine preaching the destruction of everything decent and desirable and the creation of a world-wide totalitarian tyranny. The headquarters of this criminal conspiracy was Moscow, and the Soviet system was the horrible model of the kind of regime its rulers wished to create world-wide. This popular image, expressed in newspaper editorials and scholarly writings, as well as in the pronouncements of Presidents and Secretaries of State, was based on ignorance of Marxism, on gross over-estimation of Soviet strengths, resources, and capabilities, and on paranoid concern with the brittleness and vulnerability of American institutions.

The result of this was a mood that can only be characterized as national hysteria. It expressed itself in the commonly held attitude that anyone studying the Soviet Union or Marxism was suspect. "Do you want to live in Russia?" I was asked by a student in Cambridge, Massachusetts, who had heard me lecture on the topic in 1947. "If not, why do you talk so much about it?" Well into the 1960s, students in my courses on Soviet politics or Marxist theory would tell me that their parents did not—and should not—know that they were studying communism. Nor can I forgo re-telling my encounter with an MIT graduate student who, on learning that I was writing a dissertation on Lenin, looked at me coldly and said, "Well, I guess I disagree with you 100%." That was in 1948 or 1949.

Much has been written about McCarthyism, but the roots of its popularity and success remain largely unexplored. I would suggest that it was, among other things, the Republican Party's revenge against the New Deal and the entire progressive tradition, which were now declared to be un-American. Every aim to criticize American institutions and practices, any attempt to bring about humane or democratic reforms, was labeled subversive and serving the cause of communism. Since progressives, liberals, and other people left of center had at one time or another made favorable comments about Marxism, Socialism, or some aspect of Soviet life and institutions, or had collaborated with communists in the struggle for reform or the resistance to fascism, it was easy to establish guilt by association for many people who were neither Marxists, nor communists, nor loyal to the USSR. In defense against this hysteria, the American "liberal" establishment panicked and scrambled to purge its organizations of anyone ever connected with anti-fascist, socialist, Marxist, or similar causes. American liberalism thus helped do away with much of the progressive tradition—that specifically American form of democratic radicalism. From this self-castration, American politics has never recovered.

The effect of this national mood on scholarship in the field was deplorable. First, it was easy for all of us to chime in with the denunciation or critical portrayal of the many negative features of Soviet reality. They were obvious, and we stressed them dutifully and often sincerely. But it was difficult to mention, much less praise, positive features which were also present, but easily overlooked. Similarly, it was difficult to make any statement, within the context of Soviet studies, that implied criticism of the United States. Clyde Kluckhohn, the Director of the Russian Research Center, was booed when he told an audience at a Harvard alumni association in 1952 or 1953 that a surveyed group of Soviet refugees had expressed disappointment about life in the United States about which they had given much more positive responses when surveyed in Germany before coming here.

Reactions of this kind from presumably well-informed people made scholars in the field practice self-censorship. We became cautious in our judgments or simply repressed sympathetic urges. Now, caution is a desirable attribute in a scholar. Rash statements and unsupported generalizations should properly be avoided. But in the social sciences and humanities, where there are many methods and models, different approaches and interpretations, no school of thought ought to be declared taboo, and the researcher ought to be as open as possible to conflicting critical ideas. The caution that a laboratory experimenter must exercise is profoundly different from that imposed by a vindictively censorious political climate.

Closely related to the disapproval of everything Soviet, one could sense the generally held wish that the system should fail. That wish openly expressed itself in the prevailing custom, in the 1940s and 1950s, to call those prognoses which predicted economic failure or political instability in the Soviet Union "optimistic," while those that predicted stability and economic successes were called "pessimistic."

To be sure, there were those, like myself, who deplored the cold-war climate and its effect and believed that the generally accepted totalitarian image of the Soviet Union was a caricature of reality. From early on, I called myself an anti-anti-communist. People of this orientation were subject to self-deceptional thinking of their own. For instance, those of us who sought to present a more balanced view of the USSR instinctively distrusted much of the information offered by former communist activists or former Soviet officials. Today we know that much of their material was true. In this fashion, those like myself who opposed knee-jerk anti-communism may have succumbed to some knee-jerk reactions of their own.

Kindly note the sources of Kluckhohn's information about the opinions of former Soviet citizens: it came from the Harvard interview project sponsored by the US Air Force as "target research." That pioneer project was the first major challenge to the generally accepted perception of the Soviet Union. Many of its findings were in conflict with the images conveyed by the totalitarian model. In their survey work, the members of the Harvard team discovered informal behavior and informal organizations underneath the totalitarian facade, a second economy, beginnings of a civil society, social stratification, including the persistence of pre-revolutionary status advantages, role conflicts, and ethical notions opposed to Party doctrine. In short, the findings of the Harvard project were a major challenge to the prevalent American ideology about the nature of the Soviet Union; and on the basis of subsequent research work sponsored by the US military establishment and the CIA, I would be inclined to generalize that while the political climate fostered cold-war ideology, the military were interested in realistic appraisals of strengths and weaknesses.

In this connection, it is significant that the Air Force contract with Harvard expressly specified that in the research to be done up-to-date methods developed by sociology, anthropology, and psychology should be favored over the traditional approaches of history and political or ideological studies. Similarly, the research program administered by Margaret Mead which the US Navy had sponsored stressed the application of methods then used in anthropology and psychology.

These initiatives notwithstanding, the relationship between Soviet studies and the several social science disciplines has been uneasy and troubled. By and large, the disciplines and the leading departments representing them have been hostile to specialists in the field; have been prone to declare their work substandard methodologically, and have been reluctant to give them tenured appointments. I have heard it argued by senior political scientists that acceptable work in Soviet studies is impossible because acceptable data cannot be gathered. That judgment is based, of course, on a very narrow definition of the kind of information that students of politics may properly use. By thus excluding a vast amount of interesting information, this insistence on dealing with quantifiable data greatly impoverishes the social sciences. I have argued this at some length in my contribution to a discussion of the relationship between area studies and general political science published in 1973. Incidentally, it is interesting to watch these same methodological purists plunge headlong into Soviet and East European studies now that these societies have rid themselves of communist rule.

A variation on this theme is the argument heard occasionally that area studies in general are too subjective and too anti-disciplinary. The well-rounded student of Soviet society necessarily deals with more information than one discipline can properly digest and order; and since nobody can be expected to master the methodologies of all the several disciplines, some of the work of the Soviet specialists is bound to be found dilettantish. The broad view we should properly expect of any specialist in Soviet studies is a carryover from a humanistic tradition that most of the pace setters in our contemporary social science disciplines consider illegitimate.

Another argument advanced by some highly respected colleagues at least in my discipline, political science, is that it is politically naive and, indeed, insulting to our own society to treat the Soviet Union as if it were comparable to other societies. The Soviet Union, it is asserted, is not a state like any other states; indeed I have heard a senior political scientist argue that even to call it a state would be misleading. George Kennan, in his famous Mr. X article, suggested that it was not a society either, because he denied that under the hard crust of party dictatorship there was any social life or any social structure. A senior colleague of mine in a recent conversation with me angrily denounced Gabriel Almond and James Coleman for suggesting that their structural-functional model of the political system was universally applicable and thus also to the Soviet Union, when in fact there were no comparable institutions and processes in the USSR.

For many years Sovietologists behaved as if they were in agreement with the notion that the categories, models, and methods developed by the disciplines did not apply to the study of the USSR. This assertion of uniqueness for the Soviet system or for communist states in general was rarely if ever based on the Slavophile Romanticism expressed in Fyodor Tiutchev's little poem:

Umom Rossiyu nye ponyat;
Arshinom obshchim nye izmerit.
U ney ossobennaya stat:
V Rossiyu mozhno tolko verit.[1]

Instead, it expressed the Westerner's desire to draw as sharp a line as possible between their society and our own. Political scientists studying the USSR therefore applied models and categories to their studies which the profession would not generally use. The totalitarian model was one such model; and enough ink has been spilled in controversies over its usefulness. Another model, the applicability of which was widely accepted as self-evident, was one that I call "ideological determinism." A one-time popular book by a crusading Christian anti-communist, Rev. Frederick I. Schwartz, pithily stated the gist of this theory in its title: *You Can Trust the Communists . . .*

To Do Exactly As They Say. But, the only evidence for its validity was the claim made by a communist party ideologist that the Soviet Union was the application of principles allegedly established by Marx, Engels, and Lenin, whereas in fact the relationship between the original ideas and the political practice was expressed very nicely by Shlomo Avineri (a student of Marx at the Hebrew University of Jerusalem) a few years ago when he suggested that Marx was to Stalin as Jesus Christ was to Torquemada.

Perhaps the most pervasive method studying Soviet politics has been "kremlinology," i.e. the study of political leaders, their careers, their pronouncements, and their relations with their peers. Who would be the next General Secretary and how the current Number One had risen above his rivals were questions of abiding interest, and in the quest for answers no tidbit of information about Politburo members seemed unimportant. The work of kremlinologists seemed to me to be similar to that of eighteenth century diplomats, whose reports to their own sovereigns painstakingly listed all the rumor and gossip they had heard at their diplomatic posts about the host sovereign's sexual habits and digestive disorders. No other political system was studied in this fashion; why the Soviet Union?

One explanation is that data about the top leadership were available. Their careers were public knowledge. Their public speeches could be subjected to what is euphemistically called content analysis. At times we could obtain knowledge about their past affiliations with other prominent leaders. Second, the totalitarian model of politics suggested that top leaders were the only actors worth studying and made the system seem to be nothing else than their personal creation. At best, the Soviet system was portrayed as ruled by a mafia-like gang, a narrow power elite, self-appointed and self-perpetuating and, in some studies, driven by a delusionary world image akin to paranoia. It is something like this model that led Nathan Leites to write his highly influential analysis of the Soviet leaders' mind set; it also underlay psychoanalytic studies of Lenin and Stalin and the many currently fashionable studies of clientelism in the Soviet leadership.

Yet another method of stressing the uniqueness of the Soviet Union has been to explain its political institutions and practices by the heritage from tsarist times; and if this heritage was seen as burdensome, undemocratic, or retarding, this was yet another way of emphasizing the differences between the USSR and our own supposedly civilized world. In short, attention paid to the Russianness of the Soviet system can be based either on Romantic admiration of the Russian past or on liberal-democratic revulsion against it. In both those cases it is highly charged with political judgments and also poorly integrated with the general discipline.

Within the field, however, there were always scholars who sought to move Soviet studies out of this isolation from the disciplines and to learn from their colleagues in other fields. The motivation of these, often younger, colleagues may have been complex. One reason for their attempt to integrate their studies with the general discipline may have been the compulsion exercised by the discipline. All social science disciplines function like traditional art academies in that they set certain standards of performance by which works and their creators are judged. Whoever wants her articles and books published, whoever wishes to attain tenure in his department, had better display familiarity with the currently recognized methods and models and apply them to the study of Soviet society, if only by using the currently fashionable tool kit of terms.

But speaking the language of contemporary political science or sociology may often have had a political motivation: comparing the Soviet Union to other systems, especially Western ones, was a provocation rooted in reaction to the cold-war ideology. Any attempt to apply, say, the Almond-Coleman model of politics, a post-Weberian theory of bureaucracy, or Dahl's model of group pluralism to the Soviet Union implied that there were institutions and processes in the USSR which, in whatever fashion, corresponded to those in other countries, even if for the time being they existed in rudimentary form or were hidden from view. In short, the application to the USSR of concepts and methods used to analyze Western societies implies that the Soviet system is not outlandish or monstrous, but human, that it is run by human beings who in some fashion respond to human needs and demands.

At the same time, genuine comparison of Soviet with Western institutions or processes not only implicitly renders the Soviet phenomena more acceptable but also casts a critical light on the analogous things in the West. Comparing the obkom secretary to the French préfet may appear both as a rehabilitation of the secretary and a slander of the préfet. Analogous statements can be made about other studies in which Soviet institutions or processes are compared with Western ones.

I do not, however, mean to create the impression that in order to overcome cold-war images of the Soviet Union it ought to be analyzed in terms now current in general political science. On the contrary, I would like to point out that there is not all that much that Soviet studies can learn from our colleagues in the discipline. Political science as taught in the leading departments tends to prefer methodologies that are so firmly committed to quantification that important qualified information either is lost to our view or is distorted to fit into quantitative molds. Moreover, the overarching models of political systems are mostly abstractions—and idealized ones at that—from Western history and institutions. That diminishes their usefulness to a student of the USSR while it enhances their value for ideologists. When Soviet reality is judged by its failure to come up to Western myths about their own political systems, it is bound to be found wanting.

The best guard against that kind of politicization of Soviet studies is an approach that combines institutional or behavioral analysis with cultural empathy. I find such an approach exemplified in some of the contributions to the recent *Festschrift* for Vera S. Dunham, herself a pioneer of this method. In these contributions, the writers analyze various phenomena that in our own society would be considered dysfunctional but in the Soviet context may well be eufunctional, so that features which look like weaknesses in the social fabric may in fact lend it strength. Conversely, those who now set out to study ongoing democratization processes in the USSR and Eastern Europe would be well advised to be aware of the price these societies are likely to pay, in social dislocation, economic hardships, and political unrest, to name just a few, for the blessings of a more open system.

I have said nothing about Marxist and neo-Marxist schools of Soviet studies that have always existed, though primarily outside or on the fringes of our academic institutions. They are by definition charged with political points of view; but in their appraisal of the Soviet system they have diverged as widely as non-Marxist schools. And surely I need not remind anyone that developments in the last several years have opened floodgates of scholarly self-analysis in the Soviet Union which have brought forth a broad spectrum of theories to diagnose the roots of the current crisis and to define methods for its resolution. Here the close links between method of analysis and the writer's political agenda usually are quite obvious.

I began this paper by asking why scholarship on Soviet politics and society had such a poor record of forecasting the most recent developments. From what I have said so far, in somewhat rambling fashion, one might conclude that I blame this seeming failure on the intrusion of political ideologies into our research: cold-war hysteria, knee-jerk anti-anti-communism, and the blindness of dominant social science methodologies to non-Western cultures.

Let me point out, however, that the batting average for prognoses by our colleagues in other areas is not any better. What has happened during the last 20 years in the Philippines, in Iran, or in Chile, in Spain and Portugal has equally caught the specialists by surprise. So has the rapidity of the decolonization process since the end of World War II, the effects of *perestroika* in Africa, the rapid decline of the United States as a world power, or the Ronald Reagan phenomenon.

The fact is that the study of society and politics is not a science in the strict sense of the word but is at least to some degree an art. Now art works, too, may be infused with political or social biases and nonetheless be considered great. At the same time, art that seeks to be pure, unpolitical play with abstract forms may by that same token run the risk of becoming arid and empty. But in the final analysis socially engaged art and pure formalism are likely to influence and enrich each other as long as the practitioners in the many genres are open to the work done by their colleagues.

From this my own position seems obvious: since all social studies are conducted within a political context, they are likely to express the student's political attitude. Politics and methodology inevitably are intertwined. Whatever the negative effects of that relationship, they can be mitigated by uncovering the political implications of any methodology, both in those with whom we disagree and also in our own work. Beyond that, my musings suggest that we should welcome and encourage methodological pluralism. In social science as in other genres of art, the rule of any academy promotes stuffiness and stagnation. These pursuits flourish when there is a profusion of styles. Let a hundred flowers bloom . . .

NOTE

1. One cannot understand Russia cerebrally:/Nor measure her with a common yardstick./She stands out all alone:/In Russia one can only believe.

BIBLIOGRAPHY

Gordon S. Wood, "Americans and Revolutionaries," in *New York Review of Books,* Vol. XXX, No. 14, p. 33.

Charles O'Connell, *Cold War Social Science: Soviet Studies at Harvard* (University of California Press, forthcoming).

Alfred G. Meyer in Lucian Pye, ed., *Political Science and Area Studies: Rivals or Partners?* (Indiana University Press, 1975).

Nathan Leites, *A Study of Bolshevism* (1953).

8

THE HARVARD PROJECT
AND THE SOVIET
INTERVIEW PROJECT

American scholarship on the USSR expanded rapidly after World War II. The critical obstacle to research at the time was the paucity of data, particularly reliable data, on Soviet society. The publication of a national statistical abstract had been discontinued in the mid-thirties, and the last full population census dated back to 1926. Few foreigners were admitted to the country for purposes of observation, study, or research. Under those circumstances the several million former Soviet citizens living in the West were an invaluable source of information about the society that they had left during the turbulence of the war. They provided the raw data gathered by the Harvard Refugee Interview Project, which produced a set of publications that greatly enriched Western understanding of Soviet society in those years.

The volume of data available on Soviet society today is vastly greater than in those lean years. In 1956 the publication of an annual statistical abstract resumed, and three decennial population censuses have been published since then. Hundreds of foreign students and scholars have lived and worked in Soviet universities, institutes, libraries, and archives under various cultural and scientific exchange programs. Journalists and businessmen have established relationships that have enabled them to penetrate fairly intimately into parts of the society. A large volume of social and economic research by Soviet scholars on Soviet society is available in the West, as are the unofficial research and data published as *samizdat.*

Then, with detente, came a new large wave of emigration from the USSR during the 1970s. In the light of the greatly expanded volume of data available on the USSR, the question for the scholarly community was whether a large-scale survey research project on the new emigrants was worth the effort and expense. After a period of extensive discussion in government and academic circles, the answer was clear. Although the volume of Soviet data and other information is far greater than in the dark postwar years, it is still very much less than that which is available on most Western societies. It also contains large gaps on matters that Western scholars regard as interesting aspects of societies in general and of the USSR in particular. It was that view that led to the organization of the Soviet Interview Project (SIP).

The differences between the Harvard Project and SIP reflect the remarkable change in the state of Soviet studies in the quarter-century between them. In the young field of the late 1940s, for example, there were very few professors and many graduate students; in the mature field of today there are many professors and relatively fewer graduate students. Consequently, a great deal of the work of the Harvard Project was conducted by graduate students gathering material for dissertations, under the direction of a few senior scholars. Virtually all the work of SIP, by contrast, was conducted by experienced scholars, many with substantial records of published research. The difference mirrors the change in the state of the Soviet studies, from one in which the incremental contribution of Ph.D. dissertations was substantial to one in which it is now relatively modest.

The two projects also span the period that Soviet writers used to call the scientific-technical revolution. The Harvard Project prided itself in using state-of-the-art data-processing technology, which consisted of a shiny new IBM card sorter housed in an office called the "shop." Chi-squares and correlation coefficients were produced by fast new Monroe calculators with what seemed like machine-gun speed. A quarter-century later, survey research data collection and management had become so technical a business that SIP decided to employ the services of a specialized research service organization: the National Opinion Research Center (NORC). The new computer technology made it possible for SIP analysts, like contemporary quantitative analysts generally, to employ methods that were infeasible in the past. Multivariate regression techniques, for example, were far beyond the capacity of even the fastest Monroe calculators of that time.

Survey research itself was a young discipline in the postwar years, and the Harvard Project was at the cutting edge of the art, through both its own personnel and the consultants upon whom it drew for counsel and criticism. That edge has done a lot of cutting in the intervening years, however, and is far less accessible to the nonspecialist than in the past. The training of the graduate student interviewers (it was my good fortune to be one of them) occupied a considerable number of sessions and produced interviewers who regarded themselves as quite sophisticated in the art. That training time, however, was but a fraction of that which NORC requires today to produce interviewers competent in the art as it has developed to this time.

One major difference involves not the passage of time but the logistics of interviewing. Most of the postwar emigrants had been living for some time in temporary "displaced persons camps" in Germany and neighboring countries. They were easy to locate, and they had a surfeit of time on their hands. The opportunity to tell the story of their lives to a sympathetic outsider was a welcome diversion. In contrast, the SIP respondents were scattered all over the United States. Most of them were living active lives and holding full-time jobs, and did not regard it as a great privilege to give up a couple of nights for the sake of science. Consequently, the time and cost of locating respondents and persuading them to be interviewed were much greater. The Harvard interviewers were able to spend two to three days with each respondent, whereas the SIP interviews consisted on average of one three-hour session. SIP, however, conducted personal interviews with a much larger number of respondents.

In one dominating respect, however, the two projects are quite similar, despite the passage of time. Both had to confront the crucial question of whether reliable knowledge about Soviet society can be obtained from the testimony of people who must be regarded as hostile to the political system.

The Harvard Project had a somewhat easier task. Many of its respondents had not left the USSR voluntarily because of disaffection with the system; some had been prisoners of war, and some had been seized by the German authorities in occupied Soviet territory and shipped to Germany or Austria as involuntary laborers. Almost all the SIP respondents, however, had left voluntarily, and some had faced harsh sanctions for having announced their wish to emigrate. Second, the Harvard Project respondents were almost all Slavic, mostly Great Russian by nationality. The SIP respondents, in contrast, come predominantly from the Jewish nationality, which is a small minority in the USSR that suffers from discrimination. Fortunately, there is a sufficient number of respondents of other nationalities to provide a basis for assessing the extent to which the responses and experiences of the Jewish respondents may differ from those of other nationalities.

Both projects devoted a massive effort to the detection of bias of various sorts in the testimony of the respondents. The wide acceptance of the findings of the Harvard Project signified that the scholarly community by and large was persuaded that their testimony, as analyzed by researchers sensitized to the problem of bias, did provide an acceptable basis for drawing inferences about the parent Soviet society. SIP had available the accumulated experience of several additional decades of survey research in dealing with bias. The Harvard Project, for example, devoted considerable attention to the precision of the translation of its interview questions from English into Russian, but it did not have available the "double-blind translation" method employed by SIP. With the care and ingenuity with which the SIP researchers dealt with the bias problem, they have good reason to expect that their data will be regarded as a reasonable basis for the inferences they have presented about Soviet society.

Perhaps more important than the inferences that are drawn about Soviet society are the inferences that are deliberately not drawn. The proportion of respondents who accept regime norms, for example, provides no basis for an estimate of the proportion of the parent Soviet population that accepts regime norms. However, the finding that older people in the sample are more likely than younger people to accept regime norms, other things equal, does support the inference that a similar relation between age and acceptance of regime norms is to be found in the Soviet population. That is an important finding about Soviet society, although it tells us far less than could be learned if it were possible to survey the Soviet population itself.

The findings in any research project reflect the questions that the analysts seek to answer. Those questions emerge from the state of knowledge and the research agenda at the time. In the postwar years Western views were heavily influenced by Soviet claims about the nature of their own society. Those claims were challenged by critics abroad, but the research base for assessing the controversies was very small, because of both the paucity of reliable data and the small number of researchers with the requisite language and analytic skills. The Harvard Project provided a unique opportunity to develop a body of data for illuminating that debate.

A central question at the time was the extent to which the abolition of private ownership of the means of production had eliminated the basis of the division of society into social classes, as Marx predicted and as the Soviets claimed. Was it in fact a society of a new kind, unlike those with which we are familiar, in which social class is the predominant predictor of life chances, lifestyle, attitudes, and so forth? A major thrust of the project was the exploration of that issue, and the conclusion was strikingly clear. On question after question the variable that best explained the distribution of responses was social class—not nationality, not age or sex, but social class. In most respects Soviet society reflected the characteristics of a class society of the Western industrial kind. That conclusion is perhaps the principal contribution of the Harvard Project to the advance of knowledge at the time.

It is therefore worthy of note that social class does not emerge in the SIP volume as a major analytic variable. The largest differences among groups in the SIP sample are those between the younger and the older. Education, occupation, income, sex, and nationality distinctions also show up, but it is age differences that dominate the social fabric.

Like the dog that didn't bark, the variable that does not appear may provide the clue to an interesting difference in the state of knowledge at that time and now. Several conjectures may be offered. First, the Harvard Project contributed decisively to the advancement of knowledge by settling the question that occupied center stage at the time; the class nature of Soviet society became the conventional wisdom, and the question disappeared from the agenda of subsequent research. It is simply no longer an interesting question. Second, the subject of social class, which occupied so central a role in general sociological theory and research a few decades ago, is perhaps no longer at the core of disciplinary interest. Third, contemporary data-processing power may have diminished the usefulness for social research of so aggregative a concept as social class. Traditional measures of social class like socioeconomic status scales consisted of a set of scores on such underlying variables as education, income, occupation, and so forth. It is now so easy and inexpensive to investigate the separate effects of those variables that little is gained by the use of the composite measure (I am indebted to Paul Gregory for this interpretation). It is a mark of the passage of time and of the advance of knowledge that a curiosity about the influence of social class on Soviet society reveals not one's knowledge but one's age.

The Harvard Project researchers enjoyed some of the advantages and excitement of pioneering; one did not have to be particularly ingenious to discover or explore a new terrain at that time. The age of pioneering, however, has long been over. As in all developed fields of endeavor, genuinely new contributions are rare, and it takes greater talent and training to find an important new property of a society that so many earlier researchers had overlooked. Therefore, one should not expect to find startling new insights into Soviet society that had somehow escaped the microscopes of several generations of dissertation and monographic research. One should expect rather to find those kinds of insights that could not be obtained or verified by any methods other than the surveying of substantial numbers of people who have been members of the society. The Harvard Project and SIP are the only two bodies of data in the world (excluding the USSR, though possibly including it as well) to have produced the kind of data that could support those insights.

The finding that will perhaps attract the greatest attention, as reported by James R. Millar in the next chapter, is the remarkable reversal in the relation between age and support for the regime that occurred between 1940 and 1980 (the years on which the two projects focused attention). In the earlier period it was the younger who were most supportive and the older who were most hostile. In 1980 it was the other way around. Another striking finding is the extent to which education level has come to dominate the factors determining social position and attitudes. In question after question, education level emerges as the variable that explains the largest proportion of the variation in responses. Education, of course, was a major component of the social class variable that occupied a similar dominant role in the Harvard Project study, so that there may not have been so great a change in this respect. However, the gradual attenuation of the significance of such characteristics as one's social origin, which played an important role before the war, may well have elevated education to the dominating position that the SIP study finds it to occupy today.

The political significance of this finding is that education, like age, bears a strong negative relation to support for the regime. As Brian Silver's analysis reveals, however, given the level of education, support for the regime *increases* with income level. Coming at a time when a new leader has undertaken to transform Soviet society, these and other SIP findings will provide a valuable basis for the assessment of the prospects for that program of reform.

What counts as a contribution to knowledge is to a great degree a matter of taste. For scholars of a more intuitive disposition, many of the findings will be regarded as not interesting because they are not new. The intuitionist needs no survey research project to inform him that Soviet youth are hostile to the regime; any reader of Soviet novels, or even *Pravda,* knows that is true, as does anyone who has lived in the society. Well, says the survey researcher, maybe it is, and maybe it isn't. And if it is, is it as true of female youth as of male youth? And is it as true of highly educated male youth as of less educated? And among the more highly educated male youth, is it more true of those who earn higher income than of those who earn less? The intuitionist may find something of interest in questions like these, but he may be more interested in the second set of SIP studies, which are based on in-depth interviews with emigrants with particular experiences, such as factory management or the law. The results of those studies will begin to appear shortly.

Twenty-five years elapsed between the first emigrant interview project and the second. Will there be a third, sometime in the next millennium? If Secretary General Gorbachev's policy of *glasnost',* of openness, plays itself out, there may never be a third. If the time comes when Soviet scholars are free to design their own research projects, there is no doubt that they would undertake to look into the social structure of their own society as scholars around the world look into their own. If that research were published, there would be no need for foreign scholars to do that work, much less with such unrepresentative respondents as emigrants. Extracting valid results from a biased sample is an intriguing exercise, but no one would mourn if it never needed to be done again.

9

HISTORY, METHOD, AND THE PROBLEM OF BIAS

At the most general level the Soviet Interview Project (SIP) General Survey raises a perennial issue in Soviet studies: Is the Soviet socialist system fundamentally different from the industrial and postindustrial societies of the West? Does it represent a different genus of social, political, and economic system? Or is it instead merely a different species of the Western systems that we know much more about because they are more open societies? This issue has troubled Western social science from the origins of Soviet studies. At stake is whether standard tools of analysis of the various social science disciplines are appropriate for study of Soviet society. If not, new and quite different methods would have to be applied in its analysis.

SYSTEMIC SIMILARITIES AND DIFFERENCES

The SIP General Survey protocol was designed on the hypothesis that the Soviet social system *is* amenable to analysis with standard Western disciplinary tools. The assumption is that the obstacle to standard disciplinary analysis has been the absence of data, not the intractability of the system to standard types of analyses. The SIP General Survey constitutes, therefore, a test of this hypothesis. Nonsense results, or routinely extreme values for the variables, would constitute falsification, other things equal. The SIP essays demonstrate unequivocally that Soviet society differs in quite specific ways from other societies but that the differences are in degree rather than in kind. This is, perhaps, our most fundamental finding.

Max Weber's explanation of class, or social stratification, as a function of wealth, power, and prestige, for example, seems to offer a better explanation of actual prestige rankings in the Soviet Union than does Karl Marx's analysis, which viewed social class as derived from relationship to the means of production. What is more, despite heavy advertising for the dignity of manual labor and championing of the blue-collar worker, members of the working class do not fare better in prestige ranking than in the West. Status is conferred instead on the basis of attainments such as occupational level, party membership, and education, with the highest status ascribed to lawyers, doctors, writers, professors, engineers, and army officers, in that order.

Similarly, the distribution of income and wealth in the Soviet socialist system may be more equal than in most Western mixed economies, but the difference is not radical. It appears more as a moderate outlier than as an observation associated with a different distribution. The distribution fluctuates also, as it does elsewhere, according to social policy. Poverty is still widespread, and the data indicate a trend toward the feminization of poverty in the USSR, much as has been noted in the United States and in other mixed economies.

Members of the research team are frequently asked what our most surprising findings are. There have been some surprising findings, such as the relatively high degree of satisfaction with housing that two-thirds of our respondents reported for their last period of normal life in the USSR, or the differential impact of unconventional behavior on white- and blue-collar workers. In general, however, our aggregate findings confirm theories or predictions that some scholar somewhere in the West or East has offered at some time. This is not unexpected given the intensity with which Soviet society has been studied in the West over the last three decades. As Joseph Berliner put it at a conference at Airlie House, reviewing SIP first findings, if there were to be major "surprises" in SIP's findings, Soviet specialists in this country "ought to be fired." Confirmation of results or discrimination among hypotheses put forward by other methods and using other sources is no mean feat even if it were the only result of SIP.

Fortunately, it is not. Perhaps the single most significant "surprising" finding at the macro level that emerges from the General Survey is what appears to be a transformation in the structure of support for the Soviet regime since the Harvard Project. Harvard interviewers found the young and well educated to be the most supportive, relatively, of the Soviet system. The older and less well educated were by far the more critical. Those who had benefited the most from the Bolshevik Revolution were, therefore, the least alienated of the refugees interviewed (Inkeles and Bauer, 1959). The SIP General Survey has yielded exactly the opposite result, for the younger, more educated members of the sample are the most alienated from some of the fundamental characteristics of the system. They are much less likely to have been satisfied with the quality of their lives, and they are more likely to have been critical of the system's economic performance. This was true despite the fact that, by their own admission, the younger and better educated were disproportionately reaping the material benefits of Soviet socialist society in the 1970s.

Where SIP findings are most generally surprising, however, is along dimensions about which we have had little or no information, as, for example, at the micro level of Soviet society. It has been essentially impossible to analyze the impact of gender, generation, education, income, class, unconventional behavior, size of city, and so forth, upon behavior and attitudes in Soviet society because of the absence of sufficient well-defined data in adequate detail. As one reviews the SIP essays, several factors stand out as crucial for an understanding of the structure and dynamics of contemporary Soviet society. Most significant at this stage appear to be generation, educational attainment, material incentives, and political conventionality.

THE GENERATIONAL FACTOR

SIP findings indicate clearly that there are significant elements of regime support among the older generation, among blue-collar workers, and among the less educated. The strength and direction of generational differences may be the single most significant finding to date. Generational differences surface in almost all analyses, and the differences being found are true generational differences and not merely life-cycle effects. The older generation is unforgiving of Stalinism and correspondingly more forgiving of contemporary problems. Thus, the older generation regards Stalin's era as the "worst" and Khrushchev's as the best, with the Brezhnev period somewhere in between. The young agree that Khrushchev's era was the best, but they regard Brezhnev's as the worst. They are completely unimpressed, it would appear, with the economic progress that has been achieved since Stalin and impatient with the economic slowdown of the late 1970s. The generational factor offers, then, a challenge for Soviet leadership and one that is likely to increase over time.

The General Survey reveals relatively high rates of criticism among the young at all educational levels. Significantly, as their educational attainment increases, the young tend to become more critical and more inclined toward unconventional activities. The pattern that emerges is that the young, much more so than those who are older, judge the regime on the basis of its current performance. They are generally more critical and less inclined to accept present conditions just because they are an improvement over the past.

The older generation, which experienced one or more of the many traumatic events in Soviet history, is apparently more philosophical about current failings of the Soviet economy. After all, taken as a whole, the years since Stalin have been peaceful and relatively prosperous also. The young and successful are clearly less philosophical about the recent stagnation of the economy. They may also be victims of the rewriting of Soviet history. Having never experienced Stalinism, and having been taught only a sanitized version of the Stalin era, the realities of Stalinism carry much less weight with them than with the older members of Soviet society. Thus it is that if there are neo-Stalinists today they are among the young.

THE EDUCATIONAL FACTOR

Perhaps as important as the generational factor is the educational factor. The General Survey reveals an unambiguous and negative relationship between the level of educational attainment and the level of support for various political and economic institutions of the Soviet system, other things equal. The level of support for state control and management of major sectors of the system declines with each increase in the level of education attained, and this is true even for attainments in primary and secondary school. The same pattern is evident in responses to questions that juxtapose individual rights and the power of the state, such as the provision of civil liberties. As education increases, support for state power relative to individual rights decreases.

This is not to suggest that material rewards do not matter, for they do. Other things equal, support for regime values and for the institutional structure of the Soviet social system increases with increases in material rewards. The problem, however, is that material benefits do not keep pace. As the young are also, relatively speaking, the best educated, generational and education effects reinforce one another. Hence the significance of providing adequate material rewards for education and hard work. Hence also the importance of getting the Soviet economy moving again. This conclusion is underscored by the fact that workers on the shop floor indict the system of material incentives as explanation for the poor productivity performance of Soviet industry. Widespread "time theft" from employment supports this conclusion also.

THE PARTICIPATION FACTOR

It is equally significant to note that the fact that SIP respondents endorsed strongly some key features of the Soviet system while sharply criticizing others enhances confidence in their candor and in the reliability of the survey's findings generally. Even those who were extremely hostile to the regime (to judge from their responses to other questions on the survey) did not reject everything about the system. Those who believed, for example, that the United States can learn nothing from the USSR still strongly favored, for example, state-provided medical care (48 percent), and nearly three out of ten reported that they favored state ownership of heavy industry.

Ironically, the young, successful generation reported itself as the most highly "mobilized" of any generation ever in the formal sense of the word. They reported belonging to the correct social and political organizations, and they participated at higher rates than did less successful and less well-educated members of their cohort. Yet this same group of "the best and the brightest" also was the most likely to be involved in "unconventional" behavior—refusing to vote, listening to BBC and other foreign broadcasts, reading and distributing *samizdat*, reading foreign fiction and nonfiction, and participating in other unsanctioned activities.

There is also evidence to suggest that a gradual "privatization" of personal life has been taking place since Stalin. The use of *blat* (connections and influence) to avoid undesirable activities such as military service or to obtain advantageous choices, such as a good job, has increased steadily and significantly over time. A long-term trend toward privatization is evident, which shows up not only in the evasion of mobilization efforts by state agencies but also in the economic realm. The study reaffirms the pervasiveness of illegal as well as legal private economic activity.

The early findings of the Soviet Interview Project suggest a strategy that the Soviet leadership might develop to regenerate and strengthen popular support. Because support is weakest among the best educated and the young, it follows that educational opportunity could be maintained to constrain educational attainment more closely to employment possibilities. Greater effort would need to be made to validate the differentiation of incomes; that is, goods and services would have to be made available to those who have worked hardest to earn higher incomes. And the young would have to be cultivated especially intensively—partly by linking the current regime to the progressive aspects of the Khrushchev period. This would have to be done, of course, without calling up memories of Khrushchev's often boorish public behavior. Pressures for economic progress, for access to Western culture, for "private," quiet lives, and, thus, for reform are therefore likely to grow as the "best and brightest" of the young generation replace generations with indelible memories of Stalin and his time.

FUTURE RESEARCH

The Soviet Interview Project has recently launched three additional projects. One involves recoding available materials from the Harvard Project. A second involves systematic interviews with a probability sample of Soviet emigrants who have arrived in the United States since the first General Survey was conducted, that is, since May 1982. The purpose of the second General Survey is to investigate change over time in contemporary Soviet society. The second survey will also permit the clarification and amplification of certain findings of the first. The second survey is shorter, and the questionnaire is not partitioned. With few exceptions, questions are stated exactly as they were in the first survey.

The third survey being fielded is devoted to an investigation of the Soviet military and focuses upon the "human face" of the Soviet military system and upon a comparison of civilian and military sectors of the Soviet social system. The instrument is being administered to a probability sample drawn from the sample frame from which the first General Survey was drawn.

Additional publications on the SIP General Survey I and reports on these new initiatives will appear in the future, and the data and associated materials will be placed in the public domain for the benefit of all scholars in the field. In planning the Soviet Interview Project, we discovered to our great disappointment that the Harvard Project data cards had been lost.[1] We decided that every effort should be made to insure that SIP materials are properly archived for the benefit of current and future scholars. We have even made an effort to recover what we could from the Harvard Project. All of these materials will be carefully archived both at the University of Illinois at Urbana-Champaign and, where appropriate, with the Inter-university Consortium for Political and Social Research.

NOTE

1. For a description of what materials remain of the Harvard Project, see Balzer, 1980.

REFERENCES

Anderson, Barbara A., and Brian D. Silver. 1986a. "The Validity of Survey Responses: Insights from Interviews of Multiple Respondents in a Household in a Survey of Soviet Emigrants." Soviet Interview Project Working Paper No. 14, University of Illinois at Urbana-Champaign.
_____.1986b. "Descriptive Statistics for the Sampling Frame Population: The Eligible Population for the Soviet Interview Project General Survey." Soviet Interview Project Working Paper No. 2, University of Illinois at Urbana-Champaign.
Bahry, Donna. 1985. Oral presentation. Soviet Interview Project Report to Sponsors, Airlie House, Airlie, VA, October 27.
Balzer, Marjorie. 1980. "Guide to Materials for the Project on the Soviet Social System (Harvard Project/Soviet Refugee Interview and Questionnaire Data, 1950–1953)." Soviet Interview Project Working Paper No. 1, University of Illinois at Urbana-Champaign.
Edwards, W. Sherman. 1983. "Interviewer Training for the Soviet Interview Project General Survey." Soviet Interview Project Working Paper No. 3, University of Illinois at Urbana-Champaign.
Gregory, Paul R., and Janet Kohlhase. 1986. "The Earnings of Soviet Workers: Human Capital, Loyalty, and Privilege." Soviet Interview Project Working Paper No. 13, University of Illinois at Urbana-Champaign.

Inkeles, Alex, and Raymond A. Bauer. 1959. *The Soviet Citizen* (Cambridge, MA: Harvard University Press).

Millar, James R. 1985. "The Impact of Trade Interruption and Trade Denial on the US Economy." In Bruce Parrott (ed.), *Trade, Technology, and Soviet-American Relations* (Bloomington: Indiana University Press), pp. 324–50.

Ofer, Gur, Aaron Vinokur, and Yechiel Bar-Chaim. 1979. "Family Budget Survey of Soviet Emigrants in the Soviet Union." Rand Paper P-6015 (Santa Monica, CA: Rand Corporation).

The Soviet Interview Project General Survey Codebook. 1986. University of Illinois at Urbana-Champaign.

ROBERT T. HUBER
SUSAN BRONSON

10

THE AUGUST REVOLUTION
AND SOVIET STUDIES

The failed coup d'état in the Soviet Union on August 19, 1991 accelerated and brought into even sharper focus the immense social, economic, and political issues facing Soviet society. The August Revolution also provided the American scholarly community one more jolting reminder of the need to reassess its own ways of conducting research on the Soviet Union[1] and the means for organizing that research.

Long before the events of this past August, it was increasingly clear that revolutionary changes in the Soviet Union required a perestroika of Soviet studies. Recognizing this need, in March 1990, the presidents of the Social Science Research Council and the American Council of Learned Societies, through their Joint Advisory Committee on International Programs (JACIP) and the Joint Committee on Soviet Studies (JCSS), recommended that a panel be commissioned to "clarify the future challenges and opportunities for the Joint Committee on Soviet Studies, and the Councils more generally, in the field of Soviet studies over the next five to 10 years."[2]

The request from the Councils' presidents also stressed that the JACIP panel provide "as clear a sense as possible of the infrastructural or institutional arrangements that will foster research on the Soviet Union, maximize interaction with scholars in that country, and with those elsewhere in the world who study the Soviet Union."[3] The panel was constituted in the spring of 1990 and was headed by Blair A. Ruble, director of the Woodrow Wilson Center's Kennan Institute for Advanced Russian Studies.[4] After a long period of consultations with a large number of scholars in the field as well as with the members of the JCSS, the panel released its results in September 1990.

NEW CHALLENGES AND RESEARCH AGENDAS

The JACIP panel stressed that political and economic changes in the Soviet Union since 1985 were transforming the conduct of scholarly

191

research on the Soviet Union. The study of Soviet society, politics, and economics could now fruitfully incorporate public opinion polling, survey research, and new access to historical and political archives. These opportunities have suggested new ways for scholars to use the Soviet experience as a means for illuminating and contributing to our understanding of core issues in the social sciences and the humanities. In turn, more scholars in the field have begun to put their work in a comparative context, much like research communities that study other complex regions of the world.

As a result of new research opportunities and the evolution of the perestroika era in the Soviet Union itself, the JACIP panel identified eight areas of study for further development by the JCSS and other research organizations in the Soviet studies field. These include:

Reconceptualizing paths to modernity. The collapse of the Communist Party has placed greater emphasis on the need to revise and transcend a rigid periodization of Russian and Soviet history that placed preeminent emphasis on 1917 as defining the Russia of the past and the Soviet Union of the present. In particular, historiography of the pre-Soviet period must move away from studies of the Russian revolutionary movement and the emphasis on the imperial period as part of the "march to the Revolution." This sort of teleology has shaped both imperial Russian history and the history of the Soviet period.

As the Bolshevik revolution loses significance as a paradigmatic event and as the center around which the history of Imperial Russia and the Soviet Union has been written, historians are faced with the challenge of finding new ways of understanding the history of the Russian empire. A fundamental effort at reconceptualization is in order as the very concepts and categories used as tools of analysis in historiography are now inevitably called into question.

The struggle over the past. The future direction of political and economic reform is often debated with an eye toward interpretations of Soviet history since 1917. As Soviets seek to understand the past in an effort to reclaim their history, and attempt to find models upon which to construct a future order, the danger of new myths arising as replacements for the old is ever present. The potential for abuses of history, albeit from another perspective, remains great.

Collaborative arrangements for access to party and internal security archives may prove valuable in helping to clarify and inform the complicated struggle over versions of history. The integration of Soviet scholars into the world academic community is also of enormous importance.

Thinking about civil society. The struggle over the formation of political institutions was a key element in creating alternative sources of power that ultimately proved critical to the success of the August Revolution. Nonetheless, the processes of legitimation are critical to understanding (1) the struggle for sovereignty in the former Soviet republics, (2) the authority of a bewildering array of municipalities to exert control over economic decision making, and (3) the nature of party formation, legislative activity, and executive-legislative directions. Rigorous studies of these factors are only now developing. Scholars should aggressively pursue opportunities to study indices of institutionalization in a comparative context as well as the sociological and normative political foundations of institutionalization.

Bringing culture(s) back in. The significance of culture could hardly be better studied than in the laboratory of the Soviet Union. Until recently, outside the field of anthropology, culture has largely been treated as a residual category, to be considered when the explanatory value of other variables has been exhausted. New research in sociology and anthropology which stresses the role of cultural variables must be further expanded and encouraged as both local and transnational contacts, allegiances, and sources of identity are rediscovered and reasserted. In addition, other disciplines in the social sciences must learn to incorporate culture into their understanding and interpretations of society.

New challenges for humanistic research. The devolution of authority toward the republics and away from central government has demonstrated the need for in-depth study of the roles played by theater, literature, art, music, religion, and other forms of human expression in fostering alternative identities that have endured, and even thrived, within the framework of a common and highly centralized political, economic, and ideological system. The meanings and significance of popular culture and its relationship to high culture both in the pre- and post-revolutionary periods are also critical areas of study. Of particular importance are non-Russian literatures, music, art, theatre, and cinema both on elite and mass levels. Finally, the relatively sudden freedom from censorship in the cultural world, accompanied by a corresponding loss of official place and state support for cultural enterprises, will have important consequences and pose new challenges for scholars in the years ahead.

Decolonization, regionalism, nationalism, and inter-ethnic relations. As foci of analysis and graduate training shift away from a Moscow- or Russo-centric approach, the range of issues for scholarly consideration is immense. The phenomena of ethnic identity formation and political reform must be disaggregated in the non-Russian republics due to differing historical experiences, social composition of ethnic groups, population and migration patterns, and variegated policies of center-periphery cooperation and coercion. Studies of these processes must also be undertaken with a focus on differing levels of institutional development in the various regions of the Soviet Union, the turmoil that is likely to arise not only between Russians and non-Russians but among different non-Russian ethnic groups, and the prospect that the disassembling and reassembling of political forms may take many years to resolve and stabilize. The international relations and trade policies of the newly emerging states and their capacity for carrying on such policies also need scholarly attention.

Transition to a market economy. The scientific challenge of developing modeling techniques for the transition from a command to a market economy is considerable. Theoretical development in this area may well be advanced by a rigorous consideration of both classical liberal and neo-Marxist approaches, particularly given the legacy of support for both individual liberty and welfare state measures that confronts policy makers as they deal with the collapse of state socialism. Research on issues such as monetary overhang, capital formation and credit reform, and the regulation of markets will benefit from comparative research not only in economics, but political science as well.

New thinking in foreign policy. The remarkable changes in the practical direction of Soviet foreign policy since 1985 have shattered ideologically based conceptions of its "permanently operating characteristics." These changes place new demands on the study of Soviet foreign policy. Those conducting research and training on Soviet foreign policy now need to be brought in contact with broader theoretical developments in the study of foreign policy. Studies of new foreign policy institutions, the role of ideas and beliefs in policy change, and the increasing intertwining of foreign policy objectives with domestic realities and imperatives will demonstrably add to our understanding of the operation of Soviet foreign policy as well as to our comparative understanding of the foreign policy effects of economic and political liberalization.

RECENT JCSS INITIATIVES IN TRAINING, FELLOWSHIPS, AND RESEARCH

In addition to a number of ongoing research and training programs, several new JCSS initiatives are designed to begin reconceptualizing the field. The medieval Russian history workshop has stressed interdisciplinary analysis of early Russian society and promotes new analytical and comparative methods. The goal of the workshop is to promote innovation by challenging existing paradigms, with particular attention to research incorporating issues of gender, economy, intellectual life, and significance of non-Russian interactions with Muscovite society, and the integration of theoretical perspectives from anthropology, sociology, semiotics, literary theory, and social history.

The project on "Reconstructing the History of Imperial Russia" was initiated to stimulate new research and new theoretical approaches in the study of the period. This project will bring together a small working group of senior scholars to explore new conceptualizations and set an agenda for future conferences and workshops. The history of the imperial period assumes new political significance today as Soviets look to the past in order to understand the present and seek models for the future.

The new workshop in sociology and anthropology was modeled after successful workshops in Soviet domestic politics, Soviet and East European economics, and Soviet popular culture and literature. The workshops are designed to counteract the isolation felt by young scholars in these disciplines and to enhance scholarly communication and mentoring between senior and junior scholars. Participants in the sociology/anthropology workshops are conducting important research on a wide range of topics including ethnic identity and social movements in non-Russian republics, the response of the Russian diaspora to nationalist resurgence in non-Russian areas, and levels and trends in infant mortality in various republics.

A new fellowship program has also been created to complement the three long-standing multidisciplinary fellowship competitions for graduate training, dissertation write-up, and postdoctoral research. The first-year fellowship program, targeted at the disciplines of sociology and anthropology, enables universities to apply for institutional grants to fund incoming first-year graduate students with undergraduate Soviet area studies backgrounds. These fellowships are designed to build a cadre of scholars who are prepared to take advantage of new opportunities for sociological and anthropological research on the Soviet Union, and to address the many new agendas which have grown out of recent events there.

Finally, a new program of support for research and development in Soviet studies is designed to fund meetings, conferences, workshops, and pilot programs devoted to initiatives and innovations in the field. Proposals are accepted from all disciplines in the social sciences and humanities for seed grants which will allow organizers to focus ideas on a particular project and promote sustained participation.

The JCSS is particularly interested in funding projects which involve graduate students along with senior scholars, and Soviet scholars along with Western scholars. Among the projects funded to date, one has supported the development, for both American and Soviet researchers, of reliable statistical methods for assessing Soviet election results; and another, the preparation and publication of inventories of various archival materials from the pre-revolutionary and Soviet periods.

INFRASTRUCTURAL CONSIDERATIONS
AND JCSS PROGRAMS

The JACIP report raises very difficult, even intractable issues of infrastructure and organization of the Soviet studies field and of counterpart Soviet institutions which will have to be addressed squarely. Among the most serious issues are the requirements of language competence, disciplinary and area studies approaches to knowledge, facilitating field access, and addressing the collapse and uncertain remaking of Soviet partner institutions.

The requirements of language competence for the changing field of Soviet studies are imposing indeed. The field is overwhelmingly Russian in its language competence, and disciplinary scholars also often lack language training to ground their solid methodological background in social and political context.

With one republic after another declaring independence in some form from the old Soviet structure, scholars will find that local language skills will become even more critical. Falling back on Russian as the lingua franca, or hoping to conduct research in English will no longer suffice in the current and former republics of the Soviet Union. Many such republics have or likely will adopt the language of the titular nationality as the official language for transacting business, commerce, legal relations, and scientific research. Support for scholars at all stages in their careers for intensive study of Russian and non-Russian languages will also be an important infrastructural priority for both research and teaching.

To address critical shortcomings in training in the languages of the Soviet Union, the JCSS has maintained a program to provide support for summer language institutes. Of particular importance has been the increase in funding for non-Russian languages of the Soviet Union including Azeri, Georgian, Kazakh, Kazan Tatar, Tajik, Ukrainian, and Uzbek.

Building both discipline and area-based competence in the scholarly community is clearly another important infrastructural priority. In the past, limited availability of data required a stress on the study of political personalities and hermeneutical textual analysis. Recently, dramatically enhanced access to data has facilitated and given life to the concept of the Soviet Union as a vast new laboratory for social science research. To use the assets of the laboratory requires training in the tools of science and a stress on replicability, intersubjective verifiability, and a comparative focus for interpreting results. Opportunities for training in statistics and quantitative analysis are more crucial than ever and require funding.

Over the long term, building competence in both disciplinary and area-based skills requires a commitment to the support of young scholars at the outset of their graduate careers, particularly in disciplines like sociology and anthropology, which have typically been underrepresented in Soviet studies. Such underrepresentation is in many ways an artifact of long-enforced prohibitions on field access beyond large Russian cities. As such prohibitions are eased there is a clear need to develop sustained expertise on such poorly understood but increasingly important issues as ethnicity and ethnic relations, and the effects of population distribution and social structure on social conflict, welfare, and societal values in the Soviet Union. Young scholars in graduate programs will need to bring research results from other societies to bear on the study of Soviet society, and will require extensive conceptual and methodological training best initiated at the outset of a graduate career. In addition, political scientists, economists, and historians will require training and a new blend of skills in order to take advantage of opportunities in the Soviet Union.

With regard to field access, the perestroika era has ended the need for American institutions to emulate centralized Soviet structures as a means of insuring field research opportunities for junior and senior scholars. In recent years, an enormous number of ad hoc institutional arrangements between American and Soviet institutions has arisen. Individual universities—major centers as well as smaller institutions—have signed agreements enabling personnel, data, and equipment to flow in both directions, expanding definitions of scholarly reciprocity. Such a development has moved the organizational pattern of cooperation in the Soviet studies field more into the mainstream of normal scientific activity that has been practiced in other fields of international research. As such, the trend is a welcome one although the field now faces a variety of institutional and ethical questions as a result of this trend.

The explosion of new institutional arrangements to facilitate field access does not eliminate the need for some network of national, peer review, pass-through mechanisms to establish the highest standards for social science and humanistic research. Moreover, new university-based patterns of cooperation do not typically support long-term research for junior scholars in the same scope and intensity as national programs.

While many have expressed relief over the collapse of centralized structures which controlled field access, these structures have not yet been replaced with clear-cut alternative ones. As of this writing, the USSR Academy of Sciences is seeking a new role for itself. At the same time proposals for independent academies of sciences at the republic level are being put forth and, in some cases, implemented. Finally, efforts are under way to construct a peer review national organization patterned after the US National Science Foundation. On the whole, there is near unanimous agreement that whatever structural arrangement emerges, the rapidly declining economic situation guarantees significantly reduced funding for basic research.

Given this bleak short-term outlook, scholars in the Soviet studies field in the West and those wishing to conduct research in the Soviet Union confront several dilemmas. Roaring inflation and the collapse of the old infrastructure call into serious question the ability of Soviet institutions to deliver basic services such as food, housing, and appropriate stipends to visiting scholars. Even in those instances where practical considerations are not so problematic, it is unclear that sponsoring organizations have legitimacy and authority to speak for institutions and individuals they supposedly sponsor. American institutions which negotiate agreements with central Soviet institutes can no longer assume that such institutions can credibly speak for research scholars in the non-Russian republics. As such, considerable care must be taken in negotiating with Soviet partners to specify in detail the criteria for eligibility, including place of residence and nationality. To an increasing extent, direct, separate agreements with republic-level institutions should be pursued, with thought given to the advisability of quotas for participation and eligibility.[5]

The increasingly chaotic institutional framework for the support of basic research also demonstrates the need for continuing national programs on the American side. To name but a few, the International Research and Exchanges Board (IREX), the JCSS, the Kennan Institute for Advanced Russian Studies, and the National Council for Soviet and East European Research all are capable, in varying degrees, of assessing the intellectual soundness and practical viability of proposals for collaborative research partnerships. Such capability becomes even more important given a collapsing Soviet infrastructure.

Research Materials. The internal organizational confusion and decline in the USSR is further compounded by the lack of support, both in the United States and the Soviet Union, for maintaining the integrity of research materials and enhancing the ability of research scholars to use them. In the United States, as the amount of materials reaching major research libraries has dramatically increased in the perestroika era, cataloging backlogs are reaching immense proportions.

Slavic research libraries in the United States have uncataloged backlogs of Soviet materials estimated at 250,000–300,000 volumes. Most of these are inaccessible, resulting in a tragic waste of resources and knowledge. Making such sources available is currently just beyond the reach of the Soviet studies field, due to critical funding limitations in Slavic libraries. To deal with this problem, the JCSS, through its Subcommittee on Bibliography, Information Retrieval, and Documentation (BIRD), is in the implementation stages of a program to create a system of smaller grants to libraries in the United States with significant collections of Slavic materials. A program announcement has been issued announcing grants to support funding for specially designated units of library personnel and equipment dedicated to making materials more accessible to users and developing long-term strategies to prevent recurrences of backlogs.

Efforts to promote bibliographic studies, most notably the American Bibliography of Slavic and East European Studies (ABSEES), have also been stymied by chronic shortages of funding. ABSEES represents a unique research tool for scholars. No other bibliography covers book chapters and collected essays, or gives such extensive space to dissertations and book reviews.

The JCSS has received funding to oversee the relocation of ABSEES from the Library of Congress to the University of Illinois, and provides ABSEES with a small staff dedicated to its compilation, an asset it has never had and which is critical to keeping ABSEES current and contemporary. Working with the university, and the American Association for the Advancement of Slavic Studies (AAASS), which sponsors, supervises, and arranges for the publication of ABSEES, a long-term plan has been devised which will provide a current version of ABSEES in printed format in 1991, and an on-line computer format in subsequent years thereafter. In addition, the university will explore the possibility of adding analytic and interpretive introductions to the various sections of the bibliography, and will work toward eventual integration of ABSEES with sister-bibliographies in Europe, including Eastern Europe and the Soviet Union; the anticipated result being a shared database for use by scholars, librarians, and all those concerned with current information about the Soviet Union and Eastern Europe.

While the severity of the state of research materials and their bibliographic control in the United States is considerable, the problem is truly one of crisis proportions in the Soviet Union. The decline of the Soviet academic infrastructure, which has been under way for several years, has in turn accelerated the collapse of the archival and library infrastructure. In the process, much of the cultural heritage of Russia and the former Soviet republics is being destroyed.

Conditions in Soviet libraries and archives are seriously undermining collections around the country and collections of research materials are literally rotting away. The main public library in St. Petersburg is in catastrophic condition and book treasures are being destroyed due to leaks and mechanical breakdowns. A major fire at the Library of the Academy of Sciences in February 1988 resulted in the loss of some 400,000 volumes and water damage to another 3,500,000. The Lenin Library in Moscow is in a critical state of disrepair and structural renovation may force it to close.

The August Revolution has added further administrative chaos to the already high levels of bureaucratic incompetence. The budgets of cultural institutions, including libraries, have been dramatically reduced as more powerful agencies crowd them out for shrinking allocations and access to hard currency for acquisitions. These cutbacks have also led to a dramatic reduction in personnel, resulting in a complete breakdown of the system of cataloging and bibliographic control. In addition, the transition to new forms of book publishing has driven up the prices libraries must pay for books.

At present, an effort is under way to fund a new JCSS project aimed at improving the conditions in Soviet libraries and archives. This project would call for joint projects between a Western institution and a Soviet partner to preserve important research materials, insure adequate access, and assist in training Soviet personnel in methods of preservation and documentation.

ETHICAL CONSIDERATIONS

Changes in the research environment in the Soviet Union since 1985 have confronted Western researchers with a bewildering array of opportunities for access to data in the humanities and social sciences. Unfortunately, the dramatic relaxation of traditional Soviet restrictions on permissible research activities has prompted some Western and Soviet researchers to engage in practices whose long-range consequences could be detrimental to the health of scholarly research on the Soviet Union, its history and its culture. The dramatic events of August have intensified the "anything goes" atmosphere which has accompanied the collapse of the academic system.

These concerns were voiced during a round table discussion at the Fourth Annual SSRC Workshop on Soviet Domestic Politics and Society held in June at the University of Toronto. Workshop participants formed a committee to draft guidelines in the interest of safeguarding the long-range outlook for academic research. The central issue of concern had to do with the principle of equal access to archives, libraries, institutes, and research data. The explosion of demands for currency and technology in exchange for access threatens the ability of all scholars, regardless of rank or affiliation, to do research in the Soviet Union. Other important areas of concern included the role of scholars and the importance of distinguishing between observer and participant in the Soviet sociopolitical arena, the principle of reciprocity, and the principles of collegiality and collaboration in relations among researchers.

These guidelines, which will be distributed widely, are intended to discourage practices which could jeopardize fair and equal access to data for the academic community as a whole. They are also intended to highlight principles and norms of behavior deemed to be in the best interest of preserving a spirit of scholarly investigation and collaboration over the long haul, through periods of intense geopolitical upheaval and socioeconomic change.

CONCLUSION

In many respects, this article has suggested that the era of perestroika and the events of August have left the field of Soviet studies in as much disarray as the Soviet Union itself. Yet we may also view the failed coup as a signal which emphasizes that the reorientations and reconceptualizations already under way in the field were appropriate and necessary. Both the desperate conditions in the Soviet Union and the multitude of new research agendas confronting the field create enormous problems. Yet, these conditions also pose new opportunities and challenges.

For historians, the origins and meanings of the 1917 revolutions may now be displaced as the intellectual center of the field. Access to previously restricted archives may present opportunities for entirely new histories to be written. For political scientists, the availability of information has provided opportunities for greater integration of research into the discipline of political science as a whole, while requiring a closer study of newly emerging political actors, institutions, and processes. Sociologists and anthropologists, unable to conduct the most basic research in the past can now open our eyes to a whole new complex of perspectives, issues, interpretations, and information. Economists now have a tremendously important laboratory for the creation and testing of models and for understanding transitions to a market economy. Through a variety of means described in this article, the Council and the JCSS are addressing these multidisciplinary challenges. The effectiveness of these programs will play an important role in sorting out complex phenomena, making more informed explanations about outcomes, and increasing the likelihood that scholarly consideration of a variety of foci of analysis will make outcomes less surprising and more predictable.

During the chaos of transition, with all its accompanying trials and tribulations, it seems that as practitioners in the field we often want to throw up our hands in despair. At times, a sort of strange nostalgia for "the bad old days" creeps into discussions, echoing the sentiments of many a Moscow cabbie who longs for the past when "at least we knew where we stood." As the citizens of the former Soviet territories reconstruct their social reality, social science and humanistic research that seeks to explain that reality must be reconstructed as well.

NOTES

1. We are using the term "the Soviet Union" to refer to the territory of the Soviet Union as it existed before the events of August 1991. This is

purely for convenience and for want of another single name for describing this region.

2. The Review Committee on Soviet Studies, "Beyond Soviet Studies," a report prepared for the American Council of Learned Societies and the Social Science Research Council, July 1991, preface.

3. Ibid.

4. Other members of the review panel included, in alphabetical order, Carol Avins, Northwestern University; Nina Garsoian, Columbia University; Abbott Gleason, Brown University; Robert Huber, Social Science Research Council; David Szanton, Social Science Research Council; and Myron Weiner, Massachusetts Institute of Technology.

5. For more on these points, see Brian D. Silver and Barbara Anderson, "Concerns about International Exchanges with the Soviet Union," *Items,* 45 (1), March 1991, p. 11.

Part Three

EMPIRICAL THEORY AND UNDERSTANDING THE PRESENT

DANIEL DEUDNEY
G. JOHN IKENBERRY

11

SOVIET REFORM AND THE END OF THE COLD WAR:

Explaining Large-Scale Historical Change

INTRODUCTION

After years of retirement in the academy, macro-historical commentary on contemporary events has returned to fashion. Radical domestic changes in the Soviet Union and Eastern Europe and new patterns of East-West relations—in short, the collapse of communism and the end of the Cold War—mark the end of an era and present an invitation to international theorizing.[1] Few would deny that these changes are momentous, but there is little consensus concerning their origins, trajectory, and implications. Explaining these events will necessitate a reweighing of fundamental theoretical issues. The size and speed of these changes were largely unexpected, reminding us how primitive our theories really are and encouraging us to broaden our theoretical perspective. To capture these events, theorists must reach across the disciplinary divides of Sovietology, international relations theory, political economy, and political sociology.

This paper has two objectives. First, we survey and develop a range of theories relevant to these events. Second, building on these theories, we advance an explanation for these recent events and speculate on their likely trajectories. In doing this, we hope both to illuminate recent historical events and to help define the direction of contemporary international theorizing.

The first half of the paper—examining theoretical alternatives—draws from several relevant disciplines in order to provide the building blocks for explaining events of this scope. Theoretical perspectives are rarely easy to categorize; schools of thought often blur together; they differ in coherence, parsimony, and scope. Yet fundamental theoretical alternatives can often be captured in simple taxonomies. Three broad theoretical families—realism, globalism and socioeconomic theories of democracy, capitalism and industrialism—are examined for the claims that they make about the character of world politics, the sources of historical change, and their relevance to the recent events in question.

In the second half of the paper we draw on several of these theories to construct our own explanation for the sources of the Soviet crisis and the directions of Soviet response. Explaining these events requires combining domestic and international factors, or in the language of international theory, "second image" and "second image reversed" sources of change.[2] In our view, the fundamental source of the Soviet crisis is a mismatch between Soviet command political and economic structures and the imperatives of advanced industrial production. This crisis has been exacerbated, but not fundamentally caused, by international forces. But in explaining Soviet responses, we emphasize the ways in which the pressures and opportunities of the international economic and security environment have both foreclosed some options and made others more appealing. Thus, several previously neglected or marginal theories (particularly industrial modernism) have new plausibility, while reigning ones (particularly some variants of realism) turn out to be less useful. Given the magnitude of these events, those theories with the most explanatory power can expect renewed prominence.

THEORETICAL ALTERNATIVES

Each of the three broad traditions we examine has many variants as well as shared assumptions. Three variants of realism (hard realism, soft realism, and statism) share assumptions about the primacy of the state, power, and conflict in world politics. Three variants of globalism (nuclear one-worldism, international institutionalism, and ecological environmentalism) share the view that the state-centric world order has been rendered less viable by powerful and broad underlying trends and forces operating on a global scale. And four socioeconomic theories (democratic liberalism, capitalism, neo-Marxism and industrial modernism) have in common the idea that the spread of original Western political and economic institutions is propelled by deep historical forces.[3]

Realism

Realism is an old and powerful theoretical tradition with many adherents who disagree about many things. But the common core of realism is an emphasis on power, the state, and conflict.[4] For purposes of discussion it is useful to distinguish three variants of realism. The first, hard realism, has a harshly Hobbesian view in which coercion, domination, and power-maximization define international life. The second, soft realism, gives more weight to the balance of power, and sees a role for power variables that are non-coercive and assumes that states are essentially optimizers. The third, statism, is a political sociological version of realism that emphasizes the persistence of the state as an organization separate from society and focuses on their relationship.

Hard Realism. By this term we mean a view of international life in which state interests are irreconcilable, power and coercion are dominant, international institutions are ephemeral, and states are precarious and relentless power maximizers. The hard realist assumes that other nations are acting as though they are in a Hobbesian state of nature, and urges the Western Alliance to do so as well. Scholars in this tradition also tend to be deeply suspicious of the competence of democratic states.

This position lacks a single authoritative theorist, but its main tenets can be found in readings of Hobbes, Thucydides, and Machiavelli. Such images of international life have been articulated by German theorists of *realpolitik* and *geopolitik,* such as Trietschke and Haushofer. This view is also found in the writings of American figures such as Nicolas Spykman, Colin Gray, Robert W. Tucker, and Edward Luttwak.[5]

Prior to the ascent of Gorbachev, the hard realist saw the Soviet Union as expansionary and expected the regime to cope with internal crises with international aggression.[6] During the early Gorbachev era the hard realists, looking at Soviet force structure, doubted that much had changed and dismissed "new thinking" as rhetoric. As change became undeniable, the hard realists have tended to attribute change to the Reagan era reassertion of American power—Star Wars in particular. Skeptical about the potential for reconciliation between states, the hard realists still suspect that the Gorbachev reform program serves the needs of the General Staff.[7] Their underlying assumption is that any changes the Soviets are making are intended to serve their power interests. Consequently, these new directions must be resisted as vigorously as more traditional Soviet power pursuits.

The perfectly consistent hard realist recommendation would be that the Western Alliance should take advantage of Soviet weaknesses while they last and maintain the policies that have brought the Soviet Union to this position. The fact that this position seems to have so few proponents suggests the limited character of its view of the world. At the same time, given their attitudes toward democracy, they do not really expect a democratic state, such as the United States, to pursue such advantages.[8]

Soft Realism. Another version of realism, richly developed by figures such as Morgenthau, Aron, Bull, and Kennan, holds that states are driven to optimize among a wide range of interests (which can often be an expression of regime type), that power is a multifaceted phenomenon embracing a range of material and ideological resources. Soft realists hold that international institutions, particu-

larly the balance of power, are vital for national security, and that
sudden alterations in power balances are threats to international
stability and, thus, are to be avoided. Soft realists see liabilities in
democratic governance, but not paralyzing ones. Moreover, soft realists posit that aggressive states seeking to change the status quo
will be checked by balancing behavior of other states, and eventually
moderate their foreign policy goals. An associated idea, developed
by Hedley Bull, is that interstate institutions such as diplomacy
constitute a type of "society" complete with its own norms and
capable of socializing deviant states.[9]

The classical soft realist position on the Soviet Union, as developed by George Kennan, argued that Soviet expansionary tendencies
were rooted mainly in domestic revolutionary ideology, but that the
regime would "mellow" eventually if the West thwarted their expansion without jeopardizing core Soviet interests.[10] This view would
seem to be prophetic: recent changes in Soviet foreign policy appear
to involve both a Soviet recognition that expansionary efforts will
be met by Western countermeasures, and a more general process of
socialization in which the Soviets have come to internalize the norms
of international society.[11] If the Soviet Union is changing from a
revolutionary to a status quo power (even if for reasons outside their
theory), the soft realist envisions new opportunities for stable management of international life, ranging from regional conflict management, nuclear arms control, and renewed roles for international
organizations.

Unlike the hard realists, the soft realists fear Soviet weakness as
much as Soviet strength. Perhaps, above all, they fear disintegration
of the Soviet political structure and the possible emergence of civil
war, Stalinist restoration, or the breakdown of civilian control over
the military.[12] Despite rhetorical ambivalence and pressures from
militant anti-communists, the United States policy response during
the late Reagan and early Bush administrations has been a sluggish
and halting version of soft realist grand strategy.

Statism. This theoretical tradition emphasizes the organizational
features of states and the problematic character of their need to
mobilize power from civil society. A key theme of statist theory is
that the capacities (or "strength") of states as organizations vary
greatly, with significant effect on their behavior.[13] Like other realists, statists recognize system position also to be a source of demands
on the state and, thus, on society. Domestic crisis and revolution can
be triggered by external demands that exceed the capacity of the
state to mobilize from society.

This image of the state and state crises has been developed by
such historical sociologists as Charles Tilly and Theda Skocpol. Tilly
captures the dynamic relationship between the geopolitical imperatives of early state builders and the wealth creating institutions of
civil society.[14] In Skocpol's treatment of the great revolutions in

France, Russia, and China, the collapse of the old regime was triggered by the failure of the state apparatus to extract resources from society, typically manifested as defeat in war or prohibitively expensive competition.[15] To cope with these demands, domestic class and state relations must be recast. Of course, all states restructure in the face of external pressure, but in some of them an ossification of state-society relations forces episodic-revolutionary rather than routine-incremental changes.

In this view the Soviet changes stem from the failure of the Brezhnevian system, in the face of a continuing dynamic external environment, to mobilize resources. Such a pattern is not new to Russian history. To play the role of a Great Power, Peter the Great introduced far reaching changes in state–civil society relations, a pattern which repeated itself after the Crimean War in the reforms of Alexander II, after the Russo-Japanese war in the revolutionary upheavals of 1905, during World War I with the collapse of the Czarist system, and, of course, Stalin's great push can be read as anticipation of renewed German aggression.

The statist view takes seriously the notion that Soviet society may have entered into a domestic revolution,[16] a set of events best understood by comparative historical theory. The experience of other revolutions suggests the spectre of increasing instability and complete collapse of the old order, followed by coups and dictatorship. To what degree can the West affect this trajectory? Given the statist assumption that earlier strategic threats from the West and elsewhere played such a major role in the formation of the Soviet state, it can be expected that diminished hostility from the West (to say nothing of direct aid) will bolster the prospects for reform short of revolution.

Conclusions on Realism. Realism (particularly the hard variant) is better at explaining the consequences of the recent events, than in explaining their origins.[17] An important exception is Robert Gilpin's attempt to incorporate processes of economic and technological change into a general theory of international change.[18] Relatedly, the explanatory power of realist theory is greatest when it incorporates "second image" variables in its analysis. Moreover, the very diversity of policy recommendations that emerge from the several variants of realism only underscore the heterogeneous character of realism itself.

Globalism

The central proposition of globalism is that a scale shift in human activity has occurred over the last century, with extremely broad and profound implications for all levels of human association and organization.[19] Globalists maintain that the fundamental source of this process is scientific and technological evolution. The different branches of globalism focus upon different aspects of this scale shift. Globalists posit both materialist and idea-based explanations of world political change. Although the ideational variables are often focused upon as necessary means to needed reforms or desired end-states, the characterization of the problem driving change is almost always materialist in character. In contrast to the dominant realist and liberal traditions in international theory, the globalist perspective on these issues is more inchoate, more diverse, and broader in scope.

For purposes of comparison and analysis it is necessary to focus on a limited set of globalist propositions, specifically what we label nuclear one-worldism, international institutionalism, and ecological environmentalism. By "nuclear one-worldism" we mean the proposition that the development of destructive technology, particularly thermonuclear explosives, has made it impossible for even the largest and most powerful states to achieve security, and generally requires international security organizations of new types and prominence. By "international institutionalism" we mean an older and broader proposition that human interconnectivity is occurring to such an extent that a world civic society is emerging and the autonomous nation-states are being augmented and enmeshed in broad networks of international civil associations and intergovernmental organizations. And by "ecological environmentalism" we refer to arguments linking the fate of industrial production to natural resource constraints.

Nuclear One-Worldism. Nuclear one-worldism, the narrowest and most specific globalist theory, simply holds that an epochal alteration in the availability of violence capability has occurred, thus presaging either the destruction of civilization or the end of war as a final arbiter among states. In this view, state apparatuses charged with achieving physical security previously could employ war as a routine tool but now must make the avoidance of nuclear use their paramount goal. The question of whether the adoption of deterrence is a sufficient adjustment to these new realities is an issue about which nuclear one-worlders do not agree.[20] But all agree that Great Power war as an instrument of national security policy has become suicidal. Thus, it is expected that certain forms of aggression will cease to be a significant feature of Great Power politics. An additional consequence is that the traditional comparative advantage of command systems, such as the Soviet Union, over liberal systems—their ability to mobilize and use military force—has now been eroded.

Powerful public statements of this claim have been made in the nuclear era by dozens of public figures ranging from Einstein to Eisenhower. Theoretical treatments of this view are found in the works of John Herz and Kenneth Boulding.[21] Eminent realists such as Hans Morgenthau and George Kennan have voiced this proposition, but have never convincingly related it to their more conventional realist views.[22] The nuclear one-worldist proposition is at odds with the hard realist emphasis on the inevitability of international conflict, but its counsel of moderation is congenial with the more general value that soft realists place upon stability.[23]

The reality of nuclear weapons has major implications for the Soviet Union's global position: territorial aggression has ceased to be either a major threat or a means of expansion.[24] Foreign invasions—by the Mongols, Napoleon, and the Nazis—punctuate Russian and Soviet history, creating a recurring problem of territorial insecurity and profoundly shaping state institutions and foreign policy. In the nuclear era, invasion is radically less plausible. At the same time, the Soviets' ability to engage in successful territorial aggression has been similarly foreclosed. This amounts to a profound alteration in the Russian relationship to the rest of the world.

The nuclear one-worldists interpret the recent changes in Soviet nuclear statecraft as vindication of their expectation that a process of nuclear learning will occur.[25] For much of the post-war era, Soviet nuclear strategy—not unlike American—has been a contradictory mixture of pacific declarations and attempts to use nuclear weapons for political and military gain. At the same time, Communist Party doctrine on nuclear war has evolved from Stalin's position that nuclear war was still governed by the class principle to the view, adopted in the 1970s and early 1980s, that nuclear war was species suicide, requiring deep disarmament and stronger international organization.[26] Gorbachev's "new thinking" appears to be an attempt to bring Soviet force structure and negotiating positions into line with party doctrines. This trend follows a trajectory predicted by the nuclear one-worldist.[27]

Some realists dismiss these declaratory statements and diplomatic initiatives as either cynical ploys to mislead the West or as responses to shifting power variables. Nonetheless, such realists have a hard time explaining why Soviet efforts to delegitimize nuclear weapons have accelerated as the Soviet arsenal has expanded, and particularly with the recent erosion of other Soviet power assets. The consistent hard realist position would seem to be that the Soviets would cling to nuclear weapons as their other power assets declined.

To the nuclear one-worldist, Gorbachev's initiatives are a major step forward, but hardly the arrival of the millennium. The internal destabilization of the Soviet system creates a major new danger—eroding central control over the roughly 25,000 Soviet nuclear weapons.[28] Conventional deterrence theory assumes the continuity of state apparatus control of nuclear weapons, but revolutions and social upheavals frequently split military organizations. Nuclear one-worldism, like soft realism, implies a profound American interest in the stability of the Soviet state.[29]

International Institutionalism. This second variant of globalism argues that changes in communication and transportation have produced the potential for large-scale cultural, political, and economic exchange between previously separate peoples. International institutionalists typically argue that an essentially cosmopolitan world civic society, and a matching transnational governmental structure, is both emerging and needs to emerge in response to these globalizing pressures and opportunities. It is often also held that nationalist sentiment is a powerful impediment to international institution building. This view is broader and older than nuclear one-worldism and encompasses both its diagnosis and solutions without giving them priority.

Ideas about world civic society are presaged in many religious traditions and found their first secular expression in the cosmopolitanism of the Stoics and the Hellenistic age. Since the nineteenth century, such views have flourished among American and British writers. Assumptions about melting nationality into ethnicity and belief in reasonable accommodation (as many realists point out) are essentially projections of domestic political experiences and liberal ideals to a world scale. Early twentieth-century writers, such as Leonard Woolf, H.G. Wells, Norman Angell, and Ramsey Muir, made the essential point that the national grouping had to be integrated with broader confederative, federative, and functional organizations.[30] Since World War II, a variety of formulations have been advanced to describe or explain such phenomena: "spill over," "integration," "informal penetration," "linkage politics," "incremental functionalism," and "complex interdependence."[31] Despite this variety, theorists of international institutionalism share an essentially common view of the forces and trajectories shaping international life.

In explaining changes in the Soviet Union, international institutionalism would point to increased communication and travel and the resulting spread of ideas. It is notable that the reforms were set in motion by members of the Communist Party apparatus who had been extensively exposed to the West.[32] Furthermore, proponents of this view would emphasize that the proliferation of East-West civil association and media accessibility—dimensions of both the populist peace movement and "movement anticommunism" easily overlooked by realist state-centric approaches—has been an important factor in US-Soviet reconciliation.[33] It is not easy to separate the emergence of these international norms from the appeal of liberal democratic capitalist society, a topic to which we will return.[34]

A potentially important contribution of international institutionalism is in the area of national reconciliation within the Soviet Union and Eastern Europe. The emerging clash of nationalities in the postcommunist era perhaps can be remedied by many of the same measures (de-emphasis on nationality issues and genuinely confederative structures) that were successful in solving nationality problems in Western Europe and North America.[35] The realist convention of speaking of the triumph of the nation-state form may fail to do justice to the dilution of nationality and the success of internationalism in the extended Western alliance. Pursuing the idea of autonomous nation-states would seem to be no more feasible on the shores of the Baltic than on the North Sea and Great Lakes.

Ecological Environmentalism. The idea that humans and their institutions are fundamentally shaped and limited by the physical environment (climate, fertile land, earth minerals) is as old as political science.[36] In recent years the general proposition that human societies are increasingly faced with "limits to growth" has been advanced by many environmental thinkers.[37] Opinion varies widely on the severity, urgency and correctability of such problems, with some holding that industrialism is doomed and others holding that relatively inexpensive technical fixes can solve the problems. There is, however, wide consensus that resource-intensive economic growth has reached its limits.

Two environmental claims with direct relevance to Soviet events are that extensive economic growth is increasingly nonviable, and that comparative advantages of resource exchange rise as scarcities emerge.

The Soviet Union has traditionally pursued extensive economic growth (in which higher levels of output result from increased inputs of labor, land, and raw materials) and this system is ceasing to work as it once did. The classical Soviet vision of limitless economic growth has been underpinned by the widely held assumption that, as the British geographer Halford Mackinder prophesized, and successive generations of Westerners have fearfully repeated, "the spaces within the Russian Empire and Mongolia are . . . vast and their potentialities in population, wheat, cotton, fuel, and metals . . . incalculably great."[38] Unfortunately for the Soviets, these expectations have proven inflated, and in the last two decades the easily accessible resources have been increasingly exhausted. Since the late-1970s, the energy sector, particularly oil exploration and extraction, have consumed steeply increasing shares of Soviet industrial investment while output has remained stagnant.[39] The chronic failures of Soviet agriculture continue despite vast investments in capital.[40] And expectations of rapid Siberian development continue to be frustrated by climatic barriers.[41] Environmentalists thus offer an important insight into the *timing* of the Soviet economic impasse: the fact that extensive economic growth stalled in the 1970s and 1980s, rather than decades ago or decades hence, is rooted in natural resource endowments.

The second environmentalist proposition relevant to the Soviet situation is that the opportunities for comparatively advantageous exchange increase as natural resource scarcity increases. In line with these expectations, the exchange of raw materials across the Iron Curtain has grown over the past twenty years and has drawn the West and the Soviets into increasing interdependence. It is notable that even the hard-line Reagan administration quickly restored grain exports to the Soviet Union. And the construction of the pipeline to carry Siberian natural gas to Western Europe, carried out despite strenuous resistance from Washington, deepened Soviet-NATO economic interdependence at the worst period of the Second Cold War. The resource dimension is also present in the recent Soviet acquiescence in the de-communization of Eastern Europe. Since the Soviets had underwritten this regional economic sphere with petroleum sold to COMECON at well below world market prices, they can look forward to increased earnings from this export given deregulation of prices.

Conclusions on Globalism. Unlike traditional international relations theory, globalist theories see the relations of states embedded in and fundamentally governed by a larger set of processes. They are the product of interlocking forces operating within human civilization and between human society and nature. The basic implications of these global trends is to create significant interdependencies between the Soviet Union and the rest of the world.[42] In contrast to those realists who emphasize the success of containing the Soviet Union, globalists stress that it is increasingly difficult to partition the world effectively and that Soviet changes are significantly driven by this permeability. In debates between realists and globalists that have been prominent in international studies for the last two decades,[43] the hard case for globalism was the East-West divide. If globalists are correct in attributing the recent changes to various types of interpenetration and interdependency, then the theoretical primacy of realism will have been dealt a serious blow.

Democracy, Capitalism, and Industrialism

The most popular characterization of the recent events in the Soviet Union is that it represents an historic failure of state socialism, single-party politics, and illiberalism. The spectacle of the greatest Marxist state suddenly abandoning its historical mission of world revolutionary leadership to embrace the values of liberal democracy unmistakably marks an epochal turn that must surely impress even the most world-weary observer. In this view, the basic change that is occurring is in the nature of the Soviet domestic regime, and all other changes, including international ones, stem from this basic change.

Explanations that emphasize socio-economic transformation can be grouped into four broad classes. First are those which trace their lineage back to Kant and simply posit that the desire for freedom and democracy is universal in humans and history is the process of its progressive triumph. In this view, the Soviet crisis is caused by dictatorship and popular demands for democratic rights. Second is a tradition traced back to Adam Smith that emphasizes the superiority of market over command economy. In this view, it is the economic failure of socialism in a world of expanding capitalism that triggered the reforms in the Soviet Union. Third is Wallerstein's variant of Marxism that also emphasizes the globalizing tendencies of capitalism. This view suggests that Soviet withdrawal from and prospective reintegration into the world economy is part of an ongoing unfolding of the capitalist world-system. Finally, we examine contemporary versions of industrial society theory (often associated with anti-liberal conclusions) that explain the changes in the Soviet Union as the result of the functional imperatives of advanced industrial production. In this view, pluralism and democratization follow from the productive system's needs for an educated workforce, extensive flow of information, and decentralized decision-making.

Democratic Liberalism. Since the eighteenth century, a democratic natural rights tradition has postulated that the desire for freedom and a corresponding desire to organize politics democratically is constitutive of rational human beings, and so the desire for democracy is universal. Whether found in the polemical writings of Thomas Paine or the philosophy of Immanuel Kant, the democratic natural rights argument has enjoyed wide popularity in the West. In these views, political life is both primary and largely autonomous from socioeconomic setting. The democratic theory of international relations, most powerfully developed by Kant, holds that relations between democratic states tend to be pacific and the spread of democracy is equivalent to the spread of an enduring peace system.[44]

In the American political scene this argument about the primacy of democratic norm-driven historical change is given its classic statement by Woodrow Wilson and in recent years it has been advanced by such "neo-conservative" figures as Patrick Moynihan, Irving Kristol, Jeane Kirkpatrick, George Will, and Ronald Reagan. The recently widely-discussed essay by Francis Fukuyama employs this essentially Kantian (not Hegelian) position and postulates its emergent universalization.[45] Although the current standard-bearers of this view are identified with the Right or Center in the United States, a similar intense commitment to democratic norms is also characteristic of the American Left.

Since democratic natural rights theorists believe that the demand for democracy is rooted in human nature, they have difficulty explaining variations in the occurrence of democratic institutions. To explain historical events, believers in democratic natural rights often rely upon voluntaristic theories of history in which change is driven by a "war of ideas": political regimes rest upon legitimacy and legitimacy derives from ideologies that rise and fall in the market place of ideas. Such extremely voluntaristic theories are particularly prevalent among American neo-conservatives, many of whom were shaped by sectarian Marxism of the 1930s.[46] This is a curiously elitist theory of historical change: democracy is resurgent because of the strength of the democratic intellectuals in discrediting their adversaries. In idea-driven visions of history, change can happen very suddenly. Indeed, it is striking that as recently as 1975, Daniel Patrick Moynihan worried that democracy had a dim future in a world of resurgent Leninist states and Third World dictatorships.[47]

Two different characterizations of the Soviet Union can be found among those who emphasize democracy as a motor of history. One characterization of the Soviet experience emphasizes the primacy of Leninist party dictatorship, and that the economic policies, such as agricultural collectivization, served to crush alternative bases of power in Soviet life. In this view, the end of the party monopoly of power is the end of the Leninist experiment.[48] An implication of this view is that the move to real democracy will inherently involve the disintegration of the Communist Party.

Another characterization of the Soviet Union holds that the Marxist tradition has always contained a strong rhetorical commitment to human emancipatory norms which have been subverted by a variety of factors: the Russian political culture, the demands of rapid modernization, and the state's precarious international environment. For those who emphasize the demands of industrialization and the international system, it was just a matter of time before the demand for democracy would emerge within the party itself.[49] For those who emphasize the pervasiveness of Russian political culture as a barrier, the prognosis is not so bright.[50]

In explaining the pressures toward East-bloc democracy, Americans have tended to emphasize the attractiveness of Western democracy and ideological promotion by the United States, particularly during the Reagan years. Initiatives such as Radio Free Europe and the Helsinki Process are seen as undermining Soviet ideological indoctrination and control.[51] This model better fits events in Eastern Europe, where popular resistance spearheaded change, than in the Soviet Union, where democratizing initiatives originated from the party leadership.

Those who see the events in the Soviet Union as a democratic revolution would anticipate that the US-Soviet hostility will be diminished in proportion to the success of democratization. The ultimate trajectory, in this view, is a world in which US-Soviet relations resemble those of US-Canadian relations. With regime congruence a wide array of international institutions and common efforts become not only possible but a routine matter of statecraft.

The immediate consequence of Soviet democratization may be instability and mass authoritarianism. As the experience of the Weimar Republic demonstrated, it is easier to erect democratic institutions than it is to instill a democratic political culture among a people whose political experience has been so exclusively authoritarian. Moreover, if economic growth is not achieved, the democratic processes may simply be vehicles through which radical discontent can express itself, thus endangering the democratic reforms themselves. Finally, democratization may well simply permit the expression of anti-Western sentiments of Russian nationalism in addition to anti-Russian sentiments of non-Russian peoples in the Soviet Union, in which case democratization might inflame international relations in ways inconsistent with Kant's vision.

Capitalism. Another powerful strand of liberal thought, capitalism, concerns the nature of the productive system rather than political values. Capitalism is both a description of an economic system in which relatively free markets and private property play dominant roles and the proposition that such systems are both natural to humans and the most effective means to wealth generation. Capitalist arguments are made both about the fundamentals of political economy and their international manifestations.

Among the basic propositions of capitalist political economy, as set forth by Adam Smith and the classical political economists, are that markets will spontaneously arise if people are free from coercion and control, and that market arrangements will encourage a specialization and division of labor, thus generating more wealth. Moreover, it is held that markets are inherently more efficient as a mechanism for organizing production than command alternatives.[52] However, most capitalist political economists recognize that for market relations to be more than primitive and marginal social phenomena, quite distinct cultural values (acceptance of inequality) and political structures (state protection of property rights) are necessary.[53]

Over the last five centuries, capitalism has been highly dynamic and expansionary. Gains from trade and the search for profitable investments have drawn more and more regions into the world capitalist system. Even critics of capitalism, such as Karl Marx, projected that this process would break down all "Chinese walls of exclusion" and eventually become universal. As regions come to produce for the world market, divisions and specializations of labor arise with wide-ranging ramifications for state sovereignty and economic welfare. In addition to having its own logic, the interaction between states and capitalism has been important for the power-position of states as well as the rate and direction of capitalist penetration. Just as the state must guarantee property rights, so too world-scale capitalism has political presumptions and supporting institutions, such as GATT and the IMF in the contemporary era.[54]

In the capitalist view, the Soviet domestic failure is occurring at two levels. Domestically, the command economics of communism are increasingly incapable of providing labor incentives, efficient allocation of capital, and stimulants to innovation. During the earlier period of Soviet industrialization, command economics succeeded, despite its efficiencies, in building an industrial economy because of the vastness of untapped labor, land, and natural resources. However, as these initial endowments have been exhausted, the command economy is inherently incapable of generating wealth through increased efficiency and innovation.

Since the Bolsheviks set out to beat capitalism at its own game of wealth production, the Soviet regime has staked its legitimacy upon its ability to keep up with the West in the production of wealth, unlike previous non-capitalist societies.[55] The Soviet people's willingness to accept sacrifice and the absence of liberties ultimately depended upon the expectation that socialism would steadily improve material life. Not only did the regime rest upon a standard of material life borrowed from the West, but also it rested disproportionately upon this standard and so its collapse was complete when this standard could no longer be met. History produces a rich irony: the Soviets were able to physically withdraw from the world capitalist system, but took with them a consumerist—and thus narrowed and impoverished—social ideal from the West.

The economic stagnation also affects the Soviet Union's security situation. The economic growth and technological dynamism of Western capitalist society has provided Western militaries with a large and increasingly sophisticated base from which to draw. In contrast, economic malaise in the Soviet Union has forced more painful trade-offs between guns and butter. This strategic competition gives Soviet economic underperformance its particularly significant consequences.

Although economic stagnation has triggered the crisis, the current direction of reform efforts, from the perspective of capitalist theory, has not yet come to grips with the real causes of the problem. The absence of agricultural decollectivization, the ambivalent steps toward market reform of the service sector, and the continuing absence of private property rights, all reflect a persistent belief among key Soviet elites that socialism needs to be fixed rather than eliminated. Gorbachev seeks "reform socialism" rather than capitalism. At the mass level, Soviet political culture remains deeply hostile to the inequalities and risk taking that inevitably accompany capitalism. From the perspective of capitalist theory, the absence of a program to move toward capitalism will frustrate economic growth and thus jeopardize democratic liberalization.

The prognosis for capitalism in the Soviet Union is mixed. Should the transition from socialism to capitalism in Eastern Europe bear fruit, the demonstration effects in the Soviet Union may be profound and lead toward more radical economic reforms. Moreover, the large number of joint ventures, the move to make the ruble convertible, and the move to join Western economic organizations mean that market forces have a significant beachhead in the Soviet economy. These wedges and the disintegration of the old order suggest that the Soviet Union has embarked upon a path that will not easily be reversed. Given the popular resistance to the introduction of market reforms, the establishment of a strong executive, and the continued presence of a strong state apparatus committed to change might facilitate market reforms and, by so doing, help insure the ultimate viability of democratic initiatives.[56]

In framing American policy responses, some advocates of market values argue that nothing should be done to aid the Soviet Union until the turn to genuine capitalism has been made. In this view, aiding the Soviet Union now will only prop up a moribund economic structure and delay true reform. Such a view, however, fails to acknowledge the interdependent relationship between political change and economic reform.[57] In this view, the Soviet Union has entered upon a slippery slope away from the old order, and the choice is between general collapse and staged reform. A step towards capitalism is a step toward capitalism.

Marxism. The developments in the Soviet Union seem to have dealt a death blow to Marxism as a political and intellectual force in world history. Given the degree to which Marxists and their opponents have polarized world politics in the last century, the "death of communism" is a major historical watershed. Although Marxist ideology seems thoroughly discredited, not all of the myriad variants of Marxist theory have been disproven. Socialism—particularly state socialism—has lost its appeal, but Marxist theory of the capitalist world system may provide powerful insights into the failure of Soviet socialism.[58]

Like Smith and the classical political economists, Marx held that capitalism exhibited a powerful globalizing tendency. To Marx, capitalism was a dynamic modernizing force breaking down traditional societies and creating the preconditions for the true socialist societies.[59] This view that the road to socialism was through the most advanced stages of capitalism has been at variance with the general tendency of Marxist political movements in the twentieth century to resist the encroachments of the world capitalist system and to by-pass the capitalist stage.

Building on these views of Marx, Immanuel Wallerstein has advanced a theory of the world capitalist system arguing that capitalism must become universal before true socialism is possible.[60] Unlike Marx and Smith, but like turn-of-the-century theorists of imperialism, Wallerstein argues that the state plays a critical role in shaping the pace and direction of capitalist expansion. Where Smith and the classical political economists argue that capitalism is associated with minimum state powers, Wallerstein argues that capitalism both needs and produces strong states and that the cutting edge of capitalist accumulation are coercive practices such as piracy, slavery, and land grabs.[61] Wallerstein claims that the world capitalist system is stratified into three economic zones: the core (the metropolitan capitalist states); the periphery (composed of weak states and dependent economies); and the semi-periphery (composed of a diversity of rising and declining states, but also including relatively strong states that have largely withdrawn from the capitalist system). These zones contain distinctive class structures with different orientations toward the world market as well as states of divergent capacities that largely reflect class interests. Importantly, differences in strength of states within the world system (i.e., strong states in the core and weak states in the periphery) serve to insure the domination of the leading capitalist classes by enforcing the transfer of economic surplus to the core.

Critics have found Wallerstein's global vision excessively reductionist and deterministic: the structures of socioeconomic life flow rather mechanically from the imperatives of the world market and the capacities and policies of states overwhelmingly reflect the interests of the dominant class.[62] Wallerstein's claim that the world capitalist system ultimately serves to maintain and expand the system has also been faulted for being excessively functional.[63] Despite these limitations, the model sheds light on the nature of large-scale change and the possibilities for movement of particular states within the global capitalist system. In Wallerstein's scheme, one of the paths to the privileged core of the capitalist world system is through semi-peripheral withdrawal and quasi-autarkic development rather than a direct ascent from the enforced underdevelopment of the periphery. In this way, the semi-periphery becomes a region where states can escape complete domination and build their capacities to reenter the capitalist system.

This neo-Marxist theory can provide an interpretation of the entire Soviet experience. In the Soviet era, the Russians have been pursuing a semi-peripheral strategy: the Bolsheviks withdrew, Stalin autarkically developed, and now Gorbachev seeks reintegration into the world economy as a vehicle to enter into the core.[64] Unlike Third World regions that have remained at the underdeveloped periphery, the Soviet state was strong enough to avoid permanent backwardness. This view suggests that the Soviet experience has not been a complete failure, but has been a necessary prelude to joining the ranks of the advanced capitalist states. The Soviets left the capitalist world with a largely peasant society and they return with a developed educational, scientific, and industrial infrastructure. Seen in this light, "socialism in one country" is part of the dynamic of the capitalist world system rather than an alternative to it.

Industrial Modernism. Finally, as a candidate for understanding events in the Soviet Union, we examine recent versions of industrial society theory. The core of all industrial society theory is that the functional imperatives of the industrial mode of production determine social and political outcomes. In effect, the structures of social and political life conform to the requirements of the particular stage of production. In its starkest formulation, this theory posits "base" determination of "superstructure" and, therefore, it is a variety of historical materialism.[65]

Industrial society arguments come in three main varieties. Two strands of theory posit that authoritarian, collectivistic, and antidemocratic formations are required by industrial production. In Marx's classic account, democracy and liberal social formations are to be inevitably replaced by proletarian collectivism. Early-twentieth-century writers such as Mosca, Michels, and Pareto argue that industrial production required authoritarian social and political arrangements. In James Burnham's theory of the managerial revolution, industrial society is said to be evolving toward a world order dominated by a handful of authoritarian, imperial states.[66] These theories share a characterization of the industrial mode of production in which the scale of enterprise is vast, the workforce is homogeneous, and the breakdown of pre-modern sources of authority demands organized coercion.

A third variety of industrial society theory, which has roots in nineteenth-century political economy[67] and was extensively developed in the 1950s and 1960s by Western social scientists such as Ralf Dahrendorf, Raymond Aron, Clark Kerr, W.W. Rostow, Seymour Martin Lipset and others, sought to explain how liberal and democratic societies had not only survived (contrary to Marxist and authoritarian expectations) but had proven remarkably robust as industrialization advanced.[68] During the 1970s, Alain Touraine and Daniel Bell advanced a "late-industrial" (sometimes exaggerated into "post-industrial") variant of this argument, emphasizing the advent of a new stage of industrialism characterized by an educated workforce, free flow of information, and complex decision-making.[69]

Industrial society has three features that are particularly salient. First, human capital—an increasingly highly educated workforce—is a factor of production that looms ever larger in importance. Second, the rapid flow of vastly increased amounts of information is characteristic of advanced industrial production. And third, the increasing specialization and complexity of industrial production renders centralized control and direction cumbersome and ineffective. Effective control over production is diffused throughout a network of complex organizations.[70] These new features of industrial society are expected to produce a populace that is increasingly heterogeneous, well informed, and difficult to coerce. Such a populace is incompatible with authoritarian governance and vigorously demands democratic rights. The argument is not that democracy is a functional imperative of the new industrial order but that social formations are produced by industrial production that lead inevitably to democracy.[71]

An important theme of industrial modernism was the expected convergence of all industrial societies, implying that the Soviet Union and the United States would come to increasingly resemble each other.[72] The main thrust of this school's reading of the Soviet Union is captured in W.W. Rostow's claim that communism is merely "a disease of the transition" to industrialism and cannot survive the age of "high mass consumption."[73]

Late-industrial society theory suggests that the economic and political crisis in the Soviet Union is caused by the increasing incongruity between Stalinist command structures (which might have been viable in an early stage of industrialism) and imperatives of late industrial production. In this view, the product of Stalinist industrialization is a society that "pushes" for liberalization; and the attractions of the new stage of industrialization "pulls" for it.

The old command order is impeding industrial modernization while, at the same time, industrial modernization is undercutting the old command order.[74] The traditional, politically motivated straight-jacket on typewriters, telephones, and mimeograph machines—to say nothing of word processors, personal computers, and photocopying—is a massive drag on Soviet economic performance. And every new information technology empowers civil society and loosens the control of the state. As sociologist Lewis Coser notes, "You cannot have a closed society based on computers and fax machines."[75] Modern industrial requirements of an educated workforce have created a populace that is increasingly immune to ideological indoctrination. It is no accident that the scientific and technological elite has been in the vanguard of the reform movement.[76] The complexity-driven decentralization of industrial production creates a populace accustomed to the exercise of independent judgment which is difficult to insulate from the political sphere. Ironically, a variety of historical materialism, a tradition usually linked to authoritarian and socialist outcomes, explains the failures of authoritarian and socialist systems.[77]

The industrial society theory suggests that the demands for change in the Soviet Union are deeply rooted and not likely to disappear or be diverted by momentary political setbacks. An important implication of this theory is that the changes in the Soviet Union are not the result of the embrace of democratic values, but rather that democratizing tendencies are the product of deeper material forces.

Summary on Democracy, Capitalism, and Industrialism. Kantian and Smithian liberals posit that democracy and market society are rooted in human nature and, consequently, their universalization is ultimately assured. But neither theory is very effective at explaining historical variation in the appearance of these liberal outcomes. Since it roots liberal outcomes in material forces, the industrial modernism theory is good at explaining historical variations. But such a functional-materialist argument does not explain why people widely desire democratic and market rights regardless of their stage of development.

Realists tend to see questions of democracy and capitalism as domestic regime phenomena that color international life but do not decisively shape it. Conversely, the basic thrust of democratic and capitalist theories is that international relations are embedded in and significantly shaped by social and economic systems. The current events set up a test of this clash of views: if East-West relations are radically ameliorated by the change in Soviet and East European domestic regimes, then the Kantian and Smithian images of history may explain more about the fundamental character of world politics than realism and other international theories have allowed.

CONSTRUCTING AN EXPLANATION

The second goal of this paper is to construct a convincing explanation for Soviet reforms and the end of the Cold War. In the previous section we examined ten theories with potential relevance to these events, some of which are well known, others of which we extended. Not all these theories, however, are equally persuasive; nor are all seeking to explain the same phenomenon.[78] These events are clearly too multifaceted to be subject to simple explanation, or attributed to any single variable.

Here we advance composite explanations for the crisis and the Soviet response, incorporating both international and domestic variables. In our view, the most decisive source of the crisis is Soviet economic failure, best explained by industrial modernization theory. International forces have exacerbated but have not primarily caused this crisis. In explaining the responses we believe international forces play a much more determining role by foreclosing some alternatives and creating others.

Explaining the Crisis

Virtually every commentator of these events—from Mikhail Gorbachev to his American Right-wing critics—points to economic stagnation as the decisive catalyst to change. The most convincing explanation for this, we believe, is to be found in the theory of industrial modernism. These connections are summarized in Figure [11.]1.

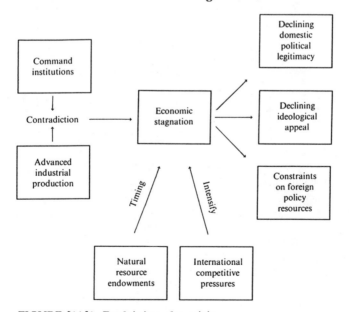

FIGURE [11.]1 Explaining the crisis

The implications of economic stagnation for the Soviet Union are three-fold. First, and most importantly, the domestic regime is perceived both by the leadership and the people as a failure, undermining its legitimacy. Secondly, economic stagnation means that the Soviet Union has fewer resources to mobilize for military and foreign policy purposes. Thirdly, the failure of the Soviet economy has diminished the Soviet Union's role as a model of development for both its allies and Third World nations.

Industrial modernism provides the best explanation of the Soviet crisis because it connects a relatively specific characterization of the material forces of production with liberal political and economic outcomes. Because it links outcomes to phases of industrial development, this theory has more explanatory value than Smithian and Kantian universalism.

International variables, particularly the Western military competition, are not convincing explanations for the crisis itself, but they are useful in explaining its timing and intensity. The timing of the crisis also has roots in natural resource constraints.

Explaining Responses

How the Soviet Union has responded to this crisis requires a separate set of explanations. The major avenues of potential responses are summarized [in Figure 11.2]:

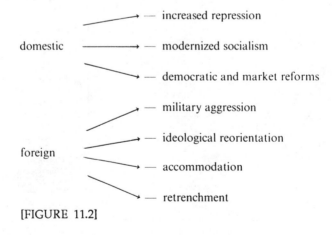

domestic — increased repression
— modernized socialism
— democratic and market reforms

foreign — military aggression
— ideological reorientation
— accommodation
— retrenchment

[FIGURE 11.2]

In general terms, the Soviet Union during the first five years of the Gorbachev era (1985–1990) responded to this crisis with a mixture of internal liberalization and external accommodation and retrenchment, rather than increased domestic repression and foreign aggression. The strongest explanation for the choice of liberalization over renewed repression is that further repression would only intensify the fundamental contradiction between the imperatives of production and political organization. Important additional supports for liberalization over repression are to be found in the international environment. Moreover, the strongest explanations for the choice of accommodation and retrenchment over aggression are to be found in the constraints and opportunities of the Soviet's external environment. These links deserve closer examination.

The primary explanation for why the Soviet domestic response has been away from repression and toward modernized socialism and liberalization is that repression would intensify rather than alleviate the contradiction.[79] Initially, Gorbachev's plan of *perestroika* was an attempt to modernize socialism. All indications are that this remedial program has been unsuccessful in revitalizing the economy, suggesting that the modernization of socialism is not a viable response to the crisis.[80] This failure produces tremendous pressure to either introduce far-reaching market reforms or to attempt a return to the old system. This basic thrust of Soviet domestic reform has also been sharpened and intensified by a complex pattern of international constraints and opportunities.

The Soviet choice of accommodation and retrenchment over aggression is even more fundamentally rooted in a complex mixture of international pressures and possibilities which have changed over time. A listing of the old and new environment and the implications of the new environment is provided in Figure [11.3].

Since at least the eighteenth century, the Russian empire and then the Soviet Union have lived in a world in which dynamic Western capitalist states have repeatedly posed challenges that have required successive political and economic restructurings. Since World War II, the number of successful capitalist states in the world has increased, with profound implications for Soviet foreign policy and domestic politics. In the economic realm, capitalist states have demonstrated superior wealth creation capacity and technological innovation. Thus the wealth and technology base from which the Soviets must draw is declining relative to their traditional adversaries. In such a world, the Soviets must either extract more from society, dramatically restructure the economy (including integration into the world capitalist economy), or seek accommodation with traditional adversaries.[81]

An important feature of the Soviet's external environment related to the health of capitalism concerns the changing status of opposition to capitalism within the West. Propelled by structural crises and deep inequalities, Western societies in the first half of the twentieth cen-

226

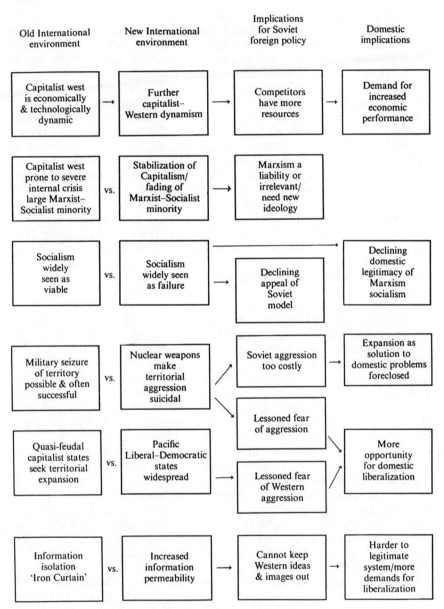

FIGURE [11.3] Implications of the changing international environment

tury were riven between a dominant capitalist group and a large and restive socialist working class opposition. Since World War II, the movement of peoples in Western colonial possessions toward national independence also created a deep fissure in the West. In this environment, the official Soviet ideology of socialism and the rhetorical identification with the oppressed both in the metropol and the periphery gave the Soviet Union powerful political supporters. In the last twenty years, the waning of proletarian movements in the West and the success of national liberation movements in the Third World have reduced the foreign policy value of socialist ideology to the Soviet state.

Seen in this context, Gorbachev's "new thinking" can be understood as an attempt to refurbish the Soviet state's ideological appeal in the world.[82] The globalist content of "new thinking"—on nuclear weapons, on international institutions, and on ecological responsibility—resonates with a large and growing segment of Western political opinion. Like socialism in an earlier era, globalist ideology puts the Soviet state in the vanguard of international progressivism, thus creating allies beneficial to Soviet foreign policy. But, unlike revolutionary Marxist ideology, "new thinking" offers the basis for a cooperative relationship with the Western powers.

Closely associated with the status of socialist movements outside the Soviet Union is the track record of centralized socialism as an economic model. Prior to the last quarter of the twentieth century, socialism could be seen as either an untried or successful economic system, with wide appeal to those dissatisfied with capitalism. However, the simultaneous stagnation of centralized economies throughout the socialist world during the 1970s has seriously undermined the appeal of socialism everywhere. For the Soviet state the role of socialist standard-bearer has been transformed from an asset to a liability.

The Soviet Union's military and strategic environment has also changed with important implications for both domestic and foreign policy choices. To begin with, the provision of physical security for its people and territory has been a primary shaping force for the Soviet state. For much of Russian and Soviet history, invasion and territorial appropriation has been a recurring problem. The development of nuclear weapons profoundly alters this situation, with a two-fold impact on Soviet foreign policy options: the cost of Soviet aggression has now become prohibitively high, while at the same time, the cost for the Soviet Union to defend itself against aggression has fallen greatly. Moreover, the emergence (or re-emergence) of powerful neighboring states in the post-war era, particularly Germany, Japan, and China, has also increased the costs of aggression for the Soviet Union. Thus, a large military is no longer useful for aggression or necessary for defense.

For much of their histories, the Russian empire and Soviet Union had as neighbors pre-modern or modernizing states whose domestic regimes were oriented toward imperial territorial aggression. By the mid-twentieth century, the Soviet Union's major adversary, the United States, was a liberal democracy, in contrast to its previous great adversary, Imperial and Nazi Germany. And the successful emergence of liberal democratic institutions in Germany also profoundly altered the Soviets' immediate security environment. This spread of liberal democratic states alters the Soviet environment because such regimes are not as likely to pose as great a threat of aggression as dictatorial and authoritarian states. Despite occasional Soviet rhetoric conflating Hitler's Germany with Reagan's America, the reality is that the United States is a far more benign and less aggressive Great Power than any of the European states with which the Tsar or Stalin had to contend. Gorbachev's decision to accept domestic political change in Eastern Europe stems, in our view, from a judgment that these Western states will not militarily advance into this traditional buffer zone.

This new security environment produced by the advent of nuclear weapons and the predominance of liberal democratic regimes as Soviet adversaries also had significant domestic consequences. First, expansionary solutions to domestic problems are foreclosed. Second, there is more opportunity for domestic liberalization. The Soviet state is no longer faced with acute security threats that force quick and dirty state mobilization of resources.[83] This means that they have less immediate pressure to change, thus permitting slower and perhaps less authoritarian reform programs. Moreover, as the state's claims on society's resources for security needs become more difficult to justify and cease to yield their traditional payoff, competing groups and interests are in a relatively stronger position.[84] In short, a world dominated by liberal states affords remaining illiberal states both a need and an opportunity to liberalize.

Another prominent feature of the changed international environment is the highly developed state of communication technology that makes possible broader and deeper information flows. In contrast to the Tsar's and Stalin's ability to close off the Russian people from the rest of the world, the Iron Curtain has proven permeable to Western radio and television penetration. Because they know so much about what goes on in the rest of the world, Eastern bloc people are less easy to mobilize through indoctrination and tend to demand Western-style rights and living standards. Thus a new and persisting source of demand for change exists in socialist societies.

Taken all together, the international environment is a source of a complex mixture of demands, opportunities, and constraints. These forces do not all cut in the same direction. Some (nuclear weapons and the increased strength of neighboring states) close off the path of expansion that previous Russian regimes pursued. Others (prevalence of liberal democracies and information permeability) strengthen the societal claims for political expression and consumption. Some (nuclear weapons and the prevalence of liberal democracies) reduce the security demands for extraction, in direct contrast to others (dynamic capitalism and diffusion of power) that increase the need to generate power resources. Because of the longer time frame available, this clash (for more power resources and for less) probably resolves itself in favor of resource mobilization through liberal reform rather than increased coercion. In the final analysis, the net impact of all these environmental forces on Soviet domestic and foreign response is substantially in favor of change toward liberalization and accommodation, in contrast to so much of Russian historical experience.

CONCLUSION

This article has examined theories relevant in explaining the origins of the Soviet crisis and the direction of responses to it. This conclusion makes two general observations about viable strategies for theorizing about such large-scale events.

First, no one theory can explain the causes and consequences of these contemporary events—no one key fits all the locks. Perhaps the correct theory has not been formulated, but it seems more likely that this inadequacy stems from the irreducibly plural nature of the historical phenomena. Paradoxically, the shortfall of each of the theories reveals a theoretical insight, namely that these events are *conjunctural:* the outcome of multiple, distinct processes. In the Soviet case, such large-scale logics as the expansion of capitalism, the maturing of industrialism, the intensification of global human interaction, and the balancing processes of the state system are all evident. Each tells much, but none tells all. In short, it is difficult to discern the plot of this unfolding drama because three or four plays are being performed on the same stage at the same time.

Second, several theories lying outside the mainstream of international relations study appear to have explanatory power. The way in which the field of international relations studies has defined itself is not broad enough to encompass many of the central processes of world historical change, forcing theories to go outside of the field to get theoretical purchase on large-scale phenomena such as the changes now unfolding. Like most American social scientists in the post-war era, international relations specialists have tended to ignore macro-historical theorizing in favor of more discrete and seemingly more tractable research questions. But when major events occur, such as those unfolding in the Soviet Union, macro-historical theorizing shows its value.

The revolutions currently underway promise to transform the intellectual as well as the political landscape. Just as Axis aggression and the Cold War altered the intellectual balance between idealism and realism, so too these contemporary events may well alter the relative appeals of realism, globalism, and socioeconomic theories such as industrial modernism.

NOTES

The authors would like to acknowledge helpful comments and suggestions by Michael Doyle, Randell Forsberg, Joseph Grieco, John A. Hall, Atul Kohli, Richard Matthew, Andrew Moravcsik, James Rosenau, Jack Snyder, Richard Ullman, and seminar participants at Columbia University and Princeton University. Research for this paper was supported by the Center of International Studies, the Peter B. Lewis Fund, and the Center for Energy and Environmental Studies, Princeton University.

1. For overviews of Soviet foreign policy change under Gorbachev, see Matthew Evangelista, "The New Soviet Approach to Security," *World Policy Journal*, 3, 1 (1986), pp. 561–99; Robert Legvold, "The Revolution in Soviet Foreign Policy," *Foreign Affairs: America and the World*, 68 (1988–1989); and Bruce Parrott, "Soviet National Security Under Gorbachev," *Problems of Communism*, 37 (1988), pp. 1–36.

2. Peter Gourevitch, "The Second Image Reversed," *International Organization*, 32 (1978), pp. 881–912.

3. We only look at theories that try to explain recent Soviet events in terms of patterns operating generally. Thus, unique patterns of Soviet political culture and history are not considered. These varieties are not equal to any one person's view. They might best be thought of as ideal-types, labels for relatively coherent clusters of assumptions, propositions, and expectations. These varieties are meant to capture the range of alternative theoretical propositions, rather than to locate or classify individual theorists. For an alternative taxonomy, see R.D. McKinlay and R. Little, *Global Problems and World Order* (London, 1986).

4. For other discussions of the varieties of realism, see Michael Joseph Smith, *Realist Thought from Weber to Kissinger* (Baton Rouge, 1987); and Michael W. Doyle, "Thucydidean Realism," *Review of International Studies*, 16 (1990), pp. 223–38.

5. Nicholas John Spykman, *America's Strategy in the World: The United States and the Balance of Power* (New York, 1942); Colin Gray, *Geopolitics in the Nuclear Age: Heartlands, Rimlands, and the Technological Revolution* (New York, 1977); Colin Gray, *The Geopolitics of the Super Powers* (Lexington, 1988); Robert E. Osgood and Robert W. Tucker, *Force, Order and Justice* (Baltimore, 1967); and Edward Luttwak, *Strategy* (Cambridge, MA: 1987).

6. Edward Luttwak, *The Grand Strategy of the Soviet Union* (New York, 1982).

7. For a general discussion of the Soviet military and the Gorbachev revolution, see Bruce Parrott, "Soviet National Security Under Gorbachev," *Problems of Communism*, 37 (November/December, 1988), pp. 1–36.

8. A perfectly consistent hard realist might lament the Gorbachev reforms, for freeing Soviet power of the millstone of communism.

9. Hedley Bull, *The Anarchical Society: A Study of Order in World Politics* (London, 1977).

10. X, "The Sources of Soviet Conduct," *Foreign Affairs*, 27 (July 1947), pp. 566–82; John Lewis Gaddis, *Strategies of Containment: A Critical Appraisal of Post-War American National Security Policy* (New York, 1982). For a useful discussion of theories of Soviet decline, see Robert P. Beschel, Jr., "The Long-term Moderation of Soviet Foreign Policy," in J.S. Nye, Carnesale, and Allison (eds.), *Fateful Visions* (Cambridge, 1988).

11. For an overview of Soviet foreign policy changes, see David Holloway, "Gorbachev's New Thinking," *Foreign Affairs*, 68 (1988–1989), pp. 66–81.

12. Soft realists are open to Havel's "paradoxical advice" that the United States should, within limits, assist Soviet reforms. For a discussion of the potential threats to the West stemming from Russian weakness, see Kurt Campbell, "Prospects and Consequences of Soviet Decline," in Nye *et al.* (eds.), *Fateful Visions*.

13. Stephen Krasner, *Defending the National Interest: Raw Materials Investments and United States Foreign Policy* (Princeton, 1978); Peter B. Evans, Dietrich Rueschemeyer, and Theda Skocpol (eds.), *Bringing the State Back In* (New York, 1985); G. John Ikenberry, *Reasons of State: Oil Politics and the Capacities of American Government* (Ithaca, 1988).

14. See Charles Tilly, "War Making and State Making as Organized Crime," in Evans, Rueschemeyer, and Skocpol (eds.), *Bringing the State Back In*.

15. Theda Skocpol, *States and Social Revolutions: A Comparative Analysis of France, Russia, and China* (New York, 1979).

16. Seweryn Bialer has recently noted the possibility of widespread instability in Soviet society: "By 1989, Gorbachev had lost control over events in all spheres of Soviet life. . . . Moreover, the most dangerous challenge that he faces is not for a coup at the top that may force his resignation, but from spontaneous forces—political, economic, and social—generated outside of the power establishment which may sweep away both him and his reforms." "The Passing of the Soviet Order?" *Survival*, 32 (March/April 1990), p. 107.

17. Others have noted the weakness of conventional realist theory in dealing with problems of change. See Robert O. Keohane, "Theory of World Politics: Structural Realism and Beyond," in Ada W. Finifter (ed.), *Political Science: The State of the Discipline* (Washington, D.C., 1983), pp. 503–40; R.J. Vincent, "Change and International Relations," *Review of International Studies*, 9 (1983), pp. 63–70.

18. Robert Gilpin, *War and Change in World Politics* (New York, 1981).

19. The globalist perspective is captured by John Ruggie: "the globe itself has become a region in the international system, albeit a *nonterritorial* one. Thus, global does not mean universal. Instead the concept refers to a subset of social interactions that take place on the globe. This subset constitutes an inclusive level of social interaction that is distinct from the *international* level, in that it comprises a multiplicity of integrated functional systems, operating in real time, which span the globe, and which affect in varying degrees what transpires elsewhere on the globe." "International Structure and International Transformation: Space, Time, and Method," in Ernst-Otto Czempiel and James N. Rosenau (eds.), *Global Changes and Theoretical Challenges:*

Approaches to World Politics for the 1990s (Lexington, MA, 1989), p. 31. See also Mike Featherstone (ed.), "Global Culture," Special Issue of *Theory, Culture & Society*, 7 (June 1990).

20. Some hold that the international system has adjusted, others hold that its adjustment will require a process of major institutional change, ranging from arms control through deep disarmament through the establishment of intrusive international monitoring and peacekeeping capabilities.

21. Kenneth Boulding, *Conflict and Defense* (New York, 1963); and John H. Herz, *International Politics in the Atomic Age* (New York, 1959).

22. Hans Morgenthau, "The Fallacy of Thinking Conventionally about Nuclear Weapons," in David Carlton and Carlo Schaerf (eds.), *Arms Control and Technological Innovation* (New York, 1976); George Kennan, *The Nuclear Delusion: Soviet-American Relations in the Atomic Age* (New York, 1982).

23. Although easily confused with the older normative critique of war, nuclear one-worldism has at its root a Hobbesian fear or physical fear of insecurity and assumes that the same imperatives leading to state formation in the pre-nuclear era will push toward global nuclear security in the contemporary period. Since the nuclear one-worldists assume that war as a process of institutional change has been blocked, it is expected that learning and anticipation (by both states and publics) eventually will cause institutional change.

24. An early statement of this position is found in Klaus Knorr, *On the Uses of Military Power in the Nuclear Age* (Princeton, 1966). See also Evan Luard, *The Blunted Sword: The Erosion of Military Power in Modern World Politics* (New York, 1988).

25. For an interpretation of detente driven by nuclear interdependence, see Steve Weber, "Realism, Detente, and Nuclear Weapons," *International Organization*, 44 (Winter 1990), pp. 55–82.

26. Stephen Shenfield, *The Nuclear Predicament: Exploration in Soviet Ideology*, Chatham House Papers 37 (London, 1987).

27. The nuclear one-worldist position is reflected in Gorbachev's speeches. See Mikhail Gorbachev, "Realities and Guarantees for a Secure World" (Moscow, 1987). For further discussion see A. Gromyko, M. Hellman *et al.* (eds.), *Breakthrough: Emerging New Thinking* (New York, 1988), particularly Alexander I. Nikitin, "The Concept of Universal Security: A Revolution of Thinking and Policy in the Nuclear Age."

28. Leonard Spector, "The Nuclear Inheritors," in *Going Nuclear* (Cambridge, 1987).

29. In his recent assessment of American strategy, Senator Sam Nunn pointed to this danger. "[T]he long-standing danger of unauthorized or accidental nuclear weapons use has been heightened by turmoil and tension in the Soviet Union," *Aviation Week & Space Technology*, April 16, 1990, p. 7.

30. Leonard Woolf, *International Government: Two Reports Prepared for the Fabian Research Department* (London, 1916); Norman Angell, *The Great Illusion* (London, 1911); H.G. Wells, *The Idea of a League of Nations* (Boston, 1919); Ramsey Muir, *The Interdependent World and its Problems* (1933; Port Washington, NY, 1971).

31. David Mitrany, *The Functional Theory of Politics* (London, 1975); Ernst Haas, *Beyond the Nation-State; Functionalism and International Organization* (Stanford, 1964); Andrew Scott, *The Revolution in Statecraft: Informal Pene-

tration (New York, 1965); James Rosenau (ed.), *Linkage Politics: Essays on the Convergence of National and International Systems* (New York, 1969); Richard Falk, *A Study of Future Worlds* (New York, 1975); Robert O. Keohane and Joseph S. Nye, *Power and Interdependence: World Politics in Transition* (Boston, 1977).

32. Of course, internationalism is not just a recent import from the West, but was an essential feature of Marxism at various stages of its intellectual and political development.

33. For a discussion of the general phenomenon of unofficial diplomacy, see Maureen R. Berman and Joseph E. Johnson, "The Growing Role of Unofficial Diplomacy," in Berman and Johnson (eds.), *Unofficial Diplomats* (New York, 1977), pp. 1–33.

34. The importance of simultaneous domestic and international "modernization" of politics is stressed in Edward Morse, *Modernization of International Relations* (New York, 1976).

35. This point is made by Zbigniew Brzezinski: "Central Europe is ripe for, and badly needs, regional cooperative arrangements of the type that Western Europe takes for granted." "Beyond Chaos: Policy for the West," *The National Interest* (Spring 1990), p. 11.

36. Clarence Glacken, *Traces on the Rhodian Shore: Nature and Culture in Western Thoughts from Ancient Times to the End of the Eighteenth Century* (Berkeley, 1967).

37. Harrison Brown, *The Challenge of Man's Future* (New York, 1954); Robert Heilbroner, *An Inquiry into the Human Prospect* (New York, 1974).

38. Sir Halford J. Mackinder, "The Geographical Pivot of History," *Geographical Journal*, 23 (April 1904). Valuable synoptic analyses of Soviet resource prospects are found in W.H. Parker, *The Superpowers: The United States and the Soviet Union Compared* (New York, 1972); and George Cressey, *Soviet Potentials: A Geographic Appraisal* (Syracuse, NY, 1962).

39. Thane Gustafson, *Crisis Amid Plenty: The Politics of Soviet Energy Under Brezhnev and Gorbachev* (Princeton, 1989), esp. pp. 22–62.

40. James R. Millar, "Post-Stalin Agriculture and Its Future," in Stephen F. Cohen *et al.* (eds.), *The Soviet Union Since Stalin* (Bloomington, 1980), pp. 135–55.

41. Alan S. Whiting, *Siberian Development and East Asia: Threat or Promise?* (Palo Alto, CA, 1981).

42. An early attempt to think about East-West interdependencies and their implications is found in Walter C. Clemens, Jr., *The USSR and Global Interdependence: Alternative Futures* (Washington, DC, 1977).

43. K.J. Holsti, *The Dividing Discipline: Hegemony and Diversity in International Theory* (Boston, 1985).

44. See Michael Doyle, "Liberalism and World Politics," *American Political Science Review*, 80 (December 1986), pp. 1, 151–69.

45. Francis Fukuyama, "The End of History?" *The National Interest* (Summer 1989), pp. 3–17.

46. John P. Diggins, *Up from Communism: Conservative Odysseys in American Intellectual History* (New York, 1975); Sidney Blumenthal, *The Rise of the Counter-Establishment: From Conservative Ideology to Political Power* (New York, 1986).

47. Daniel Patrick Moynihan, "The United States in Opposition," *Commentary* (March 1975).

48. The widely discussed argument of "Z" [Martin Malia] emphasizing the Leninist character of the Soviet Union and the undesirability of helping the Soviet Union has been surpassed by events, particularly Gorbachev's epochal move to repeal Article VI of the Soviet constitution. Z, "To the Stalin Mausoleum," *Daedalus* (Winter 1989–1990).

49. See Stephen F. Cohen, *Bukharin and the Bolshevik Revolution* (New York, 1980).

50. Robert C. Tucker, *Essays in Historical Interpretation* (New York, 1977).

51. For an early study of these processes, see W. Phillips Davison, *International Political Communication* (New York, 1965); see also James L. Tyson, *U.S. International Broadcasting and National Security* (New York, 1983).

52. The capitalist case against socialism has recently been summarized in F.A. Hayek, *The Fatal Conceit: The Errors of Socialism* (Chicago, 1988).

53. See D.P. O'Brien, *The Classical Economists* (Oxford, 1975).

54. The classic statement of this view is Karl Polanyi, *The Great Transformation: The Political and Economic Origins of Our Times* (Boston, 1944).

55. As Lenin proclaimed: "In the final analysis the competition and struggle between capitalism and socialism will be resolved in favor of the system that attains a higher level of economic productivity." Cited in Seweryn Bialer, "Gorbachev's Program of Change: Sources, Significance, Prospects," *Political Science Quarterly,* 103 (Autumn 1988), p. 410.

56. Contemporary theorists, on both the left and right, argue that strong states are crucial to the success of market-oriented reform. See Guillermo A. O'Donnell, *Modernization and Bureaucratic-Authoritarianism: Studies in South American Politics* (Berkeley, 1973); and Jagdish N. Bhagwati, "Rethinking Trade Strategy," in John P. Lewis and Valeriana Kallab (eds.), *Development Strategies Reconsidered* (Washington, DC, 1986), esp. p. 101. For an overview, see Atul Kohli, "Politics of Economic Liberalization in India," *World Development,* 17 (1989), pp. 1–30.

57. Jack Snyder, "International Leverage on Soviet Domestic Change," *World Politics,* (October 1989).

58. See the discussion of the "socialist" model in R.D. McKinlay and R. Little, *Global Problems and World Order.*

59. Shlomo Avineri, *Karl Marx on Colonialism and Modernization* (Garden City, NY, 1969).

60. Immanuel Wallerstein, "The Rise and Future Demise of the World Capitalist System: Concepts for Comparative Analysis," *Comparative Studies in Society and History,* 16 (1974), pp. 387–415.

61. Immanuel Wallerstein, *The Modern World-System: Capitalist Agriculture and the Origins of the European World-Economy in the Sixteenth Century* (New York, 1974); *The Modern World-System II: Mercantilism and the Consolidation of the European World-Economy, 1600–1750* (New York, 1980); *The Modern World System III: The Second Era of Great Expansion of the Capitalist World-Economy* (San Diego, 1989).

62. See Theda Skocpol, "Wallerstein's World Capitalist System: A Theoretical and Historical Critique," *American Journal of Sociology,* 85 (1977), pp. 1075–90; Aristide R. Zolberg, "Origins of the Modern World System: A Missing Link," *World Politics,* 33 (1981), pp. 253–81; Tony Smith, *The Pattern of Imperialism: The United States, Great Britain, and the Late-Industrializing World Since 1815* (Cambridge, 1981).

63. As Theda Skocpol describes the model, "once the system is established, everything reinforces everything else." Skocpol, "Wallerstein's World Capitalist System," p. 1078.

64. For another conceptualization of the Soviet Union's political economy in terms of Wallerstein's world-systems theory, see Timothy W. Luke, "Technology and Soviet Foreign Trade: On the Political Economy of an Underdeveloped Superpower," *International Studies Quarterly*, 29 (1985), pp. 327–53.

65. For discussion of the distinction between "capitalist society" and "industrial society," see Ralf Dahrendorf, *Class and Class Conflict in Industrial Society* (Stanford, 1959). See also Anthony Giddens, *Sociology: A Brief but Critical Introduction* (London, 1982), pp. 29–53.

66. James Burnham, *The Managerial Revolution: What is Happening in the World* (New York, 1941). See also James Burnham, *The Machiavellians: Defenders of Freedom* (Chicago, 1943).

67. An early version of these ideas was set forth by Jean-Baptist Say, the famous French political economist whose work Marx polemicized against. Say argued that the progress of industry could produce not a polarization between capitalist and proletariat, but rather a much more complex cluster of largely cooperative classes which he labelled the "industriat." Jean-Baptist Say, *A Treatise on Political Economy* (1803), trans. by C.R. Prinsep, 2 vols. (Boston, 1821). See also discussion of Say in Edmund Silberner, *The Problem of War in Nineteenth Century Economic Thought* (Princeton, 1946), pp. 69–91.

68. Dahrendorf, *Class and Class Conflict in Industrial Society.* Clark Kerr et al., *Industrialism and Industrial Man* (Cambridge, MA, 1960). This view has been strongly criticized by others, such as Reinhard Bendix, for ignoring national variations in paths to development caused by the persistence of pre-modern social formations that prove to be partially adaptive. See Reinhard Bendix, *Nation-Building and Citizenship* (New York, 1964).

69. Alain Touraine, *The Post-Industrial Society* (New York, 1971); Daniel Bell, *The Coming of Post-Industrial Society: A Venture in Social Forecasting* (New York, 1973).

70. See John A. Hall and G. John Ikenberry, *The State* (Minneapolis, 1989), pp. 80–83.

71. While the link between late-industrial society and democratic institutions appears to be strong in the contemporary era, the possibility cannot be foreclosed that a country with different historical traditions, class configurations, and international pressures might arrive at a non-democratic formation that was at the same time industrially functional. Michael Mann argues that an authoritarian capitalist model was pioneered and widely admired in pre-1914 Germany, that this non-democratic variant of capitalism could well have proved viable, but that it was destroyed by the war. Mann, "Citizenship and Ruling Class Strategies," *Sociology*, 21 (1987).

72. Brezezinski and Huntington describe convergence expectations thus: "The Communists believe that the world will converge, but into an essentially communist form of government. In the West, on the other hand, the widespread theory of convergence assumes that the fundamentally important aspects of the democratic system will be retained after America and Russia 'converge' at some future, indeterminate historical juncture. Although probably there will be more economic planning and social ownership in the West, the theory sees the Communist Party and its monopoly of power as the real victims of the historical process: both will fade away. Thus on closer exami-

nation it is striking to discover that most theories of the so-called convergence in reality posit not convergence but submergence of the opposite system. Hence the Western and the communist theories of convergence are basically revolutionary: both predict a revolutionary change in the character of one of the present systems. The Communists openly state it. In the West, it is implicit in the prevalent convergence argument." *Political Power: USA/USSR* (New York, 1964), p. 419. For a critique of convergence theory as it relates to the Soviet Union, see Bertram D. Wolfe, *Revolution and Reality: Essays on the Origin and Fate of the Soviet System* (Chapel Hill, 1981).

73. Walter W. Rostow, *The Stages of Economic Growth: A Non-Communist Manifesto* (Cambridge, 1965), pp. 162–64.

74. This argument has been made recently by several Soviet academics: "[A]s the completion of the stage of industrialization in economic development approached and the transition to the next scientific-industrial, technical-technological stage of production began, the administrative economy, devoid of any market elements, became an obstacle to the development of those very economic spheres whose accelerated development had once constituted justification of the system. At the scientific-industrial stage of technological development, the deformed socialist relations of production, of the state monopoly type, clashed with the forces of production engendered by scientific-technological progress." L. Gordon and A. Nazimova, "Perestroika in Historical Perspective," *Government and Opposition,* 25 (Winter 1990), p. 18.

75. Lewis A. Coser, "The Intellectuals in Soviet Reform," *Dissent* (Spring 1990), p. 183.

76. Soviet scientists were indispensable to the regime and, as a result, had more independence than any other group in Soviet society. The atomic designer, Pytor Kapitsa, was one of the few men to defy Stalin and live to tell about it. And, of course, Andrei Sakharov had similar independence and was therefore able to play a catalytic role in Soviet reform.

77. As Brzezinski and Huntington argued in 1964, the theory of industrial modernism is, "in effect, anti-Soviet Marxism: the forces of production will shape the social context of production, which in turn will determine the political superstructure." Zbigniew Brzezinski and Samuel P. Huntington, *Political Power: USA/USSR* (New York, 1964), p. 10.

78. Comparing and testing these theories is not a straightforward proposition because these theories differ greatly in scope and are attempting to explain different aspects of these contemporary events. Often proponents of different theories dispute factual claims. For example, the hard realists and the nuclear one-worlders do not agree upon what Soviet nuclear policy is. Perhaps more importantly, these theories are not just competing explanations of agreed-upon facts, but differ about what facts are important to explain.

79. Noting the difficulties of a return to repression, Lewis Coser argues that "[t]he fact that the intelligentsia is no longer dispensable in the Soviet sphere is among the prime reasons why a return to a totalitarian regime or to military solutions is unlikely." "The Intellectuals in Soviet Reform," *Dissent* (Spring 1990), p. 183.

80. Seweryn Bialer, "The Passing of the Soviet Order?" *Survival,* 32 (March/April 1990). See also Padma Desai, *Perestroika in Perspective: The Design and Dilemmas of Soviet Reform* (Princeton, 1989), p. 138.

81. For a discussion of the range and logic of state adjustment choices, see G. John Ikenberry, "The State and International Strategies of Adjustment,"

World Politics, 39 (October 1986); and Michael Mastanduno, David A. Lake, and G. John Ikenberry, "Toward a Realist Theory of State Action," *International Studies Quarterly,* 33 (Winter 1989), pp. 457–74.

82. Sylvia Woodby, *Gorbachev and the Decline of Ideology in Soviet Foreign Policy* (Boulder, 1989). For an analysis of the evolution of Soviet theories underpinning "new thinking," see Margot Light, *The Soviet Theory of International Relations* (Brighton, 1988).

83. This situation is noted by Seweryn Bialer: "Never in their history have the Russians been as secure from external danger as they are now and will remain in the foreseeable future. . . . A Soviet Union that understands that it is extremely secure may be less hostile to the West." Bialer, "Gorbachev's Program of Change: Sources, Significance, Prospects," *Political Science Quarterly,* 103 (Autumn 1988), p. 459.

84. Of course, security demands may decline but they will not disappear. And the security organs, forged in an earlier environment, may persist in making disproportionate claims, despite changes in the environment.

12

POLITICAL DYNAMICS OF THE POST-COMMUNIST TRANSITION:

A Comparative Perspective

There is an understandable tendency among observers of recent transformations in the communist world to be impressed by the uniqueness of the entire phenomenon. While earlier attempts at limited reform of communist polities and economies are numerous, the dismantling and disintegration of communist structures witnessed in the 1980s have never before been successfully attempted and achieved on such a scale. Although there remain important differences in the degree to which communist institutions have been displaced in various countries, the scope and depth of change have, on the whole, been sufficient for many to now speak of a "post-communist" era or even "the end of history."[1]

However unique these developments have been on one level, the transition from communism may, nevertheless, be usefully viewed as a sub-category of a more generic phenomenon of transition from authoritarian rule. In recent decades, efforts to liberalize and democratize authoritarian regimes in Latin America and Southern Europe have been quite numerous and have achieved varying degrees of success. Students of communist and post-communist regimes can learn a great deal from those cases and from the efforts that have been made to generalize about the transition process and the dilemmas and choices to which it gives rise.[2]

In this paper the focus will be on the still uncertain process of transition currently under way in the USSR. The goal is to bring a comparative perspective to bear in order both to provide new insight into the dynamics of the disintegration of the communist order and to consider the prospects for successful Soviet democratization. In the process, a case will be made for a more comparative approach to the issue of post-communist transitions in general. Before moving to substantive issues, however, a brief digression on the issue of comparability is necessary.

THE QUESTION OF COMPARABILITY

The debate over the importance of the unique versus the universal in history is certainly not new, and it is not the intention here to reiterate the old and ultimately unresolvable arguments made in that regard. Instead, what follows is addressed to those who accept that there are elements of both the unique and the universal present in every situation, who believe that comparison can, in principle, illuminate common patterns of behavior across disparate political cultures, but who may question whether—in comparing transitions from communist authoritarianism to transitions from non-communist authoritarianism—one is really looking at the generically same phenomenon. As political scientist Giovanni Sartori has noted, the higher one climbs the "ladder of abstraction" (i.e., the more extensive the class of phenomena one labels with the same conceptual apparatus), the greater the risk of "conceptual stretching" in which the extension or denotation of a concept is expanded by "obfuscating the connotation."[3] Comparing the Soviet case and other instances of post-communist transformation with transitions from non-communist authoritarian regimes raises this problem of conceptual stretching on three different levels.

In the first place, there may be significant differences in the goal of the regime transition. Although "democratization" is a common theme in cases of transition in Latin America, Southern Europe, and the communist world alike, the meaning of that term can vary tremendously. Numerous Western observers have argued that the goal of the transition initiated by Gorbachev in the USSR was never democracy in the Western sense but merely a less "totalitarian" and, perhaps, more enlightened form of authoritarian rule.[4] Assuming that to be the case, one might view the transition under way in the USSR as a transition *to* rather than *from* the kind of authoritarian rule that other nations in Europe and the Third World have been trying to transcend.

Comparison of such diverse efforts would thus appear to be quite problematic were it not for the fact that the goals of the transition, as articulated by those factions of the old regime responsible for the initiation of change, may ultimately prove to be of little consequence. As will be discussed in more detail later, most efforts to transform authoritarian regimes take on a life and dynamic of their own that quickly sweep away the most carefully laid plans of the architects of reform. Goals change as once-cautious reformers become more daring and come to accept changes that far exceed those initially intended.

A second problem in comparing such events is related to differences in the process of regime transition. Is it useful, for example, to compare the Soviet transition initiated by civilian reformers within the ruling elite to the Portuguese case in which a military coup overturned the old regime and allowed the issue of democracy a place on the political agenda? In raising that question, however, it follows that one must also ask whether the process of transition in the USSR can be compared to that of Romania or Hungary, where the specifics of the post-communist transition process have differed both from one another and from those of the USSR. Similarly, can the Portuguese situation be usefully compared to that of Spain, which, in many respects, resembles the Soviet case more than that of its Iberian neighbor? As one observer has summarized the Spanish reform process:

> It was a question of reformist elements, associated with the incumbent dictatorship, initiating processes of political change from within the established regime. Equally, it was a question of reformists seizing and, for some time, maintaining the initiative in the face of opposition from both their own backward-looking colleagues and from the dictatorship's opponents who were dedicated to a complete break with the old order.[5]

That characterization of the Spanish situation should sound more familiar to students of the Gorbachev era than to observers of the Portuguese case.

Since there appears to be as much variability in the transition process on each side of the communist/non-communist divide as there is across it, the issue of the comparability of transitions from communism to transitions from other forms of authoritarian rule seems, in this respect, to be beside the point. Instead, the concern should be to delimit a universe of potential cases for comparison by identifying characteristics of the transition process common to each. In this paper, the interest is with efforts of nonrevolutionary transitions from authoritarian rule in which elements of the old regime play an important role in the initiation and/or direction of political change. This definition is not meant to exclude the probability of societal pressures for reform or the possibility that reforms initiated from above can eventually be overtaken by revolution from below. Rather, the focus here is simply on those forms and periods of transition in which reformist segments of the old order have a part to play and which are, by definition, distinct from periods of systemic stability, on the one hand, and mass revolutionary movements, on the other.

Thus defined, all of the cases noted above (the Soviet, Romanian, Hungarian, Spanish, and Portuguese) could, despite their differences, be included, as can many others from the Third World and Europe. To use Sartori's terms once again, the "extension" of the concept of postauthoritarian transitions has been achieved not by obfuscating the connotation of the concept but by limiting it. That is, we have enlarged the class of things to which this concept refers by reducing some of its attributes while, at the same time, making sure to be reasonably precise about those common attributes that remain.[6]

The final problem of comparability to be addressed—and perhaps the place where the perception of conceptual stretching is potentially the greatest—is related to the nature of the authoritarianism being transformed. Proponents of the "totalitarian" model in communist studies have always at least implicitly argued that totalitarianism was different not only from democracy but from old-fashioned authoritarianism as well.[7] In essence, the latter distinction was rooted in the perceived ambition and success of totalitarian regimes in regard to the extension of state power and initiative. Whereas traditional authoritarianism built walls to demarcate the boundaries beyond which civil society could not tread, totalitarian regimes aimed to crush the preexisting civil society altogether.

As an ideal type, totalitarianism certainly differs from forms of authoritarian rule common in much of the non-communist world. As an empirical concept, totalitarianism also retains utility as a distinct variation on the authoritarian theme. Nevertheless, the distinction should not be exaggerated. Communist regimes have not only failed to achieve the total control envisioned by the totalitarian model but, especially in the post-Stalin era, have also scaled back those ambitions.[8] Even in the economy where the conceptual distinction between authoritarian and totalitarian regimes is sharp, the reality is much more muddled. It has been estimated that in the USSR of the late 1970s the proportion of income per capita derived from the private sector (legal and illegal) ranged from roughly 20 percent in the eastern RSFSR to more than 60 percent in Armenia.[9] At the same time, state economic ownership and control is hardly unique to self-proclaimed communist regimes.

Even where important empirical differences between communist totalitarianism and other forms of authoritarian rule remain, they should not be viewed as a barrier to comparison. While the concern over conceptual stretching is legitimate and must be kept in mind, "conceptual constriction" that ultimately reduces all phenomena to exclusive sets of single, unique entities should be of equal concern. Successful use of comparative political analysis requires the coexistence of both commonality and diversity in the cases to be examined. In fact, there is a case to be made for maximizing diversity insofar as claims to the universality of common patterns of political behavior are thereby strengthened.[10] Then again, to the extent that the patterns of political behavior differ, the distinctions in the cases examined may provide clues toward an explanation. In the discussion to follow, sensitivity to and explanation of points of both convergence and divergence in the politics of regime transition across the communist/non-communist divide is the goal.

THE DYNAMICS OF DISINTEGRATION

Transitions from authoritarian regimes actually involve two analytically distinct but empirically interrelated phenomena. On the one hand, there is the process of breaking down the preexisting structures of authoritarian rule. On the other hand, there is the task of creating new structures to take their place. In pursuing the transition, the stated goal of many reformers is to provide for a more democratic process of government, but successful dismantlement of the old order does not guarantee a democratic outcome. The former is a necessary but not a sufficient condition of the latter. The February 1917 revolution in Russia ended tsarist rule but failed to establish the foundations for an effectively functioning democracy. Similarly, by the end of 1990 Gorbachev's reforms had stripped the Communist Party of much of its power, yet the prospects for democracy seemed as remote as ever.[11] In accordance with this analytic distinction between the destructive and constructive components of regime transition, the disintegration of Soviet communism will be examined first and will be followed by an analysis of the dilemmas of democratization.

The Initial Decompression

It was under the banner of glasnost that the reformist spirit of the Gorbachev era was first introduced. In its original and most narrow sense, "glasnost" referred to a policy aimed at increasing access to information, thereby reducing the veil of censorship and secrecy that had long smothered Soviet society. In short time, however, the "glasnost era" came to represent a larger package of liberalizing reforms that included greater protection of individuals from the coercive power of the state, expanded freedom of political expression and association, easing of some restrictions on travel and emigration, and a new tolerance toward religious activity.

While glasnost did involve a significant increase in the flow of information and liberty, it was Gorbachev who maintained his hand on the control valve. Consequently, as numerous Western and Soviet observers have noted, glasnost shared little in common with the Western idea of "freedom of information" and even less with Western notions of democratic, constitutional government. As if to underline those distinctions, some observers have emphasized the Russian heredity of Gorbachev's policy. One author began an article on the subject by promising to place glasnost "in a broader context by tracing the origins of glasnost to nineteenth century Russia."[12]

Another observer has stated simply, "Glasnost has Russian national roots."[13]

Without denying the existence of Russian precedents in this regard, the fact remains that glasnost is not a uniquely Russian phenomenon. In a recent study of more than a dozen cases of transition from authoritarian rule in Latin America and Southern Europe, it was found that in every case the transition began with a period of glasnost-like liberalization.[14] This liberalization, often referred to in discussions of the Latin world as *decompressao* (decompression) or *apertura* (opening), typically involves the institution, restoration, or strengthening of the civil rights and liberties of individuals and groups. Guarantees of protection from arbitrary state power are introduced, the rights of free expression and association are strengthened, and access to information is increased.

For opponents of authoritarian rule, the decompression is typically viewed with some ambivalence. While a clear and welcome departure from past practices, liberalization is clearly not democratization. At a minimum, democracy involves both the provision of means to pursue the representation of diverse interests in government and the institutionalization of mechanisms to hold rulers accountable to the public will—including mechanisms that allow for the peaceful removal of governments from power. Furthermore, democracy precludes the possibility of altering outcomes after the fact. As Adam Przeworski has noted, everyone in a democracy, including rulers, must live with the fact that the outcome of political competition is uncertain and unalterable except through another round of equally uncertain democratic political struggle.[15] In a regime of "liberalized authoritarianism," in contrast, not only does the power apparatus remain intact but it retains "its capacity to control outcomes ex post."[16] Thus, the liberalization enjoyed always feels somewhat tenuous and insecure. It is granted and controlled from above and is potentially subject to revocation at any time.

Invariably, this liberalization process begins with a split within the ruling regime between reformers (soft-liners) and conservatives (hard-liners). Of course, even during more routine periods of authoritarian rule, divisions within the elite over issues of power and policy tend to be a constant. In periods of significant liberalization, however, not only are such divisions deeper but they lead some members of the regime to seek support outside the ruling elite.[17] In December 1976, just five months after assuming office, Prime Minister Suarez of Spain held a referendum to garner public support for his constitutional reforms.[18] In the USSR, Andrei Sakharov's return from banishment in Gorky in December 1986 and the cultural thaw that was, in effect, the first wave of glasnost were both clear efforts by Gorbachev to appeal for support to the country's intelligentsia. As time went on, Gorbachev's appeals for outside support would become even more direct. During the course of a February 1989 visit to the Ukraine, he appealed to his public supporters to help fight enemies of reform in the following terms: "You keep up the pressure. We'll press from the top, and you keep pressing from the bottom. Only in that way can perestroika succeed."[19] While common in democracies, such calls for support outside the regime constitute a radical change in the practice of authoritarian politics. While modern authoritarianism is distinguished by its efforts to mobilize the entire society behind the regime and its cause,[20] efforts to enlist outsiders as weapons of internal factional battles are generally taboo. In the Soviet case, the Leninist tradition of "democratic centralism," with its emphasis on demonstrating a united front vis-à-vis the larger society, is a very explicit statement of this principle.

Reformers within a liberalizing authoritarian regime often vary in their views of how far the process of reform should progress. While some might be satisfied with a liberalized authoritarianism, others might envision further movement in the direction of democratization. However, in comparison with regime hard-liners (who reject all but the most cosmetic changes) and opponents of the regime (who want a complete and immediate break with the past), reformers in the regime, by definition, occupy the position of the political center. While this centrist position carries with it the risk of alienating both hard-liners and regime opponents alike, at least in the early stages of the liberalization process the advantages of occupying the political center seem to outweigh the risks.

On the other hand, the reformers are initially in a strong position in relation to more radical opponents outside the regime. Emerging from the repression and persecution of authoritarian rule, the opposition is likely to be weak and disorganized. Perhaps even more important is the fear of political regression. Reflecting on the Latin American and Southern European cases, O'Donnell and Schmitter note:

> Their [the soft-liners'] ace in the hole is the threat that if the opposition refuses to play according to the rules they propose initially—usually a modest liberalization confined to individual rights and a restricted democratization with tight limits on participants and a narrow agenda of permissible policy issues—they will simply cancel the game and return to the authoritarian status quo ante. This tends to weaken and divide the proponents of further democratization. Some believe the threat and, preferring to avoid the worse outcome, agree to play the soft-liners' game.[21]

In the USSR, this logic provides part of the explanation for the failure of the radical Inter-Regional Group of Deputies in the Congress of People's Deputies to transform itself into an organized political party. According to one Western analyst who has worked with the group, there was a fear among some of its members of a return to "extreme discipline and an iron hand."[22] Although he never abandoned his principles, it is this logic that may have led Andrei Sakharov to give Gorbachev's policies his qualified support and to work for greater change within the reformed political institutions of the Gorbachev era. Similarly, in Lithuania, where the independence movement developed most rapidly, a parliamentary declaration of independence did not take place until March 1990, by which time Soviet toleration of the disintegration of its East European empire had raised questions as to how far Gorbachev would go to preserve his internal empire.

In the early stages of liberalization, the position of reformers vis-à-vis regime hard-liners also tends, for a time, to become increasingly strong. In the first place, the initial restraint and disorganization of the opposition lends support to reformers' claims to have the situation under control.[23] While conservatives, like Ligachev in the USSR, continue to harbor doubts, and though they may persist in their attacks on the reform process, they tend to remain on the defensive. That Ligachev's criticisms of the direction of change rarely attacked Gorbachev directly and almost always included pro forma endorsements of the general idea of glasnost and perestroika were good indications of the weakness of his position.

A second important weakness of conservatives stems, ironically, from the fact that the authoritarian structures, norms, and psychology of the old regime often make it surprisingly easy for reformers in positions of power to dismantle that regime from within. Despite the presence of large numbers of conservative opponents of reform, a resolution promoting the democratization of the USSR passed unanimously at the nineteenth conference of the CPSU in June 1988, with only two abstentions.[24] A few months later the Supreme Soviet voted overwhelmingly to approve new laws on elections and constitutional reform that, in effect, denied to many of those who had voted their status, power, and perquisites.[25] Similarly, in 1976 the members of the Francoist rubber-stamp legislature, the Cortes, voted 425 to 15 for political reforms in what one observer called an act of "collective suicide."[26]

Aside from these political dynamics, the strength of reformers within the regime is also a function both of the context of the larger environment and of the political leadership skills of key reform leaders. The existence of serious unresolved political, social, and economic crises is what leads to splits inside the authoritarian regime in the first place, thereby setting off the political dynamic discussed above. At the same time, political skills are necessary if reformist leaders are to take advantage of the opportunities at least temporarily available. Thus, Gorbachev was able to go further in his reforms than had Khrushchev, both because the problems facing the USSR in the 1980s were much more severe than those of the 1950s and because of Gorbachev's superior skills in playing the strong hand that the political center initially holds in such circumstances. It is this interaction of structural, political, and individual factors that explains the puzzle of Gorbachev's rapid consolidation of political authority in the mid-1980s.

Collapse of the Political Center

Just as surely as reformers in the regime are favored with certain political advantages in the early stages of the transition process, so too, in turn, do those advantages eventually begin to wither. The political center, once such an asset, can rapidly become a liability and can bring down reformist leaders who fail to adjust. The cause of this shift can best be understood through a consideration of the relationship between legitimacy and stability. As Przeworski has emphasized, while legitimacy may be a sufficient condition of regime stability, it is not a necessary condition.[27] The inability of the Communist Party to demonstrate public support in the new political milieu of the Gorbachev era certainly raises doubts as to the legitimacy of communist rule; yet, prior to Gorbachev, the political stability of the communist regime was not in question.[28] Similarly, relatively quick mobilization of support for democratic change in Portugal, Spain, and Brazil in the 1970s suggests a lack of legitimacy of authoritarian rule in those countries as well, yet, in these as in the USSR, change had to be initiated from within the regime itself. In none of those cases did there exist significant prior threats to authoritarian rule from outside the regime.

The explanation for the political stability of unpopular regimes is that stability is often less a function of legitimacy than of the perceived lack of availability of preferable alternatives.[29] Put somewhat differently, legitimacy itself may be less an *absolute* than a *relative* concept conditioned by the array of feasible alternatives present. Unpopular regimes can maintain their domination of society through repression that makes the cost of opposition very high, thus making the possibility of significant change seem remote. Compared with a return to harsh Stalinist rule, which for most Soviet citizens must have been seen as the only possible alternative, Brezhnev's comparatively mild dictatorship might even have gained some relative legitimacy. With the onset of liberalization, however, not only do the costs and risks of opposition begin to fall but alternatives to the status quo ante that once seemed impossible now appear to be within the realm of possibility. As a result, one often encounters the paradox of rising absolute legitimacy coupled with a decline in relative legitimacy and increasing instability. This comes about because increases in absolute regime legitimacy derived from the process of reform are outmatched by a sense of the expansion of the possible.

Failing fully to appreciate the dynamic at work here, reformers often overestimate both the support and the goodwill that limited liberalization has brought them as well as their ability to keep the process of change they unleashed under their control. According to O'Donnell and Schmitter, this was true of "the Argentine military in 1973, the Brazilian generals in 1974, the Portuguese MFA in 1975, the Uruguayan junta in 1980, [and] the Turkish military in 1983."[30] Gorbachev was, perhaps, more sensitive and realistic in this regard than most in his position. He was, for example, openly critical of those on his team who, by mid-1989, had begun to express surprise and alarm at the instability reform had produced. In his concluding remarks to a July 1989 conference in the CPSU Central Committee, Gorbachev asked in a rhetorical fashion: "Is it really necessary to panic when revolutionary processes become a reality? It is we who brought them about with our policy. Didn't we understand that when all this was being discussed?"[31] Likewise, his unwillingness to stand for direct election to the presidency of the USSR was another indication of a realistic estimate of the strengths and liabilities of his position.

Still, to understand the forces at work is not necessarily to control them. Maintaining control through the threat of reversing the reform process becomes less believable over time, insofar as the political fate of those who initiated liberalization becomes increasingly tied to its continuation. Indeed, the reformers' threat to reverse the process has been characterized as little more than a bluff from the outset.[32] Once called on that bluff, reformers' leverage with the opposition is reduced, and they often find themselves accepting changes that were once anathema to them. In Spain, Prime Minister Suarez was to find himself in a battle with the opposition over control of the transition and was forced to make a number of concessions, including legalization of the Spanish Communist Party.[33] Likewise, in Brazil, the Geisel government found that its plans for a closely controlled process of liberalization in the 1970s were under constant pressure from an opposition emboldened to push for quicker and more sweeping changes.[34] In a variation on the same theme, the radical leaders of the 1974 Portuguese coup were to play midwife to the birth of a liberal democratic order that they had not originally envisioned.[35]

In Gorbachev's case, it would certainly be an exaggeration to suggest that he had lost all control over events or that his reform strategy had degenerated into a completely ad hoc response to crisis. Equally exaggerated, however, are assertions that developments in the USSR have all gone according to Gorbachev's grand design.[36] At the end of 1989, Gorbachev was still resisting calls to eliminate the constitutional guarantee of the leading role of the Communist Party and to create a multiparty political system.[37] Continued pressures for reform, however, were soon to force a dramatic reversal. In

March 1990 the Congress of People's Deputies, with Gorbachev's consent, formally abolished article 6 of the Soviet constitution, which guaranteed the CPSU's monopoly on power, and this began to clear the way for the emergence of other parties.

Just when it seems that the pressures for change from below are irresistible, however, previously moribund hard-liners within the regime typically appear to be granted a new lease on life. By late 1980 and early 1981 many observers of Brazilian politics began to speak of the irreversibility of the liberalization process, only to have this optimism destroyed by subsequent reports of military terror against the opposition.[38] In Spain, the growing optimism of the opposition led directly to ever more defiant and determined cooperation between military and civilian critics of change.[39] Likewise, in the USSR, the conservative resurgence of 1990–1991 followed closely on the heels of the challenge to the one-party monopoly, the discussion of a five-hundred-day plan to marketize the economy, and the rapidly developing challenges to the very existence of the multinational union. The timing here is not fortuitous. Given the concessions made by regime soft-liners, conservatives are less convinced than ever of the ability or will of soft-liners to rein in an increasingly assertive civil society. Feeling that their conservatism has been vindicated by events, they are reenergized in their struggle against reform.

The upshot of this entire process is a society increasingly polarized, and, in such a context, the centrist position of the reformist leadership becomes increasingly untenable.[40] Briefly seen by conservatives as insurance against popular rebellion and by radicals as the main obstacles to a conservative coup, the reformist center quickly becomes the object of scorn and distrust from both sides. The Gorbachev government in the USSR, the Suarez government in Spain, and the Geisel government in Brazil each came to face this dual challenge to its authority.[41] Indeed, critics on both ends of the political spectrum, feeling equally betrayed by regime soft-liners, typically come to spend more time and energy attacking those reformers than they do each other.

At such points in time, the entire process of reform might be said to reach a crossroads. It often appears that the only possible outcomes are the reversal of the liberalization process (with or without the support of regime reformers) or further descent into chaos and, perhaps, civil war. For supporters of democracy, these are often times of pessimism. The reemergence of conservative forces and the polarization of society do seem to bode poorly for democracy. Observers of the Soviet situation in early 1991 certainly had cause to adopt this mood of pessimism.

However, the political dynamics at work here do not always guarantee the failure of the democratization process. The chaos, polarization, conflict, and tension that characterize this period of the transition can sometimes be seen, in retrospect, to have been the birth pangs of a more democratic order. As Dankwart Rustow argued in his seminal 1970 article on democratic transitions, "What infant democracy requires is not a lukewarm struggle but a hot family feud."[42] Indeed, many nations in Latin America and Southern Europe have managed to maneuver through these powerful political currents toward relatively democratic outcomes.

It is not the intention in this paper to make any firm predictions as to whether the USSR can ride those currents to a similarly positive conclusion. Instead, in the pages that follow, the intention is to go back to the literature on regime transition outside the communist world, to examine the factors that make a successful transition to democracy more or less likely, and to apply the lessons learned to the Soviet case in a manner that emphasizes less the certainty of future trends than one that analyzes what has already transpired and examines the possibilities thereby spawned.

DILEMMAS OF DEMOCRATIZATION

In the literature on transitions to democracy, some analysts emphasize variables of context while others stress those of process. Included among the former variables are the level of economic development, the character of the national political culture, the degree of national integration, and the nature of the country's class structure. These factors are usually discussed in the course of considering the "preconditions" or "determinants" of democracy.[43] In contrast, those who stress process adopt a less structuralist approach, preferring, instead, to focus on the "making" of the democratic transition and the choices and strategies adopted by key actors.[44] Still others have argued the need to draw upon and integrate the lessons of both approaches.[45] It is this latter advice that guides the present effort to understand the issue of Soviet democratization.

The Democratization Process

The first tentative steps from a process of liberalization to one of democratization were taken by the Gorbachev regime in mid-1988. At the CPSU conference held in June of that year, a resolution entitled "On the Democratization of Soviet Society and Reform of the Political System" was adopted.[46] A few months later, two laws designed to spell out and implement the political changes embodied in the spirit of that resolution, the "Law on Elections of USSR People's Deputies" and the "Law on Amendments and Additions to the USSR Constitution," were approved by the Supreme Soviet.[47] Taken together, the two laws provided, at both the all-union and local levels, for multiple candidate elections to legislative bodies whose powers and authority were significantly increased. At the all-union level, for example, there would be popular election of a new Congress of People's Deputies that would, in turn, select from among its membership a new stream-lined Supreme Soviet of 542 members. Most significantly, the new Supreme Soviet would meet in regularly scheduled spring and fall sessions each of three to four months' duration. In effect, the USSR seemed to be at least hesitantly groping its way toward a system in which the articulation and representation of diverse interests were legitimized and which institutionalized some means of promoting the responsiveness of political leaders.

Of course, as both Soviet and Western observers noted at the time, this new version of Soviet democracy was an imperfect one at best. As designed and implemented by the Gorbachev leadership, the reforms contained a number of elements intended to circumscribe electoral outcomes and to protect the interests of the traditional Soviet elite. Most important in this respect were the refusal to legal-ize the creation of competing political parties; the broad and often vaguely defined powers granted to electoral commissions to oversee the nomination, registration, and election of candidates;[48] and the reservation of one-third of the seats in the Congress of People's Deputies for election by such pro-regime social organizations as the Communist Party, the trade unions, and the Komsomol.[49] Further-more, the simultaneous expansion of the powers of the newly rede-signed Soviet presidency led some, including the writer of these lines, to argue that the main purpose of the political reforms was to increase Mikhail Gorbachev's power and independence of action.[50]

Despite these limitations, an examination of paths to democracy in other parts of the world suggests that regime insistence on main-taining decidedly undemocratic elements in the early stages of the postauthoritarian transition does not necessarily render democratiza-tion either a fraud or a failure. On the contrary, the historical record suggests that those initial limits on democracy are often a necessary part of the road to a successful and stable democratic system. In an examination of attempted transitions from authoritarian rule in Latin America, Terry Lynn Karl found that political democracies have tended most successfully to emerge from transitions from above in which "traditional rulers remain in control, even if pressured from below, and successfully use strategies of compromise or force—or some mix of the two—to retain at least part of their power."[51] By way of contrast, she notes that in Latin America "no stable political democracy has resulted from regime transitions in which mass actors have gained control, even momentarily, over traditional ruling classes."[52]

The explanation for this pattern is related to the need to assure members of the old elite that their vital interests will not be threat-ened, thus decreasing the chances that they will attempt to subvert the process of reform. Hence, democratization requires some initial institutional compromises, often taking the form of explicitly negotiated pacts, which contain one or more of such obviously undemocratic components as restrictions on participation, a limited policy agenda, or limited contestation.[53] In an earlier period, undemocratic compromises of this sort were a crucial aspect of democratization in Western Europe and North America as well. Property requirements attached to the franchise, indirect elections, the protection of less democratic Upper Houses were just a few of the means utilized to protect certain strata and interests from the "excesses" of democracy.[54] In reflecting on the early history of existing Western democracies, Robert Dahl has noted that the transition to democracy (or polyarchy, to use his term) has tended to be most successful when the transition was taken slowly, initially limiting political contestation to a small stratum of the population.[55] Viewed in the light of this historical pattern, the much-maligned undemocratic elements of Gorbachev's political reforms take on a very different hue as a crucial component of a potentially historic compromise on the path of democratization.

Admittedly, the problem of finding and maintaining a workable compromise acceptable to the old ruling stratum remains inherently more difficult in the transition from communist rule than in other cases. In capitalist economies, former rulers and bureaucrats can often retreat from positions of political power to the world of wealth and property. In communist systems, however, wealth and property are directly tied to one's political position.[56] Thus, the communist *nomenklatura* potentially has more to lose and less to fall back upon than elites in other authoritarian systems undergoing transition. Except for the unlikely possibility that some way will be found to institutionalize the privileges of this class in a post-communist era, resistance to democratic compromise will often be intense.[57]

While this situation makes successful institutional compromise and pact making more difficult, it is not impossible. While many party and state officials in the USSR have been reluctant to subject their privileges and status to the uncertainties of even a restricted democratic process, others supported Gorbachev's democratization program. Even more important to emphasize is that it is less the civilian bureaucrats than those who control the instruments of state violence whose attitudes are most vital. It is the willingness of the military establishment to tolerate liberalization and democratization that has typically been crucial to the fate of postauthoritarian transitions around the world.

In this regard, Soviet democratization efforts actually enjoy certain advantages in comparison with Latin American attempts. In the latter case, military establishments often bear direct responsibility for the repression and policies of the authoritarian regime.[58] In many cases the military *was,* in fact, the old regime, having forcibly taken political power directly into its own hands. Despite the close relationship in the USSR between the military establishment and the CPSU, the former has generally avoided direct participation in the political process. One can more easily envision, therefore, a process of pact making in which the vital interests of the military as an institution are protected from the feelings of popular retribution so common in Latin America. Indeed, the most recent evidence of military discontent with Soviet reform notwithstanding, military tolerance of the reform process in the USSR through at least the first five years of reform—despite steadily growing political and economic chaos—was noteworthy.

What then has gone wrong? If Gorbachev's cautious and compromising approach to democratization was appropriate in light of historical experience and if there was at least a temporary willingness of key sectors of the Soviet elite to engage in the process of institutional compromise, why then, in early 1991, did the democratization process appear in jeopardy?

One part of the answer to this question is found in the fact that conservative forces were not positioned to participate very successfully in a democratic polity. The results of the March 1989 elections, the first semi-free elections since 1917, must have given many party officials a jolt. Overwhelming electoral victories for key reform leaders such as Sakharov and Yeltsin and the stunning defeat of virtually the entire Leningrad party/state apparatus were certainly bad omens in this regard.[59] Still, the combination of the formal election rules and the informal pressures Communist Party officials could bring to bear did allow for significant representation of conservative and centrist forces in the Congress of People's Deputies and Supreme Soviet. While not quite the rubber-stamp legislatures of old, each of these newly elected bodies has, in fact, proven itself sufficiently malleable in Gorbachev's hands. As a result, it took yet another round of elections a year later, this time to elect deputies to republic-level soviets, for the writing on the wall to become crystal clear. In many of the republics, the formal and informal mechanisms for manipulating the electoral outcome were of little effect in preventing either the poor showing of establishment candidates or the strong performance of pro-independence forces.[60]

The great paradox here is that the prospects of democratization would, over the long haul, have been improved had conservative forces fared better.[61] As it was, the electoral results eroded any conservative confidence that the continuing ban on opposition parties, the reservation of legislative seats for loyal social organizations, and the other institutionalized limits on democratic "excesses" could successfully protect their vital interests or, perhaps most importantly, the integrity of the union. Some even began to call for an electoral change that would emphasize voting based less on territorial districts than on production units, on the assumption that such a change would produce outcomes more favorable to conservative candidates.[62] Although that proposal was not adopted, it reflected a declining tolerance for the centrist compromise that Gorbachev has tried to forge.

While the problem confronting conservative forces has been that of a large head (the party/state machine) with a relatively small body of popular support, the problem facing the democratic opposition has been that of a large body without a head. Unlike the Polish case, where Solidarity and Lech Walesa provided Jaruzelski with a partner in pact making, Gorbachev had no one to bargain with in making such a pact. In fact, his democratization program was not a pact at all but rather a set of reforms imposed by him unilaterally. In doing this Gorbachev simultaneously acted as representative of the old regime and of the reformist elements. While some have characterized his role as that of both Pope and Luther, the more contemporary analogy would be to see Gorbachev as both Jaruzelski and Walesa.

The problem posed by this situation is that the reforms never received the legitimation that pact making can provide. The democratic opposition never signed on to those reforms as such, and there was no commonly recognized opposition organization with the leadership to provide guarantees to the Gorbachev regime that the boundaries of the compromise would be respected. There is, in fact, some speculation that Gorbachev was looking to reach some such agreement with opposition forces in early 1990. In June there was a report of a secret meeting between representatives of the democratic opposition and two top Gorbachev advisers who were looking to cut a deal.[63] Gorbachev's role and intentions in that regard remain unclear; but, even assuming the very best of intentions, it is not clear who—if anyone—could bargain for and make concessions in the name of the opposition. The only conceivable possibility in this regard was Boris Yeltsin. However, his stormy, almost operatic relationship with Gorbachev (combined with the fact that, as leader of the Russian Republic, Yeltsin headed what is, in effect, a rival government) made cooperation between the two extremely difficult at that point in time. As a result, whatever inclinations Gorbachev may or may not have once had, he probably decided by the end of 1990 that an escape from the collapsing political center in the direction of the opposition would be a jump into a political abyss, while an escape in the other direction into the arms of conservative forces left some hope, however slim, that his centrist policies might eventually be salvaged.

By the spring and early summer of 1991, however, a resurrected emphasis on radical economic reform and a shaky yet hopeful truce in the war of words between Gorbachev and Yeltsin were but two manifestations of a radical reversal of the political current. This shift in direction may be a tactical move on Gorbachev's part, designed to re-create a viable political center. By zigzagging from right to left his hope may be to continue, on average, along the moderately reformist political course that he has long advocated but that lacks much of a base of support in the polarized politics of the era. More optimistically, the January resistance and bloodshed in Vilnius, the bold yet disciplined March demonstration in Moscow in defiance of Kremlin orders, and the impressive June electoral victory of Boris Yeltsin may, in demonstrating the growing confidence of the democratic opposition, have collectively provided both an indication of the high costs of further repression and, at the same time, a new opportunity to deal with an opposition whose organization and leadership have become more impressive over time. As of mid-summer 1991, it remained unclear whether it was the former short-term shift in tactics or the latter longer-term shift in strategy that was at the root of Gorbachev's renewed courtship of radical reformers.

The Question of Preconditions

While the analysis to this point has focused on issues of political process and dynamics, it would be inappropriate to conclude without considering whether the problems and obstacles most recently encountered along the path of Soviet democratization reflect objective conditions not yet sufficiently ripe for democracy. It should be noted at the outset of this discussion that an examination of the Soviet Union's relatively unique combination of structural characteristics does not contradict the previous emphasis on the political dynamics common to all liberalizing regimes. The road of liberalization has multiple exits, some leading toward greater democracy, others circling back to (or near) the point of origin. While the USSR has joined other liberalizing regimes in traveling the common road, with all of its predictable twists and turns, the exit it ultimately chooses to take remains a subject of speculation. Consideration of the "preconditions" of democracy may, when applied to the Soviet case from a comparative vantage point, provide some clues.

In the literature on political development and democratic preconditions, the variable that has, perhaps, received the most attention is a country's level of socioeconomic modernization. Reflecting a widely held view among political scientists, Robert Dahl has argued that

an advanced economy automatically generates many of the conditions required for a pluralistic social order. And as a pluralistic social order evolves . . . some of its members make demands for participating in decisions by means more appropriate to a competitive than to a hegemonic political system.[64]

In terms of this one criterion of socioeconomic modernization, the USSR would certainly seem to be ripe for political reform. Moshe

Lewin, Jerry Hough, and other Western students of the USSR have attempted to explain and, in Hough's case, to predict the reforms of the Gorbachev era as a consequence of the increased education, urbanization, and stratification that economic development has produced.[65] However, without denying that those trends have led to strains in communist systems or that they are at the root of recent reform efforts, the fact remains that in other respects the conditions for a successful democratic outcome in the USSR are, at least in the short run, much less favorable.

First, it must be emphasized that while all existing democracies are not equally modern, they are all characterized by largely private enterprise, market economies. Charles Lindblom explains this connection between democracy and markets by noting that democratization has historically been the means by which a rising middle class of entrepreneurs and merchants sought to protect its wealth, property, and economic freedom from arbitrary state action.[66] To be sure, it is clear that this middle class does not always commit itself to democratization. There are many existing market systems where the business classes feel their interests are adequately protected from the state without democracy. Indeed, in the twentieth century the business class often feels the need to be protected by the authoritarian regime from leftist and populist movements from below. Nevertheless, successful democratic transitions in Spain, Brazil, and elsewhere have been facilitated, if not determined, by the support of at least some segments of the business community.[67]

Thus, the question is whether it is modernization or, more specifically, capitalist modernization that is most important for the evolution of democracy. While, as previously noted, communist regimes have lacked the ability and desire to eliminate all private economic activity (thereby failing to maintain complete, totalitarian control over the large society), they have managed to preempt the emergence of any potential political challenge from a rising capitalist elite by effectively monopolizing control of the commanding heights of their industrial economies. Whether a substitute stratum (the managerial class? intellectuals? foreign governments and capital?) can emerge to fill the historic political role of the merchant and entrepreneurial classes remains to be seen. In advocating a Chilean or South Korean model of marketization under strong authoritarian guidance, some Soviet observers seem to have concluded that such substitution of roles is impossible and that democracy will, at best, have to await the development of a new stage in the relations of Soviet production.[68] Perhaps the best test case here will be Poland, where an experiment in simultaneous marketization and democratization is currently being pursued most seriously.

Whatever the Polish outcome, adding a consideration of "political preconditions" of democracy into the analysis leads one to conclude that Soviet democratization will remain a still more difficult nut to crack. Most importantly, while Poland is an ethnically homogeneous society, the USSR is a state that has not been able to forge a unified Soviet nation. It is difficult to exaggerate the extent to which this factor complicates efforts at democratization.[69] Of greatest significance here is the fact that political energies released by the process of regime liberalization are diverted from the quest for democracy by traveling down the road of national separatism instead. One can even point to cases, such as the Basque separatist movement in Spain, where radical elements, fearing a legitimation of the existing regime, have sought to undermine the democratization process through terror.[70] Even in less extreme situations, independence rather than democracy often comes to be seen as the primary guarantee of protection from the repression of the old regime. In this respect, a transnationally minded capitalist elite driven by the economic logic of economies of scale and the unimpeded movement of goods and capital is particularly missed.

As for the antidemocratic forces of reaction, national strife plays right into their hands. The threat of the country's disintegration not only provides a pretext for renewed repression but also divides the democratic opposition. What O'Donnell and Schmitter refer to as the "popular upsurge"—that fleeting moment that sometimes occurs when a sense of public empowerment and unity arises as the ultimate challenge to the existing order—has difficulty materializing.[71] Moreover, whatever tolerance might once have existed for institutional compromise among conservative and even moderate forces is now undercut. As noted previously, the results of the March 1989 elections, while threatening to the conservative forces in some respects, were sufficiently mixed so as to sustain, perhaps, the institutional compromise Gorbachev had forged. With the strong showing of separatist candidates in local elections in 1990, however, that possibility seemed to evaporate.

Finally, prospects for Soviet democratization are also complicated by the relative lack of a Russian democratic tradition. The problem here involves more than a question of political attitudes and values. In many countries of Latin America, Southern Europe, and even Eastern Europe, the issue on the political agenda is best described not as democratization but as redemocratization. In many of those cases, the initial stages of liberalization allowed for long-repressed political organizations to reemerge in relatively short order. In the USSR, in contrast, building an organized democratic opposition has had to proceed almost from scratch. Unlike neighboring Poland, where a history of challenges to communist governments provided a well-prepared soil for the birth and development of Solidarity, the USSR lacks a history of even unsuccessful democratic movements. It is, thus, not surprising that Gorbachev would have had trouble, as noted previously, in finding partners in pact making who could both speak for and restrain a fledgling democratic opposition.

To be sure, in considering the preconditions of democracy, one should avoid extreme determinism insofar as the emergence (or lack thereof) of democracy has not always corresponded to our theoretical understanding of the optimal objective conditions. In Latin America, for example, one can point to a number of exceptions where democratization has either lagged or outpaced expectations generated by an overly deterministic emphasis on structural preconditions.[72] So, too, in the USSR it is at least possible, if not probable, that a combination of skillful political leadership, external support, and good fortune may combine to surprise the most pessimistic observers. Taken as a whole, however, this consideration of democratic preconditions suggests that in the short run such a surprise remains a long shot, at best.

CONCLUSION

As noted at the outset, this paper had two objectives. The first was to make the case for the profitability of examining the issues of regime transition in the communist world from a comparative perspective. As such, this paper was intended as a beginning more than an end. Many of the topics considered, including the role of the military in the transition process, the relationship between regime hard-liners and soft-liners, and the issue of democratic preconditions, deserve to be examined in the context of the Soviet and other post-communist transitions in much more detail than is possible in a single article. For students of communism, these topics represent opportunities to initiate what is, in many cases, a long-postponed reintegration with the field of comparative politics.

At the same time, a second objective has been to provide some immediate insights into the political dynamics of Gorbachev-era Soviet politics. Indeed, the two objectives are closely intertwined insofar as the best way to make the case for the utility of comparison is to produce at least a sample of what a comparative analysis can provide. In this instance, the comparison demonstrated that the dynamics of the liberalization process in the USSR adhere to a model of political change previously manifested in other parts of the world. It has, thereby, helped to cast new light on some of the key political and intellectual puzzles of the Gorbachev era.

First, in analyzing the initial strengths of regime reformers, the comparison helps to explain what was for most observers an unexpectedly rapid consolidation of Gorbachev's authority in his first few years in power. Second, the subsequent decline of Gorbachev's centrist political agenda appears, from this broader perspective, not simply, as Martin Malia argues in his well-known "Z" article, a result of a uniquely futile effort to salvage some type of "soft communism," but as a generically similar dilemma of all efforts to reform authoritarian regimes.[73] Third, the comparative analysis suggests that Gorbachev's post-1988 political reform program, harshly criticized by proponents of more rapid and thorough democratic change, was an appropriate step in the process of democratization. Finally, and related to the above, the analysis suggests that the apparent failure of that democratization program was ultimately rooted in structural characteristics of Soviet society that even the wisest leadership would have had difficulty in overcoming.

Beyond the specifics of the Soviet case, the discovery of common patterns *across* such diverse cases may ultimately contribute further to the development of a generalized theory of postauthoritarian transitions. In the interim, students of the communist world, armed with a comparative perspective from the beginning, might not have been so frequently caught off guard by the developments of the last several years. In the early days of reform, when many Western observers questioned the stability of Gorbachev's political position, the literature on regime transitions could have helped point to sources of strength. Likewise, at a point when some began to speak of the irreversibility of reform, a comparative perspective might have provided greater caution.

In conclusion, it must be emphasized that comparison is not meant to substitute for case studies of transition politics. Rather, each approach is most likely to be successful when informed by the other. Nor does comparison imply an expectation of similar outcomes. As was made clear throughout the paper, the purpose of a comparative approach is as much to illuminate differences as it is to confirm similarities. The fact that there were similar political dynamics at work in post-Franco Spain and in the post-Brezhnev USSR does not mean that Spain's present is the Soviet Union's future. Indeed, the ultimate fate of regime transitions has been and will continue to be varied among the nations of both Latin America and Southern Europe. Nevertheless, an examination of the Spanish and other cases does help one to better understand the possibilities and probabilities with which the Soviet Union is faced.

NOTES

The author would like to thank Mark Ruhl for his helpful comments on an earlier draft of this paper.

1. Francis Fukuyama, "The End of History?" *National Interest* 16 (Summer 1989), pp. 3–18.

2. Students of the USSR and other communist regimes in transition have not made much use of these cases or of the literature on postauthoritarian transitions that they have spawned. Noteworthy exceptions are Thomas F. Remington, "Regime Transition in Communist Systems," *Soviet Economy* 6 (April–June 1990), pp. 160–90; and George W. Breslauer, "Evaluating Gorbachev as Leader," *Soviet Economy* 5 (October–December 1989), pp. 299–340.

3. Giovanni Sartori, "Concept Misformation in Political Science," *American Political Science Review* 64 (December 1970), pp. 1040–41.

4. See, for example, Seweryn Bialer, "Gorbachev's Program of Change: Sources, Significance, Prospects," in Seweryn Bialer and Michael Mandelbaum, eds., *Gorbachev's Russia and America's Foreign Policy* (Boulder, CO: Westview, 1988), pp. 256–58, 299. Also see Jerry Hough, *Russia and the West: Gorbachev and the Politics of Reform* (New York: Simon and Schuster, 1988), pp. 209–12.

5. Kenneth Medhurst, "Spain's Evolutionary Pathway from Dictatorship to Democracy," in Geoffrey Pridham, ed., *The New Mediterranean Democracies: Regime Transition in Spain, Greece and Portugal* (London: Frank Cass, 1984), p. 30.

6. Sartori (fn. 3), pp. 1041–42.

7. For the classic exposition of the concept of totalitarianism, see Carl J. Friedrich and Zbigniew Brzezinski, *Totalitarian Dictatorship and Autocracy* (Cambridge, MA: Harvard University Press, 1956). For the most well known recent effort to distinguish authoritarian from totalitarian regimes, see Jeane Kirkpatrick, "Dictatorships and Double Standards," *Commentary*, November 1979, pp. 34–45.

8. For a more detailed critique of the concept of totalitarianism, see Amos Perlmutter, *Modern Authoritarianism* (New Haven, CT: Yale University Press, 1981), pp. 62–75.

9. Gregory Grossman, "Roots of Gorbachev's Problems: Private Income and Outlay in the Late 1970s," in U.S. Congress, Joint Economic Committee, *Gorbachev's Economic Plans* (November 23, 1987), pp. 213–29.

10. Frederick W. Frey, "Cross-Cultural Survey Research in Political Science," in Robert T. Holt and John E. Turner, eds., *The Methodology of Comparative Research* (New York: Free Press, 1970), p. 200.

11. The conservative reaction of late 1990 and early 1991 appears less the result of a resurgent Communist Party than a military-KGB-Gorbachev alliance. See summary of Alexander Rahr's presentation to the Kennan Institute for Advanced Russian Studies by Peggy McInerny, "Democratic Opposition at the Crossroads" (Meeting Report 8:7, Washington, D.C.).

12. Natalie Gross, "Glasnost: Roots and Practice," *Problems of Communism* 36 (November–December 1987), p. 69.

13. Victor Yasmann, "Can Glasnost Be Reversed?" *Radio Liberty Report on the USSR* 3 (February 1, 1991), p. 28.

14. Guillermo O'Donnell and Philippe C. Schmitter, *Transitions from Authoritarian Rule: Tentative Conclusions about Uncertain Democracies* (Baltimore, MD: Johns Hopkins University Press, 1986), p. 10. The influence of the O'Donnell and Schmitter volume permeates much of the analysis contained in this paper even though only the most direct references will be footnoted as such. (Note that the reference here is the fourth volume in a series on transitions from authoritarian rule. The four were published both separately and in a combined edition. All the page references to the four volumes in this paper are from the combined edition.)

15. Adam Przeworski, "Democracy as a Contingent Outcome of Conflicts," in Jon Elster and Rune Slagstad, eds., *Constitutionalism and Democracy* (Cambridge, MA: Cambridge University Press, 1988), pp. 61–62.

16. Ibid., p. 61.

17. Adam Przeworski, "Some Problems in the Study of the Transition to Democracy," in Guillermo O'Donnell, Philippe C. Schmitter, and Laurence Whitehead, eds., *Transitions from Authoritarian Rule: Comparative Perspectives* (Baltimore, MD: Johns Hopkins University Press, 1986), p. 56.

18. Medhurst (fn. 5), p. 37.

19. *New York Times,* February 21, 1989, p. A3.

20. On this point, see Perlmutter (fn. 8), esp. chap. 1.

21. O'Donnell and Schmitter (fn. 14), p. 24.

22. McInerny (fn. 11).

23. O'Donnell and Schmitter (fn. 14), p. 26.

24. *Pravda,* July 2, 1988, p. 12.

25. TASS, December 1, 1988. Reported in "Constitutional Amendments Approved," Foreign Broadcast Information Service, *Daily Report: Soviet Union* (December 1, 1988).

26. Paul Preston, *The Triumph of Democracy in Spain* (London and New York: Methuen, 1986), p. 101.

27. Przeworski (fn. 17), p. 51.

28. For an alternative view of communist legitimacy that was written before the Gorbachev era, see Seweryn Bialer, *Stalin's Successors* (Cambridge, MA: Cambridge University Press, 1980), chap. 9.

29. Przeworski (fn. 17), p. 52.

30. O'Donnell and Schmitter (fn. 14), p. 58.

31. *Pravda,* July 21, 1989, p. 1.

32. O'Donnell and Schmitter (fn. 14), p. 24.

33. Preston (fn. 26), p. 95; Medhurst (fn. 5), p. 34.

34. Thomas E. Skidmore, "Brazil's Slow Road to Democratization: 1974–1985," in Alfred Stepan, ed., *Democratizing Brazil: Problems of Transition and Consolidation* (New York: Oxford University Press, 1989), pp. 10–19.

35. Thomas C. Bruneau, "Continuity and Change in Portuguese Politics: Ten Years After the Revolution of April 25, 1974," in Pridham (fn. 5), p. 73.

36. Jerry Hough comes closest to this position among Western analysts. See "Gorbachev's Endgame," *World Policy Journal* 7 (Fall 1990), pp. 639–72.

37. See *Pravda,* November 26, 1989, pp. 1–3.

38. Luciano Martins, "The 'Liberalization' of Authoritarian Rule in Brazil," in Guillermo O'Donnell, Philippe Schmitter, and Laurence Whitehead, eds., *Transitions from Authoritarian Rule: Latin America* (Baltimore, MD: Johns Hopkins University Press, 1986), p. 86.

39. Preston (fn. 26), p. 96.

40. Dankwart A. Rustow notes that the hallmark of the preparatory phase of the transition to democracy is "polarization rather than pluralism." See Rustow, "Transitions to Democracy: Toward a Dynamic Model," *Comparative Politics* 2 (April 1970), p. 354.

41. On the Spanish case, see Preston (fn. 26), p. 96. On the Brazilian case, see Martins (fn. 38), p. 84.

42. Rustow (fn. 40), p. 355.

43. A predominant (although not exclusive) emphasis on the structural preconditions of democracy can be found in Larry Diamond, Juan J. Linz, and Seymour Martin Lipset, *Democracy in Developing Countries,* 4 vols. (Boulder, CO: Lynne Rienner, 1989).

44. The volume by O'Donnell and Schmitter (fn. 14) is the best example.

45. See Terry Lynn Karl, "Dilemmas of Democratization in Latin America," *Comparative Politics* 23 (October 1990), pp. 1–21.

46. For the text of the resolution, see *Pravda,* July 5, 1988, p. 2.

47. For the text of the two laws, see *Pravda,* December 4, 1988, pp. 1–3.

48. The authority of the electoral commissions was spelled out in the "Law on Elections" and in an article in *Pravda,* January 24, 1989, p. 2.

49. The specific allocation of seats in the Congress for each social organization was not written into law but is to be determined in each election by the Central Electoral Commission. The CPSU and the trade unions were the largest recipients the first time around with one hundred deputies each. The smallest recipients were allocated one deputy each and included organizations such as the All-Union Music Society and the All-Union Society for the Struggle for Sobriety. The complete list was published in *Izvestiia,* December 28, 1988, p. 1.

50. Russell Bova, "Power, Efficiency, and Democratization: The Faces of Soviet Political Reform" (unpublished paper presented at the Mid-Atlantic Slavic Conference, Carlisle, PA, April 1, 1989).

51. Karl (fn. 45), pp. 8–9.

52. Ibid., p. 8.

53. For examples of each, see ibid., pp. 11–12. Breslauer (fn. 2), pp. 323–24, also applies this logic to the Soviet case.

54. See Przeworski (fn. 15), pp. 68–69.

55. Robert Dahl, *Polyarchy: Participation and Opposition* (New Haven, CT: Yale University Press, 1971), chap. 3.

56. Przeworski (fn. 15), pp. 74–75.

57. For an interesting pre-Gorbachev era discussion of the institutionalization of elite privileges, see Alexander Yanov, *Detente after Brezhnev* (Berkeley, CA: Institute of International Studies, 1977), pp. 1–16. Note also the attempts of party and state officials to lay claim to state property in the course of the transition currently under way in Eastern Europe.

58. For a discussion of this point in the Latin American and Southern European contexts, see O'Donnell and Schmitter (fn. 14), pp. 28–29.

59. For a summary of the March 1989 election results, see Dawn Mann and Julia Wishnevsky, "Composition of Congress of People's Deputies," *Radio Liberty Report on the USSR* 1 (May 5, 1989), pp. 1–6.

60. For a summary and analysis of these results, see Commission on Security and Cooperation in Europe, *Elections in the Baltic States and Soviet Republics* (Washington, D.C., December 1990).

61. For an elaboration of this logic in a non-Soviet context, see Przeworski (fn. 15), pp. 71–74.

62. See, for example, the interview with Mikhail Popov, one of the initiators of the proposal, in *Moscow News* 34 (August 27–September 3, 1989), p. 12.

63. Elizabeth Teague, "Gorbachev Advisors Meet Secretly with Opposition Leaders," *Radio Liberty Report on the USSR* 2 (June 22, 1990), pp. 1–2.

64. Dahl (fn. 55), p. 78.

65. Moshe Lewin, *The Gorbachev Phenomenon: A Historical Interpretation* (Berkeley, CA: University of California Press, 1988); and Jerry F. Hough, *The Soviet Leadership in Transition* (Washington, DC: Brookings Institution, 1980).

66. Charles E. Lindblom, *Politics and Markets* (New York: Basic Books, 1977), pp. 161–69.

67. O'Donnell and Schmitter (fn. 14), p. 20. For a more skeptical view of the role of the business community in contemporary transitions to democracy, see Fernando H. Cardoso, "Entrepreneurs and the Transition Process: The Brazilian Case," in O'Donnell et al. (fn. 17), pp. 137–53. Even Cardoso admits, however, that this group gave at least limited support to the transition process.

68. Yurii Prokofiev, first secretary of the Moscow party organization, is among those reported to favor this model. Soviet Computer Network, *RFE-RL Daily Report* 25 (February 5, 1991). Note that the Chilean reference, although frequently encountered, is a bit of an exaggeration. Not even the strongest advocates of Soviet marketization expect the kind of laissez-faire, Chicago school approach to the market that the Chilean junta attempted. In the Soviet context, therefore, advocates of a Chilean model are simply those who seek marketization now while postponing democracy until some indefinite point in the future.

69. Rustow, for example, sees national unity as the single most important background condition for democracy. See Rustow (fn. 40), pp. 350–52.

70. Donald Share, *The Making of Spanish Democracy* (New York: Praeger, 1986), pp. 170–71.

71. O'Donnell and Schmitter (fn. 14), pp. 53–56.

72. See Karl (fn. 45), pp. 4–5.

73. Z, "To the Stalin Mausoleum," *Daedalus* 169 (Winter 1990), pp. 295–344.

THOMAS F. REMINGTON[1]

13

REGIME TRANSITION IN COMMUNIST SYSTEMS:

The Soviet Case

INTRODUCTION

The remarkable changes in the communist world since 1989 raised certain fundamental issues about the reformability of communist political systems. Scholars addressing these issues differ over the degree to which communist regimes are capable of adapting their institutions to new requirements. One school of thought holds that the highly integrated and self-preserving character of communist political and economic structures breeds reform efforts that are too feeble to achieve the desired improvements in productivity and living standards; accumulated frustrations and resentments eventually convert a limited opening in the political system into a radicalized and rebellious society. Accordingly, this "pessimistic" school argues that communist regimes cannot be reformed, but only destroyed. Another, more "optimistic" school asserts that long-term processes of social change (rising levels of education, urbanization, communications, and diffusion of professional qualifications) create ultimately irresistible pressures for democratization of the political regime. The optimists predict that such orientations infiltrate the regime and allow it to reform itself, while providing a social base for peaceful transition to a new order.

The weight of evidence thus far supports the pessimists' view that communist institutions (political monopoly of the party, state ownership, etc.) are ultimately incapable of accommodating the explosion of demands for participation that follows a liberalization of political rights. The general tendency has been for a confrontation between regime and populace to reinforce a generalized popular antagonism toward the ruling partocratic elite. In some cases, alienation has been converted immediately into demands for ethnic-national autonomy; in others, it has been expressed in a burst of labor or regional demands. In part, that alienation is rooted in

265

deterioration of social conditions, including growing structural imbalances between occupational qualifications and the labor market, worsening corruption, and the long-term consequences of wasteful and destructive strategies of industrialization. Always, however, the popular anti-establishment movement opposes the concentration of power and privilege in the political elite of the communist regime. Thus, the pessimists' claim that these regimes cannot be reformed gains some support from trends in Eastern Europe and particularly in the USSR as it looks toward the end of 1990.

And yet, within Eastern Europe, the USSR, and the communist world more generally, we have witnessed substantial diversity of outcomes during the past two years. Romania, Bulgaria, Serbia, and many areas of the USSR have experienced changes that have been far less revolutionary than those in other parts of the USSR and those in Poland, Hungary, Czechoslovakia, Slovenia, and Croatia. One lesson of this diversity has been that the nature of the political demands placed on the regime by a rebellious society has depended in part on the distribution within the population of democratically inclined leadership, interpersonal trust, and civic values.

Another lesson has been that the greater the degree of pluralism in society under the old regime, the more rapid the spread of *organized* opposition when the crisis occurs. A democratic outcome requires that popular movements take the form of organizations capable of including individuals with diverse interests and priorities. Mobilization of people along a single cleavage line (region, ethnicity, class) may not do. Toward this end, the development of broadly inclusive political parties is critical. Their function is to challenge governments, combine broad social interests, and channel political activity into electoral competition. A particularly important condition of a successful democratic transition, therefore, is the availability of democratically inclined counter-elites to lead the new social movements, and to convert them into broadly based political parties.

The *scale* of social pluralism also influences the distribution of democratic outcomes. When channels of organization, communication, and collective action are weak at the central level but strong in the localities (cities, regions, or national territories), the transition process will yield different outcomes in different territorial units. Such has been the case in the USSR and Yugoslavia in particular.

This paper will set forth arguments that the outcome of a transition from communist rule will depend on (1) the regime's willingness to liberalize and (2) the degree of autonomous self-organization *and* self-restraint within society. An unwillingness to liberalize may result in bloody repression of social protest. But the willingness to liberalize in a society that lacks either social pluralism, cross-cutting cleavages, or values fostering self-restraint may result in either limited change or extreme social polarization. In the latter case, this can provide fertile ground for anti-democratic, populist movements of backlash. Thus, in contrast to both the pessimistic and the optimistic schools, I contend that a more meaningful theory of transition of communist regimes requires an account of the *interaction* between social and political change. My contention is the raison d'être for this paper, which will focus on the Soviet case at a time of mounting uncertainty.[2]

COMMUNIST SYSTEMS
IN COMPARATIVE PERSPECTIVE

Earlier studies of communist regimes often advanced two- and three-stage models of development, generally predicting that fundamental transformation and consolidation of society is followed by steady-state forms of authoritarianism. In the final, "third stage," an accommodation between rulers and the ruled softens the harsh and coercive outlines of the revolutionary period. Social elites are coopted into the ruling party, the system devotes a rising share of attention to the security and welfare of its subjects, and avenues of popular participation gradually allow the masses to voice certain demands.[3]

Many if not all scholars who failed to foresee a Gorbachev or the events of 1989 tended to "normalize" the study of politics in communist systems by adapting concepts borrowed from the noncommunist world. They concentrated on the statics of systems that had reached post-Stalinist periods and neglected to consider their dynamics. As Gabriel Almond and Laura Roselle correctly observed, analytical approaches to the study of communism have all been imported from other disciplines and area studies, so that "the only internally generated model . . . was the totalitarian one" (Almond and Roselle, 1989, p. 206).

The emphasis on dynamics came after Gorbachev and other communist leaders began to carry out their drastic reforms. Was meaningful reform possible without inducing violent convulsions? Western scholars who emphasized the ideological-totalitarian dimension in communist politics[4] denied the possibility of painless transition.

But while the concept of totalitarianism was being abandoned in the West, it became increasingly popular among East European intellectuals. Martin Malia took it upon himself to "present a historicized update of the original, and [admittedly] too static, totalitarian interpretation." The more communist systems attempted to reform and "soften" their political structures, the more they aggravated the systemic crisis they intended to alleviate. "The system itself," he argued, "cannot be restructured or reformed . . . , [it] can only either stagnate or be dismantled and replaced by market institutions" ("Z," 1990, pp. 301, 338, 337).

As George Breslauer suggested, the degree to which one is sanguine about the communist system's ability to reform without catastrophic breakdown depends to a large extent on one's view of existing trends in society and politics, and their impact on the distribution of values, beliefs, and expectations (Breslauer, 1990, p. 5). Optimists and pessimists differ in their view of the relationship between social and political change. Pessimists emphasize the absence of historical experience with self-government (civic associations, local governments, competitive parties, respect for law, pluralistic tolerance, etc.), arguing that transition is likely to precipitate breakdowns of the old regimes and reequilibration under some new form of authoritarian rule. Indeed, writers such as Zbigniew Brzezinski (1989; 1989/90) insisted that communist rule exacerbated nationalist conflicts by intensifying intolerance and resentment among ethnic communities because of destruction of social structures (such as the business class or aristocracy) that historically tempered mass-level chauvinism.[5]

The pessimists can support their view by invoking past communist efforts to reform their economic and political systems. Typically, the reforms either unleashed revolutionary forces or were so weakened in implementation that they failed to produce the desired impact on bureaucratic behavior. Examples of the latter in the USSR include the Kosygin reforms of 1965, the production association reform of 1973, the planning indicator reform of 1979, and the 1987 Law on the State Enterprise. The leadership groups in communist systems are not able to select some hypothetical point on a continuum between Stalinism and capitalist democracy and move the society to such a point by streamlining the mix of incentives and rights accruing to planners, enterprises, farmers, workers, consumers, regions and nationalities. Powerful self-equilibrating forces tend to keep administrative systems intact, so that reforms granting nominal rights in order to reward efficiency-seeking innovation are vitiated by the pressures of various supplementary directive targets or guidelines, which in effect substitute one form of inefficient or obstructionist behavior for another (e.g., see Campbell, 1988, pp. 89–90; Durasoff, 1988; Ofer, 1987, pp. 1805–6). Such forces then impede an economy's ability to embark on an "intensive" growth path. Even in the Hungarian case, involving what is regarded as the most advanced example of economic reform within the communist model, the effort to place state enterprises on a market footing during the New Economic Mechanism did not succeed.[6]

On the other hand, some openings spark popular uprisings, which are usually suppressed with brutal violence; other openings elicit ideological innovations that go well beyond the modest, within-system criticisms the regimes were willing to tolerate. The uprisings in 1956 prompted by de-Stalinization of the former GDR, Hungary, and Poland; the Russian workers' strike in Novocherkassk in 1962; the Romanian miners' strikes in 1977 (and the traumatic Timisoara rebellion in 1989); the Polish workers' strikes in 1970, 1976, and 1980; the student movement in China in 1989 and other episodes illustrate the pattern of mass popular protest and violent suppression. In contrast, China's "Hundred Flowers" Movement, the Prague Spring in Czechoslovakia, and the resilience of dissent under Brezhnev after Khrushchev's limited thaw show that it was nearly impossible for communist regimes to find a mutually acceptable point on the continuum that accommodates intellectuals' demands for honest and open expression and the regime's desire for ideological uniformity. With a few exceptions, such as the Czechoslovak Musicians' Union Jazz Section, or the Moscow branch of the USSR Writers' Union (in the late 1950s), state-recognized membership organizations never gained enough autonomy to win the confidence of their memberships during periods of confrontation and to truly represent society in bargaining with the regime. Hence, most protest movements tended to be extra-systemic, either in the form of anomic mass outbursts or channeled through strike committees, human rights defense groups, and *samizdats*. In only one case prior to 1989, namely that of Poland's Solidarity in 1980, did an autonomous organization manage to achieve a negotiated agreement with the regime.

The characteristic dilemma of reform, then, is that there is either too much or too little of it. Either an attempt by the regime to rationalize the cumbersome and inefficient system of administrative state control yields insufficient change or it invites controlled social mobilization. There is a high threshold to successful reform. Short of it, economic and political power is bundled together in bureaucratic structures controlling the allocation of capital resources. Beyond that threshold, a radicalization of social demands for change can quickly overwhelm the limited capacity of existing channels of participation.

SOCIAL CHANGE AND POLITICAL INSTITUTIONS

There are reasonable objections to the foregoing perspective because it places political regimes outside the reach of history, as if they were impervious to everything except their own inadequate efforts at reform. For one thing, it neglects the importance of leadership, specifically the ability of a "transformational leader" to adapt political institutions to a changed environment (Breslauer, 1989). An alternative approach considers liberalization as a product of modernization. For this school, change in political institutions is largely a function of long-term processes over which political elites have little direct control and which, in the end, they must accept. Although there may be a temporal lag before political structures catch up with social change, the regimes must bow to the impersonal forces of history. For the Soviet Union, these include:

1. The shift from a society which was 80 percent rural in 1917 to one that is 66 percent urban in 1990;
2. The remarkable accomplishments in education, whereby in 1987, one-half of the Soviet population over 10 years of age had a secondary school education (a proportion similar to that in the United States) and 9 percent a higher education (nearly the U.S. rate);
3. The transformation of the occupational structure, specifically the rapid increase in the number of individuals employed in professional and specialist occupations, whom we might label "suppies"—Soviet urban professionals;[7] and
4. The rapid spread of access to media, including communication by print, as well as radio and television broadcasting.[8]

A number of analysts have argued that the accretion of these quantitative changes gave birth to a qualitative change in society. Fred Starr, for example, claims that urbanization, the dispersion of professional skill, the penetration of a variety of communications technologies (that enable people to associate as autonomous and equal individuals), and the enormous evasion of state structures (through informal mechanisms of economic coordination and cultural expression) had already established the outlines of a civil society. Reform under Gorbachev has meant no more than clearing away the bureaucratic impediments to a liberal society (Starr, 1988, 1989). Moshe Lewin (1988) reinforced that view by highlighting the informal but sturdy milieux both within and outside official structures that sustained independent public opinion and behavior. And, as noted by Blair Ruble, Soviet society during the Brezhnev period underwent a "quiet revolution."[9] Generalizing about the global trend away from authoritarianism, Lucian Pye wrote that "the forces of modernization have made it harder for political willpower to mobilize and dominate a society" (Pye, 1990, p. 9).

The statistical evidence for significant social change is so powerful, and the record of Gorbachev's reforms still so breathtaking, that it is tempting to consider the social modernization thesis as one that is clearly established. But it is troubling that there is no agreement on the precise nature of the link between the two sides of the equation—social change and political change. In the logic of theories which posit relatively little autonomy of political factors vis-à-vis society, it makes little difference whether communist regimes accommodate civil society or surrender to it after a confrontation. They tend to treat political reform as a "sequel"[10] to the more fundamental, longer-term, and presumably irreversible effects of modernization.[11] Given the individuation and differentiation of society, a political regime attempting to govern the society eventually had to enfranchise the newly mobile, self-aware, and culturally enfranchized urban middle classes (Lapidus, 1989). These groups and the incipient consolidation of their status created a natural constituency for democratic politics, and their presence explains what is otherwise an anomalous level of success by liberal democratic candidates in the elections of 1989 and 1990.

It should be noted that optimists differ in the degree of their determinism, and allow for a wide range of possible causal mechanisms for linking the social to the political (e.g., leadership strategies, social learning, relative deprivation, and international pressures). However, since they assign relatively less weight to political than to social variables, the optimists argue that peaceful transition through reform is possible. Indeed, Lewin predicts that the one-party system will survive on the grounds that "the party is the main stabilizer of the political system. . . . The party, especially if it refurbishes its image, is the only institution that can preside over the overhaul of the system without endangering the polity itself in the process" (Lewin, 1988, p. 133).

MODERNIZATION AND DECAY

The historical optimism of modernizers overlooks some troubling questions. What, if anything, explains backsliding? Lucian Pye offers a cultural explanation: modernization occurs "in the context of constant battling between two nearly sovereign forces—the impersonal and universalistic requirements of the world culture and the particularistic passions of politics and of group identity" (Pye, 1990, p. 12). Thus, highly vulnerable and threatened national cultures may, at least temporarily, favor the advent and rise of nativist backlash movements. The student democracy movement of China may seem to be predestined by the diffusion of a universalistic, democratic political culture that was reinforced by China's decade of successful economic growth. But a different explanation must be invoked to account for the brutal enforcement of party ideological conformity after Tienanmen Square. This backlash might have been induced by structural problems associated with the "successes" of economic reform: inflation, rising inequality, stagnation, unemployment, corruption, speculation, and other pathological effects of partial marketization. It may well be that modernization theory explains little beyond suggesting that a particular direction of political change is probable, with a wide margin of indeterminacy with regard to pace and timing. No functional theory can establish with any degree of accuracy the threshold of social change which would trigger political change or would overload the capacity of political institutions to accommodate new demands. That is, no such theory can tell us how much modernization is *enough,* and how much is *too much.*

How are variations in the level of modernization within and across systems related to variations in the outcomes of political change? Neither Poland nor Hungary were the most modernized of the communist states, but they were the first ones to institute power-sharing arrangements between communist rulers and the organized opposition. One might point out that both countries are not only ethnically homogeneous but also among the most urbanized of the East European states. These factors facilitated cohesiveness of the political opposition groups, and reduced the capacity of old regimes to suppress them. As a result, the strength of popular opposition movements in Poland and Hungary in the 1970s and 1980s had more to do with the high degree of national unity than with economic or social modernization.[12] Similar social changes may have different effects on different populations, depending on the nature of the relevant social cleavages. *At any given level of modernization,* therefore, the crucial determinant of a successful democratic transition is the ability of the opposition (through superior organization and capacity to rally popular support) to raise the regime's costs of suppressing it.

Needless to say, there are also problems with the modernization hypothesis on empirical grounds. Evidence points to stagnation and decline rather than progress in several crucial indicators of modernization. For example, infant mortality rates as well as those among males aged 20 to 40 rose in the USSR throughout the 1970s (Anderson and Silver, 1990).[13] Similarly, Bulgaria, Czechoslovakia, the former GDR, Hungary, Poland, and Romania registered increases in death rates for males over the age of 30; for men in their fifties, death rates rose by over one-third (Eberstadt, 1987, pp. 230–31). We lack objective measures to assess the spread of corruption and privilege, but if we were to accept the view that Soviet national income did not grow during the 1979–1982 and 1981–1985 periods, then privilege and corruption must have caused a substantial redistribution of income favoring people with political influence (e.g., see Åslund, 1990; Ericson, 1990; CIA, 1988).

Pessimists tend to overrate the autonomy of the political sphere, whereas optimists underplay it. The former rule out the possibility of a successful radical reform policy, such as China's policy after the Tenth Plenum, or Gorbachev's radicalism after 1987–1988. On the other hand, optimists overlook the fact that communist political institutions perform crucial social functions and leave a destabilizing vacuum when they collapse. An adequate model of the transition from communist rule therefore must accurately describe trends in the social environment and also provide better insight into the complex relationship between social and political change.

MODERNIZATION AND ITS DISCONTENTS

The optimists have imported into their studies of the Soviet Union only one variant of modernization theory, namely one that is based on a linear conception of change. Yet for each indicator of modernization cited above—urbanization, educational attainments, occupational structure, and communications—the relationship between social and political processes is neither obvious nor linear. Theories of *discontinuous* change, in contrast, focus on the discontent generated by different paths to modernity, and the ability to mobilize that discontent during the transition process. A few indicators of modernization are reexamined in this light below.

Urbanization and Environmental Degradation

The nature of urban life in the Soviet Union and Eastern Europe has been shaped by a development strategy that placed industrial production facilities in the immediate vicinity of cities. Hence, as cities grew outward, large pockets of the urban population were exposed to severe and cumulative doses of toxic pollution.[14]

The Bashkir ASSR is a case in point. Bashkiria is a heavily industrialized region with a broad spectrum of industries, including oil refining, chemicals, and machine building. Reports in 1988 were sounding the alarm about environmental degradation and a crisis in public health. An article in *Zhurnalist* by *Pravda's* correspondent for Bashkiria cited a letter from Ufa to the effect that pollution levels in the city were higher than the allowable norms (by a factor of 10 and more), and that in the northern part of the city, where the petrochemical industry is concentrated, only 24 percent of infants are born healthy (Prokushev, 1988). In another example, two Soviet physicians correlated several indicators of public health (infant morbidity, mortality, and particularly an epidemic of nervous ticks) with the emission of toxic pollutants in the neighboring city of Salavat located to the south of Ufa. They noted that Salavat contains 94 industrial enterprises and 459 sources of atmospheric pollution, and that no more than 62 percent are captured by emissions controls (Lupandin and Kakorina, 1988).[15]

The consequence of this catastrophic environmental deterioration has been growing popular protest. As early as the summer of 1988, an environmental initiative group in Ufa organized a rally to demand immediate action to clean up the city (and in particular to stop construction of a major new petrochemical plant). Since then Bashkiria's environmental crisis has grown still more acute, and public protest has spread. Residents of Ufa have suffered contamination of their drinking water by phenol already twice in 1990, and in June 1989, over 500 people in the region were killed in an explosion of natural gas caused by a train accident on the Trans-Siberian Railway. As a result, several more massive popular demonstrations have occurred. In one that took place in April 1990, protestors formed a continuous chain some 40 to 50 kilometers in length. The radicalization of the populace prompted the advent of alternative political groups, such as the Bashkir Voters' Association, the Society for the Defense of Nature, the Tamai Club, and the Bashkir Club. Eventually these groups managed to form a "radical-democratic bloc" and (in February 1990) demand and successfully rally support for the resignation of the republic's party leadership (*Russkaya mysl'*, February 16, 1990). A provisional party bureau was formed after the resignation of the *obkom* bureau, with coopted representatives of two Tatar and Bashkir national informal organizations (*Izvestiya*, February 14, 1990, p. 2).

This formation of an alternative civic leadership was a response to the immiseration brought about by the regime's focus on urban industrial development. Autonomous organizations emerged from the widespread anger and frustration, mobilized the populace, and fought the established party leadership. The Bashkir case tends to illustrate hundreds if not thousands of similar movements protesting over environmental problems, shortages of food and consumer necessities, ethnic-national issues, and other causes (Remington, 1989a).

Environmental, labor, and national grievances often coincide and overlap, generating a cumulative antagonism to the system fed from a variety of sources. For example, before the strikes in the Donets basin during the summer of 1989, coal miners had been aggrieved at the build-up of toxic wastes (including phenol, chlorobenzene, and cyanide) in the groundwaters of the region. Their protests had gone unheeded by the authorities (Kiss, 1990). Environmental grievances thus joined with anger over housing problems and food shortages to spark the massive strike wave. For this reason it is often hard to distinguish working class from environmental or ethno-national movements in communist societies. The system itself spawns a generalized popular alienation and resentment, fertile ground for the mobilization of protest once political controls are loosened sufficiently to allow opposition to organize.

Education and Occupation

Soviet educational and occupational accomplishments have also generated social discontent that can affect the course of the transition. The increase in the number of Soviet specialists with tertiary education is often cited as evidence of the rise of a new "middle class." Indeed, the supply side of the social equation is in many ways an impressive story, presenting a picture of expanding educational opportunity and continuing upward social mobility for millions of workers and peasant youth. But along with the impressive growth in the number of educated specialists, particularly in science and technology, there are considerable problems of underutilization and devaluation.

To understand what happened to the Soviet professional classes, it is also necessary to examine the demand side, that is, the structure of actual employment in the economy and, in particular, the capacity of the economy to find appropriate and useful employment for the steadily growing contingent of VUZ (higher educational institution) and *tekhnikum* (specialized secondary school) graduates. Here the picture is one of near-stasis: the decline in the number of auxiliary and unskilled jobs is painfully slow[16] and the increase in the number of jobs requiring a specialist's training lags far behind the output of specialists. As a result, many specialists work in manual jobs well below their level of qualification (Kochetov, 1988, pp. 9–10).

A meaningful study of several enterprises found that less than half the actual working time of engineering personnel consisted of operations requiring an engineer's qualifications (Senyavskiy, 1984, p. 188). The director of one Soviet enterprise who had attended an engineering institute reported that when his graduating class of 25 met for its tenth year reunion, only three were working in the fields in which they had been educated.[17] *Tekhnikum* graduates tend to be pulled into manual jobs which were once performed by PTU (vocational-technical school) graduates. Indeed, *tekhnikums* have increasingly come to be regarded as a pool of skilled manual labor, a situation which has "not only lowered the prestige of specialized secondary education, but in fact has led to the dequalification of many engineers (specialists with higher education), who are forced to perform the functions of a technician, a foreman, a lab assistant, etc." (Kochetov, 1988, p. 11).

Estimates attempting to establish the number of trained engineers and technicians who hold manual jobs tend to vary. Two Soviet authors cite a figure of 1.7 million for 1975 (or 2.5 percent of the working class) and indicate that this proportion tripled from 1959 to 1975 (Selunskaya and Sivokhina, 1982, p. 118). Another pair, counting both agriculture and industry, projected in 1976 that by 1980 approximately 3 million graduate specialists would be employed in mainly physical labor occupations (Rutkevich and Filippov, 1976, p. 196). Meanwhile, a significant share of young blue collar workers have acquired VUZ and *tekhnikum* degrees (7.5 percent in 1973 as estimated by Senyavskiy, 1984, p. 197), further blurring the old distinction between "worker" and "intelligentsia." One consequence of this trend is a declining competitiveness of the admissions process to VUZy, which has been falling rather steadily since the late 1970s (Kochetov, 1988, pp. 9–10). Another effect is the demoralization of much of the technical and managerial staff in enterprises. Studies reported by Tat'yana Zaslavskaya indicate that most managers would prefer less responsible positions because appropriate recognition for what they do is not forthcoming (Zaslavskaya, 1986, p. 64).

There is evidence that the professional classes (particularly in branches of material production) experienced a significant "squeeze" during the 1960s and the 1970s. This was due to:

1. Continuous expansion of the ranks of intelligentsia, above all because of entrants from blue collar classes, to whom VUZ and *tekhnikum* degrees became increasingly accessible.[18]
2. Slow structural change in the economy, which was unable to absorb the stream of newly graduated specialists.[19]
3. Loss of skills by many graduates forced to take manual shop-floor and low-level supervisory jobs not corresponding to their specialized skills.[20]
4. Greater social proximity between manual workers and technicians traced to replacement of the PTU by the *tekhnikum* as a source of manual labor.[21]
5. Convergence in relative earnings accompanying convergence in job content between specialists and manual workers. Indeed in some regions and certain job categories (e.g., hazardous jobs) skilled workers earned more than specialists.
6. Shifts of specialists to entirely unrelated occupations prompted by depreciation of their status (brought about by the above trends)—a net drain on the nation's human capital.

In short, the old ideological notion that Soviet society was losing its class divisions, becoming more "homogeneous" through the "intellectualization" of physical labor, seems to express a perverse kernel of truth. For the trend has been toward a de-differentiation of the workforce brought about by a combination of technological stagnation and the overproduction of specialists with tertiary degrees. It is only by putting together these two sides of the equation—the hyperactive supply side with the anemic demand side—that one sees how modernization can produce social change that breeds extreme discontent.

There is considerable evidence that the social frustrations resulting from these trends have directly influenced the nature of the interests and demands articulated since Gorbachev's *perestroyka* became radicalized. In many professions, a burst of effort to regain lost recognition and esteem was in evidence in 1988. In September 1988, for example, teachers founded the "Soviet Association of Pedagogues and Researchers." In February of that year, a founding congress established a new "Union of Engineering and Scientific Societies of the USSR," which, it was hoped, would be recognized as a creative union and become a successor to the old Russian Technical Society of the late nineteenth century. This united some 48 (subsequent reports said 26) existing professional societies, representing 12.8 million members.

In accordance with the revised electoral law, the union was allocated 10 seats in the USSR Congress of People's Deputies. Other efforts involved designers who formed a new creative union and were allotted five seats. Lawyers (*advokaty*) also have sought to organize themselves as a professional association.[22] Both the association of sociologists and the union of journalists have sought to enhance public and self-esteem by adopting codes of professional ethics. In view of the deterioration of stature and autonomy that much of the intelligentsia experienced in the past, it is hardly surprising that so many professions have seized on the present moment to assert their corporate interests.

Communications as a Factor

The final commonly cited indicator of modernization is the communications revolution. According to Starr (1989) and Mickiewicz (1988), new communications technologies facilitate links among individuals and groups that subvert the regime's controls over the dissemination of information. That much said, however, it is still necessary to inquire into the role of new communications links (newspapers, journals, news services, broadcast organizations, publishing houses, newsletters, private schools, etc.) in facilitating collective action. Few scholars who emphasize this factor analyze the relationship between communications and ideology in a system where ideology prevented the formation of opposition by linking elites across divisions of ethnicity, region, generation, and sector. In such a system, with its high degree of administrative segmentation of ethnically defined territorial subdivisions, the removal of ideological controls could only favor the rise of nationalistic counter-ideologies. Indeed Moshe Lewin never discusses nationality as a cleavage in Soviet society, and, incredibly, declares that "few groups would back measures likely to erode the integrity of the entire union or the centralized state" (Lewin, 1988, p. 133). Underestimating the importance of even a defunct ideology to political integration in the communist state, the optimists failed to foresee that separatist national movements would be likely to fill the void left by official Marxism-Leninism.

THE CONCENTRATION OF GRIEVANCES

The urgency of radical reform, and the speed with which movement toward liberalization is overwhelmed by mass demands for democratization, is better explained by the intensity of accumulated popular grievances against the old regime than by the theory of a rising urban professional class. As O'Donnell and Schmitter (1986, p. 26) observe, the opening of an authoritarian regime "usually produces a sharp and rapid increase in general politicization and popular activation—the 'resurrection of civil society'." In the case of communist regime change, the most characteristic impulse in the protest movements is populist (and often ethnic or national) opposition to the power and privilege of the partocratic elite.

The drive to turn out the old ruling group helps explain why it is generally impossible for communist regimes simply to expand the political arena and find some acceptable formula for sharing power with opposition forces. Only rarely is the opposition leadership in a position to constrain the maximalist demands of the popular movement; leaders arise spontaneously in the heat of the moment or are recruited from among the "prestige elite"—journalists, writers, scientists, musicians.[23] Commonly an initial gesture (such as roundtable talks to decide on new formulae for elections) is followed by a stronger wave of mass demands for full popular sovereignty. In the USSR these waves have been especially forceful at the republican and regional levels, and have mobilized powerful regional and national loyalties. This bodes ill for the success of a democratic transition.[24]

The populist revolt against a communist regime draws its strength from the deeply felt antagonism of the populace toward the political elite—those who entered the *nomenklatura* as department heads, directors, administrators, deputies, committee members, party secretaries, and other leading cadres. The concentration of political and social power in this elite helps to unite the several streams of popular opposition into a broad movement against its rule. Now, as during the Stalin period, those close to the sources of political power are widely held to form a distinct social class. It will be recalled that Alex Inkeles and Raymond Bauer found that by far the most deeply and universally cited distinction in Stalinist society was that between "party people" and "nonparty people" (Inkeles and Bauer, 1968, p. 300). In recent decades this hazily conceptualized but intensely felt cleavage has taken the form of attacks on the privilege, corruption and conservatism of the *nomenklatura*. A 1989 article in *Ogonyok* identified the *nomenklatura* (as it is popularly termed) as the political class which had been since Stalin's time identified by privileged access to benefits unavailable to ordinary persons. Most interesting in the analysis was the author's reference to popular perceptions of the *nomenklatura,* as captured in expressions such as "so and so 'fell into the *nomenklatura*'," "that is a *nomenklatura* position," the "*nomenklatura* list," as well as his comment that "if there was an atheist heaven, the *nomenklatura* would find a little fenced-off spot for itself there as well" (Kostikov, 1989, pp. 12–15).[25]

Let us leave aside the question of whether by some objective criterion there is, in fact, a "new class" or a "*nomenklatura*." What is important is that this group occupies a distinct and thoroughly resented place in popular consciousness. In the new environment of competitive elections and *glasnost',* a great deal of evidence can be

cited on this point. Surveys of voter opinion before the 1990 republican Soviet elections found a strongly hostile attitude toward candidates identified with the party-government apparatus. In one
survey conducted across 8 cities in 3 republics, only 2 to 7 percent
of respondents expressed any sympathy for candidates from CPSU,
government, Komsomol, and related organizations, and the vast majority of respondents expressed deep hostility toward the apparat
(Rukavishnikov and Kotov, 1990, pp. 21–22). Likewise, the single
strongest determinant of voter intentions—an outlook held in many
localities by a majority of the citizens—was a populist desire to vote
against candidates considered to be part of the "bureaucracy" and
to vote for those opposing it (Levinson, 1990, p. 4). Similarly, a poll
taken in 1989 by the All-Union Center for Study of Public Opinion,
disclosed that nearly 40 percent of respondents cited "bureaucracy"
(understood to be a definable group of people) as the number one
cause of the country's problems (*Izvestiya,* April 11, 1990). A poll
reported by Tat'yana Zaslavskaya, conducted by the same Center in
1989, asked 1,583 respondents to comment on the stock shibboleth
that those in power are servants of the people. The following answers to the question, "Which of these comes closest to expressing
your point of view?" are given below (Zaslavskaya, 1990, p. 27):

1. People selected by us for positions of power soon forget about
   our concerns and do not consider the [best] interests of the
   people—44.7 percent;
2. The leadership is a special group of people, an elite, which lives
   only [to benefit] its own interests; it has nothing in common
   with us—31.1 percent;
3. Our organs of power are truly popular; they have the same
   interests as you and I—14.2 percent;
4. I have no opinion—10.0 percent.

While such data support the proposition that concentration of
economic and political power in a privileged elite fosters a broad
and intense opposition (once controls are lifted), it does not necessarily follow that a victory of such opposition would produce a
democratic transition. To the extent that the popular movement is
undifferentiated and unstructured (united only in opposition), its
moment of political triumph is also the point at which the struggle
among the movement's own latent competing interests would begin.

PATHS TO TRANSITION

Optimistic and pessimistic theories are misleading because each
adopts a partial view of the relationship between the Soviet regime
and the society it has ruled. A theory of transition from communism

should instead be based upon an understanding of how the regime
and the society influence and penetrate each other, and how that
relationship changes during the transition itself. O'Donnell and
Schmitter (1986), for example, offer a simple version of such a model:
influenced by various pressures, including factional divisions, ruling
elites loosen certain political controls in order to find new allies and
allow the population to vent steam. In response, the populace mobi-
lizes and demands still more opportunities for participation. Eventually the rulers negotiate surrender through pacts that provide for
power-sharing and civil peace. A transition theory for communist
systems, therefore, should look for ways in which long-term, sys-
tem-generated processes foster particular discontents; these are mobilized once political opposition gains the opportunity to express
itself.

There are three dimensions here. One is the willingness of the
ruling leadership to tolerate opposition activity by independent political forces ("liberalization"). The communist world has witnessed
considerable variation in the 1980s on this score. Hard-line regimes
in a number of Soviet republics and communist countries resisted
the pressure to imitate Gorbachev's policies of *perestroyka* and *glasnost'*.

A second dimension is the level of social pluralism as opposed to
atomization in society.[26] Here the key questions involve society's
capacity to form structured organizations and generate legitimate
leadership despite the party's efforts to penetrate and control. How
do intimate circles of opposition-minded intellectuals join forces with
one another and with broader social strata? What induces people to
act in concert when their actions run the risk of repression? How
do opposition movements mobilize their workplaces, residential districts, universities, professional associations, elected councils and
committees? When do people establish new organizations for collective action, rather than attempt to capture existing organizations?
What are the characteristics of successful opposition leadership? This
dimension is concerned, then, with the degree to which people are
able to convert private interests into public demands by coordinating
their efforts.

A third dimension of this problem is the scope of oppositional
action—at what level of the territorial hierarchy does the capacity
for collective action exist? It is one thing for a strike committee to
arise in Gdansk or Kemerovo. If it can find common cause with
workers throughout the country, that is quite another. It is probably
safe to say that in the USSR there is much more self-organization
in the cities, regions, and republics than across the union as a whole.

The capacity for self-organization and collective action will be
affected by the nature of the social ties that exist in a society. A
striking feature of communist societies (which distinguishes them
from more open, market-oriented societies) has been the importance

of primary ties, such as family and friendship, in shaping social opinion and behavior. Certainly in the Soviet Union, there is a good deal of evidence on the crucial role of such bonds in oppositional and unofficial behavior. As a number of studies have shown, friendship is exceptionally important as a medium of communication and solidarity in Soviet society. Evidence from Soviet surveys demonstrates the continuing centrality of face-to-face means of gathering information and forming opinions, despite the penetration of society by modern print and electronic communication (Remington, 1981, 1988). In the words of Vladimir Shlapentokh (1989), friendship and other primary bonds are valued in Soviet society primarily because they are milieux within which trust is established outside and sometimes against the state.[27]

But family and friendship can go only so far in organizing oppositional activity. There must be other institutional bases for more impersonal organization and leadership. Because of the communist party's efforts to penetrate and control society, choose its leaders, regiment its activity, and shape its ideological loyalties, oppositions in communist societies pay a relatively high price when they attempt to organize independent associations. Experience suggests that they are more willing to pay the price under several conditions:

1. When there are precedents from earlier periods of liberalization (such as the Khrushchev thaw, the Solidarity period, or the Prague Spring) during which moral and organizational leadership emerged and established links among groups and broader popular followings;
2. When there is a resilient national consciousness,[28] generally sustained by historical memories of past national oppression;
3. When a strong and organized religious community serves as a vehicle for expressing varied secular interests, as was the case with the Catholic Church in Poland, Lithuania, and Czechoslovakia, or the Evangelical Church in the former GDR; and
4. When a vigorous and indigenous cultural life is represented by scientists, writers, poets, musicians, dramatists, and other members of the intelligentsia who enjoy broad popular followings and are widely considered to be voices of the "nation."[29] Prominent members of these professions frequently become political counter-elites in a period of broad societal confrontation with the communist authorities.

These and other factors contribute to shaping the transition from communist rule. A society that is atomized and lacks many of these attributes will usually be capable only of spontaneous and localized protest. Alternatively, a society that has many of these attributes will usually develop organizational capacities that facilitate the mobilization of opposition, that represent and restrain it during negotiations on power sharing with the government, and that tap it for electoral support in parliamentary elections.

Regimes in the Soviet Union and Eastern Europe (c. 1988) could be arrayed in a two-by-two matrix that distinguishes liberalizing from hard-line regimes and atomized from pluralizing societies (Table [13.]1).

Once the process of transition has gained momentum and an organized society has forced the state to negotiate terms of representation, accountability (and the like), the next step in the direction of structuring a democratic order will be a process of party building. The importance of political parties is that they build political associations that often cut across the cleavages of ethnicity, region, and class. Given the passions unleashed by transitions from communist rule, this may be the main hope for preventing centrifugal forces from fragmenting the country into a diversity of small or exclusive units.[30] When one surveys the Soviet scene before the events of December 1990, it is most encouraging to notice the speed with which parties and party-like groups have formed: parliamentary fractions; electoral coalitions of candidates for deputy; micro-parties resembling discussion forums; inter-regional coalitions of popular fronts; and, increasingly, broad aggregative political organizations devoted to winning elections through the mobilization of voters.

BUILDING POLITICAL PARTIES
IN THE USSR

The channeling of populist protest in the USSR from "the street" into organized politics was prompted by the two successive rounds of elections sponsored at Gorbachev's behest in 1989 and 1990. These elections stimulated three processes: (1) the turning of populist protest against specific political incumbents at the national, republican, and city levels; (2) polarization of ideological trends into contending

TABLE [13.]1 Communist Regime–Society Matrix (c. 1988)

Society	Regime	
	Liberalizing	Hard-line
Pluralizing	Poland, Hungary, Baltic Republics	Czechoslovakia, GDR, Moldavia, Belorussia
Atomized	Rest of USSR?[a]	Romania, Bulgaria, Albania

[a]The Soviet case is ambiguous partly because there are very wide disparities in societal capacity for self-organization across the regions of that vast country.

streams of establishment conservatism and liberal democracy; and (3) the beginnings of the transformation of popular movements into political parties and electoral coalitions that span regions.

Political movements in the USSR during 1988–1990 have had strong regional and national bases; almost none has developed an organizational base cutting across ethnic-national communities. As a result, many popular movements have focused on demands for territorial (regional or republican) sovereignty against the union center, and for hegemony vis-à-vis internal ethnic minorities within the territory. Claims to sovereignty for the territorial unit give the popular movement a unifying focus against the center, particularly, of course, when territorial sovereignty can be identified with a national cause, such as redemption of lost statehood or assertion of full cultural identity.

In the Russian Republic, with its enormous ethnic diversity and numerous internal autonomous units,[31] regional associations of democratic forces have united behind demands for both republican sovereignty and decentralization to sub-republican levels. In Yaroslavl', a congress of the popular fronts of the Russian Republic representing eight cities met in October 1989. Roughly three months later, in Voronezh, a conference of representatives of the Popular Fronts of Voronezh, Tambov, Orel, Kursk, Lipetsk, Yaroslavl', and Ryazan' met, and agreed to establish an information agency for the Central Black Earth region (*Russkaya mysl'*, February 9, 1990). In February 1990 a meeting of deputies from the Far East and Siberia was convened by the Far Eastern Division of the Russian Popular Front. It called for a new, independent Far Eastern Republic that would enjoy autonomy, possess its own convertible currency, customs service, and constitution, and attempt to attract investment from Japan, China, and the United States (*Atmoda,* January 29, 1990; *Radio Liberty Daily Report,* February 15, 1990; Kommunisty, 1990, pp. 31–36). The popularity of this idea has influenced programs of a variety of informal groups and candidates in the region, including the Khabarovsk communist party organization, which in its electoral platform (adopted in November 1989) called for a more independent Far Eastern region with stronger foreign trade ties, more joint ventures and free economic zones (Vybory, 1990, p. 85).[32] Another example is the Interregional Association of Democratic Organizations, created in Chelyabinsk in October 1989, to which over 90 organizations belong (*Moscow News,* 1990, No. 7, p. 9). Its birth was attended by members of the Interregional Group of Deputies, who helped develop its platform (Kommunisty, 1990). The association held a second conference in Vilnius in early February 1990, at which 120 member organizations were recorded (Davydov, 1990).

In turn, these local and regional associations created an organizational basis for the most notable electoral phenomenon of 1990; the coalescing of local candidates with liberal-democratic outlooks into a broad cross-regional movement called "Democratic Russia."[33] For our purposes, it is noteworthy that in Moscow, the movement's ideological opponent received no more than 2 to 3 percent of the popular vote and represents only 2 percent of the deputies in the Moscow city soviet; the opposition did still worse in Leningrad. Democratic Russia candidates, on the other hand, won 30 to 40 percent of the seats in the Russian republican congress, and took majorities in the Moscow, Leningrad, Sverdlovsk, Ryazan', Omsk, Saransk, and Irkutsk city soviets, which have now formed an "Association of Russia's Democratic Cities." Their alliance with Boris Yel'tsin, and their skillful identification of republican sovereignty with radical democratization, gave them a dominant voice in the Russian Republic parliament during the summer and fall of 1990.[34]

As of late 1990, Democratic Russia was taking steps toward institutionalizing itself as a political party. It held a founding congress on October 20–21 in Moscow, and declared itself open to both group and individual members. Among its organizational participants are Memorial, the writers' club *Aprel'*, the Democratic Party of Russia, the Social-Democratic Party, Democratic Platform, and the Christian Democratic Movement. Although reluctant to form a permanent staff, and refusing to consider itself a "universal" or "vanguard" party, it had formed a governing board (the "Council of Representatives") which was to form a coordinating council to rule it. The newly formed party had also succeeded in reaching agreement with its counterpart in the Ukrainian parliament, "the People's Council," based on mutual acceptance of republican sovereignty as the foundation for future relations (*Izvestiya*, May 8, 1990, p. 3; *Izvestiya*, August 29, 1990, p. 3; *Argumenty i fakty*, 1990, No. 20, p. 8). Similar trends are visible in the merger of other small parties into blocs, such as the "Centrist Bloc," which was formed in June 1990 from the merger of the Liberal-Democratic Party, the Russian Democratic Forum, and other small democratic parties. Conservatives had formed a parliamentary group called *Soyuz*.[35] Certainly, pressures for forming large-scale, structured organizations have met counterpressures traceable to democratic and populist disdain for "bureaucratic" or "machine" politics. This issue has split the group seeking to create a "Democratic Party of Russia." A majority, following Nikolay Travkin, accepts the need to develop an internal party organization in order to win electoral victories, while a minority resists bureaucratization and demands an "open" and democratic structure for the new party (Meerovich, 1990, pp. 14–15). Apart from the widespread antipathy to machine politics, the general vacuum of governmental authority means that successful parties have few patronage or policy benefits to dispense. They have accordingly tended to rely on purely ideological motivations for members and activists.

The electoral success of the Democratic Russia coalition owed a great deal to the organizing efforts of the first and most important of the parliamentary fractions at the center—the Interregional Group of Deputies. Identified with one of its founding fathers, Andrey Sakharov, it comprises over 300 of the democratically inclined deputies in the All-Union Congress of People's Deputies (Murashov, 1990). Although it has played an active part as a bloc or fraction in Union-level politics, its greatest importance lies in its role as a source of programmatic ideas and organizational advice for local democratic organizations and electoral coalitions, particularly in the Russian Republic (Kommunisty, 1990; Davydov, 1990). More than any other organized element, the Interregional Group was responsible for the coalescence into the "Democratic Russia" bloc of democratic candidates in the 1990 Russian Republic elections. Its deputies also have played a mediating role in confrontations between the center and peripheral regions, for example, after the Tbilisi massacre in April 1989 or the Sverdlovsk unrest at the end of December 1989.

The Interregional Group frequently also has supplied leadership to local political movements.[36] Nevertheless, although the group plays an important coordinating, advisory, and legitimating role, it has done no more than to provide a political and ideological focus for the profusion of grass-roots political activity in the country. The number of organizations active in the March 1990 elections can only be estimated very roughly, but it certainly exceeds one thousand. A research report published in early 1990 by *Moscow News* (1990, No. 7, p. 9) estimated that there were about 140 municipal popular fronts in the USSR at the beginning of 1990. At a conference on informal groups held in Novosibirsk in December 1989, estimates were presented of the number of groups in various regions: Sverdlovsk, over 3,000; Primorsk, 250; Chelyabinsk, 30; Novosibirsk, over 100. Many, obviously, are micro-organizations. Sverdlovsk's 3,000 groups were thought to have 120,000 participants. All these figures, of course, are estimates, and they do not distinguish between active and occasionally active members of groups. But the conservative estimate by *Moscow News* of the number of political groups—2 to 3 thousand, with a membership of 2 to 2.5 million—seems plausible in light of reports from major cities (*ibid.*).

The elections also demonstrate that the social gap between intelligentsia and populace is narrower today than at any time in Russian history (Levada, 1990). Both the 1989 and 1990 elections attest that, while the populace was eager to repudiate the ruling bureaucratic elite, it was not inclined to reject candidates from among the "prestige" elite. Eighty-six percent of the candidates, and 93 percent of the winners, held higher educational degrees. Indeed, nearly 20 percent of the deputies were from the spheres of education, health, journalism, and the arts.[37] These figures suggest that the availability of credible counter-elites with strong popular followings and democratic inclinations (which I consider to be a condition for successful transition to democracy from communism) is indeed met in the USSR by the existence of a "national" intelligentsia in many of the national republics. In the Russian Republic, the organizational successes of the democratic forces have resulted to a considerable extent from growing popular respect for the prestige elite, and from the skill of counter-elites in translating popular resentment of the regime into support for democratic and market-oriented change. Boris Yel'tsin's enormous popularity among all strata and the strength of popular support for republican sovereignty also have helped to bridge the remaining gap between *narod* and intelligentsia. But it must be remembered that the politics of resentment and alienation is stronger than support for liberal principles.

CONCLUSION

In fashioning a theory of transition from communism to democracy, it is insufficient to concentrate on the political or the social domain to the neglect of the other, since what is crucial is an understanding of their interaction as they evolve. A regime-centered account can illuminate the consequences of a communist system's fusion of economic and political power. Reform programs typically have attempted to avoid undermining that fusion, and have therefore been limited in their results. In cases when real liberties are granted to sub-central governments, opposition parties, producers, and parliaments, the Communist Party's monopoly on power breaks down. Points intermediate between a loosened, softened version of the Stalinist institutional framework and a democratic, market-driven system prove to be inherently unstable and soon yield either to a conservative consolidation or to a revolutionary rising against the regime.

The social modernization school, on the other hand, underscores the enormous impact of education, urbanization, professionalization, and communications in breaking down traditional structures of political control, facilitating independent and alternative forms of opinion and behavior, and unintentionally producing a shift in consciousness in the direction of individualism and autonomy. Without this analysis we could not explain the successes of the democratic movement in 1989 and 1990. This school of thought, however, while positing a growing gulf between "state" and "society," fails to anticipate just how difficult the transition will be, for it does not focus on the distinctive features of Soviet modernization.

Inequalities of power and privilege, the calamitous decline in the quality of life, the vast carelessness and wastefulness with which the regime deploys human and material resources—all contribute to the accumulation of anti-system resentments that make it all the more difficult for the communist system to reform itself peacefully. Nor does this literature pay sufficient attention to the nature of *group* identities that fill the void left by the breakdown of a sterile doctrine of proletarian collectivism, and that form the basis for new political movements. Given the amorphous character of class identities and the strength of primordial attachments, the very structure of the Soviet state, with its ethnically defined territorial jurisdictions, nurtures ethno-national counterideologies and territorial sovereignty claims. Political transition, consequently, should be analyzed as the mobilization of discontent, the outcome of which is determined by the degree to which existing channels of social cooperation can help create cohesive, autonomous, and broadly based organizations that mediate between the regime and the populace. In the Soviet case, these capacities exist, but not at the level of the USSR itself; rather, they are concentrated in the regions.

A society with a low level of social pluralism and a highly repressive regime is likely to see a long build-up of popular frustration followed eventually by an outburst of mass rage; there is little reason to expect a democratic outcome following the explosion. Where social pluralism is high, both in the center and throughout the country, even a short transition period can result in a peaceful, negotiated transfer of power to an organized opposition. If, however, the system is composed of national communities that define themselves in irreconciliable opposition to a larger and surrounding community, then the transfer of power at the territorial level gives way to a new struggle for independence against the center.

The USSR at present illustrates a number of different patterns simultaneously. As our theory would predict, political opposition movements are most highly developed where social pluralism is greatest—at the level of republics, cities, and regions. As a result, at least partial transition from Communist Party rule has occurred in the Baltic Republics, Georgia, Armenia, Lvov and Kiev (and increasingly in other parts of the Ukraine), Moscow, Sakhalin, and elsewhere. At the same time, in many of these places a situation of "dual power" obtains, with old political machines continuing to wield administrative power, and claiming the right to uphold Moscow's authority in locales in which political insurgents have declared regional autonomy. As a result, there is a struggle of the new democratic politics against the inherited structures of the old regime (the economic bureaucracy, the party apparatus, the security apparatus).

Profiting from the conservatives' inability to free themselves from the increasingly discredited structural and ideological framework of the old regime, democratically oriented groups are building their bases of ideological mobilization and patronage in the newly elected city and republican soviets. Spearheading the movement for regional economic and political autonomy, they are reviving an older tradition of local civic responsibility. They have several assets. In Yel'tsin they have an immensely popular leader, and other attractive democratic leaders have emerged in many cities, regions, and republics. Early on, in 1989 and 1990, they learned the importance of careful tactical and organizational work to win open electoral contests. They are far more effective at mobilizing populist resentment of the bureaucratic establishment than are their opponents, and they therefore prefer to face those opponents in open electoral contests (Remington, 1989b). But the process of transition has also unleashed a struggle of order against anarchy, as all institutions, old and new, are losing authority amidst accelerating economic chaos and disintegration.

Will anarchy defeat order? To say the least, it is not unreasonable to wonder a day after Shevardnadze's resignation and after Kryuchkov's ominous warnings. But to answer this question with a longer time horizon than that of the daily deadlines, one should focus less on the policymakers at the top and more on the basic processes by which new local political structures build authority in the wake of the breakdown of CPSU controls. In addition to studies of the rise of new parties and pressure groups,[38] studies of local government are badly needed. How are the new soviets asserting power and autonomy in light of the many political centers encroaching on their authority?[39] How do they balance popular demands for immediate action to clean up the environment with popular demands for preservation of the local economic and employment base?[40] Whatever emerges from battles in Moscow over Gorbachev's authority or survival after the events of December 1990, or over a union treaty, or over yet another "compromise" economic reform program, the long-term transition to democracy will be decided by the processes of institution-building taking place far from the center. A democratic transition hinges on the gradual consolidation of meaningful *local* power, legality, parliamentarism, and pluralism.

NOTES

1. The author wishes to express his appreciation to the Harriman Institute for Advanced Russian Studies at Columbia University and to the Emory University Research Fund for sustaining support of the research on which this paper is based, as well as to George W. Breslauer whose valuable comments facilitated revisions of an earlier draft.

2. This paper went to press during the last week of December 1990, within days following Vladimir Kryuchkov's hard-line speech at the Congress of People's Deputies (*The Washington Post,* December 23, 1990, pp. A1, A22).

3. See, for example, Huntington (1970), Dallin and Breslauer (1970), Johnson (1970), Jowitt (1977), Bauman (1976), and Lowenthal (1970). George Breslauer's concept of "welfare-state authoritarianism," emphasizing a tacit "social contract" between regime and populace, remains the most insightful and lasting of the analyses of regime dynamics in the mature, "system-management" phase. The "social contract" describes the premises underlying the ruling elite's relations with the main sectors of society (Breslauer, 1978). He observes that the Brezhnev leadership redefined the contract, by offering to

improve consumer welfare, so long as the populace kept its demands limited and maintained a certain level of productivity. Like most foreign observers of Soviet society, Breslauer viewed pressures for democratization and liberalization as emanating mainly from the intellectual elite; the masses were thought to aspire only to material and security goals. While Breslauer emphasized the highly restricted opportunities available for citizens to pressure government, Jerry Hough argued that the "Soviet Union obviously is a participatory society, with . . . a very large number of settings in which citizen participation can take place." Hough's argument is based on a view that there are many channels through which individuals can press their demands. Many individuals avail themselves of these channels; citizens can voice complaints and suggestions; and for those willing to make the effort, the system is responsive to demands for change. Hough concluded that citizen participation is not different in kind from that in a liberal democracy (Hough and Fainsod, 1979, pp. 314–19). Other studies emphasized the social benefits and reduction in income equalities. These analyses conclude that the legitimacy of communist systems was strongest where popular norms of social justice (egalitarianism, state provision of welfare benefits) were most fully realized. David Lane, for example, offered a simple two-by-two matrix to contrast the USSR with Poland. The USSR scored high in regard to state legitimacy but low in the cohesiveness of social associations. Poland, on the other hand, scored low on state legitimacy and high on social cohesiveness. No evidence whatever was provided to justify the claim that legitimacy of the Soviet state was high. Similarly, Lovenduski and Woodall argued that the ideological principle of social equality had become the defining criterion for regime legitimacy in Eastern European societies. Regimes, such as that of the former GDR (that met their socialist principles most fully), were most legitimate, while those in which privilege and corruption frustrated popular demands for equality (as in Poland) experienced repeated turmoil. Scholarly assessments of class equality and social welfare in the communist world tended to agree that: (1) the level of social welfare benefits in socialist states was generally higher than in noncommunist states at similar levels of development; and (2) that communist states had achieved higher levels of income equality than noncommunist states. The studies tended to overlook the areas of popular discontent that became focal issues in the late 1980s: worthlessness of wages and benefits in the face of severe shortages of consumer goods and food; popular resentment of the ruling elites' privileges and corruption; deterioration in the quality of life, including environmental protection and public health; and the inability of the general population to influence important state policies (Lane, 1986, pp. 326–45; Groth, 1986, pp. 346–60; Echols, 1986, pp. 361–79; Lovenduski and Woodall, 1987, pp. 430–31).

4. As opposed to the rational and modernizing features (Moore, 1954).

5. Brzezinski's argument echoes the "mass society" theories explaining the rise of totalitarianism in the shattered, déclassé societies of post-World War I Europe.

6. In the words of Kornai (1990, p. 59), "direct bureaucratic regulation of the state sector was replaced by indirect bureaucratic regulation. State authorities found a hundred means to meddle in the life of firms."

7. Prior to World War II there were not quite one million specialists with higher education employed in the economy. By 1970 there were close to 7 million, and nearly 10 million with specialized secondary education. Of these

the number of engineers rose in the same period from a still smaller base of not quite 300,000 with higher education to nearly 2.5 million. Meanwhile, technical personnel more than doubled their share of a fast growing stratum, the group with specialized secondary education, increasing from 324,000 out of 1.5 million to 4.3 out of nearly 10 million (Senyavskiy, 1973, pp. 317, 439–45). We can add to these "industrial" categories of specialists two other very rapidly growing groups: those employed in science (whose numbers roughly quadrupled in the 1960s and 1970s to 1.3 million by 1980) and the group made up of planners, economists, and statisticians, who increased their ranks sixfold during the same period and numbered 3 million by 1980 (Senyavskiy et al., 1984, pp. 184–85).

8. As a major CPSU resolution noted in 1979, a majority of Soviet families were now receiving three newspapers, listening to radio, and watching television (Remington, 1988, p. 3). Television, in particular, is almost universally available to the Soviet population, and has rapidly become the dominant medium through which the populace receives images and information about the world. But the saturation of Soviet society, long an objective of the Soviet leadership, had had some unintended consequences. Ellen Mickiewicz argues that "the television revolution in the Soviet Union, though initiated and administered under tight central control, has created a new and mobilized public" and one which is especially focused on information about the West (Mickiewicz, 1988, pp. 4–5). Television's greatest effect may be concentrated among the least educated groups of the population, for whom newspapers and other sources of information may be hard to understand or inaccessible, and whom television has, in effect, "brought into the modern world" (ibid., p. 209).

9. The "revolution" evolved as newly formed social strata with new aspirations and energies enhanced individualism and fatally weakened official structures of ideological indoctrination and control (Ruble, 1990, p. 86). Emphasizing the consistent strain of radical democratization in Gorbachev's political program, John Gooding observes that the Soviet political culture is less conservative than virtually all outside observers believed. The constituency for radical change, he believes, is the large urban educated class which is receptive to Gorbachev's efforts to inject competitiveness, personality, and individualism into Soviet politics (Gooding, 1990, pp. 217–18).

10. To cite a term used by Moshe Lewin (1988, p. 49).

11. Including formation of new habits, tastes, values, and aspirations, and modification of the interests and demands pressed by the population.

12. In his seminal article, Dankwart Rustow calls national unity a necessary background condition for democratization (Rustow, 1970, pp. 350–51).

13. Anderson and Silver's most recent findings indicate that actual infant mortality rates were considerably higher than the reported ones (by a factor of 23.5 percent).

14. D.J. Peterson estimates that the Soviet Union, with a GNP no more than half that of the United States [and likely less], produces approximately 80 percent as many tons of pollution annually, of which much is concentrated in cities. Peterson goes on to say that "the basic conclusion from Soviet reports is that there seems to be no major industrial city in the Soviet Union in which air pollution norms are generally observed" (Peterson, 1990, pp. 7–8).

15. The physicians conclude that the problems of Salavat, a city of 150,000 in southern Bashkiria, are "simply the tip of an enormous iceberg," the roots

of which lie in the 1930s. It was the simplistic mentality of that time that is "responsible for the use of old technologies dangerous to the environment and human life, for the chaotic concentration of harmful production in various cities, for serious miscalculations in the location of residential and industrial facilities. . . . The cheap philosophy of the general approach to siting economic facilities is costing us dearly" (Lupandin and Kakorina, 1988, pp. 54–55).

16. One estimate is that the decline was about half a percent per year between 1965 and 1979 (Foteyeva, 1984, pp. 93–94).

17. Personal communication, Moscow, 1990.

18. Indeed, although the tempos have slowed in the 1980s, a senior Soviet scholar projected that if present rates were to continue, the "specialist" category would account for over one half of the employed population by the year 2000 (Senyavskiy, 1984, p. 188).

19. Averaging slightly more than a million per year during the 1960s, 1970s, and 1980s.

20. Directors reinforced this trend (traced to the above two) by overstating their need for specialists in order to expand the wages funds (Kochetov, 1988, p. 11).

21. The low prestige of unskilled manual jobs as well as of vocational training in PTUs (combined with universalization of secondary education) played a role. This was reinforced by arbitrary reclassification of many skilled laborers' jobs to positions requiring specialized secondary training.

22. The lawyers, however, encountered a measure of resistance from the Ministry of Justice, which formally disbanded the original organizing committee and created another in its place (Wishnevsky, 1989, pp. 15–16).

23. Boris Yel'tsin, party official turned populist hero, is an extraordinary exception. Almost no other communist leaders have become such champions of an anti-establishment cause.

24. As Robert Dahl has argued, when a society is marked by deep regional or ethnic cleavages that have been suppressed for a long time by a dominant group, conditions are especially unfavorable for the development of democratic institutions. Efforts to draw such deeply alienated groups into a democratic political framework typically involve granting veto powers to the contending groups, which in turn fosters deadlock in the policymaking process. Alternatively, argues Dahl, "the price of territorial unity may be a hegemonic [i.e., non-democratic—TR] regime" (Dahl, 1971, pp. 219, 121).

25. A more substantial analysis of the "new class" was offered by a scholar from Voronezh University in an issue of *Kommunist* devoted to the 120th anniversary of Lenin's birth. The author argued that the swallowing of Soviet society by the state led to replacement of the economic classes of capitalism by the stratification of society into two fundamental groups: those who produce surplus value, and those who redistribute it. The latter enjoy their privileged position by virtue of their status in the *nomenklatura,* but tend to become a closed caste or "estate corporation." They associate with "their own kind," they are distinctive in dress, housing, and way of life, and they share a consciousness of their common privilege and access to power. There is an enormous psychological gulf between them and the direct producers of value, a mentality captured by the concept, "we/they." The power of the privileged class derives from the convergence of political power within the state and the state ownership of the means of production. The ability to dispose of the means of production in turn is delegated to a number of

groups performing functions for the state and possessing their own controls over the allocation of resources. Their senior echelons share a common interest in preserving the privileges and constitute a more or less cohesive social entity. On the other hand, the primary producers are heterogeneous and easily set at odds with one another in competition for the state's benefits (Starikov, 1990).

26. In this context, social pluralism means not diversity of latent interests, but the degree of social cooperation and organization outside the state's control.

27. Direct testimony on how friendship networks allowed *samizdat* to survive and to increase the capacity for organized activity by the democratic dissent movement in the Soviet Union is offered by Ludmilla Alexeyeva: "Under Stalin, when informing had become the norm, unofficial contacts between people had been reduced to a bare minimum. As a rule, two or three families would associate only among themselves, and there were very few homes where many people gathered. After the fear of mass arrests had passed, people threw themselves at each other, deriving satisfaction from merely being together. A normal Moscow circle numbered 40 to 50 'close friends.' . . . All these circles were connected with other similar circles and the links led to Leningrad, Novosibirsk and other cities. . . . Large groups that fostered mutual trust created ideal conditions for the spread of samizdat. . . . At least in the early stages of the [human rights] movement, this informal structure demonstrated its effectiveness. . . . Tasks were coordinated between friends, and this ensured mutual trust without which organized activities would be impossible under conditions of constant surveillance. This system made it possible to fill vacancies frequently created by arrests: someone close to the arrested would take over his responsibilities. Ties of friendship also made penetration by provocateurs difficult. Over the past 20 years, a few activists have been pressured into giving evidence against their friends while under arrest, but there is not one known instance of a KGB agent successfully infiltrating human rights groups" (Alexeyeva, 1985, pp. 269, 270, 283).

28. As opposed to a clan-based, tribal, or denationalized and assimilated consciousness.

29. Examples include Arpad Goncz, Vaclav Havel, Adam Michnik, Vytautas Landsbergis, Andrey Sakharov, Vyacheslav Chornovil, Valentin Rasputin, Zvyad Gamsakhurdiya, Ion Drutse, Kurt Masur, Olzhas Suleymenov, and many others.

30. Some writers believe that competitive political parties are indispensable to successful democratic transitions from authoritarian regimes (e.g., Cardoso, 1989, p. 301; Powell, 1982, p. 7; O'Donnell and Schmitter, 1986, p. 58). At the same time, however, building such parties must keep pace with the rate of social and political disintegration of the old regime, for the transition can generate its own discontents. In the USSR, the breakdown of political order and elementary economic well-being is occurring very rapidly. Inflation and food shortages have become the most acute problems in public opinion at a time when the capacity of the old administrative structures to solve problems has been undermined by the collapse of their authority. A poll of 36,000 residents of the RSFSR, reported in *Argumenty i fakty* (1990, No. 20, p. 4), found that between 1985–1986 and 1989 the proportion calling inflation and food shortages a top priority problem rose some 30 percent. In the first half of 1990 alone, over 500,000 members of the CPSU either quit

the Party or stopped paying dues (*Radio Liberty Daily Report*, August 3, 1990). This was before the publicized withdrawals from the CPSU of Boris Yel'tsin, Anatoliy Sobchak, Gavriil Popov, Sergey Stankevich, and other heroes of the democratic opposition. By the end of 1990, over 1.5 million Party members had left and membership stood at 17.7 million (*Glasnost'*, November 3, 1990, as cited in *The New York Times* [national edition], November 4, 1990, p. 12).

31. Over half the Russian Republic's land area lies within autonomous, nationally-based territories.

32. None of this saved the *kraykom* first secretary from defeat in the 1990 legislative elections, forcing his resignation as first secretary of the territorial party organization.

33. I have discussed this group and its ideological opponent, the Bloc of Public and Patriotic Movements of Russia, in greater detail in a forthcoming publication (Remington, 1991).

34. However, they face the challenge of defining more concretely their attitude toward the political demands of cities, regions, and autonomous units within the republic.

35. Its visibility was greatly enhanced by Shevardnadze's resignation.

36. An example was provided by an *Izvestiya* correspondent for the Yakut ASSR, a member of the Interregional Group, who decided to start a voters' club in Yakutia after returning from the first session of the Congress of People's Deputies. Following the formation of the club in Yakutsk, which attracted about 100 members, similar clubs sprang up in a half dozen other cities of the autonomous republic, usually with a few dozen members each. In turn these clubs formed a Union of Voters' Clubs. In November 1989, the union decided to publish a newspaper, which appears in 1,000 to 3,000 copies whenever paper and facilities are available. Its chief editor is A.A. Loginov, a member of the coordinating council of the local Social-Democratic Association (*Russkaya mysl'*, February 9, 1990).

37. This also explains the fact that, although 94 percent of the deputies to the Russian Republican Congress of People's Deputies were individuals elected to such an office for the first time, the incidence of Party membership rose 20 percent over that in the old RSFSR Supreme Soviet.

38. See the forthcoming article by Darrell Slider (1991) on the new associations of cooperatives.

39. These include local executive organs of the soviets, superordinate governments, local CPSU committees, local agencies of the central bureaucracy, and lower-level governments within the territory.

40. A relatively recent article by Bill Keller (*New York Times*, November 26, 1990, p. A6) details the contradictory pressures on the newly elected government of the Bashkir city of Sterlitimak. Amidst disastrous environmental conditions, the city faces increasing pressure to finance the clean-up (and maintain its employment base) from local resources.

REFERENCES

Alexeyeva, Ludmilla, *Soviet Dissent: Contemporary Movements for National, Religious, and Human Rights,* translated by Carol Pearce and John Glad (Middletown, CT: Wesleyan University Press, 1985).

Almond, Gabriel A. and Laura Roselle, "Model Fitting in Communism Studies," in Thomas F. Remington, ed., *Politics and the Soviet System: Essays in Honor of Frederick C. Barghoorn* (London: Macmillan, 1989).

Anderson, Barbara A. and Brian D. Silver, "Trends and Counter-Trends in Mortality in the Soviet Population," *Soviet Economy,* 1990.

Åslund, Anders, "How Small Is Soviet National Income?" in Henry S. Rowen and Charles Wolf, Jr., eds., *The Impoverished Superpower* (San Francisco, CA: Institute for Contemporary Studies, 1990).

Bauman, Zygmunt, "The Party in the System-Management Phase: Change and Continuity," in Andrew C. Janos, ed., *Authoritarian Politics in Communist Europe: Uniformity and Diversity in One-Party States* (Berkeley, CA: Institute of International Studies, 1976).

Breslauer, George W., "On the Adaptability of Soviet Welfare-State Authoritarianism," in Karl W. Ryavec, ed., *Soviet Society and the Communist Party* (Amherst, MA: University of Massachusetts Press, 1978).

_____, "Evaluating Gorbachev as Leader," *Soviet Economy,* 5, 4:299–340, October–December 1989.

_____, "Thinking About the Soviet Future," in George W. Breslauer, ed., *Can Gorbachev's Reforms Succeed?* (Berkeley, CA: Berkeley-Stanford Program in Soviet Studies, Center for Slavic and East European Studies, University of California, Berkeley, 1990).

Brzezinski, Zbigniew, *The Grand Failure: The Birth and Death of Communism in the Twentieth Century* (New York: Scribners, 1989).

_____, "Postcommunist Nationalism," *Foreign Affairs,* 68, 5:1–25, 1989–1990.

CIA (US Central Intelligence Agency), *Revisiting Soviet Economic Performance Under Glasnost': Implications for CIA Estimates* (Washington, DC: CIA Directorate of Intelligence, September 1988).

Campbell, Robert, "The Soviet Economic Model," in Seweryn Bialer and Michael Mandelbaum, eds., *Gorbachev's Russia and American Foreign Policy* (Boulder and London: Westview Press, 1988).

Cardoso, Fernando Henrique, "Associated-Dependent Development and Democratic Theory," in Alfred Stepan, ed., *Democratizing Brazil: Problems of Transition and Consolidation* (New York and Oxford: Oxford University Press, 1989).

Dahl, Robert A., *Polyarchy* (New Haven, CT: Yale University Press, 1971).

Dallin, Alexander and George W. Breslauer, *Political Terror in Communist Systems* (Stanford, CA: Stanford University Press, 1970). Davydov, Valentin, "Neformal'noye dvizheniye: voprosov bol'she, chem otvetov (The Informal Movement: More Questions Than Answers)," *Soyuz* (supplement to *Izvestiya*), 20:8–9, 1990.

"Demokratizatsiya partii—demokratizatsiya obshchestva (Democratization of the Party—Democratization of Society)," discussion rubric published in *Kommunist,* 3:38–39 and 4:85–89, 1988.

Durasoff, Douglas, "Conflicts between Economic Decentralization and Political Control in the Domestic Reform of Soviet and Post-Soviet Systems," *Social Science Quarterly,* 69, 2:381–98, 1988.

Eberstadt, Nick, "Health of an Empire: Poverty and Social Progress in the CMEA Bloc," in Henry S. Rowen and Charles Wolf, Jr., eds., *The Future of the Soviet Empire* (New York: Institute for Contemporary Studies/St. Martin's Press, 1987).

Echols, John M., III, "Does Socialism Mean Greater Equality? A Comparison of East and West Along Several Major Dimensions," in Stephen White and Daniel Nelson, eds., *Communist Politics: A Reader* (New York: New York University Press, 1986).

Ericson, Richard E., "The Soviet Statistical Debate: Khanin vs. TsSU," in Henry S. Rowen and Charles Wolf, Jr., *The Impoverished Superpower* (San Francisco, CA: Institute for Contemporary Studies, 1990).

Filippov, F.R., "Izmeneniya v sotsial'nom oblike i sostave sovetskoy intelligentsii (Change in Social Character and Composition of the Soviet Intelligentsia)," in W. Wesolowski and M.N. Rutkevich, eds., *Problemy razvitiya sotsial'noy struktury obshchestva v Sovetskom Soyuze i Pol'she (Problems of the Evolution of Social Structure in the Soviet Union and Poland)* (Moscow: Nauka, 1976).

Filippov, F.R. et al., eds., *Formirovaniye sotsial'noy odnorodnosti sotsialisticheskogo obshchestva (Formation of Social Homogeneity of Socialist Society)* (Moscow: Nauka, 1981).

Fotoyeva, Ye. V., *Kachestvennyye kharakteristiki naseleniya SSSR (Qualitative Characteristics of the USSR Population)* (Moscow: Finansy i statistika, 1984).

Gooding, John, "Gorbachev and Democracy," *Soviet Studies,* 42, 2:195–231, 1990.

"Goskomstat SSSR soobshchayet (USSR Goskomstat Communique)," *Sotsiologicheskiye issledovaniya,* 2:142, 1988.

Groth, Alexander J., "Worker Welfare Systems in Marxist-Leninist States: A Comparative Perspective," in Stephen White and Daniel Nelson, eds., *Communist Politics: A Reader* (New York: New York University Press, 1986).

Hough, Jerry F. and Merle Fainsod, *How the Soviet Union Is Governed* (Cambridge, MA: Harvard University Press, 1979).

Huntington, Samuel P., "Social and Institutional Dynamics of One-Party Systems," in Samuel P. Huntington and Clement H. Moore, eds., *Authoritarian Politics in Modern Society: The Dynamics of Established One-Party Systems* (New York: Basic Books, 1970).

Inkeles, Alex and Raymond Bauer, *The Soviet Citizen* (New York: Atheneum, 1968).

Johnson, Chalmers, "Comparing Communist Nations," in Chalmers Johnson, ed., *Change in Communist Systems* (Stanford, CA: Stanford University Press, 1970).

Jowitt, Kenneth, "Inclusion and Mobilization in European Leninist Regimes," in Jan F. Triska and Paul M. Cocks, eds., *Political Development in Eastern Europe* (New York: Praeger, 1977).

Karnaukhov, S., "About Privileges and Openness," *Pravda,* August 1, 1988 (as translated in *Current Digest of the Soviet Press,* Vol. 40, No. 31, August 31, 1988, p. 19).

Kiss, Ilona, "The Coal Miners: Spearhead of the Soviet Working Class," *Beszelo,* July 28, 1990 (translated in *Uncaptive Minds,* 3, 4:42–44, 1990).

"Kommunisty i samodeyatel'nyye dvizheniya (Communists and Independent Movements)," *Partiynaya zhizn',* 2:31–36, 1990.

Kornai, Janos, *The Road to a Free Economy* (New York and London: Norton, 1990).

Kochetov, A.N., "Novyye tendentsii v sovershenstvovanii sotsial'noy struktury sovetskogo obshchestva (1980-ye gody) (New Trends in Improving the Social Structure of Soviet Society [the 1980s])," *Istoriya SSSR,* 6:3–16, 1988.

Kostikov, Vyacheslav, "Blesk i nishcheta nomenklatury (The Splendor and Poverty of the *Nomenklatura*)," *Ogonyok,* 1:12–15, 1989.

Lane, David, "Human Rights under State Socialism," in Stephen White and Daniel Nelson, eds., *Communist Politics: A Reader* (New York: New York University Press, 1986).

Lapidus, Gail, "State and Society: Toward the Emergence of Civil Society in the Soviet Union," in Seweryn Bialer, ed., *Politics, Society, and Nationality Inside Gorbachev's Russia* (Boulder and London: Westview Press, 1989).

Levada, Yuriy, summary of presentation appearing in *At the Harriman Institute,* 3, 13:1–2 (New York: Harriman Institute of Columbia University, 1990).

Levinson, Aleksey, "Predictable Surprises," *Moscow News,* 10:4, 1990.

Lewin, Moshe, *The Gorbachev Phenomenon: A Historical Interpretation* (Berkeley, CA: University of California Press, 1988).

Lovenduski, Joni and Jean Woodall, *Politics and Society in Eastern Europe* (Bloomington, IN: Indiana University Press, 1987).

Lowenthal, Richard, "Development vs. Utopia in Communist Policy," in Chalmers Johnson, ed., *Change in Communist Systems* (Stanford, CA: Stanford University Press, 1970).

Lupandin, V.M. and Ye. P. Kakorina, "V chyom prichina epidemii sredi detey (Cause for an Epidemic Among Children)," *Sotsiologicheskiye issledovaniya,* 6:50–55, 1988.

Meerovich, Aleksandr, "The Emergence of Russian Multiparty Politics," *Radio Liberty Report on the USSR,* 2, 34:8–16, August 24, 1990.

Mickiewicz, Ellen, *Split Signals: Television and Politics in the Soviet Union* (New York: Oxford University Press, 1988).

Moore, Barrington, *Terror and Progress USSR* (Cambridge, MA: Harvard University Press, 1954).

Murashov, A., "Mezhregional'naya deputatskaya gruppa (The Interregional Deputies Group)," *Ogonyok,* 32:6–8, 1990.

O'Donnell, Guillermo and Philippe C. Schmitter, *Transitions from Authoritarian Rule: Tentative Conclusions about Uncertain Democracies* (Baltimore and London: Johns Hopkins University Press, 1986).

Ofer, Gur, "Soviet Economic Growth: 1928–1985," *Journal of Economic Literature,* 25, 4: 1767–1833, December 1987.

Peterson, D.J., "The State of the Environment: The Air," *Radio Liberty Report on the USSR,* 2, 9:5–9, March 2, 1990.

Powell, G. Bingham, Jr., *Contemporary Democracies: Participation, Stability, and Violence* (Cambridge, MA: Harvard University Press, 1982).

Prokushev, Vladimir, "'Kruglyy stol' . . . samoubiits ('Roundtable' . . . of Those Committing Suicide)," *Zhurnalist,* 10:4–7, 1988.

Pye, Lucian W., "Political Science and the Crisis of Authoritarianism," *American Political Science Review,* 84, 1:3–19, 1990.

Remington, Thomas F., "The Mass Media and Public Communication in the USSR," *Journal of Politics,* 43, 3:803–17, 1981.

_____, *The Truth of Authority: Ideology and Communication in the Soviet Union* (Pittsburgh, PA: University of Pittsburgh Press, 1988).

_____, "A Socialist Pluralism of Opinions: Glasnost' and Policy-Making under Gorbachev," *Russian Review,* 48, 3:271–304, 1989a.

_____, "Perestroika and Pluralism: The Soviet Elections of 1989," *Japan-US Joint Study on the Soviet Union,* Conference VI, June 16–17, 1989b.

_____, "The 1990 RSFSR Elections," in Darrell Slider, ed., *Elections and Political Change in the Soviet Republics,* 1991.

Ruble, Blair A., "The Soviet Union's Quiet Revolution," in George W. Breslauer, ed., *Can Gorbachev's Reforms Succeed?* (Berkeley, CA: Berkeley-Stanford Program in Soviet Studies, Center for Slavic and East European Studies, 1990).

Rukavishnikov, V.O. and A.P. Kotov, "Predvybornyye nastroyeniya: obshchiye cherty (The Pre-Election Mood: Broad Outlines)," in V.O. Rukavishnikov et al., eds., *Predvybornaya situatsiya: mneniya izbirateley (The Pre-election Situation: Opinions of the Voters)* (Moscow: Institut Sotsiologii Akademii Nauk SSSR, 1990).

Rustow, Dankwart A., "Transitions to Democracy: Toward a Dynamic Model," *Comparative Politics,* 2, 3:337–64, 1970.

Rutkevich, M.N., "Sotsial'naya struktura sotsialisticheskogo obshchestva v SSSR i yeyo razvitiye k sotsialisticheskoy odnorodnosti (Social Structure of Socialist Society in the USSR and Its Evolution toward Socialist Homogeneity)," in W. Wesolowski and M.N. Rutkevich, eds., *Problemy razvitiya sotsial'noy struktury obshchestva v Sovetskom Soyuze i Pol'she (Problems of the Evolution of Social Structure in the Soviet Union and Poland)* (Moscow: Nauka, 1976).

Rutkevich, M.N. and F.P. Filippov, *Sotsial'naya struktura ravitogo sotsialisticheskogo obshchestva v SSSR (Social Structure of Developed Socialist Society in the USSR)* (Moscow: Nauka, 1976).

Selunskaya, V.M. and T.A. Sivokhina, *Sotsial'no-politicheskoye yedinstvo sovetskogo obshchestva (The Social and Political Unity of Soviet Society)* (Moscow: Mysl', 1982).

Senyavskiy, S.L., *Izmeneniya v sotsial'noy strukture sovetskogo obshchestva, 1938–1970 (Change in the Social Structure of Soviet Society, 1983–1970)* (Moscow: Mysl', 1973).

Senyavskiy, S.L. et al., eds., *Aktual'nyye problemy istorii razvitogo sotsializma v SSSR (Timely Problems in the History of Developed Socialism in the USSR)* (Moscow: Mysl', 1984).

Shlapentokh, Vladimir, *Public and Private Life of the Soviet People: Changing Values in Post-Stalin Russia* (New York and Oxford: Oxford University Press, 1989).

Slider, Darrell, "The First Independent Soviet Interest Groups: Unions and Associations of Cooperatives," in James Butterfield and Judith Sedaitis, eds., *New Social Movements in the Soviet Union* (Boulder, CO: Westview Press, 1991).

Sokolova, I.F. and M.A. Manuil'skiy, "Kak stat' ministrom (How to Become a Minister)," *Sotsiologicheskiye issledovaniya,* 1:16–25, January–February 1988, No. 1.

Starikov, E., "Novyye elementy sotsial'noy struktury (New Elements of Social Structure)," *Kommunist,* 5:30–41, 1990.

Starr, S. Frederick, "The Changing Nature of Change in the USSR," in Seweryn Bialer and Michael Mandelbaum, eds., *Gorbachev's Russia and American Foreign Policy* (Boulder and London: Westview Press, 1988).

_____, "The USSR: A Civil Society," *Foreign Policy,* 70:26–41, 1989.

"Vybory v sovety: platformy partiynykh komitetov (Elections to the Soviets: Platforms of Party Committees)," *Izvestiya Tsk KPSS,* 1:75–86, 1990.

Wishnevsky, Julia, "Association of Legal Counsel to Be Established," *Radio Liberty Report on the USSR,* 1, 2:15–16, January 13, 1989.

Zaslavskaya, Tat'yana, "Chelovecheskiy faktor razvitiya ekonomiki i sotsial'naya spravedlivost' (The Human Factor in the Development of the Economy and Social Justice)," *Kommunist,* 13: 61–73, September 1986.

———, "Vesti dialog s lyud'mi (To Carry Out a Dialogue with the People)," *Narodnyy deputat,* 2:23–27, 1990.

Z [Martin Malia], "To the Stalin Mausoleum," *Daedalus,* 119, 1:295–344, 1990.

14

CONTINUITY AND CHANGE IN RUSSIAN POLITICAL CULTURE

This chapter assesses the presence or absence in Russia of a political culture compatible with the emergence of democratic institutions. It offers a test of the thesis that political culture may be an important variable linking economic development to transitions to democracy. On the basis of findings from a systematic random sample of opinions about politics in the city of Yaroslavl' in March 1990, the article finds little support for the argument that Russian political culture today is dominated by the autocratic traditions of the past. Rather, the patterns that emerge suggest that Russian political thinking comes closer to what is found in Western industrial democracies.

THE ISSUE

For students of contemporary Soviet politics, the compelling question for analysis is surely the extent to which the reform of Soviet political institutions will result in something like a Western parliamentary democracy. In short: will Soviet politics become more democratic or not? If the question can be simply stated, efforts to answer it engender controversy. One of the key issues of contention is the problem of political culture. Broadly speaking, the division of opinion is between those who feel that societal changes in the Soviet Union have produced a population supportive of democratic ideas and institutions and those who argue that the persistence of a political culture antithetical to democratic values all but ensures the restoration of authoritarian rule in one form or another. As Archie Brown writes in a recent effort to address this question: "The issue of continuity and change in ideology and political culture—although seemingly at some remove from the everyday world of political decision-making—is of critical importance for the success or failure of the project on which Mikhail Gorbachev has embarked in the second half of the 1980s."[1]

What follows is a contribution to this debate, based on a survey of attitudes about politics conducted among nearly 1,000 voters chosen by a systematic random sample in the Russian provincial capital of Yaroslavl' in the spring of 1990. The problem of how much one may generalize from such a sample is dealt with in the methodological section of this article. Here, however, let me note the related objection that any survey of views taken early in 1990 may be unduly optimistic; a survey taken a year later, say, would surely have yielded different results because of rising popular discontent. Lacking evidence to the contrary, the possibility that major differences in response would have been found has to be acknowledged. However, political culture, if it has any meaning conceptually, is presumed to change slowly.[2] Moreover, the present article attempts to weigh whether, at least at the time the survey was taken, there was sufficient receptivity in the popular political consciousness to sustain democratic institutions. Whether the populace became less receptive with the passage of time can only be answered conclusively with longitudinal data as yet unavailable.[3] At the least, the data provide a baseline against which persistence or change in Russian political thinking can be measured.

The other purpose of this research is to use the study of political culture in Russia to illuminate some larger disciplinary concerns relating political culture to the question of transitions to democratic institutions. More specifically, the data are used to examine the argument that generational changes in political culture accompany the process of modernization. This larger context will be established in the first section of the chapter, followed by a review of the literature on continuity or change in Russian political culture. The methodology and findings are then presented and some very tentative conclusions are offered in an attempt to answer the rather large questions raised at the outset.

ECONOMIC DEVELOPMENT, POLITICAL CULTURE, AND DEMOCRATIC INSTITUTIONS

While the immediate purpose of this article is to assess the presence or absence in Russia of a political culture compatible with the emergence of democratic institutions, such analysis may also contribute to our understanding of broader theoretical issues within the discipline of political science. Prominent among these is the question of why and under what conditions economically developed countries come to be democratically governed. Lucian Pye raised this issue in his presidential address to the 1989 annual meeting of the American Political Science Association. The main challenge for contemporary political science, he argued, is to analyze the transition to post-authoritarian regimes. While claiming "vindication" for modernization theory as a predictor of political change, Pye maintained that democratic outcomes are by no means assured and will depend upon clashes between national political cultures and the "world culture" of modernization.[4]

Pye appears to share the broad consensus among political scientists that the emergence and maintenance of democratic regimes is far more likely to take place in societies that are economically developed than in those that are not.[5] Yet, clearly, there have been economically developed societies that have not been democratic. The Soviet Union under Brezhnev is a frequently cited example.[6] Germany under Nazi rule is another. Economic development may be a necessary condition for the emergence of a democratic polity, but it would not appear sufficient. Why? What else is needed?

One effort to advance theories relating economic development to political democracy was recently offered by Ronald Inglehart of the University of Michigan. Based on his analysis of cross-cultural data from ten European countries, Inglehart makes a case for the persistence of distinctive patterns of political culture and directly relates this continuity to the durability of democratic institutions. Rejecting rational choice models which explain political behavior primarily as a function of economic calculation, Inglehart proposes a "complex interplay" of economics, political culture, and institutions as accounting for democratic outcomes. According to Inglehart: "Political culture is a crucial link between economic development and democracy."[7]

Perhaps the foremost contemporary analyst of democratic theory, Robert Dahl, also accords a key role to political culture. In his recent study, *Democracy and Its Critics,* Dahl identifies a political culture "favorable to democratic ideas and practices" as one of five conditions necessary if a country is "to develop and sustain the institutions of polyarchy."[8] Both arguments are consistent with the concept first advanced by Almond and Verba in *The Civic Culture* that the viability of democratic institutions rests at least in part on the existence of a congruent political culture.[9]

Following this line of thought, the theory adopted heuristically by the present chapter assumes that political culture is an important intervening variable between economic development and the development of democratic institutions. Specifically, economic development changes the way people think about politics; it predisposes them to be receptive to democratic ideas and institutions. How? Without elaborating an argument that has been made elsewhere, we suggest that because of increased intellectual and material resources available to an ever-widening circle of citizens, there is a growing expectation that the making of decisions in society will be shared.[10] In short, economic development fosters the emergence of something like a "civic culture," and the existence of such a culture is a precondition for the emergence and maintenance of democratic institutions.

But what about the Soviet Union or, at least, its Russian component? Russia was economically developed before Gorbachev came to
power, yet lacked truly democratic institutions.[11] In fact, the Russian
case provides a useful test of the theory developed above. If the
theory is correct, we would expect Soviet citizens to possess a set
of attitudes, values, and beliefs about politics more or less comparable to those found in the developed democratic systems of the
West—something like a "civic culture." Moreover, these attitudes
would have developed *independently of the authoritarian political
institutions of Soviet government.* They would come closer to being
a variant on the "world culture" of modernization referred to by
Pye.[12] If, on the other hand, we found no evidence of similarity
between the political culture of contemporary Russia and that found
in Western industrial democracies, we would have to question
whether political culture is the "crucial link between economic development and democracy" that Inglehart proposes. After all, Russian
political culture would have been unaffected by economic development. If economic development does not necessarily foster democratic values, how can political culture be a link between
development and democracy? Economic development would be
shown to be as compatible with, say, an authoritarian or "subject"
political culture as with a democratic one.

RUSSIAN CULTURAL CONTINUITY

The approach outlined here also enables us to test another major
thesis long debated by students of the Soviet Union. It is the thesis
that there is far more historical continuity than change in the way
Russians think about politics. There are a variety of explanations for
the alleged uniqueness and persistence of Russian political culture,
arising out of studies of national character traits[13] and psycho-cultural
analyses.[14] But the most comprehensive and well-developed versions
of the continuity thesis come from historians.

One of the most prominent of these historians is Richard Pipes,
whose book, *Russia Under the Old Regime,* traces the development
of "patrimonial" rule—allegedly distinctive to Russia among European nations—which culminated by 1881 in an absolutist political
system that survived unchanged, if not actually strengthened, under
the Bolsheviks.[15] Soviet officials in the Stalin period, Pipes writes
elsewhere, were "for all practical purposes directly descended from
the peasantry," a class he views as virtually without a sense of civic
responsibility: politically passive but sly, and wholly accepting of an
autocratic order.[16]

Edward Keenan provides another version of this cultural-continuity thesis. In a long and well-crafted essay, he asserts the persistence
of what he calls "Muscovite political folkways." Based on an analysis

of village, court, and bureaucratic political cultures, Keenan finds that political orientations emphasizing traditional patterns of centralization, bureaucratization, and risk-avoidance have been dominant features since the establishment of Muscovite rule in the sixteenth century. Except for the "aberrant" political culture that accompanied the initial industrial revolution (1870–1930), "it is these features that determine Soviet political culture today, as they have determined Russian political culture for centuries."[17] For Keenan, Stalinism merely marked the restoration of Muscovite political culture.

A number of political scientists specializing in the study of Soviet politics have also found the argument for historical continuity persuasive. Perhaps the most unequivocal endorsement of this view comes from Zbigniew Brzezinski who argues that "Soviet politics cannot be separated from Russian history" and that "the central and significant reality of Russian politics has been its predominantly autocratic character."[18] He identifies eight different features of this historical legacy, all of which are antithetical to the emergence of democratic institutions in Russia. Soviet political culture, he argues, combines the features of modern totalitarianism and traditional autocracy.

The most detailed attempt to date, however, by a political scientist to study Soviet political culture is found in the writings of Stephen White. In his book, *Political Culture and Soviet Politics,* White identifies the main features distinguishing what he calls the "traditional Russian political culture" and describes the "distinctive" social structure that sustained it. Among the features noted by White are the absence of institutions for communicating popular demands, a highly centralized and largely unlimited autocracy, and the highly personalized relationship between the vast majority of the population and their autocrat, the Tsar. White goes on to examine efforts by Soviet leaders to resocialize the population in the mould of the "new Soviet Man" and finds that by and large they have failed. He concludes that "an emphasis on continuity rather than change in Soviet political culture would not appear to be misplaced,"[19] a conclusion he embraces even more ardently elsewhere.[20]

It is significant that at least some political scientists accepting one or another version of the cultural-continuity thesis have maintained their view in the face of Gorbachev's efforts to democratize Soviet political institutions. Thus, Walter Laqueur argues that efforts at democratization will fail because there are not enough democrats in Russia: "Basic instincts do not easily change; the Russians never respected and loved democracy as they respected and loved autocracy."[21]

Brzezinski acknowledges that, as a "revisionist," Gorbachev has sought to change the Soviet political culture and to accommodate the emergence of new political groups. But Brzezinski is convinced that Gorbachev will fail because "Russian history and Soviet reality both conspire against restructuring." His prognosis is pessimistic. The alternatives to Gorbachev's success, which he considers "doubtful," are: "inconclusive turmoil," renewed stagnation, a coup or fragmentation of the Soviet Union resulting from some combination of these.[22] The point to be made here is that those holding to the view that there is a strong continuity in Russian political culture are more likely than others to discount the possibility of political change in Russia in the direction of a more democratic polity.

A number of analysts of Soviet politics dispute the view that there is more continuity than change in how Russians think about politics. The thrust of their argument is that social changes resulting from the process of modernization have, in the course of several generations, produced a population qualitatively different from that found in Russia prior to industrialization: today's Russians are more educated, more urban, more middle-class, and better-off materially. Such social characteristics are generally associated with higher levels of political participation.[23]

An early proponent of the idea that generational change could be having significant consequences for Soviet politics is Jerry Hough.[24] In his more recent work, *Russia and the West,* Hough contradicts Keenan's thesis, arguing that the Bolshevik revolution and the period of Stalinism that followed it represent "not a restoration of Russian absolutism" but "an unnatural break" in the struggle of Russia to modernize. Gorbachev is best understood as a return to aspirations for a modern, Western society reaching back to Peter the Great. His arrival on the scene is a consequence of the social-structural changes that have accompanied economic development over the past fifty years.[25]

An equally compelling argument is offered by Moshe Lewin in *The Gorbachev Phenomenon.* Lewin traces the transformation of Russian society from one that was primarily rural and traditional to one that is predominantly urban and modern. The increased complexity of social structure that accompanied such a transformation could not be accommodated within the framework of an authoritarian state system. Given the growing dialectical tension between a modernized society and an anachronistic polity, reform was inevitable.[26] A similar view is offered by Blair Ruble who writes of a "quiet revolution" taking place over several decades, "a prolonged process of social differentiation and fragmentation" which seems likely to facilitate the transition from authoritarian rule.[27]

S. Frederick Starr and Gail W. Lapidus foresee these forces coming together to produce something like a "civil society" in the Soviet Union. Starr points to the role of the new communication technologies in creating a "pluralism of information" in the Soviet Union, including information from the West, which he argues greatly facilitates the development of independent networks and groups.[28] Starr and others have also pointed out that the pre-revolutionary Russian past was not so impervious to liberal democratic thought as the continuity thesis would lead one to believe.[29] Lapidus explicitly links the emergence of civil society to modernization theory, seeing in the current reforms a "long-delayed response by the leadership to fundamental social changes."[30] Drawing on Brian Silver's analysis of data from the Soviet Interview Project, Lapidus develops the intriguing hypothesis that the emergence of civil society is linked to the search by a younger and better-educated but also more alienated generation for a private, non-official sphere.[31]

One of the most thoughtful analysts of political culture in Communist systems—Archie Brown—sees both persistence and change in Soviet and Russian political culture. On the one hand, he agrees with those who emphasize continuity, noting that "the long-term authoritarian character of the Russian and Soviet state constitutes a serious impediment to political change of a pluralizing, libertarian, or genuinely democratizing nature."[32] On the other hand, Brown is convinced that the way Russians think politically is changing, and he rejects the idea that they are incapable of doing so as "thinly disguised racism."[33] Part of the change he attributes to *glasnost* and to institutional changes introduced by Gorbachev, such as competitive elections. However, Brown also acknowledges the role played by societal change, concluding that, as a result, "the climate for reform is less arid than the climate that confronted the immediate post-Stalin reformers."[34]

It is not surprising that proponents of the view that there is more continuity than change in Russian political culture are strongly critical of explanations of change rooted in some variant of development theory. Keenan and Brzezinski point to the "failure" of Khrushchev's reform attempts as evidence of the persistence of traditional political values,[35] while Brzezinski and White reject the modernization hypothesis on the grounds that development and "modernity" have not always resulted in the emergence of democratic institutions.[36] On similar grounds, these authors reject the notion that generational differences will result in political reform, White more cautiously than the others.[37] The differences between proponents and critics of the "cultural continuity" thesis are significant because they so strongly condition one's expectations of whether democratic reform in the Soviet Union will succeed or not. George Breslauer neatly captures this dichotomy when he writes:

> Counsels of hope are based on an image of Soviet society that displays the "modernizing" tendencies as actually or potentially dominant—strong to begin with and getting stronger. Optimists view the process of reform as one during which the structure of political and economic incentives reinforces modernizing attitudes. Counsels of alarm, in contrast, view the "drag" of traditional attitudes as great enough to lace the reform

process with compromises, hesitations, and contradictions that will prevent a decisive breakthrough . . . .[38]

HYPOTHESES

The literature reviewed here, and the theories they elaborate, are rich in hypotheses that, in principle, can be subjected to empirical verification. This chapter offers a step in that direction. To begin, we must identify which of these hypotheses we intend to test and then specify the methods and data we will use to arrive at our conclusions. We hypothesize that:

1. If the theory of Russian cultural continuity which emphasizes the persistence of an authoritarian culture in Russia is correct, we would expect to find Russian attitudes, values, and beliefs about politics to be markedly different from those found in Western industrial democracies. Specifically, we would expect to find a substantially lower sense of political efficacy and political trust. We would also expect to find a lower level of popular support for democratic institutions, notably elections, and a lower level of interest in politics.

2. Conversely, if the theory is correct that economic development tends to foster the acquisition of the values, attitudes, and beliefs we have come to associate with a "civic culture," regardless of the institutional framework within which development takes place, we would expect to find levels of political efficacy and political trust, levels of support for democratic institutions, and a degree of political interest in Russia roughly comparable to that in Western industrial democracies. This hypothesis, if upheld, would tend to support the view of political culture as being an autonomous and intervening variable between development and democracy.

3. If the theory that continuity rather than change is characteristic of Russian political culture, we would expect to see a consistency of political attitudes, values, and beliefs about politics across generations. Specifically, we would find no significant differences in political efficacy, political trust, political interest, support for democratic values, or political cognition between older and younger cohorts.

4. Alternatively, if the theory that modernization has produced generations with different ideas and views of politics has validity, we would expect to see differences on the measures of political culture specified in the previous hypothesis according to age and education. Specifically, we can test, at least partially, the proposition that it is among "the young and better educated" that a more critical attitude toward official norms is to be found.[39]

METHODOLOGY

Until recently, the possibility of testing empirically hypotheses about political culture in the Soviet Union did not exist, especially for Western specialists. Attempts at understanding this subject were frustrated by a paucity of reliable survey data, leading analysts to rely on indirect means or descriptive studies.[40] Now, thanks to a new attitude toward empirical sociology and the Soviet government's need to gauge public opinion accurately, opportunities for gathering data about political attitudes in the Soviet Union using surveys have become possible, even for Westerners.[41] A number of scholarly studies by Western analysts employing survey research have been conducted or are under way.[42]

The method adopted here to test the hypotheses previously listed is essentially comparative. Using questions that are widely used in the West to measure political efficacy, political trust, popular support for elections, political interest and knowledge, we compare the answers of our respondents to those found in Western studies. It may be argued that this procedure does not offer a true comparison since we are using data from a single city. This is a fair objection, which needs to be addressed.

First, Yaroslavl' is an overwhelmingly Russian city: 95 percent of the population (and 94 percent of our sample) is Russian, and the city's history as a center of Russian culture reaches back to its founding in 1010 by Yaroslavl' the Wise. Second, it is a Russian city that is outside of Moscow or Leningrad. These two cities could be dismissed as atypical because of their demographic make-up and because insurgent victories in local elections in March 1990 offer *a priori* evidence of a more "progressive" political culture. Yaroslavl' cannot. Insurgents did not take power there in March 1990, and while there is political ferment in the city so is there elsewhere in the Russian Republic. There is, in short, no compelling reason to think that Yaroslavl' citizens are very far out of the *Russian* political mainstream in one direction or another. Finally, we propose to use the "most conservative" test against which to compare our data set: the political culture of Americans, arguably the prototype of a society that is consensually regarded as having a "civic culture." The citizens of other industrial democracies except Britain generally score lower on standard measures of a democratic or participant political culture.[43] In short, if the political attitudes, values, and beliefs of those living in a Russian city that is not particularly different politically from other Russian cities appear comparable to those in the society commonly regarded as having the most highly democratic political culture, then the test we propose of our hypotheses would appear reasonable.

The data set employed in this article was made possible as a result of the new opportunities for research referred to earlier. It is based on a survey of the opinions of 975 randomly selected voters living in Yaroslavl' in March 1990. The survey was conducted by the author, who was assisted by sociologists from Moscow State University, from the Institute for Research on State Construction attached to the USSR Supreme Soviet, and from Yaroslavl' itself. It is, to the best of the author's knowledge, the first truly representative sampling of public attitudes toward politics conducted in a Russian city outside Moscow.[44]

The questionnaire consisted of eighty items measuring respondents' political attitudes, behavior, and knowledge. In addition, appropriate demographic information was collected. We intentionally included questions that would replicate as nearly as possible standard measures of political efficacy, political trust, support for elections, political interest, and political participation that are used in the United States. Certain other political questions, particular to the Soviet setting, were also asked. Among them were questions about the respondents' attitudes toward the Communist party, toward informal groups, and about government policies.

As anyone who has attempted to do so is well aware, it is no easy task to render English-language questions into usable Russian for reasons that are cultural as well as linguistic. Consequently, the author, who is fluent in Russian, worked out an initial draft with Russian sociologists in the United States who were fluent in English, prior to departing for Moscow in February 1990. In Moscow, the preliminary questionnaire was pretested and subjected to subsequent revision in consultation with Soviet sociologists at the institutions noted above. The final product was printed in a brochure format similar to that used by Soviet interviewers doing field work.

The sample was constructed using voter lists which included virtually the universe of those who were 18 or over and eligible to vote in Yaroslavl'. In 1989 Yaroslavl' had a population of 628,000, of whom 465,000 were registered. Voter lists were obtained with the help of the city's Central Election Commission. Although there was no single city-wide list, complete lists were available in three of the city's six districts (raiony) and at precincts (uchastky) in the remaining three. The author, accompanied by two Soviet sociologists, copied by hand the names and addresses of respondents using a skip interval of 372 starting with the 186th person on each list. This procedure yielded a sample of 1,222 potential respondents. The response rate of 80 percent varied little between the six districts of the city (raiony v gorode), enabling us to claim a margin of error of less than plus or minus 4 percent at a 0.05 level of confidence. Substitution of respondents was not permitted, contrary to normal Soviet practice. A comparison of the demographic characteristics of the sample with those of the population as a whole confirmed the representativeness of the sample.

Interviewing was conducted face-to-face over two and a half weeks starting on March 9, 1990. A team of 26 interviewers was chosen on the basis of professional experience and competence. All were from Yaroslavl', and most had done at least some interviewing previously. In addition, they received detailed instructions, orally and in writing, from myself and a Russian colleague prior to doing the field work. The interviewers were not students and they were not amateurs; they were, from all appearances, mature and motivated. Consequently, they were paid 7.5 rubles per 30–40 minute interview, about twice the normal rate. However, in order to ensure that the work was properly conducted, we accompanied the interviewers on a random basis and informed them beforehand that we would randomly choose a number of their respondents to confirm that the interviews had taken place. And contact was in fact made with at least one and sometimes as many as three respondents for each interviewer. This "call back" verification had to be done in person since only 30 percent of the inhabitants had telephones, but it provided a measure of confidence in our results that is unusual in Soviet polling since the Russians do not routinely introduce verification procedures. Respondents were assured of confidentiality and on the whole appeared to be cooperative, even enthusiastic, about responding. When asked if they would agree to be interviewed again, more than 80 percent said "yes"; fewer than 10 percent were unwilling.

Coding and data processing were conducted at Moscow State University's new Laboratory for the Study of Public Opinion. Coders were experienced and data entries appropriately verified. Data processing was done by the author in conjunction with a specialist in the university's competing center using an SPSS/PC+ format. The results were written on two diskettes which the author brought to the United States in April 1990 for further "cleaning" (three duplicate cases had been inadvertently introduced) and for the preparation of a code book. In sum, every effort was made at every stage of the survey to ensure that the highest possible standards were adhered to. For this reason we have confidence that the data set is what it purports to be: a reasonably accurate reflection of the political culture of Russians living in a city outside Moscow as of March 1990.

FINDINGS

The presence or absence of the cultural prerequisites of a democratic polity can be measured along various dimensions. Among these are attitudes that are not specifically political such as life satisfaction and interpersonal trust.[45] Others include tolerance for political dissent

and opposition,[46] a tolerance of ambiguity,[47] and psychological factors.[48] For those willing to accept a conceptualization of political
culture that includes a behavioral component, one may also choose
to include as a dimension levels of political participation.[49] This
study, however, confines itself to the following attitudes, values, and
beliefs: political efficacy, political trust, support for competitive elections, political interest, support for a multi-party system, and political
knowledge.[50]

Political Efficacy

The dimension of political efficacy is intended to indicate the degree
to which respondents feel they can have an impact on political
decisions that affect their lives. It is a dimension of the subjective
competence that an individual feels that he or she has in relation to
government. The converse of political efficacy is political alienation.
Those scoring high on one dimension are low on the other.[51] The
answers to the questions used in the Yaroslavl' study to measure
political efficacy in relation to local and national government are
listed in Table [14.]1 next to the answers given to the 1976 pre-election
study in the United States (NES, 1976) conducted by the Center for
Political Studies at the University of Michigan.

With respect to feelings of subjective competence at the local and
national level, Yaroslavl' voters appear to exhibit rather high levels
of political alienation. On all six items, more than half the respondents agree with statements indicating low efficacy. On only three
items do approximately a quarter of the population assert efficacious
feelings. Nevertheless, it is only on the dimension of governmental
responsiveness that we find truly striking differences between our
populations (Questions 1 and 5). These differences are further confirmed when we look at responses to the question taken from *The
Civic Culture* regarding local political efficacy (Table [14.]2). Our
Russian respondents exhibit levels of efficacy similar to those found
in Italy and Mexico, substantially lower than those in the United
States or Great Britain. American and British respondents clearly feel
they can influence what their government does; Russians do not.
How do we explain these differences? If we think in terms of Soviet
practice, at least over the last sixty years (since industrialization
began), the differences are reasonable. In fact, Soviet citizens until
recently have had little, if any, opportunity to influence what government does (external efficacy). This does not necessarily mean that
they do not think they should be able to exercise such influence or
that they feel the affairs of government are beyond their ken (internal efficacy).[52]

What is significant for the hypotheses being tested here is that,
with the notable exceptions of questions relating to efficacy as the
expectation of governmental responsiveness (external efficacy) as dis-

TABLE [14.]1 Comparative Political Efficacy Measures for Local
and National Government: Yaroslavl', 1990; American NES 1976*

Percentage political efficacy: national	Yaroslavl' (1990)	NES (1976)
1. People like me don't have much say about what government does.		
Agree	84.8	41.1
Disagree	9.0	56.3
Don't know†	6.3	2.6
	(n = 971)	(n = 2,394)
2. I don't think public officials care much what people like me think.		
Agree	55.9	51.3
Disagree	29.4	44.3
Don't know	14.7	4.4
	(n = 943)	(n = 2,388)
3. Sometimes government seems so complicated that people like me can't really understand what's going on.		
Agree	69.4	71.5
Disagree	23.2	26.8
Don't know	7.5	1.7
	(n = 966)	(n = 2,392)
4. Generally speaking, those we elect lose touch with the people quickly.		
Agree	61.0	68.2
Disagree	16.3	26.4
Don't know	22.6	5.4
	(n = 969)	(n = 2,392)
Percentage political efficacy: local		
5. People like me don't have any say about what the local government does.		
Agree	83.3	32.5
Disagree	10.4	66.3
Don't know	6.0	1.2
	(n = 965)	(n = 2,404)
6. Sometimes local government seems so complicated that a person like me can't really understand what is going on.		
Agree	59.7	50.4
Disagree	30.6	48.6
Don't know	9.7	1.0
	(n = 959)	(n = 2,403)

*The pre-election National Election Study for 1976 is used here because the author used the items as the basis for replicability, and because American attitudes regarding political efficacy have remained relatively stable over time (ICPSR, American NES, 1976).
† The 'don't know' response was noticeably more frequent among Russian respondents. This could be interpreted as reflecting greater passivity or lack of interest in matters political. However, a contrary interpretation is also possible. The 'don't know' response may represent a particularly thoughtful and interested opinion; e.g., upon reflection, the respondent really 'doesn't know' whether 'the government cares what people think', etc.

TABLE [14.]2 Comparative Political Efficacy Measures for
Local Government: Yaroslavl', 1990; Civic Culture, 1963

Percentage of citizens agreeing they could influence unjust local regulations.*

US	77
UK	78
Germany	62
Mexico	52
Italy	51
Yaroslavl'	51

* Per cent responding that they would do something when asked: 'Suppose a law was being considered by your local government that you considered to be unjust or harmful. What do you think you could do?' Almond and Verba, *The Civic Culture*, pp. 184–5.

tinct from questions related to feelings of personal competence (internal efficacy), Russian responses are on the whole similar to American. In two cases (Questions 3 and 4), the Russians actually appear to be less alienated toward their national government than Americans are toward theirs. Even in the case of political efficacy with regard to local government, our Russian sample was similar to those in Italy and Mexico, two nations normally regarded as democracies.

Political Trust

Political trust is a dimension of political culture that measures people's feelings about whether government and its officials can be trusted to perform well.[53] Low levels of political trust indicate a politically cynical population. Most of those who are cynical about politics are less likely to participate in political life,[54] with at least some degree of mass participation being essential if democratic institutions are to remain viable. The answers to questions designed to tap this dimension at both the local and national levels in Yaroslavl' are compared with answers for the American population in Table [14.]3. While similar questions were used for both samples, the response set varied somewhat. Nevertheless, the questions and answers appear to be sufficiently comparable that general conclusions may be drawn about levels of trust in the two groups.

While there is certainly a strong current of cynicism about politics present among the Russian respondents, it is not as strong as one might have expected. On no item did more than half of those sampled provide the "cynical" response. At the same time, there do seem to be some response sets that may be peculiar to Russian political culture. The respondents exhibit higher levels of trust on items that relate to distributive justice ("Is government run for the benefit of all or a few?") and on personal competence than on the question of governmental performance (making the right decisions). Whether

TABLE [14.]3 Comparative Measures of Political Trust for Local and National Government: Yaroslavl', 1990; American NES 1976

Percentage political trust: national Yaroslavl' 1990		NES 1976	
1. How much of the time do you think government makes the right decisions		How much of the time can you trust the government in Washington to do what is right?	
Almost always	18.3	Just about always	3.5
Half the time	39.2	Most of the time	29.8
Rarely or never	26.3	Some of the time	62.2
Don't know	16.2	Never (R volunteers)	1.2
		Don't know	3.4
	(n = 965)		(n = 2,861)
2. Would you say that government, when it makes decisions, takes care for the well-being of all the people or only for a few?		Would you say that government is pretty much run by a few big interests or that it is run for the benefit of all?	
Benefits all	36.3	Benefits all	24.0
Sometimes all	26.2	Benefits few	66.3
Benefits few	29.6	Don't know	9.6
Don't know	7.9		
	(n = 970)		(n = 2,840)
3. Do you feel that a majority of those running the government are capable or do you think only a few are?		Do you feel that almost all of the people running government are smart people or do you think quite a few of them don't know what they are doing?	
A majority	24.7	Are smart	43.8
About half	24.9	Don't know (or	
A minority	37.0	cynical: they know)	49.5
Don't know	13.2	Don't know	6.7
	(n = 970)		(n = 2,851)

Percentage political trust: local Yaroslavl' 1990		American NES 1976	
4. How much of the time do you think your city government makes the right decisions?		How much of the time do you think you can trust your local government to do what is right?	
Almost always	6.3	Almost always	8.0
Half the time	23.1	Most of the time	45.4
Rarely or never	36.3	Only some of the time	42.3
Don't know	34.3	Never (R volunteers)	1.9
		Don't know	2.2
	(n = 965)		(n = 2,387)
5. Would you say that your local government when it makes decisions takes care for the well-being of all people or only for a few?		Would you say that government is pretty much run by a few looking out for themselves or that it is run for the benefit of all the people?	
Benefits all	15.2	Benefits all	49.3
Sometimes all	23.3	Benefits few	41.9
Benefits few	46.3	Don't know	8.8
Don't know	15.3		
	(n = 966)		(n = 2,364)

this is a residual effect of official socialization, which contrasted communist "rule for all" with bourgeois-government rule by special interests, is not clear. The other tentatively distinctive pattern that emerges in contrast to the American responses is that Russians, at least in Yaroslavl', appear to trust their local government less than their national government (compare "cynical" responses in questions 1 and 4, and 2 and 5). Americans, on the other hand, trust their local government more than their national one. Obviously, the generalizability of these findings could be established only if comparable results were found in other parts of Russia.

Nevertheless, while the political culture of Russians living in Yaroslavl' exhibits certain characteristics that may be distinctly Russian, it would be incorrect to conclude that overall levels of political trust are widely different in the two societies. Indeed, on two of the five measures examined here (items 2 and 3), the Russians actually appear more willing than the Americans to give their government the benefit of the doubt. On the whole, the patterns of political trust found in the Russian sample would not appear to be particularly inhospitable to the emergence of a participatory or "civic" culture. Certainly, any argument that a transition to democratic institutions was impossible because of a deep distrust of government held by Russian voters would seem questionable, at least in the circumstances of March 1990.

Support for Elections

There is a broad consensus among political scientists that free elections are one of the essential prerequisites of political democracy. While elections alone do not ensure democracy, authentic elections provide people with an essential means for controlling those who govern them.[55] Until recently, elections in the Soviet Union failed to meet the tests of authenticity. While many of the constitutional requirements of free elections were met and voter turnout was nearly universal, control of the nomination process by the CPSU and the lack of alternative candidates rendered Soviet elections essentially meaningless as a mechanism for popular control of government.[56]

As a result of changes introduced in Soviet election laws in 1988 and 1989, however, Soviet voters have since then been confronted with meaningful choices at the polls. In the majority of races for the Congress of People's Deputies of the USSR in 1989, and in local and republican elections in 1990, a plurality of candidates was the norm. Establishment party candidates lost in many cases; in the Moscow, Leningrad, and Kiev city governments, among others, insurgents were swept to power.[57] Turnout in both sets of races was heavy: 89.9 percent in the national race, 60–70 percent in local races.

Despite this *prima facie* evidence of support for the electoral process, it has been argued that the Soviet electorate was only voting

against a class of candidates—the party bosses and state bureaucrats—and that the elections represented an exercise in democracy
imposed "from above," intended to further Gorbachev's political
power. In reality, this argument runs, an appreciation of the rules
of democratic politics lacks deep roots in Russian soil.[58] If this line
of thinking is correct, then our conclusions about the emergence and
maintenance of a democratic polity in Russia would necessarily be
pessimistic.

How much support is there for free elections in Russia? What
evidence is there that a degree of commitment to electoral procedures
exists within the Russian political culture that would sustain voter
involvement beyond simply a desire to "get even" with the *appa-
ratchiki?* We asked the voters of Yaroslavl' four questions commonly
used to measure a sense of civic obligation and, more specifically,
the respondent's support for electoral participation. It is a well-estab-
lished proposition that those feeling some sense of a duty to participate politically are more likely actually to do so.[59] The results are
found in Table [14.]4.

The data suggest considerable popular support for democratic elections among our predominantly Russian respondents. In all cases, at
least half actively disagree with statements indicating weak support
for competitive voting. At the same time, it is clear that the strength
of their support is lower in every case than among the American
respondents. In two cases the difference is negligible, less than 6
percent; in the remaining two cases, it is about 20 percent. In fairness, it should be noted that, although Americans score particularly
high on this dimension of political culture, actual voter turnout in
the United States is quite low compared with that in other democracies, especially in national elections. Taken together, the data suggest that, while the roots of support for democratic institutions do
not run as deeply in contemporary Russian political culture as they
do in America, neither are they absent. Most Russians—in Yaroslavl'
at least—exhibit a sense of commitment to voting.

In addition, we asked three questions particular to the Soviet
Union, which also shed light on popular attitudes toward political
competitiveness. The respondents were asked to evaluate the fairness
of both national and local elections, in which most of them had taken
part. It is possible, after all, that individuals could feel a duty to
vote, but if they judged elections to be a sham their views of the
electoral process would be likely to be cynical.[60] Another measure
of people's readiness for the emergence of a more pluralistic, competitive political process is their attitude toward the emergence of a
multi-party system. The judgments of the Yaroslavl' sample on the
issues of electoral fairness and a multi-party system are reported in
Table [14.]5.

Most Yaroslavl' voters felt that the elections were free, although
when it came to the national elections in 1989 a sizable minority,

TABLE [14.]4 Comparative Levels of Popular Support for Elections: Yaroslavl', 1990; NES 1980

Percentage support for democratic elections:		Yaroslavl' 1990	NES 1980
1. A good many local elections aren't important enough to bother with.			
	Agree	14.0	13.8
	Disagree	82.5	85.9
	Don't know	3.5	0.3
		($n = 967$)	($n = 1,561$)
2. If a person doesn't care how an election comes out, then that person shouldn't vote.			
	Agree	44.2	41.0
	Disagree	50.8	58.2
	Don't know	5.0	1.0
		($n = 964$)	($n = 1,559$)
3. So many other people vote in national elections that it doesn't matter much whether I vote or not.			
	Agree	27.5	9.0
	Disagree	68.3	90.7
	Don't know	4.2	0.3
		($n = 959$)	($n = 1,576$)
4. It isn't so important to vote when you know your party [candidate] doesn't have a chance to win.			
	Agree	28.2	7.9
	Disagree	62.0	91.7
	Don't know	9.8	0.5
		($n = 961$)	($n = 1,564$)

TABLE [14.]5 Evaluations of National and Local Elections and of Multi-party Systems: Yaroslavl', 1990 (in percentages)

1. Did R think the elections for deputy to the USSR parliament for Yaroslavl' were free?

Yes	59.1
No	26.1
Don't know	14.1
	($n = 968$)

2. Did R think the March 4 elections to the local soviets were free?

Yes	68.3
No	16.6
Don't know	11.5
	($n = 968$)

3. Does R think there should be a multi-party system in the country?

Extremely necessary	15.2
Necessary	36.5
Not necessary	7.4
Only the CPSU needed	21.5
Don't know	18.7
	($n = 969$)

one in four, did not. In addition, a substantial percentage (10–15 percent) appeared to be unsure. This may reflect dissatisfaction with election procedures which reserved one-third of the 2,250 seats in the Congress of People's Deputies for those nominated by "public organizations," notably the CPSU and the Komsomol. It is also my impression from personal observation that charges of unfairness and election violations were most frequently heard among the "democratic opposition," which expected to do better in the elections than they did. As to the large number expressing uncertainty, the lack of experience with truly free elections throughout the Soviet period may have contributed. It seems probable that a large number really "didn't know" what a free election was or whether they had witnessed one.

On the question of support for a multi-party system, our findings indicate that an absolute majority prefer more than one party. This figure is contrary to data reported by Stephen White to bolster his contention that "no clear preference for multi-party politics" existed. However, the strength of support for the CPSU, and the number of those without a clear preference, is similar to the findings reported by White (about one in five in each category). Even so, White's conclusion that such evidence "suggested that democratic procedures in general did not command overwhelming support" among the Soviet public seems premature in the light of the results reported here.[61]

Political Interest and Knowledge

The gap between the expectations of democratic theory and the evidence of empirical research regarding the attentiveness and knowledge of those living in democratic polities has been well established. It is a central tenet of classical democratic theory that, if popular sovereignty is to have meaning, citizens should be informed about the issues confronting society and should care about their resolution. It is equally clear from survey research that the American electorate, among others, exhibits rather low levels of interest in politics and knows little about either the issues being debated or the process by which they will be resolved.[62]

In an effort to find the key to this "paradox of mass politics," W. Russell Neuman proposes that there are three publics, each characterized by a different level of "political sophistication." The largest of these—about 75 percent of the population—is neither political nor apolitical but "in between." These people "can be mobilized to political action, they half-attentively monitor the flow of political news, but they run, for the most part, on a psychological automatic pilot."[63] Continuously high levels of interest and knowledge about politics do not appear to be any more essential to the functioning of democracy than are high levels of political participation.[64] Their complete absence, however, would seem to be more compatible with an authoritarian regime than with a democratic one; some minimal levels of interest, knowledge, and participation would appear to be essential.

Although the Yaroslavl' study contained questions about the respondents' levels of political participation, the discussion of this variable is beyond the scope of the present chapter. With respect to their level of political interest, however, the results are reported in Table [14.]6.

The levels of political interest found in our predominantly Russian sample are considerably higher than among American respondents. This may be attributable to the current political transformation taking place in the Soviet Union, and they may be abnormal and temporary. Nevertheless, the data would appear to contradict the image of the Russians as apolitical, passive, uninterested subjects for whom the "high politics" taking place behind the Kremlin walls is none of their business.

With respect to levels of information about politics, the Yaroslavl' electorate did not exhibit high levels of knowledge. When asked approximately how many deputies there were in the national parliament, only 31.4 percent gave a reasonably correct answer. Not quite half (46.1 percent) knew how frequently elections were held. Such answers, while indicating that many Soviet citizens do not know a lot about their governmental institutions, should be compared with an American electorate only half of whom (51.2 percent) could correctly identify the Democrats as the majority party in the US House of Representatives following the 1984 election. Only about one in four (27 percent) could do so for the Senate.[65]

A New Generation

Taken together, the findings presented thus far provide little support for the argument that continuity rather than change is the chief characteristic of Russian political culture. On all dimensions of political culture measured here—political efficacy, political trust, support for popular elections, political interest and knowledge—the evidence suggests that Russians come closer to what we find in Western industrial democracies than to what we would expect to find if the traditional cultural patterns ascribed to the period of Russian autocracy had persisted. While there do appear to be distinctive patterns of attitudes, values, and beliefs in Russian political culture, which may be enduring, they do not appear to be so distinctive as to present an obstacle to the emergence and maintenance of democratic institutions. Certainly the conclusion that "Soviet political culture, formed over centuries of autocratic rule, provided a relatively weak base for the development of pluralistic politics"[66] seems to be contradicted by what Russians think in Yaroslavl'.

TABLE [14.]6 Comparative Levels of Political Interest: Yaroslavl', 1990;
NES 1984

Percentage level of political interest*	Yaroslavl' 1990	NES 1984
Follow politics		
Most of the time	52.3	26.4
Some of the time	29.5	36.3
Now and then [rarely]	12.1	23.1
Hardly at all [never/almost never]	5.6	14.0
	(n = 967)	(n = 1,296)

*The full text of the question was: 'Some people seem to follow what's going on in government and politics most of the time, whether there's an election or not. Others aren't that interested. Would you say you follow what's going on in government and public affairs most of the time, some of the time, now and then, or hardly at all?'

If the evidence presented here does not sustain the hypothesis that little has changed in the way Russians think about politics, is there any evidence to suggest that factors of development are at work? Did the processes of industrialization and modernization produce a "new generation" of Russians who differed from previous generations not only economically and socially, but in their political expectations as well?

Evidence from the Soviet Interview Project (conducted among émigrés) strongly suggests the presence of generational differences. Donna Bahry found greater activism among the young in both conventional and unconventional political behavior, while Brian Silver's study of attitudes toward regime norms concluded that "younger cohorts were less supportive of the collective and more supportive of the rights of the individual than older cohorts."[67] Neither Bahry nor Silver explicitly links their findings on generational differences to economic development, nor are their data compared directly to any from Western societies. However, the findings offered here, that levels of political efficacy, trust, support for electoral politics, political interest and knowledge are not so dissimilar in Russia from what we find in Western industrial democracies, would tend to support a developmental hypothesis.

But what is really at work here? Why should one generation think differently politically from another as a result of development? This chapter shares the view that education is the critical intervening variable between development and political culture. Certainly one of the generational changes that accompanies economic development is that successive generations are better educated. While a better educated population may not automatically or necessarily be more democratic in its political culture, education does seem to contribute to making a democratic culture possible. It provides people with the skills necessary to understand political choices and to communicate preferences to those who make decisions. As Almond and Verba conclude in *The Civic Culture:*

> As with most other studies of political attitudes, our data show that educational attainment appears to have the most important demographic effect on political attitudes. Among the demographic variables usually investigated—sex, place of residence, occupation, income, age, and so on—none compares with the educational variable in extent to which it seems to determine political attitudes. The uneducated man or the man with limited education is a different political actor from the man who has achieved a higher level of education.[68]

The correlation between higher levels of education and the attitudinal and behavioral dimensions we usually associate with a civic or participatory culture is broadly supported in the literature.[69] It also lies, at least implicitly, at the core of the arguments made by those accepting some version of the thesis that modernization has been a source of social and political change in the Soviet Union.[70] Development produces better-educated generations, and education in turn changes how people think about politics. If this proposition has validity, we would expect to find significant differences on all the dimensions of political culture measured here according to levels of educational attainment. Absence of such differences would constitute serious grounds for questioning the generational hypothesis.

What do the data suggest? It is important first to establish whether, indeed, a relationship exists in our sample between age and education. Not surprisingly, a strong correlation was found: the younger generation (born after 1945) is far more likely to have completed secondary or higher education than the preceding generation (R = 0.45, p. 0.00).[71] The questions used in the analysis of Russian political culture presented so far were then combined to create new scaled variables, which were then correlated with education. The relationships between education and the new variables (as well as some single-question variables) are presented in Table [14.]7.

The data appear to support the following propositions. Those with higher levels of education are significantly: (a) more politically efficacious; (b) more likely to support competitive elections; (c) more in favor of a multi-party system; (d) more interested in politics; (e) more knowledgeable about government; (f) less trusting of government; and (g) less likely to think the elections were fair. Taken together these propositions would appear to disprove the null hypotheses: there are significant differences in political culture between those who are more educated and those who are not. Since education is strongly correlated with age, we can tentatively conclude that generational factors are indeed at work in ways that

TABLE [14.]7 The Relationship of Education to Political Culture Along
Seven Dimensions: Yaroslavl', 1990*

	Pearson's R	p
1. Political efficacy (6)†	0.45	0.00
2. Support for elections (4)	0.15	0.00
3. Support for multi-party system	0.28	0.00
4. Political trust (5)	0.16	0.00
5. Political knowledge (3)	0.37	0.00
6. Levels of political interest	0.24	0.00
7. Evaluation of election fairness (2)	0.14	0.00

* The direction of the relationship is specified in the text.
† The numbers in parentheses indicate the number of items used in scaled variables, where more than one question was used to create a scaled variable. Scales were created on the basis of paired intercorrelations between individual items. A minimum positive intercorrelation of 0.20 was required for inclusion. Most were higher. A similar test was performed using the NES variables to determine if American and Russian response sets were comparable. The results suggest they were.

those adhering to some variety of modernization thesis would predict.

The generational argument presented thus far is that Soviet economic development resulted in an increasingly well-educated population and that those with a higher level of education think differently about political life from those without. Specifically, they are more receptive to democratic institutions and values. Since successive generations of Soviet citizens have had larger proportions of better-educated people, the political culture of the population gradually has changed accordingly. However, in order to demonstrate more conclusively that education is the critical independent variable, it is necessary to show that the hypothesized relationships remain after controlling for age. To do this, the sample was divided into four age groups roughly corresponding to differing periods in Soviet history: those born after 1955, who came of age politically in the Brezhnev years; those born in 1945–1955, whose salient political figure was Khrushchev; those born in 1930–1945, who grew up in the post-war period of reconstruction; and those born before 1930, whose political views were developed during the height of Stalinism.[72] Multiple-regression analysis was employed within each group to see if education continued to be the best predictor of the political culture variables used in this study.

With one quite important exception, similar relationships between education and the indicators of political attitudes and values used in the present study were found regardless of age group. The exception was political trust. Here statistically significant relationships between education and trust largely disappear when we controlled for age; younger cohorts are more politically cynical regardless of education (R = 0.20; p < 0.00). Education in the aggregate, however, appears to enhance this cynicism (R = 0.20; p < 0.00). Thus, although the oldest cohort was more trusting overall, the highest levels of trust were found among the least well educated from the oldest generation; their more educated peers were less trusting. What makes these findings particularly arresting is that they reverse the relationships found among American respondents. For them, higher education correlates positively with trust (R = 0.14; p < 0.00), while age is not a significant factor. Taken together these data appear consistent with the findings of Bahry, Silver, and Lapidus cited earlier. Soviet society is distinguished by a younger and better-educated generation that is more disaffected from the politics of the past.

CONCLUSIONS

The question posed at the outset of this chapter was whether or not Russian political culture is compatible with the emergence of democratic institutions in the Soviet Union, or at least in that part of it which is Russia. What can we say about Russian political culture on the basis of the findings presented here? The predominantly Russian electorate of Yaroslavl' exhibited little confidence in their ability to influence governmental decision making (external political efficacy), yet a majority appeared willing in March 1990 to trust their government to perform their duties well. These findings are consistent with a view of Russians as subject-recipients oriented toward the implementation side of the political process.[73] However, our Russian respondents also showed substantial support for democratic values. A clear majority favored competitive elections and a multi-party system and were highly interested in political life around them. On the whole, the picture of Russian political culture that emerges from this study is one not strikingly different from what is found in Western industrial democracies.

Moreover, the weight of the evidence presented here favors the argument that support for democratic institutions in the Russian political culture is more likely to be found among the young who are also better educated. This group demonstrated significantly higher levels of political efficacy, support for elections and a multi-party system, political interest and knowledge about government than their predecessors. They are also a less politically trustful generation. It appears that a better-educated younger generation of Russians is more skeptical about government and those running it, an assessment that can reasonably be interpreted as dissatisfaction with the pace of change toward democracy.[74]

Our findings would also appear to provide support for the view that political culture plays an important intermediary role between political development and democracy. The generational differences in political culture found in our sample are clearly related to higher educational attainment, an important consequence of economic development. This suggests that Inglehart is right when he argues that the durability of democracy "seems to result from a complex interplay of economic, cultural, and institutional factors."[75] Economic development, a participant political culture, and democratic institutions are all necessary but not sufficient conditions for the transformation of authoritarian regimes into democratic ones. None of these factors will result in political democracy without the others; conversely, where all three are present, political democracy will be far more likely to emerge and to endure. If this argument has merit, one conclusion seems inescapable: democratic institutions will not flourish in countries lacking a suitable political culture, even if those countries are economically developed.

The relevance of this conclusion in assessing whether the Soviet Union will make a successful transition from authoritarian to democratic rule is considerable. Some have argued that the problem with Gorbachev's proposals to democratize Soviet society is that they have been imposed "from above"; that is, he has introduced the institutions of parliamentary democracy in a society that lacks the requisite political culture to sustain those institutions. If they are right about the absence of a compatible political culture, the prospects for a transition to democracy would indeed be bleak. However, the evidence offered here and elsewhere suggests quite the opposite: that Russian political culture, at least, would appear to be sufficiently hospitable to sustain democratic institutions.[76]

These conclusions are further buttressed by my field observations at the time of elections in both 1989 and 1990. People did not vote because they had to; they did not join independent political organizations because they were directed to from above; and they certainly did not demonstrate against the Party in Yaroslavl' and in Moscow because they had been mobilized for that purpose by the leadership. Democratic institutions cannot be imposed on an unwilling or unreceptive people from above. If they are, they will not work. It seems more reasonable to argue that the institutional reforms introduced since 1987 were congruent with a relatively participant political culture already present.

It is by no means assured that the democratic institutions that have been introduced in connection with political reform in the Soviet Union will withstand economic collapse if such a collapse is forthcoming. A return to authoritarian rule is not excluded. Even if this were to happen, however, it would not invalidate the argument being made here. While democratic institutions cannot be imposed on an unwilling population, authoritarian institutions can. What the findings presented here suggest is that the rudiments of a democratic political culture arose before Gorbachev came to power—despite an authoritarian institutional context—and that they will continue to exist even if one is reimposed. Admittedly, this case is impossible to prove conclusively, if only because we lack directly comparable data from before 1985.[77] Nevertheless, in the light of the evidence presented here and elsewhere, and given the apparent enthusiasm with which many Russians participate politically, the burden of proof for a contrary conclusion would appear to belong to those who see more continuity than change in Russian political culture.

NOTES

The author wishes to acknowledge with gratitude the Carnegie Corporation of New York and the International Research and Exchanges Board (IREX) for their support of the field research on which this article is based. He is also grateful to the Berkeley-Stanford Program for Soviet Studies and its director, Gail Lapidus, for the opportunity to spend the academic year 1990–1991 at the University of California at Berkeley during which this article was written. The field work could not have been accomplished without the help of Soviet colleagues including Valerii Korobeinikov of the USSR Supreme Soviet's Institute for State Construction and Legislation, Alex Gasparashvili, Vladimir Toumanov, Leonid Pietetskii, and Sergei Glavatskii of Moscow State University and Tatiana Rumiantseva of Yaroslavl'. Henry Brady, George Breslauer, Archie Brown, Justin Green, Jerry Hough, Matthew Kerbel, Brendan Kiernan, Gail Lapidus, Moshe Lewin, Blair Ruble, Paul Sniderman, S. Frederick Starr, Stephen White, and Frank Zinni kindly read the original version prepared for the October 1990 annual meeting of the American Association for the Advancement of Slavic Studies. The final product was much improved by their input although this in no way implies their agreement with its conclusions or any responsibility for its faults. Three graduate students, Beth Fecko, Gordon Adams, and Gavin Helf provided hours of invaluable assistance in preparing the data.

1. Archie Brown, "Ideology and Political Culture," in Seweryn Bialer, ed., *Inside Gorbachev's Russia* (Boulder, CO: Westview, 1989), p. 1.

2. It has been argued that the persistence of values over time constitutes a validation of political culture theory. See, for example, Archie Brown, "Introduction," in Archie Brown and Jack Gray, eds., *Political Culture and Political Change in Communist States* (New York: Holmes and Meier, 1977); Gabriel A. Almond, "Communism and Political Culture Theory," *Comparative Politics*, 15 (1983), 127–38. For a recent summary of the literature see Gabriel A. Almond, "The Study of Political Culture," in Gabriel A. Almond, ed., *A Discipline Divided* (Newbury Park, CA: Sage, 1990), pp. 138–56.

3. It is the author's intention to conduct another survey which will replicate the questions used here. Only analysis of similar data over time allows the researcher to begin to separate out period, generational, and other effects which may not be revealed by cross-sectional analysis. See Neal Cutler, "Generation, Maturation, and Party Affiliation: A Cohort Analysis," *Public Opinion Quarterly*, 33 (1969–1970), 583–8; Norval D. Glenn and Ted Hefner, "Further Evidence on Aging and Party Identification," *Public Opinion Quarterly*, 35 (1972), 31–49; Donna Bahry, "Politics, Generation, and Change in

the USSR," in James R. Millar, ed., *Politics, Work, and Social Life in the USSR* (Cambridge: Cambridge University Press, 1987), pp. 74–6.

4. Lucian W. Pye, "Political Science and the Crisis of Authoritarianism," *American Political Science Review,* 84 (1990), 3–19, p. 11.

5. Robert A. Dahl, *Democracy and Its Critics* (New Haven, CT: Yale University Press, 1989), p. 25; Seymour Martin Lipset, *Political Man* (New York: Doubleday, 1960), chap. 2.

6. See, for example, the treatment of the Soviet Union in Gabriel A. Almond and G. Bingham Powell, *Comparative Politics* (Boston, MA: Little, Brown, 1978); also Dahl, *Democracy and Its Critics,* p. 262. In these works the basis for viewing the Soviet Union as an exceptional case is that the society is economically developed, but authoritarian.

7. Ronald Inglehart, "The Renaissance of Political Culture," *American Political Science Review,* 82 (1988), 1203–30, p. 1219.

8. Dahl, *Democracy and Its Critics,* p. 264.

9. Gabriel A. Almond and Sidney Verba, *The Civic Culture* (Princeton, NJ: Princeton University Press, 1963).

10. Lucian W. Pye and Sidney Verba, eds., *Political Culture and Political Development* (Princeton, NJ: Princeton University Press, 1965); Almond and Verba, *The Civic Culture,* pp. 379–87; Lipset, *Political Man,* p. 39; Dahl, *Democracy and Its Critics,* p. 251.

11. The question has been raised about whether the Soviet Union can be properly considered as "uneconomically developed." In some ways, economic conditions more nearly approximate those found in the Third World, "an Upper Volta with rockets," as one reviewer put it. The position taken in this article is that the Soviet Union must be counted among the developed countries because of its level of industrialization and because of the portion of its labor force engaged in industry and in professional occupations, including the field of science. That the consumer market works badly and that the standard of living compares poorly with what is found in other industrialized societies is evidence that economic development in the Soviet Union was distorted, not that it does not exist.

12. Pye, "Political Science and the Crisis of Authoritarianism," p. 11.

13. Nicholas Berdaiev, *The Russian Idea* (London: Geoffrey Bles, 1947); Henry Dicks, "Some Notes on the Russian National Character," in Cyril E. Black, ed., *The Transformation of Russian Society* (Cambridge, MA: Harvard University Press, 1960).

14. Geoffrey Gorer and John Rickman, *The People of Great Russia: A Psychological Study* (New York: Chanticleer, 1950); Nathan Leites, *A Study of Bolshevism* (Glencoe, IL: The Free Press, 1953); Karl A. Wittfogel, *Oriental Despotism* (New Haven, CT: Yale University Press, 1957).

15. Richard Pipes, *Russia Under the Old Regime* (New York: Scribners, 1974).

16. Richard Pipes, "Detente: Moscow's View," in Richard Pipes, ed., *Soviet Strategy in Europe* (New York: Crane, Russak, 1976). Pipes's views on the peasantry and of the essential continuity between the Russian past and the Soviet period have been forcefully reiterated in his latest work: Richard Pipes, *The Russian Revolution* (New York: Knopf, 1990). For an interesting review and criticism of this book, see Terence Emmons, "Unsacred History," *The New Republic,* November 5, 1990, pp. 34–8. According to Emmons, "The continuity of political culture is Pipes' fundamental premise" (p. 38).

17. Edward L. Keenan, "Muscovite Political Folkways," *The Russian Review,* 45 (1986), 115–84, p. 169.

18. Zbigniew Brzezinski, "Soviet Politics: From the Future to the Past?" in Paul Cocks, Robert V. Daniels and Nancy Whittier Heer, eds., *The Dynamics of Soviet Politics* (Cambridge, MA: Harvard University Press, 1976), p. 337.

19. Stephen White, *Political Culture and Soviet Politics* (London: Macmillan, 1979), p. 166.

20. This thesis is stated even more forcefully in Stephen White, "Soviet Political Culture Reassessed," in Archie Brown, ed., *Political Culture and Communist Studies* (New York: M.E. Sharpe, 1984), p. 91, and in Stephen White, "Political Culture in Communist States," *Comparative Political Studies,* 16 (1984), 351–65, p. 354.

21. Walter Laqueur, *The Long Road to Freedom* (New York: Scribner's, 1989), p. 8.

22. Zbigniew Brzezinski, *The Grand Failure* (New York: Scribner's, 1989), pp. 99–100.

23. Lester W. Milbrath and M.L. Goel, *Political Participation,* 2nd ed. (Lanham, MD: University Press of America, 1977), pp. 90–110.

24. Jerry Hough, "The Soviet System: Petrification or Pluralism?," *Problems of Communism,* 21 (March–April, 1972), 25–45.

25. Jerry Hough, *Russia and the West* (New York: Simon and Schuster, 1988), pp. 121–7.

26. Moshe Lewin, *The Gorbachev Phenomenon* (Berkeley: University of California Press, 1988).

27. Blair A. Ruble, "The Soviet Union's Quiet Revolution," in George Breslauer, ed., *Can Gorbachev's Reforms Succeed?* (Berkeley: Center for Soviet and East European Studies, University of California, 1990), p. 79. A more recent version is Blair A. Ruble, "Stepping Off the Treadmill of Failed Reforms," in Harley D. Balzer, ed., *Five Years That Shook the World* (Boulder, CO: Westview, 1991).

28. S. Frederick Starr, "Soviet Union: A Civil Society," *Foreign Policy,* 70 (1988), 26–41; S. Frederick Starr, "New Communications Technologies and Civil Society," in Loren R. Graham, ed., *Science and the Soviet Social Order* (Cambridge, MA: Harvard University Press, 1990), pp. 19–50.

29. S. Frederick Starr, "A Usable Past," *The New Republic,* 200 (May 15, 1989), 24–7; Emmons, "Unsacred History," p. 38; see also portions of the debate between Fyodor Burlatsky and Anatoli Adamishin on Russian political culture in *Literaturnaia gazeta,* January 25, 1989, p. 2.

30. Gail W. Lapidus, "State and Society: Toward the Emergence of Civil Society in the Soviet Union," in Seweryn Bialer, ed., *Inside Gorbachev's Russia,* p. 121.

31. Lapidus, "State and Society," p. 128; Brian D. Silver, "Political Beliefs of the Soviet Citizen: Sources of Support for Regime Norms," in Millar, ed., *Politics, Work, and Daily Life in the USSR,* pp. 100–41.

32. Brown, "Ideology and Political Culture," p. 19.

33. Brown, "Ideology and Political Culture," p. 31.

34. Brown, "Ideology and Political Culture," p. 27. See also, Archie Brown, "Reconstructing the Soviet Political System," in Abraham Brumburg, ed., *Chronicle of a Revolution* (New York: Pantheon, 1990), pp. 46–9.

35. Keenan, "Muscovite Political Folkways," p. 175; Brzezinski, "Soviet Politics: From the Future to the Past?," p. 346.

36. White, *Political Culture and Soviet Politics*, p. 173; Brzezinski, "Soviet Politics: From the Future to the Past?," p. 344.

37. White, *Political Culture and Soviet Politics*, p. 188.

38. George W. Breslauer, "Thinking About the Soviet Future," in Breslauer, ed., *Can Gorbachev's Reforms Succeed?*, p. 10.

39. Lapidus, "State and Society," p. 127–8; Silver, "Political Beliefs of the Soviet Citizen," pp. 116–18.

40. White, *Political Culture and Soviet Politics*, p. 95; Jeffrey W. Hahn, *Soviet Grassroots: Citizen Participation in Local Soviet Government* (Princeton, NJ: Princeton University Press, 1988), p. 17. The tendency to rely on historical inference and to include behavioral evidence in some Western analyses of political culture in communist countries has been attributed to the inability of specialists to conduct survey research on political attitudes in those countries. See Stephen Welch, "Review Article: Issues in the Study of Political Culture—The Example of Communist Party States," *British Journal of Political Science*, 17 (1987), 479–500, pp. 480–2.

41. It has been argued that survey research may not be the best way to study political culture in communist countries because "the survey method puts political culture on the same conceptual level as public opinion" (Welch, "Issues in the Study of Political Culture," p. 484). A certain amount of caution is in order to avoid equating public opinion with political culture. The latter term refers to the more enduring values and beliefs about politics which members of society hold and which presumably condition their perception of government. As such they are assumed to change much more gradually than opinions about political issues and government personnel. See Brown, *Political Culture and Communist Studies*, pp. 155–64.

42. Ada W. Finifter and Ellen Mickiewicz, "Redefining the Political System of the USSR: Mass Support for Political Change in the USSR," paper delivered at the annual meeting of the American Political Science Association, 1990; James L. Gibson, Raymond M. Duch and Kent L. Tedin, "Cultural Values and the Transformation of the Soviet Union," paper delivered at the annual meeting of the American Political Science Association in San Francisco, 1990. Other major joint projects are being conducted by a team of political scientists from the University of Iowa (principal investigator, Arthur H. Miller), and by the National Opinion Research Center (field research director, Cynthia Kaplan). Results from many of these efforts are being brought together in book form: Arthur H. Miller, William M. Reisinger, and Vicki L. Templin, eds., *The New Soviet Citizen: Public Opinion and Politics in the Gorbachev Era* (forthcoming).

43. Almond and Verba, *The Civic Culture*; Inglehart, "The Renaissance of Political Culture."

44. The question may be raised as to why a single city study should be regarded as more representative than a national sample such as those conducted by the Soviet All-Union Center for the Study of Public Opinion. Obviously, a truly representative national sample would be preferable. However, aside from the problem that the Center simply has not published a comparable study of Russian political culture, there are grounds for wondering how representative their survey results are for the population as a whole. The disadvantage of the case study approach is clear: we have no way of saying scientifically whether conclusions based on a single city study are generalizable elsewhere. This is offset, however, because the serious technical

problems encountered in doing a national survey may be minimized, if not eliminated, in a single-area study thereby yielding greater confidence in the representativeness of the results. A detailed discussion of this may be found in Jeffrey W. Hahn, "Public Opinion Research in the USSR: Problems and Possibilities," in Miller *et al.*, eds. *The New Soviet Citizen.*

45. Inglehart, "The Renaissance of Political Culture."

46. James W. Prothro and Charles M. Grigg, "Fundamental Principles of Democracy: Bases of Agreement and Disagreement," *Journal of Politics,* 22 (1960), 276–94; Herbert McCloskey, "Consensus and Ideology in American Politics," *American Political Science Review,* 58 (1964), 361–82; John L. Sullivan, James E. Pierson, and George E. Marcus, *Political Tolerance and American Democracy* (Chicago: University of Chicago Press, 1982); Herbert McCloskey and Alida Brill, *Dimensions of Tolerance* (New York: Russell Sage, 1983); James L. Gibson, "The Structure of Attitudinal Tolerance in the United States," *British Journal of Political Science,* 19 (1989), 562–70.

47. Theodore F. Adorno *et al.*, *The Authoritarian Personality* (New York: Harper and Row, 1950).

48. Paul Sniderman, *Personality and Democratic Politics* (Berkeley: University of California Press, 1975).

49. There is a vigorous debate among specialists studying political culture, especially in communist countries, on this issue. Leading proponents of the view that political behavior is as important a dimension of political culture as attitudes include: White, "Soviet Political Culture Reassessed," pp. 62–6; Robert L. Tucker, *Political Culture and Leadership in Soviet Russia* (New York: W.W. Norton, 1987), pp. 5–6; and Richard T. Fagen, *The Transformation of Political Culture in Cuba* (Palo Alto, CA: Stanford University Press, 1969), pp. 6–10. Among those insisting on the need to separate the psychological dimension from the behavioral one are Brown, "Ideology and Political Culture," p. 2, and Almond, "The Study of Political Culture," p. 145. This view, which would exclude behavior from what is embraced by political culture, has been called a "subjectivist" definition and inclusion of behavior is sometimes designated an "anthropological" definition, although Brown has questioned the appropriateness of that. (See the chapters by Archie Brown and Mary McAuley in Brown, ed., *Political Culture and Communist Studies.*) My own point of view on this debate can be found more extensively in Hahn, *Soviet Grassroots,* pp. 10–11 and pp. 41–3. While my treatment in this article relies on attitudinal rather than behavioral indicators of political culture, evidence of political participation, including the activism which Soviet citizens exhibited during recent election campaigns and in street demonstrations, would seem to offer *prima facie* support for the existence of something like a "civic culture," however desirable it may be to exclude behavior as a component part of political culture conceptually.

50. Many, if not most, of the questions used were replications of those in the pioneering study of the American electorate by Angus Campbell, Gerald Gurin, and Warren E. Miller, *The Voter Decides* (Evanston, IL: Row, Peterson, 1954). There were two reasons for choosing these items. First, they are probably the most widely used measures of American political culture and, secondly, they have been repeated in the various follow-up American National Election Studies conducted by the Center for Political Studies at the University of Michigan. The relative consistency of responses to these measures suggests they are measuring political culture rather than opinion.

The results were made available through the Inter-University Consortium for Political and Social Research (ICPSR) in Ann Arbor, Michigan. The questions used are found in the codebooks for the 1976, 1980, 1984 and 1988 elections. See *American National Election Study, 1976 (1980, 1984, 1988): Pre- and Post-Election Survey File,* conducted by the Center for Political Studies of the Institute for Social Research at the University of Michigan and the National Election Studies under the general direction of Warren E. Miller, ICPSR, Ann Arbor, Michigan, 1978 (1982, 1986, 1990). Hereafter, references will be *American NES* and the year.

51. Ada W. Finifter, "Dimensions of Political Alienation," *American Political Science Review,* 64 (1970), 389–410. More recent treatments of a concept originally used in Campbell, *et al., The Voter Decides,* would include: Harold D. Clarke and Alan C. Acock, "National Elections and Political Attitudes: The Case of Political Efficacy," *British Journal of Political Science,* 19 (1989), 551–61; and Steven E. Finkel, "Reciprocal Effects of Participation and Political Efficacy," *American Journal of Political Science,* 29 (1985), 891–913.

52. The distinction between internal and external originates in Robert E. Lane, *Political Life* (New York: The Free Press, 1959), p. 149; see also Clarke and Acock, "National Elections and Political Attitudes," p. 552.

53. Robert E. Agger, Marshall Goldstein, and Stanley Pearl, "Political Cynicism: Measurement and Meaning," *Journal of Politics,* 23 (1961), 477–506; Arthur H. Miller, "Trust in Government," *American Political Science Review,* 69 (1974), 951–72.

54. Milbrath and Goel, *Political Participation,* p. 64.

55. Dahl, *Democracy and Its Critics,* p. 283; Austin Ranney, *Governing,* 3rd ed. (New York: Holt, Rinehart, and Winston, 1982), pp. 128–31.

56. Hahn, *Soviet Grassroots,* pp. 92–5.

57. Jeffrey W. Hahn, "Gorbachev Confronts His New Congress," *Orbis,* 34 (1990), 163–78; Jeffrey W. Hahn, "Developments in Local Soviet Politics," in Alfred J. Rieber and Alvin Z. Rubinstein, eds., *Perestroika at the Crossroads* (New York: M.E. Sharpe, 1991).

58. Stephen White, *Gorbachev in Power* (Cambridge: Cambridge University Press, 1990), p. 216.

59. Milbrath and Goel, *Political Participation,* p. 49.

60. Victor Zaslavsky and Robert J. Brym, "The Functions of Elections in the USSR," *Soviet Studies,* 30 (1978), 362–71.

61. White, *Gorbachev in Power,* p. 215. The data reported by White were collected by the All-Union Center for the Study of Public Opinion. While this Center is certainly one of the most professional among Soviet polling organizations, this author has reservations about the reliability of national samples taken in the Soviet Union. (See fn. 44.)

62. Bernard R. Berelson, "Democratic Theory and Public Opinion," *Public Opinion Quarterly,* 16 (1952), 313–30; Angus Campbell, Philip E. Converse, Warren E. Miller, and Donald E. Stokes, *The American Voter* (New York: Wiley, 1960).

63. W. Russell Neuman, *The Paradox of Mass Politics: Knowledge and Opinion in the American Electorate* (Cambridge, MA: Harvard University Press, 1986), p. 6.

64. Milbrath and Goel, *Political Participation,* p. 145.

65. *NES, 1984,* p. 518.

66. White, *Gorbachev in Power,* p. 216.

67. Donna Bahry, "Politics, Generations, and Change in the USSR," and Brian D. Silver, "Political Beliefs of Soviet Citizens: Sources of Support for Regime Norms," in Millar, ed., *Politics, Work, and Daily Life in the USSR.* The quote from Silver is on p. 122.

68. Almond and Verba, *The Civic Culture,* p. 379.

69. Milbrath and Goel, *Political Participation,* p. 98.

70. Lewin, *The Gorbachev Phenomenon;* Hough, *Russia and the West;* Ruble, "The Soviet Union's Quiet Revolution"; Lapidus, "State and Society."

71. This correlation simply confirms for the sample what one would expect from aggregate data showing the growth of Soviet education levels over time. See, for example, *SSSR v tsifrakh v 1984 godu* (Moscow: 1984), pp. 18–19.

72. There is considerable disagreement among political scientists as to what is learned and when, and even whether it matters very much. The assumption used here, however, is that political socialization begins in childhood and that the acquisition of affective political orientations precedes cognitive ones. It appears reasonable to assume that children have an awareness of politics and government and feelings about them by age ten. For discussions of the literature, see Alan D. Monroe, *Public Opinion in America* (New York: Harper and Row, 1975), pp. 61–78; and M. Kent Jennings and Richard G. Niemi, *The Political Character of Adolescence* (Princeton, NJ: Princeton University Press, 1974), pp. 4–25.

73. Wayne DiFrancesco and Zvi Gitelman, "Soviet Political Culture and 'Covert Participation' in Policy Implementation," *American Political Science Review,* 78 (1984), 603–21.

74. Lapidus, "State and Society," p. 127; Silver, "Political Beliefs of Soviet Citizens," p. 116; Bahry, "Politics, Generations, and Change in the USSR," p. 91.

75. Inglehart, "The Renaissance of Political Culture," p. 1229.

76. Gibson, Duch, and Tedin, "Cultural Values and the Transformation of the Soviet Union"; Finifter and Mickiewicz, "Redefining the Political System of the USSR: Mass Support for Political Change."

77. For arguments that there are elements in Russian history favoring the emergence of a more democratic political culture, see fn. 29. Beyond this, a recent article based on data from the Soviet Interview Project suggests that an attitudinal basis for expanded political participation existed before Gorbachev's reforms. See Donna Bahry and Brian D. Silver, "Soviet Citizen Participation on the Eve of Democratization," *American Political Science Review,* 84 (1990), 821–47. These findings suggest that the results from Yaroslavl' are not merely a consequence of the time or place in which they were obtained.

15

THE SOVIET ETHNIC SCENE:

A Quarter Century Later

Nothing is more gratifying to an author than to have a work remembered many years after it appeared in print. It is almost equally gratifying—although at times painful—to have the opportunity to take a fresh self-critical look at the work. Prepared just two years after the 1959 Soviet census became available, "The Ethnic Scene in the Soviet Union" could take advantage of that milestone in Soviet data availability. Hence I was able to present suggestions on data use which were then novel in the analysis of contemporary Soviet affairs. Possibly these methodological innovations, crude as they were, stimulated interest in quantitative behavioral analysis of mass phenomena in the USSR. Now, however, both the methodology and the data retain only historical interest. If, therefore, the re-publication satisfies more than antiquarian interest, it is because of the ideas presented in the article.

Other contributors to this book will, I hope, sufficiently emphasize the limitations of my conceptual framework, or, to use a currently fashionable term, "deconstruct" the writing. The author, too, has an obligation to point out what turned out to be "non-heuristic," or just plain wrong in the approach, as well as the right to suggest such vestiges of theoretical interest that his treatment retains. Before taking up these burdens, though, it will be advantageous for both deconstructors and salvagers to recall the history of the article.

In May 1965, on the suggestion of Merle Fainsod, Erich Goldhagen invited me to present the opening paper at the first conference sponsored by the Brandeis University Graduate Center for Contemporary Jewish Studies. The entry of East European Jewish studies into the broader range of Soviet nationality studies was auspicious. Goldhagen remarked that "while most other papers will treat the lives of the separate minorities, yours should be focused on the summit of Soviet power, discussing its views and treatment of the non-Russian peoples since Stalin's death." This was a very attractive mandate, for I had been broadening my discussion of the Soviet nationalities issue during the early 1960s, in *The Politics of Totalitarianism* (1961) and the first edition of the textbook *Ideology, Politics and Government in the Soviet Union* (1962). With broadening came the realization that conceptualization (i.e., a pre-theory or at least a typology) was indispensable for meaningful comparative analysis of the sprawling nationalities situation.

Moreover, such conceptualization was what I had had in mind all along. From boyhood, I had been fascinated by inter-ethnic relations, both because of my own multi-ethnic ancestry and the daily evidence of the miniature melting-pot which my native town, St. Augustine, had been for centuries. Returning to college after World War II experiences—including observation of difficult ethnic interactions like the Flemish-Walloon cleavage and briefer contacts with Soviet defectors—I decided to apply my long-range interest to the Soviet scene. Then, as today, I believed that extensive monographic seasoning is a prerequisite for producing broad conceptual schemes. So, as I approached my mid-forties, Goldhagen's challenge hastened a step I had considered—with trepidation—for some time.

As the sequel showed, my hesitations were well founded. The basic model for the article is a combination of structural functionalism and the single rational actor approach. Many may not recall how popular structural functionalism was during the early 1960s, in Talcott Parson's sociological version, in the elaboration by Gabriel Almond, and in applications to the Soviet field by Frederick Barghoorn and George Fischer. Indeed, the framework was a major heuristic force turning Sovietologists toward more sophisticated conceptualization. Nevertheless, structural functionalism raised serious logical questions.[1] I sought to avoid such quandaries by substituting the avowed teleological role of the Soviet decision-makers for what had been (in some structural-functionalist approaches) the implicit assumption of natural teleology. For many years, I have regretted this aspect of the article, without in any way losing sight of the fact that structural functionalism may be very useful for analyzing relatively unorganized Third-World systems and some elements of more advanced systems. Applying the model to the current operations of a tightly centralized system like the Soviet one, however, simply confuses matters by using terms in a situation to which they were not intended to apply.

The use of the single rational actor approach represented a lapse of judgment concerning the evolution of the Soviet system rather than conceptual confusion. The monstrous concentration of power under Stalin had come closer to the single-actor model. Khrushchev seemed to be aiming for a similar concentration. His dismissal in October 1964 should, no doubt, have warned me that the long single-actor phase of the Soviet political system had ended. However, although I identified the oligarchical impulse behind his dismissal, I did not anticipate the durability of oligarchic stagnation. If I had,

I might have expected the loss of functional rationality due to diminished initiatives and enhanced corruption.[2] Even so, I probably would not have dreamed how far the decline of ideological consistency, systemic integrity, and simple personal rationality (e.g., resort to "faith healers") would proceed during Brezhnev's final years. By that time, the notion of a single rational actor manipulating nationalities according to standards of functional utility was fanciful.

Having confessed to three ways in which the republished article is no longer pertinent, the author might be expected to retire gracefully from bat. Scholarship is not, however, a baseball game, if only because we vociferously "kill" the half-blind who aspire to be umpires. Schiller's aphorism, *"Die Welgeschichte ist das Weltgericht,"* certainly applies to theories if it applies to anything at all. In order to find the judgment of history, one must undertake examinations of (1) the explicit reception of a work by qualified critics; (2) ways in which others, perhaps novices, have found the framework useful; and (3) the extent to which events have confirmed its implied predictions. A quarter-century is a very brief period for drawing conclusions about the judgment of *Weltgeschichte;* but my own stipulation that theoretical life begins after forty means that an author will never have much longer perspective for reassessing his own work.

I realized all along that any conceptualization of Soviet nationalities policy would have few more general applications unless it was bolstered by reference to the longue durée. Gabriel Almond came to the same conclusion concerning his theories, writing that they needed to "take the historical cure."[3] My initial resort to theory-building was in exploration of comparative administration rather than ethnicity. During the 1970s, however, I began examining the historical context of a key group in "The Ethnic Scene" by publishing "mobilized and Proletarian Diasporas."[4] Reactions to this new article were gratifying, particularly when they came from men engaged in seminal monographs of their own, like the Israeli scholar Shimon Redlich. Interest in the Baltic German diaspora and among Armenians was also evident. Most important to me were comments by the late Hugh Seton-Watson, whose monumental knowledge of Eastern European affairs was combined with a pragmatist's skepticism concerning theories; yet he found my concept of mobilized diasporas useful in grappling with a recalcitrant question.

On the whole, Soviet groups I considered to be mobilized diasporas have behaved according to my model. It must be remembered that my formulation preceded the Six-Days War by nearly two years. Thereafter, an ascending spiral of Jewish self-confidence, Slavic discrimination, and Jewish apprehension produced, between 1968 and 1979, the sharpest xenophobia observed in the Soviet polity. For a while, the succession of mobilized diasporas which I had predicted appeared to be under way. Throughout the Brezhnev era, Mikoian's influence appeared to guarantee Armenian acquisition of a limited range of significant roles hitherto occupied by Jews. Armenian institutions, including the Gregorian Church, occasionally acted as auxiliaries for Soviet policy at home and abroad. Yet there were hints that the customary insecurity of mobilized diasporas threatened even the Armenians. During the late 1980s, Moscow evidenced more intense irritation concerning Armenian territorial demands, while Armenians grumbled about independence. Nevertheless, regardless of rebuffs the latter cannot afford to forego the tacit Russian alliance; it may be that further scenes of the Soviet drama will show Armenians still performing the role of mobilized diaspora.

The *colonial* category in my typology presented no terminological novelty. Still, until the 1970s Sovietologists, with notable exceptions, resisted a sharp distinction between USSR Europeans and ethnic groups of Moslem cultural background. Until very recently, the tendency was to dichotomize "Asians" (or "Central Asians") and Europeans, including peoples of European background domiciled in Asia. Commonly, the North Caucasus and Azerbaidzhan were included among European regions, or Georgians and Armenians were lumped with Azerbaidzhanis as "Asians" beyond the geographers' nominal frontier at the crest of the Caucasus range. By 1979, however, in my brief on-the-spot observations, I found Georgians and Armenians insisting that their countries are in Europe, whereas Azerbaidzhanis were just as adamant that they were in Asia. None of this demonstrates that the present civil war in Azerbaidzhan will spread to Central Asia, where Slavs rather than Armenians are the main "intruders." However—if one is to credit *Krasnaia Zvezda*—puzzling intra-Moslem feuding in Uzbekistan during June 1989 arose because a small Turkic immigrant group refused to join a conspiracy aimed at uniting Moslems in Central Asia for driving out Europeans.[5] Such a situation is reminiscent of former colonial countries, e.g., in North Africa or India, where peoples of non-European culture were far from united, but where contagion of rebellion against colonial powers spread rapidly.

Compared to the exotic types just discussed, my typological category *state nations* may appear self-evident. Clearly the subsequent history of the Baltic republics has conformed to the model, except for the rather surprising degree to which their economic innovations became a model for more limited Soviet experimentation during the late Brezhnev period. No state nation emulated the mobilized diasporas by major dispersion outside its own frontiers—even Latvians, prominent throughout the Soviet sphere during the Civil War, apparently renounced all-Union careers. Nor was the growing proportion (after my 1959 data) of Russian immigrants in each Baltic republic surprising, although it complicates present efforts at secession.

Georgians have also conformed closely to the state-nation model, through high social mobilization, avoidance of dispersion, and intense national consciousness. Somewhat less expected was the brutal Russian reaction to Georgian protests; still, repression of milder protests during the 1950s might have forewarned us. Similarly, the intensity of minority (Christian Ossetian as well as Moslem Abkhazian) resentment of Georgian dominance in their little "empire" was foreshadowed by obscure maneuvers during the 1950s.

As for *irredenta* (significant Soviet fragments of nations located outside the USSR), only the Moldavian development can be followed in detail. By exceeding, in recent months, expectations for a hitherto unmobilized, passive element, Moldavians confirm the importance of a legacy of statehood as an incitement for renewed independency during a relatively fluid situation like the present.

"The Ethnic Scene" clearly suggested that Russians were the *dominant* ethnic element, the source of the unified national culture which the elite believed it required. In the mid-1960s it appeared that Marxist-Leninist ideology exerted an influence roughly equal to Russian nationalism. I continue to believe that Khrushchev truly adhered to Marxist-Leninist millennial goals; and as late as 1968 Suslov and Brezhnev legitimized their power at home and abroad by blunt quotations from the Leninist canon. Over the succeeding two decades, such ideological influences virtually vanished; concomitantly, traditional Russian values inevitably increased among the elite. It is now fairly certain that I underestimated the non-functional elite attachments when I assumed that "the elite is not primarily motivated by Russian ethnocentrism as such." Even during Khrushchev's dominance, the proportion of Russians in the elite increased, but Ukrainians (some of whom, like Shelest and Podgorny, evidently wished to foster a distinct ethnic consciousness) grew faster. Under Brezhnev, such Ukrainian elements were eliminated. More significant, perhaps, than their near-monopoly of top positions, has been the Russians' turn toward xenophobic movements like *Pamiat.* These movements waver ominously between demanding ethnic "purification" of core Russian regions and support for Russian colonist minorities in other nations' homelands. Historically, dominant elite elements, when they lose self-confidence and a sense of direction, pose a severe hazard for peaceful evolution.

Today, as it did a quarter-century ago, my category *younger brothers* points to the crux of the ethnic predicament in the USSR. In "The Ethnic Scene," a "devious" regime policy toward Ukrainians (to a lesser extent Belorussians) was identified. Their movement into major positions was encouraged, and they were given certain symbolic gratifications. Conversely, assimilation to Russian culture was quietly fostered, and overt manifestations of national distinctiveness were fiercely repressed. Perhaps this was the shrewdest regime policy for the 1960s, while anticipating the erosive effect of the passage of time on resentments caused by memories of Stalin's anti-Ukrainian policies. After Shelest was eliminated from power (1971), the "carrot" in this policy dissipated; eighteen years later, the "stick" was largely discarded.

In contrast to non-Slavic republics, Ukrainians and Belorussians did not react immediately by producing a united national opposition to Moscow. In Belorussia, long regarded as weak in national consciousness, the relatively moderate national revival did go slightly beyond what might have been expected. But in the Ukraine, during 1941–1950 the scene of fierce resistance, manifestations were relatively muted. The sharp—although prudently peaceful—clamor for religious freedom and national cultural revival in the West Ukraine did not spread throughout the East. Instead, the vigorous miners' strikes for socio-economic reforms in the southeast (Donbas) were inspired by Russian miners' examples, and rejected Ukrainian nationalist intervention. In between, the majority of East Ukrainian provinces remained, as during the 1940s, indecisive. Certainly strong voices—some ethnic Russian—demanded greatly enhanced autonomy for the Ukraine; but it is unclear that "Rukh," the most influential organization, will press for independence. My category "younger brothers" implied that (apart from completely alienated West Ukrainians) East Slav relations resemble a family quarrel, in which bitter reactions to regime mistreatment alternate with reconciliation to the Russians. Most recent trends appear to bear out this diagnosis.

To sum up, the typology presented in "The Ethnic Scene" and many of its practical implications have held up, whereas the broader theoretical underpinnings had to be discarded.[6] Such paradoxes are not uncommon in the social sciences, where mistaken efforts to produce elegant systematic frameworks are often remedied by pragmatic diagnoses based on intimate knowledge of specific situations. For me, the lesson is to exercise caution about applying general theories to contemporary situations, while continuing the search for conceptual schemes which can be tested against the greater range of historical evidence. In the end, the *longue durée* approach may, in fact, be more productive even for policy requirements. If I had to do "The Ethnic Scene" over again, I should adopt a simpler approach. Eschewing overarching concern for the Soviet regime's intentions, I should estimate the potential utility of each major nationality in a rough matrix composed of the following axes: (1) the utility of each nation for the overall economic and geopolitical objectives of any regime installed in Moscow, ranging from very high for Ukrainians (given their strategic and economic resources) and Armenians (given their propensity for flexible enterprise) to very low for most Moslem nations; and (2) the propensity of each nation for collaboration with Russians, ranging from fairly high for Ukrainians, Belorussians, Armenians, and Georgians, to very low for Moslems and Baltics. From a strictly rational point of view, one might anticipate that such a matrix would lead Moscow to concentrate on retaining the younger brothers and the European Transcaucasians, while cutting its losses elsewhere—as it has already done in East Central Europe. But observation of Russian elite behavior has sufficiently chastened my expectations of a functionally rational policy that I would no longer anticipate such an outcome. To put the matter another way, a more modest conceptualization would produce a very similar typology—and the same indeterminate prognosis of policy outcome.

NOTES

1. Somewhat more extended discussions of structural functionalism appear in my chapter "Communist Political Systems as Vehicles for Modernization," in Monte Palmer and Larry Stern, *Political Development in Changing Societies* (Lexington: Heath, 1971), pp. 127--28 and 143--44; and *The European Administrative Elite* (Princeton: Princeton University Press, 1973), pp. 8, 202.

2. As I indicate in *ibid.,* p. 8, one may use a limited functional approach without embracing a system like structural functionalism.

3. See my review article, "Development Theory: Taking the Historical Cure," *Studies in Comparative Communism,* VII (1974), pp. 217, 223–25.

4. *American Political Science Review,* LXX (1976), pp. 393–408.

5. *Krasnaia Zvezda,* June 21, 1989, abstracted in *Current Digest of the Soviet Press,* XLI, No. 25, p. 22.

6. Conceptual frameworks should also be evaluated—to a lesser extent—by the frequent errors they avoid. In this respect, "The Ethnic Scene" has the following "negative" merits: (1) Its typology does not rest on excessive concern for *language* distinctions; (2) It notes the importance of *non-territorial* ethnic groups; (3) It did not predict *economic modernization* would blur national identities; (4) Specifically, it noted that an *"internal proletariat"* relegated to unattractive jobs in dominant ethnic urban areas had been avoided in the USSR, and did not predict that modernization would produce such a proletariat.

16

APPROACHES TO THE STUDY OF SOVIET NATIONALITIES POLITICS:

John Armstrong's Functionalism and Beyond

John Armstrong's functional typology of Soviet nationalities is the best known and most enduring of theoretical constructs used in the study of Soviet nationalities politics. First written in 1965, the essay still holds true today to an extraordinary degree, though the forms of stratification that Armstrong describes are increasingly under strain and attack.

The success of Armstrong's model can be attributed to three factors. First, Armstrong was sensitive to the enormous variety and complexity of the Soviet ethnic scene. While he viewed Soviet nationalities politics as taking place within a single institutional and ideological framework, they defied mechanistic analogies or classifications. This was so not only because of the historical, cultural, and socio-economic differences among Soviet peoples, but also because of the different relationships between these peoples and the political system. Armstrong well understood that it would be impossible to find a single analogy that would fit the variety of Soviet circumstances; any successful model of Soviet nationalities politics would have to include a multiplicity of analogies.

Second, Armstrong's model was successful because he consistently followed a holistic approach to the study of Soviet nationalities problems. Given the great variety among Soviet peoples, there has been a natural tendency among those who study Soviet nationalities to engage in excessively empirical and nation-specific research, to concentrate on describing the situation of a particular Soviet group without relating it to others. Armstrong, by contrast, understood that one cannot understand the individual parts unless they are related to each other and to the whole. It is this which constituted the center of his "functional approach," which sought to uncover how each element contributed to or undermined the entire system of ethnic stratification. Such an approach also foreshadowed the use of Soviet nationalities as the subjects of cross-cultural comparative analysis; it suggested that, much as West Europeanists, Latin Americanists, or Africanists attempt to understand politics by comparing the behavior of peoples across borders, Sovietologists as well could contribute to theory-building in comparative politics by comparing the behavior of peoples within Soviet borders.

Finally, part of the genius of Armstrong's model was its rigorous comparative focus beyond Soviet borders. Through his categorization, Armstrong directs our attention to analogies from other cultures that are relevant for understanding Soviet situations. He suggests, for instance, that Ukrainian politics might be better conceptualized by studying relations between the English and the Scots rather than the Russians and the Balts; that the situation of the Armenians had more in common with that of the Chinese in Southeast Asia than it did with the neighboring Georgians; and that Central Asian politics could best be studied by analyzing French colonialism rather than Soviet policies in Belorussia. He also understood the limited application of two common analogies often drawn in regard to Soviet nationalities politics: that of the West European model of the state-nation, which he saw as limited to the Balts, the Georgians, and to the irredenta of the Moldavians, Poles, and Finns; and that of an urban ethnic underclass or "internal proletariat," which, he correctly pointed out, did not exist in any form in the USSR.

As a predictive model of political attitudes and behavior, Armstrong's classification has held up surprisingly well against the events of the *glasnost'* period. A recent survey conducted by the USSR Academy of Sciences' All-Union Center for the Study of Public Opinion found sharp attitudinal differences toward ethnic issues along many of the lines envisioned by Armstrong. Informants were asked to identify which of several propositions they believed to be in the "good of their nation" *(dobro svoemu narodu)*. The results, presented in Table [16.]1, were not broken down by nationality, but rather by republic or region. However, assuming that these figures fairly well reflect the attitudes of the major nationalities residing in these territories,[1] the data show that attitudes toward ethnic issues roughly correspond to the categories devised by Armstrong. For instance, of those groups surveyed, only the Balts expressed a strong desire for political independence. Separatist demands in the Soviet Union have largely been limited to those nationalities classified by Armstrong as state-nations (the Balts, the Georgians, and the Moldavians), though more recently the desire for state sovereignty has spread throughout Transcaucasia.

TABLE [16.]1 Responses to Question, "Those Who Wish Good for Their Nation Should Above All . . ." (August–September 1989), by Republic (in percent)

Response	Armenia	Baltics	RSFSR	Ukraine
Be concerned about the unity and cohesion of the USSR.	10.6	10.2	63.4	30.9
Strive so that we have "a strong center and strong republics."	4.8	9.6	19.5	17.2
Concentrate all energies on preserving one's native language and culture.	52.9	25.6	8.8	20.6
Strive for the economic independence of one's republic.	26.0	43.5	14.8	32.4
Seek full political self-determination for one's republic, not excluding separation from the USSR.	17.3	47.0	9.9	20.6
Cannot say.	1.9	2.9	7.5	4.9

Source: *Ogonek*, no. 43 (October 1989), pp. 4-5. Respondents could choose more than one response, and therefore columns do not add to 100 percent.

The "younger brother" Ukrainians are still highly divided, much as Armstrong described in his essay. More than any group other than Russians, they expressed belief in the need to preserve the unity and cohesion of the country, as well as support for Gorbachev's formula of a "strong center and strong republics." However, almost an equal proportion of respondents in the Ukraine expressed support for economic independence for the republic, preservation of Ukrainian language and culture, and (to a lesser extent) political independence. While there has been a resurgence of nationalism among Ukrainians and Belorussians, nationalist movements in these areas have generally been less assertive vis-a-vis the center than those in the Baltic or Transcaucasia; their demands have been confined largely to the sphere of cultural and linguistic autonomy.

Armenians overwhelmingly expressed concern about the preservation of their language and culture—perhaps not a surprising response for a nation living in diaspora. Armstrong pointed in particular to the high degree of social mobilization among the Armenians and their potential to attract the animosity of neighboring peoples—an observation which has largely proved true. The relatively large proportion of Russians (7.5 percent) who provided no answer to the survey question is perhaps indicative of the lack of confidence that the traditionally dominant group now feels about its future. As for the "colonials," who are not represented in this survey, Armstrong believed in the possibility of a sudden explosive rebellion against Russian dominance, particularly among rapidly modernizing groups—a prediction which has, with the exception of the Azerbaidzhani insurrection, yet to be realized.

The problem with Armstrong's classification is not its "functional approach" as much as the limits of Karl Deutsch's theory of social mobilization, on which Armstrong relies heavily for his underlying explanation of ethnic conflict. Deutsch's theory would predict that those groups with the highest levels of social mobilization and lowest levels of assimilation would be most likely to assert their ethnic identities.[2] Within the Soviet context, this would be the Balts and the Transcaucasians. But Deutsch's theory cannot explain why so much conflict has at times taken place in some of the least modernized parts of the Soviet Union. For example, Deutsch's theory could not explain why Soviet Moldavians, who by nearly all standards of social mobilization (urbanization, education, geographic mobility, and level of development) rank practically at the bottom of major Soviet nationalities, have become such a source of protest, instability, and violence in the Soviet Union in recent years. Nor could it predict the violent clashes that have taken place in Central Asia. As one respected scholar has observed in reference to the application of Deutsch's theory in other contexts, "empirical efforts to confirm the role of modernization level as an intervening variable between ethnic diversity and political instability have come to nought."[3]

Armstrong's continued interest in the Deutsch approach was reflected in his subsequent work, in which he explored the powerful role of myths and symbols in the creation of ethnic identities. However, he abandoned Deutsch's stress on social mobilization and modernization, focusing instead on the factors associated with the emergence of ethnic identities over thousands of years of history.[4] This evolution of perspectives was perhaps not accidental. Armstrong's functional classification of Soviet nationalities placed undue emphasis on group attributes of modernization, deducing the strength of ethnic identities in part from the interplay between social mobilization and processes of assimilation. Armstrong's comment in his essay that the Deutsch approach "may well overemphasize the purely demographic side of the interaction"[5] hints that Armstrong was well aware of the problems posed by relying on a theorist who believed that nationalism was being gradually transcended by the forces of modernity and would eventually be replaced by "a more thoroughgoing world-wide unity than has ever been seen in human history."[6] It is interesting in this regard that Armstrong's reliance on Deutsch may well have caused him to overestimate the potential for assimilation among Ukrainians.

In line with Deutsch's emphasis on demographic rather than attitudinal factors, Soviet nationalities are largely treated in Armstrong's essay as relatively undifferentiated cultural identities. Attitudinal and behavioral differentiation among members of an ethnic group along class, regional, patrimonial, or other lines is largely unexplored by Armstrong, mirroring cultural-pluralist rather than instrumentalist assumptions about ethnic politics. One can, as Armstrong does, speak of a broad system of stratification among whole ethnic groups in the Soviet Union that implies certain roles for indigenous elites and populations in an all-Union division of political and economic labor. But such a perspective without qualification tends to reify group behavior, transforming whole nationalities (rather than their individual members) into the main actors of politics.

No better can the dangers of an excessive focus on group attributes rather than group attitudes be illustrated than in the case of the Russians, who are strangely ignored by Armstrong, though they provide a standard of reference used throughout. An informal poll of Soviet citizens published by Radio Liberty in early 1989 found that approximately a third of Russians viewed the ethnic disturbances of recent years as a positive development in Soviet society, seeing them as examples of democracy in action and as channels for airing previously suppressed demands.[7] In a more recent poll of 2000 Muscovites conducted in October 1989 by the unofficial Informal Sociological Service, 38 percent of those questioned "responded positively" to the idea of political self-determination for the Baltic republics.[8] In other words, there appears to be considerable ideological differentiation among Russians that defies stereotyping based on intergroup stratification or levels of social mobilization.

To illustrate the same point with a non-Russian group, the range of political opinions among Lithuanians today runs from the radical Lithuanian Liberty League to various wings of the Sajudis movement, and now even to Lithuanians participating in the reconstituted Communist Party of Lithuania, who oppose the decisions of the Twentieth Party Congress of the Communist Party of Lithuania to separate from the Communist Party of the Soviet Union. The relationship here between political attitudes and differential levels or rates of social mobilization within the Lithuanian population is unclear, as is the relationship with levels of assimilation.

The October 1989 Informal Sociological Service poll cited above also indicated a close correlation of class, occupation, and age with attitudes toward Baltic independence among Muscovites. Thus, 85 percent of students and 70 percent of the artistic intelligentsia favored Baltic political self-determination, while only 25 percent of workers at large industrial enterprises did—a reflection of the phenomenon of Russian working-class "internationalism." At the same time, 92 percent of military officers, 75 percent of housewives, and 100 percent of Party, Soviet, and Komsomol employees were against Baltic independence. And while more than 70 percent of respondents younger than 39 responded positively to the prospects of Baltic political independence, almost 80 percent of pensioners responded negatively.[9] In other words, ethnic attitudes can and do transcend patterns of interethnic stratification in significant ways that Deutsch's social mobilization approach cannot adequately capture.

This raises yet another issue largely glossed over in Armstrong's essay, as well as in Deutsch's work in general—the role of elites in ethnic politics and their relation to society. Some theorists of nationalism view elites (and in particular—the intelligentsia) as the main carriers of nationalist ideologies in the modern world.[10] Armstrong, however, really only addresses the role of elites in describing patterns of intergroup stratification (i.e., the use of Ukrainians and Belorussians as mediating elites for Russian domination elsewhere in the country and the prominence of Armenians within the trading and commercial elite).

Yet certainly, within each of the national contexts of the Soviet Union, the functional equivalent of "younger brothers" has traditionally existed. What theorists of imperialism have sometimes labelled "comprador elites"—i.e., collaborators drawn from the native population—have generally acted within each of the republics as intermediaries between the Russian-dominated center and the non-Russian periphery. It is precisely such elites who have become the target of animosity of nationalist movements throughout the Soviet Union—at times being swept away by massive protest against them.

In Estonia, for instance, native cadres were traditionally divided between "home communists" (i.e., those who lived their entire lives in Estonia) and "Russian-Estonians" (i.e., Estonians who spent considerable parts of their lives in the RSFSR), with *glasnost'* being associated with the victory of the former over the latter.[11] Emblazoned into the Moldavian national consciousness is the division within the Moldavian political elite between so-called "left bank" and "right bank" cadres, the former corresponding to officials originating from the left bank of the Dniestr (the territory of the Moldavian ASSR in the 1920s and 1930s), the latter corresponding to officials originating from that part of Moldavia that belonged to interwar Romania.[12] Don Carlisle has shown the ways in which regionalism, patrimonialism, and political attitudes toward de-Stalinization fused among the native cadres of Uzbekistan, as regionally-based cliques within the Uzbek elite fought over power and policy.[13] And while from the all-Union perspective Ukrainians might appear to have played the role of "younger brothers," within the Ukraine itself there was a need to find a subgroup of slightly more senior Ukrainian brothers to act as mediators between the Ukrainian population and the central authorities as well.[14]

Processes of political change at work today in the Soviet Union may well resemble the politics involved in decolonization after World War II. As Robinson described the process in Africa:

> When the colonial rulers had run out of indigenous collaborators they either chose to leave or were compelled to go. Their national opponents . . . sooner or later succeeded in detaching the indigenous political elements from the colonial regime until they eventually formed a united front of collaboration against it.[15]

In any case, there is a need for some well-developed conception of elite differentiation and behavior in analyzing Soviet ethnic politics.

The point is not that stratification in the Soviet Union is more regional, patrimonial, or class-based than it is ethnic, nor that Armstrong's classic description of patterns of national identity and intergroup stratification has somehow been transcended by events. On the contrary, it still holds true to an extraordinary degree. Rather, the point is that ethnicity is above all, in Hans Kohn's words, "a state of mind"[16] rather than a state of modernization, and Sovietologists, like other social scientists, still have much to learn about the factors that contribute to it and its relationship to other forms of consciousness and stratification in society. Two decades more of research on these questions have passed since Armstrong wrote his essay. Yet, in pursuing answers we would do well to stand on John Armstrong's shoulders.

NOTES

1. This is not a wildly distorting assumption, considering that, according to the 1979 census, 89.7 percent of the population of Armenia consisted of Armenians, 82.6 percent of the population of the RSFSR consisted of Russians, 73.6 percent of the population of the Ukraine consisted of Ukrainians, and a total of 68.5 percent of the population of the Baltic republics consisted of the titular nationalities of those three republics. See Tsentral'noe Statisticheskoe Upravlenie SSSR, *Chislennost' i sostav naseleniia SSSR: Po dannym Vsesoiuznoi perepisi naseleniia 1979 goda* (Moscow: Finansy i statistika, 1984).

2. See Karl W. Deutsch, *Nationalism and Social Communication* (Cambridge, MA: The MIT Press, 1953); Karl W. Deutsch, "Social Mobilization and

Political Development," *American Political Science Review* (September 1961), pp. 493–514. Actually, Deutsch was confused as to whether it was the level of social mobilization or the rate of social mobilization that was the key. Either approach presents clear anomalies in recent Soviet experience that cannot be explained by this theory.

3. Donald Horowitz, *Ethnic Groups in Conflict* (Berkeley, CA: University of California Press, 1985), pp. 102–03.

4. See *Nations Before Nationalism* (Chapel Hill, NC: University of North Carolina Press, 1982).

5. See *Journal of Soviet Nationalities,* I, 1 (Spring 1990), p. 29.

6. Deutsch, *Nationalism and Social Communication,* pp. 190–93.

7. Kathleen Mihalisko, "Poll of Soviet Citizens' Attitudes Toward Ethnic Unrest," *Radio Liberty: Report on the USSR,* vol. 1, no. 10 (March 10, 1989), pp. 31–42.

8. *Atmoda,* December 4, 1989, pp. 4–5. The question asked was: "What is your attitude toward political self-determination for the Baltic republics?" The reliability of the survey results may be undermined by the fact that 30 percent of those questioned refused to answer the survey.

9. Ibid.

10. See, for instance, Anthony D. Smith, *Theories of Nationalism* (2nd ed.) (New York: Holmes and Meier Publishers, 1983). For a perceptive essay on the role of elites in the formation of Central Asian national identities, see Kemal Karpat, "Introduction: Elites and the Transmission of Nationality and Identity," *Central Asian Survey,* vol. 5, nos. 3–4 (1986), pp. 5–24.

11. See Jaan Pennar, "Soviet Nationality Policy and the Estonian Communist Elite," in Tonu Parming and Elmar Jarvesoo, eds., *A Case Study of a Soviet Republic: The Estonian SSR* (Boulder, CO: Westview, 1978), pp. 120–22; Toivo U. Raun, *Estonia and Estonians* (Stanford, CA: Stanford University Press, 1987), pp. 190–93.

12. See, for instance, former Moldavian Party Second Secretary V.I. Smirnov's statement on this account in *Sovetskaia Moldaviia,* May 31, 1987, p. 2.

13. Donald S. Carlisle, "The Uzbek Power Elite: Politburo and Secretariat (1938–1983)," *Central Asian Survey,* vol. 5, nos. 3–4 (1986), pp. 91–132.

14. For my description of this process, see Mark R. Beissinger, "Nationalism, Cadres, and Neoimperial Integration: Ukrainian and RSFSR Regional Party Officials Compared," *Studies in Comparative Communism,* vol. 21, no 1 (Spring 1988), pp. 71–85.

15. Ronald Robinson, "Non-European Foundations of European Imperialism: Sketch for a Theory of Collaboration," in Roger Owen and Bob Sutcliffe, eds., *Studies in the Theory of Imperialism* (London: Longman, 1972), p. 139.

16. Hans Kohn, *Nationalism: Its Meaning and History* (Princeton, NJ: D. Van Nostrand Company, 1955), p. 9.

17

THE LOGIC OF COLLECTIVE
ACTION AND THE PATTERN
OF REVOLUTIONARY BEHAVIOR

Some expect a theory to explain all behavior. Since interest group activity and revolutions obviously take place, since emotion and irrationality are obviously a part of politics, many area specialists have had a tendency to treat works such as *The Logic of Collective Action* as theoretically interesting, but essentially irrelevant. In 1989 and 1990 when Americans have deeply sympathized with the Poles, Czechs, Lithuanians, and so forth, it is particularly unpleasant to hear someone say that the hearts and minds of those in the streets don't matter—only the attitudes and decisions of the Communist oppressors.

Mancur Olson has often responded to objections by saying that "obviously the kind of argument I made needs to be enormously enriched. I am completely conscious that I am vastly oversimplifying on the theory that this is useful and must be done if we are to think theoretically." There do, indeed, seem to me qualifications that need to be made, and I will discuss them in this article.

The area specialist should not, however, assume that because Olson's conclusions come from deductive theory, they would not be supported by any empirical work. The opposite is the case. The classic study of revolution was Crane Brinton's *Anatomy of Revolution,* and it still is one of the best. Brinton's analysis—based essentially on a study of the American, English, French, and Russian revolutions—continually emphasizes defects on the governmental side in a way that reminds one of Olson's analysis. Brinton emphasizes financial difficulties and the inadequacies of tax systems more than societal economic problems, and governmental inefficiency more than despotism.

What may be called the ruling class seems in all four of our societies to be divided and inept. When numerous and influential members of such a class begin to believe that they hold power unjustly, or that all

347

men are brothers, equal in the eyes of eternal justice, or that the beliefs they were brought up on are silly, or that "after us the deluge," they are not likely to resist successfully any serious attacks on their social, economic, and political position.

When those of them who had positions of political power did use force, they used it sporadically and inefficiently. . . . The line in actual practice of government between force and persuasion is a subtle one, not to be drawn by formulas . . . but by men skilled in the art of ruling. One of the best signs of the unfitness of the ruling class to rule is the absence of this skill among its members.

In each revolution there is a point, or several points, where constituted authority is challenged by the illegal acts of revolutionists. In such instances, the routine response of any authority is to have recourse to force, police or military. . . . Those of the ruling class responsible for such responses in all our societies proved singularly unable to make adequate use of force. . . . We can . . . with some confidence attribute the failure of the conservatives to use force skillfully to the decadence of a ruling class.[1]

Similarly, when Myron Weiner recently surveyed political change in Asia and Africa over the last 25 years, he focussed on its divergence from the earlier predictions of political scientists. There have been no more peasant uprisings or revolutions and relatively little in the way of leftist urban upheaval. Citizen political participation has been denied but this "has, surprisingly, been less a source of political instability than one might have expected. . . . Many regimes have been unstable, especially in Africa, but the instabilities can be attributed more often to intra-elite conflicts than to the imbalance between political participation and political institutionalization."[2]

Those who are particularly disturbed by Mancur Olson's assertion that governments make peoples rather than the other way around might reflect on these words of Weiner:

Hegemonic rather than accommodative ethnic politics characterize the new states. In country after country, a single ethnic group has taken control over the state and used its powers to exercise control over others. Indeed, among the multi-ethnic states, the process continues to be one of "nation-destroying," to use Walker Connor's term for the process by which the state attempts to assimilate, absorb, or crush ethnic groups that do not accept the legitimacy of the state within existing boundaries.[3]

We should not, of course, assume that a theory such as Mancur Olson's is to be applied mechanically or that it explains everything. On the contrary, the "logic of collective action" has been an extraordinarily productive theory precisely because it does not explain everything: collective action obviously does take place when it "rationally" should not. But when we take for granted political action that we should not take for granted, we do not seek explanations.

It was precisely Mancur Olson's understanding that much existing collective action is unnatural that led him to other explanations for that action, particularly to compulsion and side payments (or positive selective incentives).

It is striking how frequently this simple insight leads to quite non-intuitive explanations of concrete events. For example, American trade union leaders were very slow to support governmental social welfare measures that their members wanted precisely because they were using social welfare benefits as the side-payment to attract members and because they knew that free governmental benefits would undermine their membership drives. To gain trade union support for the Social Security Act, President Roosevelt needed to substitute compulsion (the closed shop of the Wagner Act) for the side-payments they had been using.

Similarly, the "logic of collective action" alerts us to a major current problem with membership of the Communist party in the Soviet Union—one that the American media is almost certain to misinterpret. When Lenin and Stalin structured the requirements of party membership, they showed a deep understanding of the logic of collective action. By making party membership a requirement for many jobs that were not normally considered "political," and by making participation in political activity a requirement for membership, they created a very sophisticated system of side-payments and compulsion that induced the broad administrative elite both to join the Communist party and to engage in supplementary political activity. Because of Gorbachev's reforms, however, party membership will no longer be required for a broad range of employment, and the incentive for many people to continue to pay dues—let alone engage in supplementary political activity—is going to be sharply reduced. One can predict a sharp drop in the number of party members for this reason alone, even among people who may still vote for the party's candidates. Clearly Soviet radicals and the American media will explain any decline in membership in terms of political dissidence, but this is an explanation that we will need to examine carefully.

We should employ this type of counter-factual analysis when we apply Mancur Olson's logic of collective action to revolutionary behavior. Let us not fight the compelling logic of what he says. It *is* strange that hundreds of thousands of people go into the streets of Lithuania. The costs and benefits of an independent Lithuania would accrue to all of its citizens, regardless of who does or does not participate in collective activity to achieve independence. Yet, the impact of individual participation in any mass action in Lithuania is absolutely insignificant. It would make no conceivable difference if there were only 500,000 persons in a demonstration instead of 500,001. But it is only when we accept the basic insight that revolution is not a rational consequence of popular unrest within a dictatorship that we are in a position to begin a sophisticated analysis of the factors which do work to overcome the logic of collective inaction in the real world.

As we do this, two questions are important to ask. First, why does revolutionary action take place? Olson is right in saying that the ratios of the potential costs, the potential benefits, and the potential impact of individual participation in revolutionary action strongly suggest non-participation. He is right in emphasizing that popular revolution is never able to generate enough support to stand up to an army that continues to fire its weapons. Yet, a very substantial number of people are, in fact, killed while participating in revolutionary and semi-revolutionary action. The hundreds killed in the Soviet Union in the last few years are nothing in comparison with the death toll in other countries. Sri Lanka has sixteen million people—some 5 percent of the Soviet total—but fourteen thousand have been killed in the Tamil uprising since 1983.[4] The divisions in the elite—and especially at the top of the military—may explain why the Romanian revolution was successful in 1989, but William Crowther is right to remind us that a lot of blood was shed before those divisions were visible to anyone in Romania or abroad. We need to explain why this happened.

Second, the Olson argument does not specify with any precision the point at which a country's elite will lose self-confidence to a dangerous degree. It does not explain when divisions within the elite will create the conditions for popular revolution and when (for example, in the Soviet Union in 1937 and 1957) they will not. Clearly economic problems are of crucial importance, but during the long Great Depression of the 1930s, many countries did not come close to serious political instability. Indeed, as Olson himself noted in 1963, it is rapid economic growth that is often associated with the destabilization of old regimes.[5]

This article will be devoted, first, to an exploration of the relationship of the logic of collective action to these questions, and then to an examination of the implications of the logic for the future of nationality revolt in the Soviet Union.

THE CAUSES OF "IRRATIONAL" PARTICIPATION AND THE CYCLE OF REVOLUTIONARY ACTION

As we try to explain participation in revolutionary behavior in terms of the logic of collective action, we need to begin by distinguishing between the leaders and the mass participants. It is not difficult to explain why some persons would choose to take a leadership or highly activist position in a revolutionary movement if they think it may succeed in whole or in part. If the revolution wins, those who led it will receive jobs that they never could hope to obtain in another way. Even if the movement for Lithuanian independence does not succeed, a number of those who became active in the Sajudis movement have already acquired high governmental posts.

The same is obviously true of domestic politics as well. If a person can obtain enough membership dues or other financial support from organizing a trade union or interest group to pay his or her own salary, he or she has an interest in taking an entrepreneurial role in doing so. Activists in the civil rights and feminist movements in the United States in the 1960s and 1970s acquired the political experience and contacts to move into high political posts a decade or two later.

The difficult problem is to explain why people would participate in mass demonstrations, in illegal sit-ins or boycotts, in the throwing of rocks at troops, and so forth when their individual participation in the mass activity is not noticeable but may lead to arrest or physical harm—or simply to an expenditure of time that has no impact on the final outcome.

One reason, of course, can be compulsion. In extreme cases, non-participants in revolutionary or semi-revolutionary situations can find burning tires around their necks, their houses bombed, the windows of their stores broken, or their businesses boycotted. In less extreme cases, non-participants can simply feel the sting of social ostracism. When friends and acquaintances feel strongly about an issue, most people tend to conform in their political behavior, whatever their inner reservations. If this is true in normal political life, it is even more the case in emotional revolutionary conditions.

Nevertheless, while we all know the force of conformity and social ostracism, we must be very careful in using this explanation in rational-actor analysis. If social ostracism were a sufficiently powerful source of compulsion, there would be none of the problems with collective action that are emphasized by Mancur Olson and that are observable in normal political life.

The key to explaining individual participation in mass collective action, especially mass revolutionary action, is to understand that "non-rational" factors are not limited to compulsion and traditional side-payments. Mancur Olson is an economist and has naturally been concerned with institutions such as trade unions and interest groups that arise in economic life, but there are other "non-rational" factors that can sometimes induce collective action. These play a particularly significant role in collective action of the extremely large groups that are engaged in revolutionary or semi-revolutionary collective action.

First, society devotes an enormous amount of effort to inculcate values such as collective responsibility, professionalism, and honesty that transcends individual rationality (narrowly defined) into its citizens. This effort is not totally without effect. The greatest mass participation in the United States occurs in a case—presidential elections—when the possibility of individual impact on the result is absolutely zero. The rate of participation in these elections is the

highest among the more successful and better educated who should
have the clearest sense of their rational individual interests. Socialization has to provide a substantial part of the answer.

Over two hundred years ago Jean Jacques Rousseau wrote, "the
strongest is never strong enough to be always the master, unless he
transforms strength into right, and obedience into duty."[6] Overwhelming force can compel any action, but overwhelming force can
be repulsive to an elite or can simply not be cost-effective. We
sometimes obey laws and pay taxes not simply because of compulsion, but also out of a sense of legitimacy. The compulsion embodied
in the law is often actually welcomed as a guarantee of equity, a
guarantee that others will not act as free riders.

When this sense of "right" is absent, law evasion can become very
widespread, and communities can create conditions in which laws
are collectively annulled because the police are afraid to enforce
them. The regime can bring in outsiders or break up community
pressure with mass deportations and arrests, but the costs can be
enormous. Even Stalin decided that it was not worthwhile to enforce
equality for women in the Moslem Central Asian countryside.

This sense of "right" and "duty" is particularly important to inculcate into soldiers and potential soldiers, for they must be willing
to risk death. However, when the government itself fails to promote
national goals, its former indoctrination works against it. Mancur
Olson would, no doubt, suggest that such national delegitimization
is devastating only when it affects the elite, but this factor can also
sometimes lead to individual participation in mass activity to overthrow the regime.

A second non-rational factor inducing political participation is irrationality itself. People are not simply rational beings. Emotion is part
of the human makeup, and it is part of politics. A half century ago
Harold Lasswell went so far as to say that it is the essence of politics:

> Political movements derive their vitality from the displacement of
> [unconscious] private affects upon public objects. . . . It is becoming
> something of a commonplace that politics is the arena of the irrational
> but a more accurate description would be that politics is the process by
> which the irrational bases of society are brought out into the open.[7]

We would not want to push this line of analysis to an extreme, but
to deny this irrational aspect of politics altogether is also clearly
wrong.

Without any question, people sometimes do participate in collective actions simply because they are angry and want to strike back
or to express themselves. Donald Forbes is right that there is a part
of politics (and not just nationalism) "that has to do with anger,
with indignation, with loyalties to culturally defined groups, with
pride, with identity."[8] In domestic American politics, the Supreme

Court's *Webster* decision on abortion produced an increase of money to the relevant women's organizations, and it is doubtful that a rational calculation of costs and benefits was the cause. In Miami when a black teenager was killed by a policeman, people simply poured into the streets when a cooler calculation of self-interest might have led them to non-participation. There are many examples of this type of burst of action.

A third "non-rational" factor that may lead to participation in collective action is simply enjoyment. Edward C. Banfield's famous article "Rioting Mainly for Fun and Profit" reminds us that "side-payments" are not limited to such "profits" as the liberation of television sets from stores in a riot area.[9] If 500,000 people are demonstrating in the center of town and it is safe to join them, the 500,001st person will not worry about the lack of impact of his or her participation, but will join for the sheer excitement and novelty of the "happening."[10]

Indeed, as Mancur Olson states, this factor helps to explain why, as in East Germany in 1989, the size of demonstrations often escalates with such incredible speed. Liberalization reduces the cost element in the cost-benefit equation for demonstrators, but liberalization does not increase the positive incentive for the individual to participate. Indeed, as the size of the demonstration increases, the impact of the participation of any one individual correspondingly decreases. On the "selective incentive" side of the equation, the crucial fact is not the liberalization, but the preceding repression: the more severe the old repression, the greater the novelty of the demonstration. Once it appears safe, people come out to participate in increasing numbers partly to see what is going on and to be able to talk about it with their friends.

Other types of political participation can be explained in a similar manner. In April 1990, the chairman of the Republican State Committee of Texas absolutely enthused when he talked about politics as the most exciting game in the world. For him it obviously is, and hence it is quite rational for him to participate. Similarly, if a woman has sufficient disposable income and feels good when she makes a contribution to the National Organization for Women, who is to say that this is a less rational luxury expenditure for her than a more expensive evening at the opera? It is this "luxury" aspect of contributions that helps to explain why, in the words of E.E. Schattschneider, "the flaw in the pluralist heaven is that the heavenly chorus sings with a strong upper-class accent."[11]

Clearly no reasonable rational actor analysis can fail to recognize the complexities of human nature discussed in the preceding paragraphs. Reasonable rational actor analysis should not deny the obvious, but should phrase its points in more qualified terms: (1) emotion and anger as driving forces in politics tend to fade rather quickly or at least turn into resignation; (2) the "fun" and excitement of demonstrations quickly turns to boredom as one follows another, and from a strictly empirical point of view, the proportion of the population who enjoy political activity as much as watching a baseball or football game is, alas, not that high; (3) people's willingness to be led by civic duty into actions that have no individual impact or payoff declines extremely rapidly as the cost of the activity rises. Even the higher information cost of a local election in comparison with a presidential election has a major impact on voter turnout.

It is by recognizing both the short-term force of factors such as emotion and entertainment and the long-term force of the factors emphasized by Mancur Olson that we can begin to understand a number of the regularities of revolutionary behavior that are familiar to us from reading the scholarly literature or even from following the media.

First, as we know most recently and dramatically from television reports of the rock-throwing on the West Bank of Israel or the student demonstration in Tiananmen Square in Beijing, the participants in major revolutionary action almost always are young people of high school or college age. This is true whatever the revolutionary behavior, be it participation in guerilla bands, the "necklacing" in South Africa, or the seizure of American hostages in Teheran in 1979.[12]

Virtually all of the factors discussed in this sector help to explain this pattern. The young are, of course, more susceptible to peer pressure to conform. The rites of passage to adulthood in any society often require the demonstration of bravery, and a young person—especially a young man—may feel that the costs of being branded a coward for "rational" behavior are simply too high. But, in addition, the young may simply not calculate costs and dangers in a mature manner (this certainly seems to have been the case of many of the students who stayed in Tiananmen Square). They pay no economic opportunity costs for participation if they are not employed, and they are likely to be particularly susceptible to the excitement and emotion of the moment if something new and interesting occurs. And, of course, as emotion and novelty fade, new people enter their teens every year. A critic of experimental psychology once said that its results could not be believed because they were based on experiments with rats and sophomores, and neither were human. The point was extreme, but the imperatives of the young may, in fact, be quite different from those of their elders.

Second, revolutionary bursts usually become more and more extreme with the passage of time, and usually they must either succeed in a few years or else exhaust themselves. Some kind of conservative Thermidor or separation of the moderates from the radicals takes place. If the causes of the grievances are not attacked, the revolutionary wave may form once more, but normally only after the passage of a significant period of time. Clearly anger and emotion can explain why revolutionary outbursts do occur, and their evolution in a more radical direction results from the fact that only the most emotional—the most fanatical—have staying power. This also explains why revolutions usually lose force in several years if they are not successful.

With the memories of the very quick collapses of the Central European regimes in 1989 fresh in mind, we are now too inclined to assume the fragility of dictatorial regimes. Without question, they can vanish in a moment, but we should not think that a momentary lapse, a brief period of indecision, a relaxation of controls necessarily brings the house of cards tumbling down. In fact, most mass demonstrations in favor of revolutionary change, most mass challenges to tanks and troops, end as they did in Tiananmen Square, not as in Romania, let alone East Germany. Mancur Olson is right in suggesting that the balance of selective incentives is usually on the side of a regime.

Indeed, if collective action becomes large-scale and particularly if it becomes violent and emotional, most regimes do not normally call out massive force immediately. They often play a revolutionary or semi-revolutionary burst like a big fish on a line and let it run at first. Then they begin to reel it in once it has tired itself out. In a riot in an American city, the National Guard seals off the riot areas and waits out a night or two of anarchy in the expectation that this will be enough to dissipate emotion. In a true revolutionary situation in Poland in 1980 and 1981, the regime waited nearly eighteen months to apply martial law, but then it worked with surprising effectiveness. This strategy of revolutionary control corresponds well with the assumption that a non-rational factor—emotion—is at work and that it will decline in force over time. At this stage it becomes easier to separate the "rational" moderates from the fanatics and begin to apply force to increase the potential costs to the individual participant.

THE APPLICATION OF FORCE AND
THE PATTERN OF DEMOCRATIC REVOLUTION

But when we have said all of this, it still seems to me that Mancur Olson is basically accurate. If we really want to understand the dynamics of revolution, we need to look more at the instruments of repression and those who control them than at the hearts and minds of the masses.

All theories of revolution are tautological. It is easy enough to find factors in common in the great majority of successful revolutions, for they usually have far more "causes" than are necessary to "explain" them. The real mystery is that they didn't occur earlier. In comparative perspective the surprising thing is the large number of regimes that have richly deserved to be overthrown (even by Mancur Olson's criterion of divisions within the elite and the incompetence of the regime), but that stayed in power. To repeat, dictatorial regimes are not as fragile as they appear in moments of extremism.

Unless a theory can explain why the factors that "produce" revolution in some cases do not produce it in others, it is open to the charge of post-facto, non-verifiable analysis. To say that a political leadership is in the deepest trouble if it loses control of the military is a truism. To say that a loss of faith in the elite or divisions in the elite are crucial does not explain why an elite loses faith or why some divisions lead to revolutions and others do not.

Of course, it may be that ultimately there is no real answer. Social scientists like to generalize, but to some extent Crane Brinton was clearly right when he pointed to such non-generalizable factors as the competence and skill of the leader. Machiavelli was right when he pointed to "fortuna"—luck—as being as important to a prince as skill.

Yet, because we are social scientists, we need to make the effort to find patterns and regularities, or we have nothing to guide us as we think about the fortune of countries such as the Soviet Union.

The first step in analyzing the relationship of elites and leaders to revolution is to distinguish between different kinds of revolution or semi-revolution. The elites are facing quite different kinds of people in the streets, and this affects the way that they react.

Sometimes it is the elite's own children who are rebelling. This was true in the American anti-Vietnam revolution (if we may extend the word "revolution" to those events), and not surprisingly even the few deaths of students at Kent State University had a major impact on elite attitudes. In China, the students who first went into Tiananmen Square came from elite universities and families, and the regime stayed its hand until most of them had been warned off. (At the end those students in the square were primarily from the provinces.) Indeed, the fact that revolutions rest on the young—especially students—frequently means that the elite literally must decide whether to unleash the troops on its own children.

By contrast, in other cases the elite may feel that the demonstrators are morally repugnant or otherwise totally illegitimate. Thus, conservative governments in the Third World have sometimes been extraordinarily brutal with Communists. In Indonesia the number of Communists killed in the mid-sixties reached into the hundreds of thousands. The Soviet Communists for their part saw the "kulaks" resisting collectivization as class enemies who could be (and were) treated ruthlessly. Any elite that is totally convinced of the righteousness of its cause will apply force without mercy, and Mancur Olson is correct that the likelihood of successful revolution in these cases is extremely low, especially if the military shares these beliefs.

It seems to me that Thomas Remington was too sweeping in speaking of a reciprocal relationship between an elite that provides various services and a population that accords legitimacy, but that Donald Forbes formulated Remington's point more successfully when he suggested that the attitudes of the elite and masses may be subject to the same influences. Forbes rightly put nationalism in this category, but it is not unique. Economic difficulties or defeats in war affect the thinking of both elites and masses. So can historical experiences. Surely one reason that the Hungarian and Polish elites made no effort to resist in 1989 is that both they and the masses of their age had been the students of the revolts of 1956 and that the students of 1989 were their own children. The thought of a Romanian-like bloodbath was simply too repugnant.

Conclusions such as these, however, give us little help in predicting when elites will have different attitudes, and we need to examine broader patterns of revolutionary behavior if we are to make more useful generalizations.

Several basic regularities deserve serious reflection. First, although there are exceptions, the level of economic development and education in a country seems to be strongly associated with its ability to develop stable democracy. To phrase the point differently, mass revolutionary action in favor of democracy is likely to be more successful in economically well-developed countries than in poor ones.

Second, the movement towards stable democracy in the course of industrialization was a very slow and fitful one in Western Europe. In many countries it extended well over a century. In general, however, the period of the transition seems to have been featured by more serious revolutionary activity than either the traditional society that preceded it or the fully industrial societies that subsequently emerged. In the transitional period, democratic revolts often alternated with military ones. Neither theory nor the evidence of the twentieth century gives any reason to expect that the Third World experience in the future will be any different from the European in the past.

Third, the pattern of successful ethnic or national revolt has been strongly associated with the physical location of the ethnic group in revolt. If it lives outside the "borders" of the country of the dominating ethnic group (what we often would call a colony), then the dominated ethnic group almost always achieves national independence. This earlier pattern of the non-Communist world has now been confirmed in the Communist world in Central Europe. If, however, a dominated ethnic group lives inside the "border" of a country, it almost never gets free unless the central power of the country disintegrates. Secessionists seldom succeed. Areas such as Algeria that formally were inside France create ambivalent situations, but the fact that the Algerian revolt produced the end of the Fourth

Republic is perhaps the perfect symbol of the ambivalence. The importance of borders—for whatever reason—is shown in the universally accepted assumption that the de jure incorporation of the West Bank into Israel would change the situation fundamentally from the de facto incorporation of the last quarter of a century.

Of these three revolutionary patterns, the instability in periods of the transition is perhaps easiest to explain. In an earlier work, Mancur Olson looked at this phenomenon and noted approvingly the theories of revolution that emphasized the insecurity, the anxiety, the loss of reassuring community ties, the undercutting of old values that marked people's movement from a stable rural society into the city.[13] These are all the kind of non-rational factors that should be expected to overcome the logic of collective action on a short-term basis. Action, especially collective action, could easily release psychological tension and not be "irrational" from an individual's point of view even if it is "non-rational."

This earlier article of Mancur Olson predated his book on the logic of collective action, and it did not explore the cost or repression side of the equation. His article in the *Journal of Soviet Nationalities* (Summer 1990) fills in that part of the puzzle nicely. Industrialization provides the financial means to transform the military from a small band of marauders into a well-armed, mass force, but the transition to industrialization is marked by great difficulties and ambiguities in this process. If early rulers received their financing from the rural elites, the new industrial elites ultimately have superior economic resources (or the promise of them) and can use them either to subvert the loyalty of the old army or even to create a new one. (Chiang Kai-shek provides an excellent twentieth century example of a leader who was able to defeat regionally based military leaders— "warlords"—because of the work of his finance minister, T.V. Soong, and Chiang's consequent access to far superior financing for the creation of his "national" army.[14]) During the transition, however, this process is marked by many irregularities and unpredictabilities that explain a great deal of instability.

In addition, industrialization introduces real cleavages into the former ruling elite. The old rural elites clearly do not like the level of taxation that would be required to compete for the loyalty of the army with the newly rising industrial elite. Moreover, some of the members of the old elite find the city an attractive place for investment. As a consequence, interests of the old ruling elite become very complex. Their children move into the city and are found among the students who go into the streets or join revolutionary groups. In the process, divisions arise that are qualitatively different from the simple personality and policy conflicts that are present in any ruling group. The burgeoning political science literature on the various coalitions that arise between "land" and "industry" is a reflection of the kind of cleavages that can seriously undercut the willingness of an elite to use military force ruthlessly over a prolonged period.

It is not difficult to explain why industrial elites eventually prevail over rural ones in the process of modernization. They ultimately have the economic resources that a modern military requires. But if the switch of military loyalty to the urban elites is easily understandable, why does the industrializing military dictatorship that is common to the transition period give way to democracy in advanced industrial countries? Why do democratic revolts succeed so frequently in advanced industrial countries when they often produce short-term successes at best at earlier stages?

Part of the explanation can perhaps be found at a different level than the one at which the logic of collective action usually works. If the question is resistance of a broader or even inner elite to a king such as Stalin who is willing to kill them, then the logic of collective action works as well for the elite as for the masses. The elite did not even move to overthrow Stalin as he was killing them off in 1937–1938.

But kings are as mortal as ordinary people. During successions, elites can affect the values—and the degree of ruthlessness—of the new king at least if the succession is not hereditary. They usually have a strong interest in selecting a successor who is less likely to harm them in the future. (This clearly happened in 1953 in the Soviet Union on a conscious level.)

Indeed, this process goes on well before any actual succession, natural or otherwise. Intellectuals in a dictatorship are able in various ways to undercut the legitimacy of the elite among the elite itself.[15] They can try to teach more relativistic values or the virtues of democracy for industrial growth to the students in college who will become the elite of the future. It is not purely economic interest that leads high quality universities to admit inferior students such as Ted Kennedy or Dan Quayle. Harvard University has been quite self-conscious about wanting to affect the thinking of future leaders.

Other lower members of an elite who have no individual interest in standing up to a dictator directly can take minor and quiet decisions over a lifetime that indirectly affect the outcome years later. For example, persons who have the requisite ruthlessness or ideological fanaticism to use force indiscriminately are usually sidetracked during the promotion of people at lower and middle levels of a bureaucracy, including a military one.[16] Part of the story of the Romanian revolution is the untold decisions that resulted in generals with ambiguous ideas about force being in key positions in Bucharest in 1989.

Yet, when we talk about the willingness and ability of a government to use repression, we probably should not focus on the elite level alone. As Mancur Olson said, neither the ruler nor the generals and colonels are the best marksmen. Mass revolutions are successful when soldiers refuse to obey orders to fire their weapons on the crowds or when the officers do not trust the soldiers to fire and fear to call them out. A central factor in maintaining the loyalty of soldiers is the continued ability to pay them a salary, especially in underdeveloped countries when soldiers have few other employment opportunities, but emotion and values are also important to soldiers when questions of life and death—especially their own—are involved. Studies of World War II showed that small-group loyalty was crucial in influencing the willingness of soldiers to take risks, and there have been innumerable cases when soldiers have fought more vigorously in defending their homeland than in carrying the war abroad. (For example, this was noticeable on both sides in the Iran-Iraq war.)

The attitudes of the rank-and-file soldiers are particularly important in revolutionary situations precisely because the people facing the guns and tanks are in their teens or early twenties—the same age as the soldiers themselves. If the soldiers are sociologically and psychologically very similar to the demonstrators, they are likely to have similar attitudes to the problems that brought the demonstrators into the streets. For example, one would suspect that the citizen-soldiers in the army of the GDR had much the same dislike of the Communist regime as the demonstrators and that the soldiers of the Shah's army felt the same attraction to the Ayatollah Khomeini as those in the streets. It is because the nineteen year olds in the army can become caught up in the popular emotions and refuse to fire their weapons that a revolution can unexpectedly succeed with breathtaking speed.

Indeed, it is possible—even probable—that the strong correlation between the level of education in society and the existence of democratic institutions rests as much or more on the character of the soldiers as the character of the elite. So long as the army is composed largely of poorly educated recruits, usually from the countryside, it can generally be counted upon to fire on the elite urban youth who (as in China in 1989) are likely to be the core element of a revolutionary demonstration in an underdeveloped country. But the rise in the level of education in society eventually reaches the point where the army recruits themselves come predominantly from the city and have secondary education. They become similar to the young demonstrators upon which they are supposed to fire—or at least this is so unless something reduces the sense of identity between the soldiers and the demonstrators.

THE LOGIC OF ETHNIC REVOLT

Clearly one of the major distinctions between socio-economic revolution and nationality or religious revolt is that the soldier and demonstrator may have far less of a sense of identity in the latter case than in the former. If soldiers are asked to fire upon people of a different ethnic background—and if the order is supported by emotional appeals about national unity and even national security— they almost always will do so. (Of course, for this reason the leaders of a multi-ethnic society must be very careful about the ethnic composition of their army, or they can find that it will not fire on ethnic groups they want to control.)

If the soldiers can be counted on to fire their weapons, then the key questions about the application of force against a nationality revolt concern the interests and motivations of the elite. Why then is there such a difference between the willingness of elites—at least after some time—to let colonies go and their great reluctance to tolerate national revolt within the boundaries of the country?

Elite behavior in the case of colonial revolt is relatively easy to understand. We must begin with a fact that nationalists usually try to obscure: while nationality revolts are formally directed against the political authorities of another nationality, they are also, in practice, directed against elite members of the nationality that is revolting. The American revolution, for example, was directed not only against the British, but also against the American Tories who benefitted from British colonial rule and wanted it to continue.

Soviet ideologists used to refer to "bourgeois nationalist" revolts in the Third World, and there was reason for this designation. Colonial powers often made alliances with the colony's traditional elites, but their policy inevitably created new elites associated with industrialization and foreign economic relations. The new elites learned the "imperial" language, either at home or abroad, and if they worked for the colonial administration or foreign business, they generally earned higher incomes than their compatriots. This was true not only of managers who worked in the colonial administration and in the multi-national corporations, but also of the skilled workers employed by foreign firms—the so-called "workers' aristocracy" who earned higher wages than workers in other sectors.

As these new elites begin to use nationalist appeals to mobilize revolt against the old elites and the colonial power, the officials of the latter are in a very ambivalent position. On the one hand, they resent the criticism and know that a loss of colonies may undercut them politically at home. On the other hand, their long-term commercial and investment interests in the colony are really tied with its industrializing elite. Particularly as it has become increasingly clear that colonies are not economically advantageous, the government of the colonial power does not have a long-term interest in spending enormous sums to destroy its natural long-term allies. (It is not a coincidence the pre-industrial Portuguese government was the West European country to fight the longest to preserve its colonial empire.)

If the colony is "inside" the country—if it is an Uzbekistan instead of an India—then some elements of the logic are similar, but others are different. First, the number of persons of the dominant nationality who benefit directly from the "colonial" relationship is usually much greater. Obviously the British colonial office and its officials stationed in India had an interest in preventing decolonization, but their numbers were small, and they were counterbalanced by British industrialists who only wanted peaceful political conditions in which their enterprises in India could function.

If the ethnic group being controlled is inside the borders of the country, there likely will have been much more migration of the dominant ethnic group into the "colonial" area. Indeed, the frequent pattern is for the cities of the internal "colonial area"—be they Montreal in Canada or Kharkov in the Ukraine—to be the bastion of members of the "colonizing" ethnic group and those of the local nationality or nationalities who are willing to assimilate into it. The vast majority of the members of the "colonial" population live in the countryside, speaking their own language and generally being politically quiescent.[17]

So long as the migration of the dominated ethnic group into the city is relatively slow, the dominant elite is able to demand assimilation as the price for entry, but better rural medical care (and the resulting population explosion in the countryside) and industrialization in the city produce such a flood of migrants from the countryside to the city that the assimilative processes are swamped. This is particularly so when the national group (as usual) has a different language. In 1921 Joseph Stalin placed great emphasis on the inevitability of this process, and this understanding lay at the base of his policy.[18]

> The Ukrainian nation exists and the development of its culture is the obligation of Communists. It is impossible to go against history. It is clear that if Russian elements still predominate in the Ukrainian cities, then with the passage of time the city will inevitably be Ukrainianized. Some 40 years ago Riga was a German city, but since towns grow by drawing on the country and the country is the preserver of nationalism, Riga is now a purely Latvian city. Some 50 years ago the towns of Hungary had a German character, but now they are Magyarised. The same will happen with Belorussia, in the cities of which non-Belorussians still predominate.

It is with the nativization of the cities and the rise of education levels within them that strong separatist movements tend to arise. The issue of the language to be used in education and at work is often crucial. In the countryside people of the indigenous nationality seldom meet members of other groups. They speak their own language as a matter of course and suffer little for it. In the city, by contrast, the career chances of two people of equal ability but different native languages are enormously affected by which language is used in college or at the workplace. This is far less true for unskilled workers than for those in professional and administrative posts, and this is why major unrest tends to be associated with an increase in the education level of the local population.

With separatist movements in "inner colonies" developing in this context, the central government has a much greater incentive to use force than in the case of an "outer colony." There are far more persons of the central nationality living in the "inner colony" to be protected. Moreover, since the area is fully integrated into the national economy, the economic equation is different. And the whole psychological sense of national and territorial legitimacy of the central elite is more deeply at stake.

The crucial factor in determining the strength of the separatist revolt (or that of any other disadvantaged group) is the degree to which a critical mass of persons of the aggrieved group acquire the education to warrant upward social mobility, but find their opportunity for such mobility blocked. This was true of the blacks in the American South, the Moslems in Lebanon, the Vietnamese in South Vietnam, the Catholics in Northern Ireland, the French in Quebec, the Palestinians on the West Bank (after employment opportunities in the Gulf States were curtailed).[19]

The blockage of upward mobility of talented and educated individuals is especially explosive because it is particularly galling to the young. In a burst of emotion they easily can think that they have nothing to lose. If this problem is not resolved, new youngsters enter their teens every year and feel the same personal frustration.

Yet, for a series of reasons, the guarantee of upward social mobility by the central government often is a powerful tool to control ethnic unrest.

First, the logic of collective action begins to work with special force. The upward mobility is beneficial first of all to those for whom the logic normally works less well—those among the young who are ambitious and talented enough to take a leading role in organizing and mobilizing their peers to rebel. If they see that individual advancement is possible within the system, they have little reason to take the risks or even spend the time to seek advancement outside the system.

Second, the upward mobility creates a growing group within the elite who have incentives to remain within the larger country. The ambitious French Canadian politician has the chance to become the premier of Canada, not just Quebec, and other members of the French Canadian elite benefit in various ways from being in a larger arena. In addition, the central government can provide selective incentives to reward loyal members of the elite of the minority and/or to buy off potentially fractious members in a way that divides separatist opposition.

Third, upward mobility tends to identify people within the regime that provides it. This has often been noted among groups where ethnicity is not at issue, but it can affect ethnic minorities as well. Moreover, the process of nation-building or nation-destruction described by Mancur Olson and Myron Weiner is often not without its effect psychologically. Younger French in Quebec, younger Slovenians, and younger Ibos have been socialized in a number of powerful ways to think of themselves as Canadians, Yugoslavs, and Nigerians respectively. As this becomes a part of their identity in addition to their original ethnic identity, their desire for the breakup of the larger country becomes increasingly ambiguous.

The situation with respect to the French in Quebec was typical. The French were relatively quiescent so long as they were rural and had little self-interest in the working language of Montreal. A strong separatist movement arose when large numbers of French moved into the cities and found their way upward blocked by the English— and by the requirement of a fluent knowledge of the English language as a condition for promotion. The movement subsided, at least temporarily, when French was recognized as the official language and when limitations were introduced on the rights of immigrants to have their children educated in English-language schools. The blocking of upward social mobility can be just as crucial when language is not involved: the civil rights movement in America began in the black colleges of the south, not in the poorest black areas, and it ended once affirmative action guaranteed educated blacks access to better positions.

It may well be that, as nation-states become part of larger common markets or North-American free markets, both the psychology and the selective incentives of the elite of the majority and minority will change. Slovenians, Bavarians, and French Canadians may see themselves as part of a still larger community, and the nation-state of which they are currently a part may seem less relevant. But if this is to occur, it will become politically relevant in the twenty-first century, not the twentieth, except perhaps in Yugoslavia. This latter country will be an interesting test.

THE IMPLICATIONS FOR THE SOVIET UNION

This is not the place for a long discussion of the prospects for political development in the Soviet Union, but the preceding analysis has several implications that are at least worth some reflection.

First, of course, Mancur Olson's argument always suggests the need for a bit of uncertainty in the analysis of any revolutionary situation. It follows from his work that the correct revolutionary strategy is to try to undermine the confidence of the regime. A successful revolutionary aims his arguments not just at the masses, but at the leadership.[20] For this reason the correct revolutionary strategy in the Soviet Union at the present time is precisely that being followed by the Moscow radicals: to try to create a sense at the top that the economy is totally hopeless, that perestroika cannot possibly succeed, that the Soviet Union cannot intervene in Lithuania because it would destroy relations with the West. The correct revolutionary strategy is to say that democratization is necessary for successful economic reform. Whether these assertions are accurate or not—and I think they are all inaccurate—they will produce an overthrow of the regime if they succeed in undermining the self-confidence of Gorbachev and the other members of the upper elite. If the elite throws in its cards—even if it has been bluffed—then the revolutionaries have won, and we never can be absolutely certain that this will not happen.

By the same token, however, we should be extremely sensitive to the conscious or unconscious strategy of the revolutionaries. They have a vital interest in exaggerating the difficulties of the situation. They have a vital interest in convincing American correspondents and scholars of the accuracy of their position, because exaggerated analysis that comes back to the Soviet Union on Voice of America—hopefully even with CIA endorsement—may be especially convincing. American analysts must be sensitive to the danger that they themselves—or their colleagues—will be caught up in the revolutionary situation and will consciously or unconsciously be trying to undercut Gorbachev's self-confidence themselves. In the spring of 1990 the overwhelming majority of American policy intellectuals proclaimed that Gorbachev dare not invade Lithuania because of the consequences abroad. It is hard to explain this interpretation other than as an attempt to persuade Gorbachev not to act in a situation in which the long-term foreign costs of action clearly would not have been all that high. If the revolutionary appeals do not weaken the self-confidence of the Soviet leadership, then we are left with predictions that have misled our own political and business elite.

Mancur Olson's analysis is right in suggesting that one of our central tasks in analyzing the Soviet Union is to make a judgment about Gorbachev. I must say that everything I have seen confirms Andrei Gromyko's reported statement about Gorbachev's "teeth of iron." While Soviet radicals and American analysts have talked about disintegration and chaos, Gorbachev has calmly and methodically gone about an extremely solid consolidation of power within the system. He may be foolish in his assumption that power within the system will matter, but if his self-confidence is a crucial factor, we need to be careful in accusing him of being wrong. As far as I know, he has never apologized for the use of force in Georgia and elsewhere, and his warnings to the Lithuanians have been chilling. Those who think that he will not act—or that his army will not fire on non-Russians—are making a very dubious assumption.

If we follow the example of most of the members of the May seminar at the Duke University East-West Center and see a more reciprocal relationship between mass attitudes and elite self-confidence than Mancur Olson portrays, we also have reason for caution.

First, the fact that republican unrest was permitted to express itself seriously for the first time in 1988 and has escalated very rapidly in some republics in the intervening two years does not prove that the unrest will continue in a linear fashion. On the contrary, the fact that the unrest has continued for two years may indicate that we are much nearer to the end of the revolutionary burst than we think, at least in republics with the most prolonged unrest. Since May the evidence is multiplying that this is in fact happening in the Baltics and Armenia.

Second, from the 1920s Stalin had a very clear sense that massive social mobility for non-Russians—even a policy of "korenization" or "nativization" that meant massive preferential affirmative action for them[21]—was crucial for political stability. This process has removed any problem of blockage of social mobility, and it reduces the individual gains for individual social mobility to be obtained from independence (except perhaps for peasant movement into the heavy industry working class jobs that probably would be opened up by departing Russian workers—and, of course, the replacement of one member of the local nationality by another within the political elite).

In addition, the nativization policy has created a huge urban "collaborationist" managerial and professional class whose individual interests often may not be served by independence. Lithuania, for example, is not a natural economic unit, but must be submerged in a broader economic community—perhaps the Soviet Union, perhaps the Common Market, at least the global market. The broad Lithuanian elite has a major personal investment in the Russian language, and it would have to pay extremely high information costs if it quickly had to learn the West European economic system and a West European language. Those Lithuanians in Klaiped would lose as the Russian majority in that city seceded from Lithuania.

In the 1970s Westerners often predicted revolution in Central Asia, but (except for conflict among Central Asians) it has thus far been the most untroubled area. Part of the answer is the continuing high level of rural population in the area (a situation that, alas, will be changed in the coming years, as Gregory Gleason shows), but another part may be a fear on the part of the broad educated elite, let alone the political elite, that a religious elite might seize control of a revolutionary upsurge and be hostile to the entire industrializing elite.

Gorbachev's economic reform promises massive upward mobility into very high-paying and generally high status private (or "cooperative") sector jobs. In the next twenty years some are going to make great fortunes. The group that benefits most of all from this mobility is the young—that is, precisely the group that is needed for revolutionary action. As demonstrations become old hat, as Gorbachev starts raising the individual costs to participants through repression, as economic reform reaches the point where the young are convinced that it is worthwhile and safe for them to engage in private economic activity, the incentives for the active young people to desert the revolution for economic activity will become extremely high. The economic difficulties, as in Poland in 1981, are likely to increase the popular willingness to tolerate repression rather than lead to increased revolutionary activity.

Third, it was an intelligent strategy for Gorbachev to let national unrest run a bit wild at first. This not only released much of the pent-up emotional resentment among non-Russians, but also reminded the Russians that democracy would mean national disintegration while strengthening the argument for economic decentralization. (The Russians are the most dangerous nationality, for the predominantly Russian army may not fire on Russian demonstrators.) But once the economic reform provides the outlet for upward mobility of the young, once the revolutionary burst has had time to spend itself, Gorbachev's obvious strategy is to crack down in order to increase the costs for potential participants. The logic of the situation suggests that it will be a successful strategy for at least the rest of this decade. One of the top Soviet specialists on nationalities said, "Just because the teapot is letting off steam does not mean it is breaking up." It seems to me that this is right, although the contents of the teapot are clearly changing.

NOTES

1. Crane Brinton, *The Anatomy of Revolution* (New York: W.W. Norton & Company, Inc., 1938), pp. 48–50, 105–106, and 109.

2. Myron Weiner, "Political Change: Asia, Africa, and the Middle East," in Myron Weiner and Samuel P. Huntington, eds., *Understanding Political Development* (Boston, MA: Little, Brown, and Company, 1987), pp. 45 and 57–58.

3. *Ibid.,* p. 35.

4. *Financial Times,* August 30, 1990, p. 6.

5. Mancur Olson, "Rapid Growth as a Destabilizing Force," *Journal of Economic History,* December 1963, pp. 529–52.

6. Jean Jacques Rousseau, *The Social Contract and Discourses* (New York: E.P. Dutton and Company, Inc., 1950), p. 6.

7. Harold D. Lasswell, *Psychopathology and Politics* (Chicago, IL: University of Chicago Press, 1930), pp. 173 and 134.

8. Donald Forbes, *Journal of Soviet Nationalities,* I, 2 (Summer 1990), p. 32.

9. Edward C. Banfield, *The Unheavenly City* (Boston, MA: Little, Brown, 1968), pp. 185–209.

10. The author of these lines is particularly sensitive to the power of this factor, for he was tear-gassed only once in his life—at a large demonstration in favor of the preservation of Latin on the Harvard University diploma, a political goal to which his commitment was minimal in the extreme.

11. E.E. Schattschneider, *The Semisovereign People* (New York: Holt, Rinehart and Winston, 1960), p. 35.

12. See the cover story of "Child Warriors," in *Time,* June 18, 1990.

13. Olson, "Rapid Growth as a Destabilizing Force," pp. 531–35.

14. For an excellent discussion of this, see Donald A. Jordan, *Northern Expedition: China's National Revolution of 1926–1928* (Honolulu: University Press of Hawaii, 1976), pp. 13–14 and 53.

15. For the way in which the "new way of thinking" was formed in the decades prior to Gorbachev's election, see Jerry F. Hough, *The Struggle for the Third World: Soviet Debates and American Options* (Washington, DC: The Brookings Institution, 1986). This book goes beyond its title to explore the undercutting of the old assumptions on economic reform, the relation to Europe, and the nature of politics.

16. Zbigniew Brzezinski, "Victory of the Clerks: What Khrushchev's Ouster Means," *The New Republic,* November 14, 1964, p. 18.

17. Karl W. Deutsch, *Nationalism and Social Communication* (New York: John Wiley and Sons, Inc., 1953), pp. 161–67.

18. I.V. Stalin, *Sochineniia* (Moscow: Ogiz, 1947), Vol. 5, p. 49.

19. Horowitz found that early revolt in the former colonies was often associated with resentment over the percentage of slots guaranteed a national group in the country's civil service. Donald Horowitz, *Ethnic Groups in Conflict* (Berkeley, CA: University of California Press, 1985), pp. 238–40.

20. This is also true of regime propaganda or the falsification of the history of repression; they are designed as much—and perhaps more to maintain the self-confidence and sense of righteousness of the elite as to fool the masses.

21. For this process in the Ukraine, see George Liber's forthcoming book, *The Urban Harvest: Soviet Nationality Policy and Social Change in the Ukrainian SSR, 1923–1933.*

Part Four

CONCLUSION

FREDERIC J. FLERON, JR.
ERIK P. HOFFMANN

18

POST-COMMUNIST STUDIES
AND POLITICAL SCIENCE:

Peaceful Coexistence,
Detente, and Entente

For more than half a century Westerners have claimed that Soviet society was completely different from any other and that, because of its closed nature and the paucity of reliable data, sui generis methods had to be developed to study it. Unique methods are required to study a unique system, and, of course, they give unique results. Hence, social science and Sovietology had little to offer each other.[1]

But it may be that Sovietologists were unprepared for perestroika and postcommunism because we had been influenced too little by Western social science, not because we had been influenced by it too much. Now it is fair to ask: Where are we, and where should we focus our energies?

Let us try to clarify the nature of the problem. Although we acknowledge that Soviet studies has been strengthened by multidisciplinary and long-term policy-oriented research since the early 1970s, we believe there are numerous reasons why Western Sovietologists (collectively, if not individually) are not well equipped to comprehend post-Communist systems. Here is our lengthy and open-ended list of reasons, which falls into two general categories: professional and sociocultural.

Parts of this conclusion have been adapted from Frederic J. Fleron, Jr., and Erik P. Hoffmann, "Sovietology and Perestroika: Methodology and Lessons from the Past," *Harriman Institute Forum,* 5, 1 (September 1991).

THE SHORTCOMINGS OF SOVIETOLOGY

Professional Factors

1. Sovietologists who stressed the "uniqueness" of the USSR lacked background in social science theory, philosophy of science, and comparative politics. They tended to isolate themselves from mainstream social science inquiry in the post–World War II period. The divorce of Sovietology from general philosophical, epistemological, and methodological concerns greatly weakened our collective ability to ask theoretically relevant questions. This is especially true of post-Communist democratization, disintegration, conversion, and marketization, which transcend the boundaries of geographic area specialization. By definition and in actual fact these processes reject uniqueness. Post-Communist transformation is a nomothetic (not an idiographic) revolution.[2] It is part of a worldwide cultural transformation that is fostering political-military, socioeconomic, and environmental-ecological interdependence. There is a real and perceived convergence of interests on many global issues and on some regional issues. And there is increasing consensus on international structures and norms, especially in the spheres of trade, finance, law, human rights, security, and environmental dilemmas. Hence, the theory and practice of postcommunism include some generally accepted goals, presuppositions, and methods.

2. There has been too much policy-oriented research geared to the short term (less than one year). All governments must deal with day-to-day problems, but these problems are often compounded by technocratic counsel that is neither historically grounded nor farsighted. Longitudinal studies can be of considerable practical value because they compare phenomena at different stages of their past and probable future development. In contrast, short-term policy analysis places heavy emphasis on current political personalities, top-level power relationships, and international and domestic crises rather than on the thinking and behavior of counterelites and ordinary citizens; on underlying socioeconomic and scientific-technological trends; and on policy options, policy implementation, and policy outcomes at the national, regional, and local levels. Also, short-term policy commentary is usually more focused on means than ends, more speculative than analytical, more partial to simplistic than complex explanations, more eager for quick fixes than durable solutions, more accepting of official than independent-minded views, and more cognizant of immediate political costs and consequences than eventual multifaceted costs and consequences.

3. We have been handicapped by mediocre linguistic skills. Insufficient knowledge of Russian, to say nothing of the other languages

of the former USSR, and excessive emphasis on the stilted language of official Party and government pronouncements have not prepared us well for the living language of postcommunist orders.

Sociocultural Factors

4. The personal background of most Sovietologists (mainly middle and upper middle class) has introduced certain biases into our orientations and approaches:

A. We have tended to adopt elitist values, attitudes, and beliefs. We have focused on the view from the top rather than from the bottom of the political pyramids in the former USSR and elsewhere. Hence, we have a bias toward guided reform rather than revolution. And by concentrating on the smoke-filled rooms rather than the grass-roots initiatives, we too often forget that leadership can and does come from all levels and strata of society.

B. We have tended to judge regimes by how they treat intellectuals.[3] We focused on dissidents (democratic much more than authoritarian dissidents) in the 1960s and 1970s. Also, we made the Moscow intelligentsia the chief object of our research and relied on it for our information on many topics. We frequently succumbed to the temptation to take the intelligentsia's "insider" pronouncements at face value and to presume it had much greater political influence than it did.

C. We have tended to overvalue "national interests" and to overestimate central control of regional and local politics and everyday life.

5. We are products of an Anglo-American political culture, either by birth or, in the case of the emigres among us, by assimilation. As a result, we have defined democracy in procedural rather than substantive terms. Many of us have little appreciation for the intellectual and historical traditions from which the Bolsheviks emerged—a revolutionary tradition that emphasized economic freedoms over political freedoms. It was no accident that the U.S. Constitution was framed as a political document, not an economic one. The founding fathers already had their economic freedom. Likewise, it was no accident that Petr Tkachev and the *Narodnaya Volya* held English liberalism in such contempt. What good was freedom of speech to people who were hungry?

6. Western intellectuals valued more highly the incrementalism, circumlocutions, and political oscillations of Mikhail Gorbachev than the impatience, directness, and uncompromising principles of his

reactionary and conservative opponents (e.g., Yegor Ligachev) as well as of his radical and populist opponents (e.g., Boris Yeltsin).[4]

7. We have been unable to comprehend the changing nature of localism and departmentalism and the irreconcilability of competing interests and opinions in a disintegrating party-state not grounded on the Western principles of the "rule of law" and "constitutionality."

8. We have been blinded by Weberian norms, according to which modernization is the shift from the particularism of traditional society to the universalism of legal-rational society. We have only begun to perceive the forms and pervasiveness of distinctly neotraditional societies that stand outside this Weberian dichotomy.

9. We have been unable to understand scarcity and bargaining. A weakness of Soviet studies has been our lack of empathic understanding of the linkages between economics and politics in the behavior of individuals, groups, and organizations at the national, republican, and local levels. We have found it difficult to comprehend the politics of survival in economies that are dominated by nonmarket forces and that reward *blat,* stability, conformity, and material equality rather than work, risk, creativity, and personal achievements. Because we live in consumer-oriented societies where virtually all goods and services are available to those who have the money to pay for them (i.e., societies with no nomenklatura elites), we have brought too many Western economic, social, and psychological assumptions to our analyses of Communist systems. Of course we prefer our basic political values and general economic prosperity. But if we can minimize our cultural chauvinism and intellectual biases, we will improve our ability to analyze the reciprocal influences between Communist politics and economics and to facilitate the difficult and multifaceted transition to post-Communist orders.

10. We have been unable to understand intense ethnicity and strong loyalty to native cities, towns, and villages (because of the "American melting pot" and the "American dream" as well as our considerable geographical and socioeconomic mobility, real and imagined).

11. Considerable professional opportunities in the United States reduce our ability to understand societies in which a person cannot say, "Take this job and shove it." For example, we need better comprehension of the patron-client relationships, bureaucratic resistance to meritocracy, and the "leveling mentality" that have pervaded Communist societies and are obstructing the democratization and marketization of post-Communist societies.

12. Most Western Sovietologists lack military experience, which has led to an antimilitary bias, strengthened (in the case of many American academics) by opposition to the Vietnam War. Hence, there is a general lack of interest in and understanding of military issues— including political-military relations; the role of the armed forces in society; and the "military ethos" in Soviet culture, which stemmed

from the trauma of World War II and the Communist Party's use of both the victory in World War II and the Cold War to legitimize its power and its East European empire. Such traditional military issues are being replaced by new ones. For example, sustained hostilities among the USSR's successor states would be disastrous but cannot be ruled out a priori, as the violent disintegration of Yugoslavia has sadly demonstrated.

NEW DIRECTIONS

Proper attention to the issues raised by the professional factors in the preceding list will reduce the problems created by the sociocultural factors. This is reason enough to be more explicit and rigorous in our use of theory, including linguistics and hermeneutics. But there are other important and compelling reasons as well. As the peoples of the former USSR change their polities, societies, and economies and adopt more of the ideas and accomplishments of Western countries, so must Sovietologists employ more of the theories and methods of social scientists who study political behavior in the West. The pressure on us to do so will increase as Soviet scholars and analysts make greater use of "Western" (no longer "bourgeois") social science theory and methods.

A familiar but interesting feature of perestroika was that Soviet academics provided many of the theoretical parameters of policy debates. Indeed, one of perestroika's leading documents—the Novosibirsk Report—was written by Tatyana Zaslavskaya, a sociologist attached to the Siberian Branch of the USSR Academy of Sciences. This fact is remarkable for several reasons, not the least of which is that much of the rationale (if not the impetus) for perestroika is said to have been based on the results of concrete sociological research. Such research, especially on democratization and voting behavior, marketization and regional economics, and ethnic conflict and territorial disputes, has proliferated since the mid-1980s. This has helped to reverse a potentially dangerous situation that has been noted not only by Western Sovietologists but by Gorbachev and other Soviet and post-Soviet leaders: Every reform effort since the death of Stalin has ended in failure because top national officials have not been willing or able to accumulate sufficiently accurate and generalized information about actual conditions in their own country and thereby to learn from past mistakes. As Gail Lapidus has put it: "The primitive level of economics, not to mention sociology, demography, ethnography, psychology, and the study of public opinion, and the paucity of economic and social statistics have deprived not only policymakers but society as a whole of the self-knowledge that is a prerequisite to genuine progress."[5]

But just how did the Soviet leaders go about acquiring knowledge of their own system? What categories of analysis (concepts and theories) did they employ?

1. At a very general level, we often heard Gorbachev say that the Soviet Union was a great power but did not act like one; that it was a national scandal that a small country such as South Korea ranked higher than the USSR on the list of world's exporting countries; and that the USSR "should abandon everything that led to the isolation of socialist countries from the mainstream of world civilization."[6] Such statements suggest that Gorbachev and his more reformist colleagues were familiar with some of the ideas contained in, or were intuitively aware of the issues raised by, such works as Paul Kennedy's *The Rise and Fall of the Great Powers* (1987), Richard Rosecrance's *The Rise of the Trading State* (1986), and Theodore von Laue's *The World Revolution of Westernization* (1987).

2. A few Soviet analysts have long employed "Western" social science categories, at least with regard to the international system and the Soviet place in it.[7] Even in the early 1970s, some of us were impressed by the knowledge (if not always the understanding) of Western social science literature by leading researchers at the Institute of the World Economy and International Relations (IMEMO), the Institute of the United States and Canada (ISKAN), and elsewhere in the USSR.

3. Soviet academics and policy analysts have also been reading the works of some of our Sovietologists—even adopting some of their arguments, especially with regard to the USSR's main problems in the period of "stagnation" under Brezhnev and especially after the August 1991 putsch. Soviet interest in Western economic analysis of the USSR has always been considerable. Witness the voracious Soviet appetite for the reports of the Joint Economic Committee of the U.S. Congress, compiled by John Hardt, and the Soviet translations of works by and frequent consultations with senior Western economists. And Russian interest in Western political and legal ideas is growing rapidly. Witness Yeltsin supporters' increasing attention to Western concepts such as "federalism," "separation of powers," "checks and balances," "the market," and "the rule of law."

But if some Soviet scholars and officials have been trying to better understand their own system by making increasing use of social science theory, concepts, and methodology—despite their lack of background in these spheres—can the same be said of the profession of Sovietology? To what extent were the concepts of Western social science in general and comparative politics in particular employed by Western scholars in an attempt to understand perestroika? We have all encountered the concepts "political culture," "civil society," "pluralism," and "exit" and "voice" in the now enormous literature on perestroika. But how many of these concepts were used as more than metaphors or informing tropes? For example, Gail Lapidus used

Albert Hirschman's terms "exit" and "voice" chiefly for heuristic purposes. Gordon Bengsten and Russell Bova, however, closely followed Hirschman's definitions and attempted to retest Hirschman's basic propositions in their analysis of worker power under communism.[8]

Let us approach the issues of conceptualization and theory construction from a different angle. Perestroika was much misunderstood both in the Soviet Union and elsewhere. Almost everyone was *for* perestroika, at least in public. The reason there appeared to be little public opposition to perestroika was that it meant different things to different people. This was pointed out by many Western scholars, some of whom suggested that various problems of perestroika resulted from the fact that the Soviet leaders did not have a *theory of perestroika*—that is, a theory of the politics of economic reform, as Ed Hewett put it,[9] and a theory of simultaneous transitions from a totalitarian/authoritarian to a democratic socialist or liberal democratic government and from a planned to a mixed or market economy. But Soviet officials and analysts appeared to be revising the categories of thought they were using to diagnose the USSR's problems. These reconceptualizations were part of the Soviet national and republican leaders' attempts to improve their understanding of political-administrative, socioeconomic, and scientific-technological change—an issue to which George Breslauer sensitized us in his comparison of the authority-building strategies of Khrushchev and Brezhnev about a decade ago.[10]

Now that the Soviet Union has disintegrated, what theory or theories should the new leaders (many of them former Communists) use in interpreting recent developments? What theory or theories should Westerners use in attempting to understand the political and cultural revolutions now under way in Russia and in the USSR's other successor states? Should these newly independent countries use the same theories as Westerners? And should Russians, Ukrainians, Kazakhs, Georgians, Tatars, Bashkirs, and others use the same theories?

Ben Eklof has rightly suggested that most Russians lack organizing theories such as those of Max Weber and Emile Durkheim: "The virtual absence in Soviet education of any discussion of 'middle-level' theories in social analysis, of sociological thought in the Weberian or Durkheimian traditions, leaves many emigres without coherent intellectual strategies or vocabulary (except a curiously inverted Marxism-Leninism) to deal with the complex issues they must often address as 'experts' on their own country."[11] Eklof's statement supported Hewett's observation that the Soviet leaders needed a political theory of economic reform and Lapidus's claim about the "poverty of socio-political thought" in the USSR. But Eklof affirmed the importance of middle-level theories while apparently disregarding the content of those theories. How else could one juxtapose Durkheim and Weber in such a way? One was clearly positivist; the other attempted to fuse idealist and positivist perspectives. The result is two very different schools of social thought. Therefore, it makes a big difference whether one chooses Durkheim or Weber.

Some scholars have suggested that we distinguish between positivism and holism—two methodological cultures that "coexist uneasily in the social sciences."[12] Perhaps so, but life is never simple. There are, after all, many ways to dichotomize the world (if one wishes to do so), and that is only one way. Durkheim, for example, was simultaneously a positivist and a holist: a positivist because he believed in the "objective reality of social facts" and a holist because he reversed "the perspective which makes society the result of individual behavior and insist[s] that behavior is made possible by collective social systems individuals have assimilated, consciously or unconsciously."[13]

Along with Sigmund Freud, the psychologist, and Ferdinand de Saussure, the founder of modern linguistics, Emile Durkheim "helped to set the study of human behavior on a new footing." They "saw that the study of human behavior misses its best opportunities if it tries to trace the historical causes of individual events. Instead it must focus on the functions events have within a general social framework. It must treat social facts as part of a system of conventions and values."[14]

Saussure's major contribution to the study of linguistics was to draw a "distinction between the *synchronic* study of language (study of the linguistic system in a particular state, without reference to time) and the *diachronic* study of language (study of its evolution in time)."[15] This dichotomized approach to social inquiry may produce different conclusions or important differences in emphasis. For example, Westerners have long debated whether the Soviet system could be properly understood without rigorous analysis of the historical development of that system. Stephen F. Cohen explicitly argues in *Rethinking the Soviet Experience* that such analysis is necessary.[16] Such a call for more historical studies reflects a diachronic bias (one that can be found in the work of Robert C. Tucker, Moshe Lewin, and others). But does this approach necessarily reject the more synchronic approaches of Kremlinology, the conflict model, the group theorists, public policy analysis, and so on? And what are the benefits of the more synchronic approaches of Durkheim or Saussure, perhaps especially for the study of the relatively stable Brezhnev period?

Satisfactory answers to these questions require a high degree of methodological self-awareness and abundant knowledge of cross-disciplinary theory and data. The same questions have preoccupied students of many cultures, societies, and political systems. This was reason enough for Sovietology to have rejected the view that the USSR was unique and, therefore, impervious to normal social science research methods and theory. Now it seems clear that we must attempt to study the Soviet Union and especially its successor states in most of the same ways that we study other polities. Failure to do so will perpetuate our subject as an arcanum, and it will no doubt result in our being ridiculed as irrelevant or disingenuous—perhaps especially by the Slavic peoples of the former USSR, who for the first time are widely and often uncritically emulating *ideas* Western, not merely *things* Western.

Since the mid-1980s Sovietology has been edging away from the arcane and toward the mainstream of Western social science, and since 1991 this trend has been gaining momentum, thanks in large part to the growing interest of non-Sovietologists and nonacademics in the dramatic breakup of the USSR. For example, an increasing number of studies of Soviet and post-Soviet foreign policy have contained references to general theoretical and comparative literature. And more and more Sovietologists from the social and policy sciences now see the relevance of comparative studies and theory to their work. This was not the situation two decades ago.

Furthermore, analysts of Soviet and post-Soviet politics are increasingly testing propositions derived from the study of other social systems. Three examples are the application of (1) Mancur Olson's theory of the "logic of collective action" to the nationalities question;[17] (2) theories of the transition from autocratic to democratic regimes in Iberia and Latin America to the disintegration of the USSR;[18] and (3) theories of leadership to evaluate Gorbachev's and Yeltsin's performances.[19] Whether the promise of such efforts is realized and whether this trend continues, only time will tell.

BUILDING AN AGENDA

We would like to suggest other possibly fruitful and exciting lines of inquiry. Some are quite far removed from mainstream social science, but they could nevertheless contribute to a more theoretically oriented Sovietology and post-Sovietology in the immediate future. Our list is by no means exhaustive, and we encourage readers to add to or delete from it.

1. Reevaluate or replicate some of the classic studies of Soviet politics, especially in light of information recently made available.[20] How do these studies hold up in light of new evidence?

2. Reassess the various schools or approaches that shaped Sovietology in preceding decades: Kremlinology and the conflict school as well as the totalitarian, interest group, directed society, bureaucratic ossification, institutional pluralism, social systems, and political culture approaches, among others. What did these schools and approaches add to our knowledge, and what could they have added?

3. Analyze the rejection of reform communism in Eastern Europe and the Soviet Union in light of current organization, communica-

tion, and role theories, and consider how data from the experience of the former Soviet bloc might alter those bodies of theory. For example, the role conflicts, role stress, and role ambiguities among civilian and military officials in these countries have been intense and have greatly influenced personal as well as professional relationships.

4. Apply theories of colonialization to the collapse of the Soviet external and internal empires and compare post-Communist modernization in the countries of both former empires. For instance, how important is it that colonialization began under the tsars, that one-party socialism was developed in Russia and imposed on the rest of the Soviet Union, and that Stalinist socialism was forced on Eastern Europe utilizing both tsarist and Soviet experience?

5. Apply theories of federalism to Russia and theories of confederation to the Commonwealth of Independent States. True, these theories are not settled or widely agreed on. But comity, compromise, and consensus are the essence of Western politics, and they are just beginning to take root within and among some of the USSR's successor countries. For example, federalism probably should be conceptualized as a multifaceted phenomenon (e.g., historical/cultural, political/constitutional, fiscal, and programmatic), with special attention to the role of regional governments (e.g., representation/participation in the central government and supervision of local governments), to economic issues (e.g., the pros and cons of "unified" monetary, tax, energy, defense, environmental, and foreign trade policies), and to human rights (e.g., freedoms of speech, religion, assembly, and ethnic expression).[21]

6. Read Stephen R. Burant's article on the influence of Russian tradition on the political style of the Soviet elite, and then compare it to Robin Horton's study of tradition and modernity.[22] Horton's point of departure was "Durkheim's neglected insight concerning the continuities between, on the one hand the spiritualistic thought of traditional cultures in Africa and elsewhere, and on the other the mechanistic thought of modern Western cultures."[23] In his analysis, Horton contrasts two syndromes: cognitive traditionalism and cognitive modernism. This conceptual apparatus has considerable applicability to Soviet and post-Soviet politics: The putsch leaders of August 1991, Yegor Ligachev, the Russian neo-Stalinists, many middle-level and local bureaucrats, and other *temnye liudi* represent cognitive traditionalism; Gorbachev and other reformers represent cognitive modernism to some extent and Boris Yeltsin and other revolutionaries to a much greater extent.

7. Take cues from Ken Jowitt and Andrew Walder, but beware that each may use the concept of neotraditionalism quite differently from the other, even allowing for dissimilarities between the USSR (Jowitt) and China (Walder).[24] Replicate Jerry Hough's study *The Soviet Prefects* with at least one eye open to the types of relation-

ships and processes denoted by the concept "neotraditionalism," especially in Walder's usage. This is a promising concept with implications that extend far beyond academe. As Thane Gustafson has pointed out, "If Jowitt is right and neotraditionalism is a corrupt form of Leninism, then what Gorbachev is doing is quite reasonable and may even work. If Walder is right—that neotraditionalism is the essence of Leninism and the key to its success—then Gorbachev is bursting wide open the entire working basis of the communist authority system. Not only is he going to fail; he is going to blow the whole country wide open."[25]

8. Read Clifford Geertz's classic "Deep Play: Notes on the Balinese Cockfight."[26] Your view of perestroika and postcommunism may never be the same. Deep play is an allegory, and current Soviet developments can be interpreted as a "text" that functions much like other art forms, "coloring experience with the light they cast it in."[27] In the Balinese cockfight, deep play exists when the "stakes are so high that it is, from [the] utilitarian standpoint, irrational for men to engage in it at all." By defining perestroika as revolutionary in its scope and not "just another reform," Gorbachev was trying to place his program in a deep-play context.[28] But Gorbachev's willingness to gamble with the country's future in an all-or-nothing context was much weaker and less consistent than Yeltsin's, to say nothing of the leaders of the former Baltic republics and of some other former all-Union and autonomous republics. For example, Gorbachev forced deep-play rules on the national party-state apparatuses by insisting at the January 1989 Central Committee Plenum that "the CPSU is the ruling party and therefore *bears the whole brunt of responsibility before Soviet society for the destiny of socialism and of the country*" (italics added). But Yeltsin, standing on a tank in front of the Russian parliament and calling for a nationwide strike to rebuff the "unconstitutional" power grab of the putschists, epitomized the politics of high risk and unbending principles in August 1991. Deep play is precisely this process of upping the stakes for winning and losing in a dramatically public fashion. Yeltsin's bold commitment to radical economic reform in the USSR in October 1991 and in Russia alone in November 1991, together with his lack of specifics about the abolition of price controls, foreign debt, marketization, privatization, conversion, and implementation generally, were additional high-risk gambles in an intensifying revolution. And Ukraine's vote for independence raised the stakes for the new country and the doomed USSR in a remarkably visible and irreversible way in December 1991. However, the election of former apparatchik Leonid Kravchuk rather than former dissident Viacheslav Chornovil as president reflected a modicum of pragmatism or restraint in deep play. Whereas Yeltsin combined electoral legitimacy with raw charisma and morally grounded political initiatives, Kravchuk combined electoral legitimacy with

managerial experience and instrumentally grounded consensus-building.

9. Learn the principles of hermeneutic interpretation and apply them to theories of revolution and current experience in the former Soviet Union.[29] The keys here may be the concept of preunderstanding and the distinction between the meaning and significance of a text. Employ such concepts and distinctions if you agree that one needs to know much about Russian culture before one can really understand the transformation of the Soviet polity, economy, and society. Also, make your assumptions as explicit as possible so that they can be critically scrutinized by social scientists with diverse theoretical interests and by specialists in other geographical areas, thereby improving collective understanding of what we are doing and what we could and should be doing.

THE FUTURE

The end of the Cold War poses major challenges to social science theorists and area specialists as well as to policymakers and advisors. The political-administrative, socioeconomic, scientific-technological, environmental-ecological, ideological-cultural, and military-security dimensions of modernization are tumultuously influencing one another throughout the world. Individuals are striving for greater spiritual and material freedom, societies are learning more about themselves and others, economies are becoming more and more marketized and interconnected, and polities are increasingly helping or hindering one another's development. Surely the theories and methods of Western analysts must change accordingly.

Sovietologists should more than ever try to benefit from and contribute to the social sciences. Our investigations should probably focus on theories of social change (e.g., the interconnections among technology, culture, and development), the transition from command to market economies (e.g., the privatization of national and regional economies and their integration into global markets), the dismantling of military-industrial complexes (e.g., with American and East European comparisons), the democratization of one-party political systems (e.g., with Latin American and Iberian comparisons), the creation of a civic culture (e.g., with the rule of law), and many other vital subjects.

It is time to move from peaceful coexistence or detente to entente between the social sciences and Sovietology. The emergence of post-communism necessitates post-Sovietology. And post-Sovietology entails mutually beneficial cooperation of many kinds. Researchers and officials in the fragmented USSR and Eastern Europe are eagerly exchanging data, opinions, and advice with their Western counterparts. Collaborative projects are now limited mainly by financial and professional constraints rather than by political and ideological barriers. Moreover, Western methodologies and theories can be exceedingly helpful in studying the former Soviet internal and external empires as well as in shaping the current Soviet and East European revolutions. Socioeconomic and policy-relevant information is being unearthed or generated at an unprecedented pace. Finally, Western theories can be strengthened and perhaps corrected only with fresh evidence about the "tectonic" shifts of postcommunism. As a Soviet geologist remarked to one of the coeditors of this book, "The former USSR is an extraordinary laboratory for all of the social and physical sciences. Even most of our mountains are new."

NOTES

1. For example, Richard Pipes affirms: "The fusion of traditional Russian autocracy and Marxism, adapted to Russian conditions and mentalities, produced a regime that was quite outside the experience of the West but that the West nevertheless has ever since sought to explain in Western categories. It pushed to the forefront in Russia those elements that had remained unaffected by Western culture. Here no sociological or other 'scientific' theories are of much help. The Revolution threw Russia back to its pre-Western origins, to patrimonialism, to lawlessness, to human bondage, to the sense of uniqueness and isolation." Richard Pipes, *Survival Is Not Enough: Soviet Realities and America's Future* (New York: Simon and Schuster, 1984), p. 24. These have been consistent themes in Pipes's writings. Compare, for example, Richard Pipes, "Russia's Chance," *Commentary*, 93, 3 (March 1992), p. 33.

2. For a discussion of the distinction between idiographic and nomothetic studies, see Frederic J. Fleron, Jr., "Soviet Area Studies and the Social Sciences: Some Methodological Problems in Communist Studies," *Soviet Studies*, XIX, 3 (1968), pp. 317–320. This article was reprinted in Frederic J. Fleron, Jr. (ed.), *Communist Studies and the Social Sciences: Essays on Methodology and Empirical Theory* (Chicago: Rand McNally, 1969).

3. This point was made earlier by Jerry F. Hough in *The Soviet Union and Social Science Theory* (Cambridge, MA: Harvard University Press, 1977), pp. 180, 189.

4. In his lament that "Sovietological perestroika is, alas, far behind the one in Moscow," Alexander Yanov criticizes both conservative and liberal perspectives on Soviet Russia. See Yanov's "Is Sovietology Reformable?" in Robert O. Crummey (ed.), *Reform in Russia and the USSR* (Urbana: University of Illinois Press, 1989), pp. 257–276.

5. Gail W. Lapidus, "State and Society: Toward the Emergence of Civil Society in the Soviet Union," in Seweryn Bialer (ed.), *Politics, Society, and Nationality Inside Gorbachev's Russia* (Boulder and London: Westview Press, 1989), p. 131.

6. Gorbachev's remarks to the CPSU Central Committee Plenum of February 1990, *New York Times*, February 6, 1990, p. A16.

7. See Allen Lynch, *The Soviet Study of International Relations* (Cambridge, England: Cambridge University Press, 1987).

8. See Lapidus, "State and Society," pp. 121–147, and Gordon Bengsten and Russell Bova, "Worker Power Under Communism: The Interplay of Exit and Voice," *Comparative Economic Studies*, XXXII, 1 (1990), pp. 42–72. For useful discussions of metaphors and informing tropes, see James J. Bono, "Literature, Literary Theory, and the History of Science," *Publication of the Society for Literature and Science*, 2, 1 (1986), pp. 5–9; and George Lakoff and Mark Johnson, *Metaphors We Live By* (Chicago and London: University of Chicago Press, 1980).

9. Ed A. Hewett, *Reforming the Soviet Economy: Equality Versus Efficiency* (Washington, D.C.: The Brookings Institution, 1988), pp. 10, 275–364. Hewett's statement may have been the inspiration for Hough's effort to develop such a theory. See Jerry F. Hough, "The Politics of Successful Economic Reform," *Soviet Economy*, 5, 1 (1989), pp. 3–46.

10. George W. Breslauer, *Khrushchev and Brezhnev as Leaders: Building Authority in Soviet Politics* (Boston and London: George Allen & Unwin, 1982).

11. Ben Eklof, *Soviet Briefing: Gorbachev and the Reform Period* (Boulder and London: Westview Press, 1989), p. 6.

12. Jack Snyder, "Science and Sovietology: Bridging the Methods Gap in Soviet Foreign Policy Studies," Chapter 4 in this collection.

13. Jonathan Culler, *Ferdinand de Saussure*, rev. ed. (Ithaca: Cornell University Press, 1986), p. 87.

14. Culler, *Ferdinand de Saussure*, p. 16.

15. Culler, *Ferdinand de Saussure*, p. 45.

16. Stephen F. Cohen, *Rethinking the Soviet Experience: Politics and History Since 1917* (New York and Oxford: Oxford University Press, 1985).

17. Articles by Jerry F. Hough and Mancur Olson plus discussion by others in *Journal of Soviet Nationalities*, I, 2 (Summer 1990), pp. 1–65; and Alexander J. Motyl, *Sovietology, Rationality, Nationality: Coming to Grips with Nationalism in the USSR* (New York: Columbia University Press, 1990). See Chapter 3 by Motyl and Chapter 17 by Hough in this collection.

18. See Chapter 12 by Russell Bova and Chapter 13 by Thomas F. Remington.

19. For example, see George W. Breslauer, "Evaluating Gorbachev as Leader," *Soviet Economy*, 5, 4 (October–December 1989), pp. 299–340.

20. The fine case studies and monographs of the 1960s by Carl Linden, Sidney Ploss, and Jerry F. Hough as well as the classics of Kremlinology by Robert Conquest, Michel Tatu, and Myron Rush virtually cry out for reevaluation and/or replication. Also, how does one evaluate Barrington Moore, Jr.'s two major books on modernization and change in the Soviet Union about four decades later?

21. For example, see Richard P. Nathan and Erik P. Hoffmann, "Modern Federalism," *International Affairs* (Moscow), 5 (May 1991), pp. 27–38.

22. Stephen R. Burant, "The Influence of Russian Tradition on the Political Style of the Soviet Elite," *Political Science Quarterly*, 102, 2 (1987), pp. 273–293; Robin Horton, "African Traditional Thought and Western Science," *Africa*, 37, 1 (1967), pp. 302–371; and 37, 2 (1967), pp. 155–187.

23. Robin Horton, "Tradition and Modernity Revisited," in Martin Hollis and Steven Lukes (eds.), *Rationality and Relativism* (Cambridge, England: Cambridge University Press, 1982), p. 201.

24. Ken Jowitt, "Soviet Neotraditionalism: The Political Corruption of a Leninist Regime," *Soviet Studies,* XXXV, 3 (1983), pp. 275–297; Andrew G. Walder, *Communist Neo-Traditionalism: Work and Authority in Chinese Industry* (Berkeley and London: University of California Press, 1986).

25. Thane Gustafson, quoted in "The Aftermath of the 19th Conference of the CPSU: A *Soviet Economy* Roundtable," *Soviet Economy,* 4, 3 (1988), p. 218.

26. Clifford Geertz, "Deep Play: Notes on the Balinese Cockfight," in Paul Rabinow and William M. Sullivan (eds.), *Interpretive Social Science: A Reader* (Berkeley and London: University of California Press, 1979), pp. 181–223. This paper was originally published in *Daedalus,* 101, 1 (1972).

27. Geertz, "Deep Play," p. 221.

28. Although not explicitly employing the "Deep Play" metaphor, Peter Reddaway's discussions of Gorbachev's attempts to increase the stakes in his struggles with his rivals suggest the utility of further exploration of this approach. See, for example, Reddaway's articles in *New York Review of Books,* May 28, 1987; August 18, 1988; and August 17, 1989.

29. There is, of course, a vast literature in the hermeneutic tradition and about hermeneutic interpretation. Two good places to begin are: Richard E. Palmer, *Hermeneutics: Interpretation Theory in Schleiermacher, Dilthey, Heidegger, and Gadamer* (Evanston, IL: Northwestern University Press, 1969); and Frank Kermode, *The Genesis of Secrecy: On the Interpretation of Narrative* (Cambridge and London: Harvard University Press, 1979).

ABOUT THE BOOK AND EDITORS

Beset by the USSR's closed nature and the paucity of reliable data, scholars have used unique methods to study a political system they claimed was completely different from any other on earth. However, in the first extended reassessment of Sovietology in over two decades, Frederic Fleron and Erik Hoffmann argue that the isolation of the field from the social sciences has diminished analysts' ability to explain the dramatic changes in their area of study. The editors' collection of key essays elucidates Sovietology's theories and methodologies and underscores the need to adapt them to the rapidly shifting conditions in the USSR during the 1980s and in its successor countries during the 1990s.

This important anthology is the only book to systematically review the state of Sovietology and to provide practical suggestions for new methodological approaches and conceptual orientations for all analysts of postcommunism. The book's stimulating diversity of views will make it required reading for political scientists, area specialists, policy advisers, and students who hope to understand the Communist past and the transition to a post-Communist future.

Frederic J. Fleron, Jr., is professor of political science, State University of New York at Buffalo. He is coauthor of *Comparative Communist Political Leadership*; editor of *Communist Studies and the Social Sciences: Essays on Methodology and Empirical Theory* and *Technology and Communist Culture: The Socio-Cultural Impact of Technology under Socialism*; and coeditor of *The Conduct of Soviet Foreign Policy* and *Soviet Foreign Policy: Classic and Contemporary Issues.*

Erik P. Hoffmann is professor of political science, State University of New York at Albany. He is coauthor of *The Politics of Economic Modernization in the Soviet Union, "The Scientific-Technological Revolution" and Soviet Foreign Policy,* and *Technocratic Socialism: The Soviet Union in the Advanced Industrial Era.* He is editor of *The Soviet Union in the 1980s* and coeditor of *The Conduct of Soviet Foreign Policy, The Soviet Polity in the Modern Era, Soviet Foreign Policy in a Changing World,* and *Soviet Foreign Policy: Classic and Contemporary Issues.*